Millgate, Linda

The almanac of dates

595

DATE		
11/30/78		

THE ALMANAC OF DATES

Events

of the Past

for Every Day

of the Year

THE ALMANAC OF DATES

EVENTS OF THE PAST FOR EVERY DAY OF THE YEAR

LINDA MILLGATE

Harcourt Brace Jovanovich   New York and London

Printed in the United States of America

Library of Congress Cataloging in Publication Data
Millgate, Linda
    The almanac of dates.
    1. Calendars. I. Title.
D11.5 .M565   902'.02   76-27408
ISBN 0-15-145773-5

First edition

B C D E

ACKNOWLEDGMENT

Encyclopedists, almanac compilers, historical writers of both fact and fiction, anyone who has published anything with a full date in it--thank you.

To my parents who knew I would finally succeed in spite of never knowing what I would try next.

Preface

I hated history in school. Twice a year I had to
memorize the same dates, once to pass Friday's
test, later for the final exam. None remained in my
memory, having no personal significance.

Then came an office party when they wanted something
on the cake other than "Happy Birthday" and I was
elected to find it. It took a couple of hours of
frantic research, but an almanac finally came through.
The item was so nonmemorable that it must have had
some personal meaning to the compiler, but it was the
right date and was duly inscribed on our cake. I
decided to get a date or so ready for each employee -
and you are holding the results. I got carried away,
gleaning items from everywhere, from encyclopedias to
cereal boxes.

You'll notice that the early years for each date lean
heavily on the history of the Catholic Church. Like
modern authors, the monks wrote about what they knew
best, and as they were almost the only ones who could
write at all, the results are obvious. If the calendars
of other civilizations have been worked out to corre-
spond to ours, no one has published them that way,
except for a very few items, as I have found. George
Washington saw his birthdate change, due to the incor-
poration of the Gregorian calendar, from February 11th
to the 22nd. The Julian, or Old Style, in his case
the 11th, is marked as such if I found it that way.

Without the background that went with the dates back
then, here are the old school facts, set out so you
can easily find the ones that happened on your days.

THE ALMANAC OF DATES

JANUARY

Full Moon - Wolf Moon
                 Koreans pray for a bountiful harvest
3rd Friday - Arbor Day in Florida
Last week - Bears born
Last weekend - Start of St. Paul, Minnesota Winter
                 Carnival

January 1st

              New Year's Day
              Feast of St. Benedict Bobures (Venezuela)
              Feast of St. Basil (Orthodox) (died 379)
              Circumcision Day (Protestant)
              Octave of the Nativity
              Tournament of Roses Parade (Pasadena,
                       California)
              Mummers' Parade (Philadelphia, Pennsylvania)
              College Football Bowl Games
              Chariot Racing at Kuna and Jerome, Idaho
              Turtle Dance at the Taos Pueblo, New Mexico
              Annual Swim at Newport, Rhode Island
              Druids cut and distributed sacred mistletoe
              St. Almachius (Telemachus) ended gladitorial
                       contests in Rome
4713 BC   Beginning of the Julian Period
  27   Octavian made Caesar Augustus, ruler of Rome
   1 AD   Vulgar Christian Era began
 193   Pertinax chosen Roman Emperor
 533   St. Fulgentius died
 898   Odo, King of the Franks, died
1048   St. Odilo, Cluniac abbot who started obser-
                       vance of All Souls' Day, died
1387   Charles II, "the Bad," King of Navarre, died
1473   Annobon Island discovered by the Portuguese

Year	Event

1515   King Louis XII of France died
1527   Ferdinand of Austria elected King of Croatia
1531   Rio de Janerio, Brazil discovered
1553   Seige of Metz by Charles V, Holy Roman Emperor, failed
1559   King Christian III of Denmark and Norway died
1562   Huguenots abolished Catholicism in Castres, France
1596   The first Dutch landed on Sumatra
1618   LaSalle's expedition reached the site of Peoria, Illinois
       Murillo, Spanish artist, baptized
1637   Royal Charter granted to Newfoundland colony
1651   Prince Charles Stuart of England (King Charles II) crowned King of Scotland, the last coronation at Scone
1673   Dutch captured St. Helena Island
1699   First Russian year not to start on September 1st
1713   Battle of Agra, India
1735   Paul Revere, Revolutionary rider and silversmith, born
1752   Betsy Ross, flagmaking seamstress, born
1757   British massacred at Fort William Henry (French-Indian)
1772   Thomas Jefferson married Martha W. Skelton
1776   First U.S. flag, "The Great Union," displayed
       U.S. Continental Army established
1785   London Times founded as The Daily Universal Register
1787   Arthur Middleton, signer of the Declaration of Independence, died
1788   The Times of London first appeared under that name
1801   Ceres, first asteroid, discovered
       English rulers gave up the use of the French part of their coat of arms
1808   Importation of slaves into the U.S. prohibited
1815   New Year Island discovered
1822   Greece adopted its national flag
1824   James K. Polk married Sarah Childress
1831   Genesee Farmer newspaper founded
       An abolitionist journal, Liberator, founded in Boston
1842   Thames, first Royal Mail Steam Packet, left on its maiden voyage for the West Indies
1848   John-Donkey, comic weekly, founded in New York and Philadelphia, but died in 7 months
1857   Gretna Green marriages became illegal in England
1863   Lincoln made his Emancipation Proclamation
1867   London's Metropolitan Fire Brigade formed

1869	Meteorite rain fell near Hessle, Sweden
1870	The Outlook, a religious and literary weekly begun
1886	Britain annexed Burma
1889	Solar eclipse
1894	England's Manchester Ship Canal opened to traffic
1895	J. Edgar Hoover, first head of the FBI, born
1898	The 5 boroughs became Greater New York City
1900	Xavier Cugat, bandleader, born
1904	Institute of Brewing founded in England
1909	Australia became a Commonwealth
	Barry Goldwater, Senator and presidential candidate, born
1912	China became a Republic
1913	U.S. Parcel Post began
1915	British battleship Formidable torpedoed and sunk
1919	J.D. Salinger, writer, born
	Iolaire and the 240 persons aboard lost off Scotland
1922	King Charles I, former ruler of Austro-Hungary, died
1927	The BBC founded with a Royal Charter
1931	Naval Reduction Treaty went into effect (U.S., G.B., It., Fr., Jap.)
1942	Atlantic Charter became the United Nations
1944	Syria became a Republic
1946	Britain and Thailand signed a peace treaty
1947	Britain nationalized its coal mines and communications
1948	Britain nationalized its railways
1956	The Sudan became independent
1958	European Common Market formed
1959	Castro assumed power in Cuba
1960	Cameroon became independent of France
1962	Independence granted to Western Samoa
1972	Maurice Chevalier, entertainer, died

January 2nd

	Feast of St. Macarius (the Younger) of Alexandria, a desert monk
69 AD	Aulus Vitellius became Emperor of Rome
1119	Pope Gelasius II, died
1322	King Philip V, "the Tall," of France died
1492	Moors surrendered Granada to Spain
1631	England and Spain signed a treaty against the Dutch
1666	Castle, South Africa, founded
1730	Yazoo Indians massacred the garrison at Fort St. Peter, Mississippi

1778	Esek Hopkins, first Commodore of the U.S. Navy, dismissed from the service
1788	Georgia ratified its constitution
1828	Jeremiah E. Rankin, author of "God be with you till we meet again," born
1833	St. Seraphim of Sarov, a mystic, died
1836	St. Caspar del Bufalo, founder of the Missionaries of the Precious Blood, died
1861	Frederick William IV, King of Prussia, died
1871	Nevada's legislature first met in its capitol
1890	The Persia wrecked off Corsica
1896	Jameson Raiders surrendered at Doornkop (Boer War)
1905	Port Arthur, Russia surrendered to Japan
1907	Train wreck near Volland, Kansas
1912	Ann Sothern, actress, born
1920	Isaac Asimov, author, born
1924	Simon & Schuster, publishers, founded
1926	The State of Washington adopted its flag
1942	The Japanese occupied Manila, Philippines
1950	Robert E. Vogeler, U.S. businessman, arrested as a spy in Hungary and its consulates in the U.S. were ordered closed
1955	José Antonio Remon, President of Panama, assassinated
1959	Lunik I, Russian moon probe, launched
1963	A packing plant exploded in Terre Haute, Indiana
1968	First successful human heart transplant performed
1972	Start of National "Save the Pun" Week

January 3rd

Feast of St. Genevieve, patroness of Paris, invoked against fever

106 BC	Cicero, Roman politican, born
236	St. Antherus ended his 43 days as Pope
533	St. Fulgentius of Ruspe, bishop, died
964	Roman citizens attacked the Vatican
1399	Tamerlane and the Mongols defeated Emperor Mahmud of India
1437	Catherine of Valois, wife of King Henry V of England, died
1521	Martin Luther was excommunicated
1565	Ivan the Terrible, Czar of Russia, voiced his intention to abdicate
1661	First Polish newspaper published
1694	St. Paul of the Cross born
1777	Washington defeated the British at Princeton, New Jersey

1795	Josiah Wedgewood, potter, died
1801	Port Folio, Philadelphia weekly newspaper, founded
1816	The Recorder, Boston newspaper, began publication
1820	Providence Journal, Rhode Island newspaper, founded
1826	Military Society of the War of 1812 formed
1831	First U.S. building and loan association organized
1840	First deep-sea sounding (ocean depth measurement)
1846	Broadway Journal, weekly, expired after 52 issues
1847	Yerba Buena renamed San Francisco (California)
1862	Union victory at Mufreesboro-Stones River, Tennessee
1870	Brooklyn Bridge construction begun
1879	Grace Coolidge, wife of the President, born
1883	Clement Atlee, British statesman, born
1888	Waxed paper drinking straws patented
1894	Elizabeth P. Peabody, founder of first U.S. kindergarten, died
1895	James Merritt Ives, Currier's lithography partner, died
1907	Ray Milland, actor, born
1909	Victor Borge, comedian-musician, born
1924	Food plant explosion in Pekin, Illinois
1938	"March of Dimes," anti-polio campaign, organized
	First BBC broadcast aired that was not in English
1944	U.S.S. Turner exploded off New York harbor
1946	William Joyce, Nazi broadcaster, hanged in Britain for treason
1954	Tobacco companies undertook study of smoking-cancer link
1959	Alaska became a state
1960	Moscow State Symphony became the first from Russia to play in the U.S. (New York City)
1961	U.S. severed diplomatic relations with Cuba
1970	Old Christmas Celebration (Rodanthe, North Carolina)

January 4th

----

48 BC	Caesar arrived in Greece pursuing Pompey
275	St. Eutychian became Pope
871	The Danes defeated the English at Reading
1700	Western European dress declared the rule in Russia

1754	Kings College (Columbia University) founded in New York
1776	<u>New York Packet and the American Advertiser</u> newspaper founded, lasting till 1798
	All but St. Paul's Church in Norfolk, Virginia destroyed by fire
1785	Jacob Grimm, fairy-tale writer, born
1789	Thomas Nelson, Jr., signer of the Declaration of Independence, died
1809	Louis Braille, blind-alphabet inventor, born
1813	Sir Isaac Pitman, shorthand inventor, born
1821	Mother Elizabeth Seaton, founder of the Sisters of Charity, died
1825	Ferdinand IV, King of Naples, died
1831	Edward P. Dutton, publisher, born
1832	Maine's legislature first met in its state house
1845	<u>Broadway Journal</u>, weekly, founded
1847	The U.S. government ordered 1,000 Colt pistols
1864	Designated birthday of scientist George Washington Carver
	Two of Plummer's gang hanged near Alder, Montana
1870	<u>La Nacion</u>, newspaper, first appeared in Argentina
1877	Cornelius Vanderbilt, millionaire, died
1883	<u>Life</u>, New York satirical weekly founded (sold to Time, Inc. in 1936)
1884	First recorded successful appendix removal
1896	Senator Everett Dirksen born
	Utah became a state
1933	<u>L'Atlantique</u> burned in the English Channel
1935	Floyd Patterson, boxer, born
1948	Burma became independent of Britain
1960	European Free Trade Association formed among countries outside the Common Market
1964	Pope Paul VI began his trip to the Holy Land
1966	Reconstruction of Abu Simbel temples begun on a dry site in Egypt
1969	Ifni province returned to Morocco by Spain

January 5th

	Our Lady of Altagracia (Venezuela)
	Feast of St. Simeon the Stylite who dwelt atop a pillar
	Feast of St. Telesphorus, Pope
1066 AD	Edward the Confessor, King of England, died
1371	Pierre Roger crowned Pope Gregory XI
1477	Swiss victory over the Burgundians and Charles the Bold at Nancy
1537	Duke of Florence (de Medici) assassinated by a kinsman
1589	Catherine de Medici, Queen of France, died
1762	Empress Elizabeth of Russia, died

1771	Kalmucks gathered to leave Russian oppression by returning to China
1776	New Hampshire set up a noncolonial government
1778	Explosives set afloat on the Delaware to destroy the British feet, but none of them exploded
	Zebulon Pike, discoverer of Pike's Peak, born
1781	British burned Richmond, Virginia
1782	Robert Morrison, first Protestant minister to China, born
1796	Samuel Huntington, signer of the Declaration of Independence, died
1814	Sir John Burke, originator of Burke's Peerage, born
1859	First steamboat set sail on the Red River
1867	Konrad Adenauer, German statesman, born
1875	New Paris Opera House opened
1887	First Library School in the U.S. opened (Columbia University)
1914	Workers at Ford Motor Co. granted a raise from $2.40 for 9 hours to $5.00 for 8 hours
1921	Grand Duke Jean, ruler of Luxembourg, born
1922	Sir Ernest Shackleton, Antarctic explorer, died
1925	First Woman governor in U.S. installed (Nellie Taylor Ross; Wyoming)
1933	Calvin Coolidge, U.S. President, died
1943	George Washington Carver, scientist, died
1950	Britain severed diplomatic relations with Nationalist China

January 6th

	Three King's Day; Epiphany
	Greeks dive for the Cross at Tarpon Springs, Florida
	Baptism of Christ (Orthodox)
	Installation of Governors at most New Mexico pueblos
1205	Philip again crowned King of Germany
1311	King Henry VII of Germany crowned himself King of the Lombards
1349	Third vicar appointed at Shaftsbury, England, when predecessors died of the plague
1355	Charles IV crowned King of the Lombards
1367	King Richard II of England, inventor of the handkerchief, born
1373	St. Andrew Corsini died
1401	Rupert crowned King of Germany
1412	St. Joan of Arc, born
1425	Henry IV, "The Impotent," King of Castile, born

```
1540        King Henry VIII of England married his fourth
                 wife, Anne of Cleves
1579        Union of Arras formed
1661        Fifth Monarchy men tried to take possession of
                 London
1759        George Washington married widow Martha D. Curtis
1797        Albany became the permanent capital of New York
1821        Indianapolis site chosen as Indiana's capital
1828        Ward H. Lamon, Abraham Lincoln's law partner,
                 born
1838        Telegraph first publicly tested
1857        Second Vermont legislature building burned down
1871        Henry Morton Stanley landed on Zanzibar
1872        James Fisk, financier, shot by a former business
                 partner
1878        Carl Sandburg, poet, born
1882        Sam Rayburn, Congressman, born
1898        First telephone message sent by a submerged
                 submarine
1900        Kathryn Hulme, author, born
1906        Cuban national flag officially adopted
            First Gypsy Congress held in Sofia, Bulgaria
1912        Frederick Manfred, author, born
            New Mexico became a state
1914        Loretta Young, actress, born
            Danny Thomas, comedian, born
1916        British battleship Edward VII sunk by a mine
1919        Theodore Roosevelt, U.S. President, died
            County agricultural offices created in France
1921        Cary Middlecoff, golfer, born
1922        Philadelphia-Camden Bridge opened
1927        Marines sent to Nicaragua to protect U.S.
                 interests
1941        Franklin D. Roosevelt made his "Four Freedoms"
                 speech to Congress
1946        Poland nationalized its basic industries
1950        Britain recognized Communist China
1964        Pope Paul VI ended his trip through the Holy
                 Land
            Hello Dolly opened on Broadway
1967        Trial irregularities caused espionage charges
                 to be dropped in the Coplon and
                 Gubicher case
1970        Dezome-shiki or New Year's Parade of Firemen,
                 in Tokyo, Japan
```

January 7th_____

```
            Feast of St. John the Baptist (Orthodox)
            Orthodox and Coptic Christmas
            Oriental White Horse Banquet (for a prosperous
                 year)
```

```
                Chief festival at Hongu Shrine, Japan
                        reactivating the shrine's
                        amulet
                Feast of St. Distaff
                Start of Fasching Carnival, Germany
    312 AD      Lucian, martyred Christian saint, died
                        for his faith (Feast Day)
    1131        St. Canute Lavard murdered (Feast Day)
    1285        Charles I, King of Naples and Sicily, died
    1566        Michael Ghislieri elected Pope (Pius V)
    1598        Czar Theodore of Muscovy died
    1610        Jupiter's major satellites first seen,
                        by Galileo
    1655        Pope Innocent X died
    1670        St. Charles of Sezze, lay friar, died
                        (Feast Day)
    1714        First typewriter patent issued (England)
    1761        Mogul rule in India ended
    1789        First U.S. presidential election held
    1800        Millard Fillmore, U.S. President, born
    1822        Missionaries began printing textbooks in
                        Hawaiian
    1830        Sir Thomas Lawrence, English artist, died
    1845        King Louis III of Bavaria born
    1865        Indians attempted to ambush Cavalry of Iowa
                        Volunteers at Julesburg,
                        Colorado
    1879        King William III of Holland married
                        Adelheid of Waldeck-Pyronont
    1888        "The Players," club for New York theatrical
                        people, founded
    1912        Charles Addams, cartoonist, born
    1937        Juliana, heiress to the throne of Holland,
                        married Prince Bernhard of
                        Lippe-Beisterfeld
    1944        Lou H. Hoover, wife of the President, died
    1968        Surveyor VII landed on the moon
    1970        Start of the Narcissus Festival at
                        Honolulu, Hawaii
```

January 8th

```
                Feast of St. Gudula of Belgium
                Feast of St. Pega, hermitess,sister of
                        St. Guthlac
                Feast of St. Lucian of Beauvais
    482 AD      St. Severinus of Noricum, missionary to
                        Austria, died (Feast Day)
    786         St. Abo died (Feast Day celebrated in
                        Russia)
    1081        Henry V, Holy Roman Emperor, born
```

```
1198      Pope Celestine III died and Innocent III
                   elected
1285      St. Thorfinn, Norwegian bishop, died (Feast
                   Day)
1455      St. Lawrence Giustiniani died
1506      Sigismund I elected King of Poland
1536      Catherine of Aragon, first wife of King Henry
                   VIII of England, died
1547      King Henry VIII of England died
1642      Galileo, astronomer, died
1705      Handel's first opera, Almira, premiered
1792      Lowell Mason, author of "Nearer My God to Thee,"
                   Born
1815      British defeated at the Battle of New Orleans
1862      Frank N. Doubleday, publisher, born
1884      Texas legislature called into special session
                   to settle "Fence-cutters War"
1891      William Kiplinger, founder of Kiplinger Letter,
                   born
1904      Peter Arno, cartoonist, born
1918      Mississippi became the first state to ratify
                   the Prohibition amendment
          President Wilson's "14 Points" submitted to
                   Congress
1921      Chequers, official residence of England's
                   Prime Minister, had its first
                   housewarming
1926      Ibn Saud crowned King of Arabia
1959      Castro's revolution victorious in Cuba
1962      Saba (Yugoslavia) and Dorington Court
                   (England) collided in the
                   English Channel
1971      Voyageurs National Park created (U.S.)
```

January 9th

```
          Feast of St. Julian
          Ancient Roman Festival of Agonalia
          Feast of St. Fillian
 639 AD   Dagobert, King of the Franks, died
 710      St. Adrian of Canterbury died (Feast Day)
1324      Marco Polo, traveler, died
1569      St. Philip of Moscow, Primate of the Russian
                   Church, killed by Ivan the
                   Terrible (Feast Day)
1570      Ivan the Terrible, Czar of Russia, began the
                   massacre of Novgorod
1675      Holy Roman Imperial Army defeated at Turkmeim
                   in an attempt to invade France
1684      Ivan V, Czar of Russia, married Praskovia
                   Saltvikova
1788      Connecticut ratified the U.S. Constitution
```

1793	First successful U.S. balloon flight (15 miles)
	First parachute ride in America taken, according to the rider, Blanchard
1819	William Powell Frith, English artist, born
1820	Maine adopted its state coat of arms
1861	Mississippi seceded from the Union
1867	Emperor Meiji acceded to the throne of Japan
1878	Victor Emmanuel II, King of Italy, died
1879	Dull Knife's Cheyenne Indians escaped the prison at Fort Robinson
1893	Louis Daguerre received France's Legion of Honor for his photography invention
1897	Felisa Rincon de Gautier, Puerto Rican stateswoman, born
1898	Gracie Fields, actress-comedienne, born
1900	Richard Halliburton, author, born
1902	Rudolph Bing, manager of the Metropolitan Opera, born
1908	Simone de Beauvoir, writer, born
1913	Richard M. Nixon, 37th President of the U.S., born
1938	Johnny Gruelle, creator of Raggedy Ann, died
1945	U.S. forces invaded Luzon, Philippines
1952	Freighter Pennsylvania sank in a Pacific storm
1953	Chang Tyong-Ho foundered off Pusan, Korea
1960	Construction of Aswan High Dam begun (Egypt)
1970	Fur and Wildlife Festival at Cameron, Louisiana
	U.S.S.R. launched its Cosmos 318 space vehicle

January 10th

	St. Gregory of Nyssa (Orthodox Feast Day)
681 AD	Pope St. Agatho died
987	St. Peter Orseolo, doge of Venice, died (Feast Day)
1276	Pope Gregory X died
1295	Monks of Paisley, Scotland got their charter
1430	Order of the Golden Fleece established in Spain and Austria
1532	Ruiz, conqueror, arrived in Ecuador
1737 or 1738	Ethan Allen, American patriot, born
1778	Carolus Linnaeus, botanist, died
1791	Portland Head Lighthouse begun, the first in Maine
1807	England declared all trade with France illegal
	President Jefferson received the report of the Lewis and Clark expedition
1812	Steam-powered vessel, New Orleans, arrived there from Pittsburgh
1840	England's penny-postal system established

1844	Pyramid Lake, Nevada discovered
1845	Elizabeth Barrett and Robert Browning began corresponding
1861	Florida seceded from the Union
1862	Samuel Colt, revolver inventor, died
1880	St. Botolph Club founded in Boston
1882	O. P. Brigg patented his barbed wire
1883	Francis X. Bushman, actor, born
1887	Robinson Jeffers, poet, born
1891	American Sugar Refining Company incorporated
1893	Meyer Davis, orchestra leader, born
	Ferdinand I of Rumania married Marie of Saxe-Coburg-Gotha-England
1901	Oil was discovered in Texas
1904	Ray Bolger, performer, born
1917	William F. ("Buffalo Bill") Cody, showman, died
1916	Pancho Villa raided Santa Isabel (Mexican Revolution)
1920	League of Nations begun in Geneva, Switzerland
1924	British submarine L-24 involved in a collision off Portland, England
1925	"Ma" Ferguson inaugurated governor of Texas
1946	League of Nations dissolved
	First United Nations General Assembly met (London)
	Radar beam reached the moon
1951	Sinclair Lewis, novelist, died
1952	Freighter Flying Enterprise sank in a storm off Lizard Point, England
1960	Dashiell Hammett, author, died
1962	Devastating avalanche in Peru
1966	Spanish freighter Monte Palomares sank in a North Atlantic storm
1970	Pancake Feed at Ord, Nebraska
1971	"Coco" Chanel, fashion designer, died

January 11th

	De Hosto Birthday Celebrations in Puerto Rico
	Feast of St. Balthasar, patron of playing-card makers; invoked against epilepsy
	Log-hauling and axe ceremonies at the site of the Nachi Falls Pagoda in Japan
	Ancient Roman festival of Luturna
49 BC	Caesar crossed the Rubicon
29 BC	Temple of Janus closed for the first time in 200 years (Rome)
314 AD	Pope St. Miltiades died
529	St. Theodosius of Cenobiarch died, age 105 (Feast Day)
705	Pope John VI died
802	St. Paulinus of Aquileia died (Feast Day)

1693	Mt. Etna volcano, Sicily, erupted

1693   Mt. Etna volcano, Sicily, erupted
1757   Alexander Hamilton, American statesman, born
1775   Ivanovich Pugachev, pretender to the Russian
        throne as Czar Peter III, executed
1797   Francis Lightfoot Lee, signer of the Declara-
        tion of Independence, died
1805   Michigan became a U.S. territory
1808   Jean Gilbert Victor Fialin Persigny, French
        statesman, born
1815   Sir John MacDonald, first Premier of Canada,
        born
1822   Missouri adopted its state coat-of-arms
1843   Francis Scott Key, author of the "Star-
        Spangled Banner," died
1861   Alabama seceded from the Union
1866   London foundered in the Bay of Biscay
1870   Alice H. Rice, author of Mrs. Wiggs and the
        Cabbage Patch, born
1872   Jean Gilbert Victor Fialin Persigny, French
        statesman, died
1880   Solar eclipse
1911   Hank Greenburg, baseball player, born
1912   Russ foundered in the Black Sea
1923   France and Belgium occupied the Ruhr Valley to
        enforce repatriation
1942   Japan declared war on Holland
1951   Charles W. Goddard, author of the movies
        Perils of Pauline, died
1965   Milan, Italy's cathedral completed
1968   Geos II satellite launched by the U.S.
1970   City Ice Skating Championships at Aurora,
        Illinois

January 12th --

        "Burning of the Clavie" at Burghead, Scotland
        Feast of St. Benedict (Benet) Bishop
        Feast of St. Tatiana
1519 AD Maximilian I, Holy Roman Emperor, died
1588 OS John Winthrop, first governor of Massachusetts,
        born
1632   Lazarites, or Congregation of Priests of the
        Mission, founded
1643   Warwick, Rhode Island, settled
1729   Edmund Burke, English statesman, born
1737 OS John Hancock, signer, born
1751   Frederick IV, King of Naples, born
1773   The Charlestown Museum, first in America,
        organized (S.C.)
1810   Ferdinand II, "King Bomba" of Sicily, born
1839   Iron first made with hard coal (Pennsylvania)
1856   John Singer Sargent, artist, born

```
1861    U.S. Naval Yard at Pensacola seized by Florida
            Confederates
1876    Jack London, novelist, born
        L'Athenne Louisianais, French literary society,
            founded in New Orleans
1897    Sir Isaac Pitman, shorthand inventor, died
1918    Distinguished Service Cross and Medal
            instituted (U.S.)
1919    Train wrecked in South Byron, New York
1929    Cascade Tunnel of the Great Northern Railroad
            first used by a train (U.S.)
1933    First woman elected to the U.S. Senate
            (Mrs. Hattie W. Caraway)
1950    Truculent, British submarine, sank in the
            Thames estuary
1952    Archbishop Stepinac of Yugoslavia made a
            Cardinal
1967    Northern Mexico devastated by a storm
1971    U.S.S.R. launched Cosmos 309 into space
```

January 13th

```
        Plowman's Festival
        Ides of January
        New Years' Day Old Style (OS) or according
            to the Julian calendar
86 BC   Gaius Marius, Roman general, died
533 AD  St. Remi or Remigius, apostle of France, died
1327    Edward III proclaimed King of England
1330    Frederick III, King of Germany, died
1522    King Louis II of Hungary and Bohemia married
            Maria of Austria
1609    Augsburger Abendseitung, newspaper of Bavaria,
            Germany, founded, lasting till 1934
1649    The Bastille fell to the forces of the Fronde
            (Paris)
1733    James Oglethorpe and 120 colonists arrived in
            Charlestown, South Carolina,
            headed for Georgia
1785    Samuel Woodworth, poet, born
1794    Legislation passed to add more stars to the
            U.S. flag
1808    Salmon P. Chase, U.S. statesman, born
1834    Horatio Alger, author, born
1837    Almost all of the business district of St.
            Johns, New Brunswick, Canada,
            destroyed by fire
1857    Chicago Academy of Sciences founded
        Plate fulcrum railway track scale patented
1864    Stephen Foster, composer, died (Memorial
            Day in U.S.)
1874    T'ung-Chih became Emperor of China
```

```
1875        First American dynamo completed (Cornell
                  University)
1883        Theater fire in Bendichev, Russia
1885        Schuyler Colfax, U.S. Vice President, died
1892        414 died when the Namchow was wrecked in the
                  China Sea
1898        Theosophical Society of the Universal Brother-
                  hood founded
            Emile Zola's "J'accuse" about the Dreyfus case
                  first appeared in a French
                  newspaper
1908        Rhoades Opera House movie theater burned
                  (Bovertown, Penna.)
            Henry Farnum won $10,000 for a successful
                  flight in a heavier-than-air
                  vehicle
1913        Central Italy rocked by an earthquake
1915        An earthquake shook Avezzano, Italy
1925        Gwen Verdon, musical performer, born
1961        U. S. and Brazil signed an extradition treaty
1970        Rural recognition banquet at Columbus, Nebraska
1971        Apollo 14 and 3 Americans took off for the moon
```

January 14th

```
            Russian Orthodox New Year
            Feast of St. Felix of Nola, invoked against
                  perjury
            Feast of the Ass celebrated in Northern France
            Celebration at Beauvais representing the Jews'
                  flight into Egypt (Roman Catholic;
                  France)
            Feast of St. Kentigern of Mungo
            Feast of St. Macrina the Elder
 346 AD     St. Barba'shmin, Persian martyr died (Feast
                  Day)
 936 AD     Rudolph, King of the Franks, died
1235        St. Sava or Sabas died (patron of Serbia;
                  Feast Day)
1237        King Henry III of England married Eleanor
                  of Provence
1331        Odoric, missionary to China, died
1478        Novgorod, Russia surrendered to the Czar
1639        Planters in Connecticut wrote the first
                  American Constitution
1659        Portuguese defeated the Spanish at Elvas
1730        William Whipple, signer of the Declaration of
                  Independence, born
1741        Benedict Arnold, Revolutionary War traitor,
                  born
1766        King Frederick V of Denmark and Norway died
1784        Peace treaty with England ratified by Congress
```

```
1797        French-Austrian battle at Rivoli, Italy
1814        Treaty of Kiel united Sweden and Norway
1863        R. F. Outcault, creator of Buster Brown,
                 born
1867        Jean Auguste Dominique Ingres, French
                 artist, died
1874        Thornton Burgess, author of children's
                 books, born
1875        Albert Schweitzer, doctor-missionary, born
1886        Hugh Lofting, creator of Dr. Dolittle, born
1901        Carlos Romulo, President of the Philippines,
                 born
1904        Cecil Beaton, photographer, born
1907        Kingston, Jamaica, suffered an earthquake
1908        Illinois chose its state tree (oak), and
                 flower (violet)
1926        Solar eclipse visible over the Indian Ocean
1928        Chicago, Milwaukee, St. Paul and Pacific
                 Railroad Company founded
1935        First train crossed the Lower Zambezi Bridge
                 (Africa)
1950        U.S. recalled all consular personnel from
                 Red China
1954        Nash-Kelvinator and Hudson Motor Car Co.
                 merged
1964        Blair House, the official U.S. guesthouse, was
                 completed in its restoration
1967        Korean ferry Hanil-Ho sank after a collision
1970        Thai Pongal Day (Hindus of Thailand honor
                 the Sun God)
            Pongal-Sankranti (harvest festival and New Year
                 celebrated by the Hindus in India)
1972        King Frederick IX of Denmark died
```

```
=====================================================
January 15th
-----------------------------------------------------
=====================================================
```

```
            Feast of the Child Jesus (Venezuela)
            Adults' Day Holiday in Japan
            Korean Festival of the Five Grains
            Burning the Emperor's First Writings (Japan;
                 New Year's writings)
            Feast of St. Ita, Irish abbess
            Feast of St. Macarius the Elder, desert monk
            Feast of St. Paul the Hermit (of Thebes),
                 first Christian hermit
            Start of the month-long Winter Festival at
                 Malaga, Spain
 708 AD     Sisinnius elected Pope
1208        St. Peter of Castelnau died
1485        Catherine of Aragon, first wife of King Henry
                 VIII of England, born
1559        Queen Elizabeth I of England crowned
```

1622	Molière, French drama writer, born
1701	Prussia proclaimed a kingdom
1716	Philip Livingston, signer of the Declaration of Independence, born
1759	The British Museum opened to the public
1844	University of Notre Dame founded (South Bend, Indiana)
1879	H.M.S. Pinafore, Gilbert and Sullivan operetta, had its U.S. debut
1896	Mathew Brady, pioneer photographer, died
1902	King Saud of Arabia was born, later to be ousted from ruling
1909	Gene Krupa, drummer, born
1915	Fanny Farmer, noted cook and candy maker, died
1918	Gamal Abdul Nasser, head of the United Arab Republic, born
1929	Martin Luther King, Jr., civil rights leader, born
1932	Japanese priest killed in China
1937	Margaret O'Brien, child actress, born
1943	Pentagon building completed (Washington, D.C.)
1944	San Juan, Argentina, rocked by an earthquake
1951	Ilse Koch sentenced for German concentration camp murder
1961	Texas Tower 4, a lighthouse off New Jersey, collapsed
1968	Sicily hit by an earthquake
1970	End of the Narcissus Festival at Honolulu, Hawaii
1971	Santo Nino Fiesta held in the Philippines

January 16th

27 BC	Octavian was given the title of "Augustus" by the Roman Senate
309 AD	St. Marcellus, Pope, died
429	St. Honaratus of Arles, bishop and founder of the monastery at Lerins, died (Feast Day)
648	St. Fursey, an Irish monk whose writings were the inspiration for Dante's Divine Comedy, died (Feast Day)
1066	Harold was crowned King of England
1153	St. Bernard and his companions were martyred (Feast Day)
1409	Rene I, King of Naples, Sicily, and Jerusalem, born
1547	Ivan the Terrible was crowned Czar of Russia
1556	Charles V, King of Spain and Holy Roman Emperor, abdicated
1599	Edmund Spenser, English poet, died

1605	Charles I, future King of England, made Duke of York
1775	Captain Cook discovered St. George Island
1777	Royal American Gazette, New York newspaper, founded
1794	Edward Gibbon, author of the Decline and Fall of the Roman Empire, died
1815	Brazil was decreed a kingdom, independent of Portugal
1822	"Old Grimes," a poem by Albert G. Greene, was first published (Providence Gazette)
1855	Nebraska's legislature first met
1862	J. H. Speke became the first white man to see the Kagera River (Africa)
1876	Edmund H. Sears, "It Came Upon a Midnight Clear" author, died
1883	U.S. Civil Service System was established
1888	The Order of United Commercial Travelers of America was established
1891	The first shot in Chile's civil war was fired
1906	Marshall Field, merchant, died
1909	Ethel Merman, entertainer, born
1911	"Dizzy" Dean, baseball great, born
1919	The Prohibition Amendment became part of the U.S. Constitution when Nebraska ratified it
1920	Eighteenth Amendment went into effect and sale of alcoholic beverages was banned in the U.S.
	Reginald De Koven, author of "O Promise Me," died
	The blockade of U.S.S.R. was raised
1938	Spanish insurgents began aerial bombing of Barcelona
1962	Alberta, Canada rocked by a gas pipeline explosion
1968	Cosmos 119, U.S.S.R. satellite, launched
1970	Pongal-sankranti, Indian harvest festival, ended
	Start of Sandy Shoes Festival, Fort Pierce, Florida
1972	Solar eclipse visible in the Antarctic

January 17th

	Feast of St. Sulpice, bishop
	Festival of the Little Drinking Mugs, Evora, Portugal
356 AD	St. Anthony the Abbot died, patron of monks; Mexican pets are blessed
395	Theodosius I, Roman emperor, died of dropsy

```
1328    Louis IV was crowned Holy Roman Emperor
1411    Jobst, King of Germany, died
1465    Johann Gutenberg, printing-press inventor,
                    was granted a civil pension for
                    services to Mainz, Germany
1549    Thomas Seymour, Lord High Admiral of England,
                    arrested
1562    Edict of Toleration (Protestants in France)
1706    Benjamin Franklin, statesman, born
1773    Captain Cook's 2 ships became first to cross
                    the Antarctic Circle
1781    British were defeated at Cowpens, South
                    Carolina
1785    English Channel was crossed by a manned balloon
1791    Isaac Pinto, translator of the first Jewish
                    prayerbook printed in America,
                    died
1793    A French convention voted to send Louis XVI,
                    to the guillotine
1794    Andrew Jackson,  U.S. President, married
                    Rachel D. Roberts
1860    Anton Chekhov, Russian writer-physician, born
1861    Lola Montez, mistress of Ludwig of Bavaria,
                    died
1893    Rutherford B. Hayes, U.S. President, died
1919    French Chaonia with 460 aboard lost in the
                    Straits of Messina
1920    Volstead Act, enforcing the Prohibition Amend-
                    ment, passed by Congress over
                    the President's veto
1926    Moira Shearer, ballerina, born
1949 or 1950  Great robbery of a Brinks' armored truck
                    in Boston
1959    Mali Federation formed
1961    Patrice Lumumba, ousted President of the Congo,
                    murdered
```

January 18th

```
        Feast of St. Prisca or Priscilla, virgin martyr
336 AD  St. Mark became Pope
697     Dance and Song Banquet last given by the
                    Japanese emperor
888     Charles III, "the Fat," deposed King of the
                    West Franks, died
1095    St. Wulfstan died
1256    Marie, wife of King Louis II of Bavaria,
                    beheaded
1270    St. Margaret of Hungary, Dominican nun, died
                    (Feast Day)
1514    Balboa returned to Darien from the Pacific
1535    Pizarro founded Lima, Peru
```

1671	Henry Morgan and his buccaneers attacked the city of Panama
1701	Frederick I crowned King of Prussia
1775	Georgia's Provincial Congress first met (Savannah)
1777	Mission Santa Clara de Asis, San Jose, California, founded
1778	Captain Cook first sighted Hawaii
1782	Daniel Webster, U.S. statesman-orator, born
1788	First British convicts landed in Australia
1844	Horace H. Hayden, founder of the first U.S. dental college, died
1861	John Heathcoat, lace-maker inventor, died
1862	John Tyler, U.S. President, died
1863	Said, Viceroy of Egypt, died
1871	Wilhelm I was proclaimed ruler of Germany and Prussia
1872	Publishers' Weekly, a trade journal, founded in New York as Weekly Trade Journal
1884	City of Columbus wrecked off Massachusetts
1886	Field Hockey Association formed
1904	Cary Grant, actor, born
1912	Scott's expedition reached the South Pole but never returned
1913	Danny Kaye, actor-comedian, born
1918	Harmon Helmericks, author-explorer, born
1919	Peace conferences opened in Paris
1936	Rudyard Kipling, author, died
1951	Mt. Lamington, New Guinea began 3 days of volcanic eruptions
1956	Tanker Salem Maritime exploded in Lake Charles, Louisiana
1967	Eastern Brazil hit by 6 days of flood
1970	Euzkaldunak's Muz Tournament (Basque folk game) at Boise, Idaho
	Fish Derby at Oconto Falls, Wisconsin

January 19th

	Feast of Sts. Audifax and Abachum, sons of Marius and Martha
	Feast of St. Canute IV, King of Denmark
	Feast of St. Henry of Uppsala, martyred bishop, patron saint of Finland
	Feast of Sts. Marius and Martha, martyrs
379 AD	Theodosius I, Roman emperor, named "Augustus"
1095	St. Wulfstan, bishop of Worcester, died (Feast Day)
1160	The retired Japanese emperor was kidnapped
1544	King Francis II of France was born
1736	James Watt, steam-engine inventor, born

1806	Britain took possession of the Cape Colony (South Africa)
1807	Robert E. Lee, Civil War general, born (Southern U.S. holiday)
1809	Edgar Allan Poe, writer, born
1813	Sir Henry Bessemer, steel-making inventor, born
1839	Paul Cezanne, French artist, born
1855	Mescalero Apaches ambushed the First Dragoons of the U.S. Cavalry in New Mexico
1861	Georgia seceded from the Union
1883	Germany's Cambria hit an iceberg; 389 died
1887	Alexander Woollcott, author, born
1907	Train wreck in Fowler, Indiana
1910	National Institute of Arts and Letters incorporated by an act of Congress
1927	Empress Charlotte, wife of Maxmilian, of Mexico, died
1940	Province of Osorno, Chile created
1943	Princess Margriet of the Netherlands born
1947	Greek Hemeia hit a mine off Athens and 392 died
1961	Dr. Thomas Dooley, medical missionary to Viet Nam, died
1970	Vasant Panchami (Hindu harvest festival in Surinam)

January 20th

	U.S. Presidential Inauguration Day
	St. Agnes Eve
	Feast of St. Sebastian, invoked against plague
250 AD	St. Fabian, Pope, martyred
473	St. Euthymius the Great died (Feast Day)
1320	Wladislaus was crowned king of Poland
1479	John II, King of Aragon, died
1500	Pinzon discovered Brazil
1612	Rudolph II, Holy Roman Emperor, died
1615	Portuguese again defeated by the British off Swally, India
1732	Richard Henry Lee, signer of the Declaration of Independence, born
1734	Robert Morris, signer of the Declaration of Independence, born
1779	David Garrick, English actor, died
1788	The first settlers, mostly convicts, arrived in New South Wales, Australia
1795	The French cavalry captured the ice-bound Dutch fleet
1830	Red Jacket, chief of the Seneca Indians, died
1840	Adelie Island, Antarctic, discovered by Jules d'Urville
1866	Livingstone landed in Zanzibar

1870	Jenny Lind, singer, gave her last performance
1879	New Orleans mint began manufacturing money
1880	Ruth St. Denis, dancer, born
1882	Franklin D. Roosevelt, U.S. President, born
1887	Ships Kapunda and Ada Melmore collided in Brazil
1891	Mischa Elman, violinist, born
1892	The first real basketball game was played
1894	Harold L. Gray, creator of "Little Orphan Annie," born
1918	German warship Breslau mined off Imbros Island
1925	"Ma" Ferguson installed as governor of Texas
1926	Charles M. Doughty, Arabian explorer, died
	Patricia Neal, actress, born
1936	King George V of England died of a chill
1939	El Salvador adopted a constitution
1962	Robinson Jeffers, poet, died
1969	Marble Canyon proclaimed a National Monument
1970	Grandmothers' Day in Bulgaria
1971	Meteor 7, U.S.S.R. weather satellite, launched

January 21st

----

259 AD	St. Fructuosus of Tarragona died (Feast Day)
304	St. Agnes, patron of young girls, martyred (Feast Day) (As St. Inez, patron of Cumana, Venezuela)
861	St. Meinrad died (Feast Day)
1506	Papal Swiss Guard first entered Rome
1527	Juan de Grijalva, discoverer of Mexico, died
1670	Claude Duval, English highwayman, hanged
1743	John Fitch, steamboat pioneer, born
1785	U.S. treaty signed with the Wyandot, Delaware, Chippewa, and Ottowa Indians
1793	King Louis XVI of France guillotined
1813	John C. Fremont, California explorer, born
1824	General "Stonewall" Jackson born
1829	Oscar II, King of Sweden and Norway, born
1831	Paterson-Hudson Railroad Company incorporated
1846	The London Daily News first appeared
1851	The first practical envelope-folding machine was patented
1865	Akron, Ohio, incorporated as a city
1869	PEO Sisterhood founded (Paternal Order of Eagles)
1873	Eliza H. Bordman died, having succeeded in making Washington's birthday a U.S. holiday
1879	Cheyenne Indians imprisoned at Fort Robinson escaped
1906	Aquidaban exploded off Brazil

1908	A law was passed making it illegal for a woman to smoke in public in New York City
1914 or 1915	The first Kiwanis Club was chartered Edwin Ginn, founder of Ginn Brothers Publishers, died
1918	British Louvain torpedoed in the Mediterranean
1919	Jinx Falkenburg, the first "Miss Rheingold," was born
1924	Vladimir Lenin, Russian Communist leader, died
1926	Makwar Dam on the Egyptian Nile River opened
1930	First BBC broadcast to the world aired "Buck Rogers" comic strip first published
1934	Weitung, a Chinese ship, burned in the Yangtze River
1940	Jack Niklaus, golfer, born
1941	Start of 4 days of experimental air-raid-warning tests in New England
1945	Japanese kamakazi planes killed 144 aboard the aircraft carrier Ticonderoga
1951	Mt. Lamington, New Guinea ceased erupting
1954	Nautilus, the first atomic submarine, launched
1959	Cecil B. DeMille, theatrical personality, died
1961	George Washington, nuclear submarine, completed a journey under the Arctic ice
1964	Relay II, U.S. communications satellite, launched
1966	Druid New Year celebrations
1971	Sultan's Birthday Celebration at Kedah, Malaysia

January 22nd
----

304 AD	St. Vincent of Saragossa, patron of the wine industry, died (Feast Day)
628	St. Anastasius the Persian died (Feast Day)
1498	Columbus discovered St. Vincent Island
1561	Francis Bacon, English philosopher-statesman, born
1671	Czar Alexei of Russia married Natalya Naryshkina
1788	George Gordon, Lord Byron, writer, born
1789	The first American novel, The Power of Sympathy published
1798	Lewis Morris, signer of the Declaration of Independence, died
1813	Massacre of the Raisin River (Indians; Michigan settlers)
1840	The first British colonists landed in New Zealand
1850	St. Vincent Pallotti died (Feast Day)
1873	Northfleet lost after a collision off Scotland

1879	Francis Picoba, French artist, born
1881	Obelisk raised in Central Park (New York City)
1901	England's Queen Victoria died
1903	U.S. and Colombia signed a treaty over the digging of the Panama Canal
1905	"Bloody Sunday" (protest march shootings; St. Petersburg, Russia)
1906	Valencia lost off Vancouver Island
1916	Pollentia foundered in mid-Atlantic
1922	Pope Benedict XV died
1939	Uranium atom split at Columbia University
1949	Communists took over Peiping, China
1956	Los Angeles, California, train wreck
1964	Zambia, formerly Northern Rhodesia, became independent
1965	Tiros 9, U.S. weather satellite, launched
1968	Apollo V, unmanned, sent into an Earth orbit
1972	England, Ireland, Norway, and Denmark joined the European Common Market
1973	Lyndon B. Johnson, 36th President of the U.S., died

January 23rd

	Betrothal of Mary and Joseph
	Feast of St. John the Almsgiver, patron of the Order of St. John at Jerusalem, the Knights of Malta
	Sun reappears at Hammerfest, Norway
667 AD	St. Ildefonsus died (Feast Day)
1002	Otto III, Emperor of the West, died
1264	Provisions of Oxford, English reforms, annulled
1275	St. Raymond of Penafort died (Feast Day)
1295	Benedict Gaetani crowned Pope Boniface VIII
1730	Joseph Hewes, signer of the Declaration of Independence, born
1737	John Hancock, signer of the Declaration of Independence, born
1800	Edward Rutledge, signer of the Declaration of Independence, died
1806	William Pitt, English statesman, died
1812	Great North American earthquake
1813	George Clymer, signer of the Declaration of Independence, died
1831	Belgium adopted its national flag
1832	Edouard Manet, French artist, born
1866	Thomas Love Peacock, English novelist, died
1889	The Philippines declared themselves a Republic
1893	Phillips Brooks, composer of "Oh, Little Town of Bethlehem," born
1909	Republic was sunk by the Florida off Nantucket and radio was first used in a sea rescue

1942	Japanese landed on New Britain and New Ireland Islands

```
1942    Japanese landed on New Britain and New Ireland
            Islands
1943    Alexander Woollcott, author, died
1968    Pueblo, U.S. reconnaissance ship, seized by
            North Korea
1970    Itos-1, weather satellite, launched
1973    Helgafell Island, near Iceland, erupted
```

January 24th

```
 41 AD  Caligula, Roman emperor, murdered
 76     Hadrian, Roman emperor, born
 97     St. Timothy, patron of stomach patients,
            died (Feast Day)
772     Pope Stephen IV died
817     Pope Stephen V died
1376    Richard, Earl of Arundel and former Regent
            of England, died
1458    Matthias was elected King of Hungary
1521    Magellan discovered St. Paul's Island in
            the Pacific
1556.   Shensi, China, struck by an earthquake
1692    Indians massacred and destroyed all of York,
            Maine, but the jail
1705    Farinelli, male soprano, born
1712    Frederick II, "The Great," King of Prussia,
            born
1746    Gustavus III, King of Sweden, born
1760    Discovery of the Venus's-flytrap announced
1775    Pennsylvania Evening Post newspaper began
            publishing 3 times a week
1848    Gold was discovered in California
1862    Edith Wharton, novelist, born
1870    Oneida sank after a collision off Yokahama,
            Japan
1894    Lobster thermidor first served (Paris)
1899    First rubber heel was patented
1908    First Boy Scout troops organized (England)
        Edward McDowell, composer, died
1915    British sank the German cruiser Blucher
1922    Chocolate-covered stick ice cream, Eskimo
            Pie, patented
1925    Maria Tallchief, ballerina, born
        Solar eclipse
1935    Mohawk and Talisman collided off New Jersey
1939    Chile rocked by an earthquake
1946    U.S. Army announced that a radar beam had
            reached the moon 2 weeks before
1965    Winston Churchill, English statesman, died
1967    Six days of floods in eastern Brazil ended
```

Conversion of St. Paul
Feast of Sts. Paul and Peter (Episcopal)
Feast of St. Gregory of Nazianzus (Orthodox)

98 AD	Nerva, Roman emperor, died
363	Sts. Juventinus and Maximinus died (Feast Day)
477	Gaiseric, King of the Vandals, died
817	Paschal I consecrated Pope
1325	Lithuania opened to settlement
1533	Henry VIII, King of England, married Ann Boleyn, his second (of 6) wives
1694	Natalia Naruishkina, mother of Czar Peter I of Russia, died
1759	Robert Burns, poet, born
1787	Shay's Rebellion in Massachusetts failed
1823	Edward Jenner, conqueror of smallpox, died
1839	Texas state flag adopted
1858	King Frederick III of Germany and Prussia married Victoria, Princess Royal of England
1871	William McKinley married Ida Saxton
1874	W. Somerset Maugham, writer, born
1893	Empire Theater opened in New York City
1903	Cheswich, Pennsylvania, mine disaster
1905	Bowden, in a Mercedes, set a land-speed record of 109.75 mph
1915	First transcontinental phone call (New York to San Francisco)
1917	Laurentic, a British cruiser, struck a mine off Ireland
1919	League of Nations plan adopted by the Peace Conference
1934	Dillinger caught in Tucson, Arizona
1942	Britain declared war on Siam
1944	Solar eclipse
1956	First atomic submarine, U.S.S. Swordfish, launched
1964	Echo II, U.S. communications satellite, launched
1966	Permina, Indonesian ship, sank in a storm off Sumatra
1970	Beauty Queens' Day at Easley, South Carolina Sloppy Slalom Obstacle Course Ski Race at Big Boulder, Penna.
1971	Intelsat IV F-2, communications satellite, launched
1972	Republic Day in Uganda
1973	J. Carroll Naish, actor, died

India Republic Day
Feast of St. Polycarp
404 AD   St. Paula died (Feast Day)
724   Caliph Yazid II died of grief over his favorite singing-girl
1100   St. Eystein of Norway died (Feast Day)
1108   St. Alberic or Aubrey, founder of the Cistercian monks, died (Feast Day)
1266   Charles of Anjou became King of Sicily by his victory at Benevento
1347   University of Prague authorized by the Pope
1500   Vincent Pizon, captain of Columbus's Nina, ciscovered the Amazon River
1531   Lisbon, Portugal, struck by an earthquake
1763   Charles XIV John, King of Sweden and Norway, born
1788   First settlement in Australia, Sydney, founded, a penal colony (Australia Day Holiday)
1802   Congressional Library founded with a librarian and a room in the Capitol
1808   William Bligh, captain of the Bounty, arrested for tyranny
         Rum Rebellion in Australia
1832   Rufus H. Gilbert, builder of elevated railroads, born
1837   Michigan became a state
1852   Pierre de Brazza, founder of the French Congo, born
1870   Virginia re-entered the Union
1880   General Douglas MacArthur was born (Arkansas holiday)
1885   Charles G. ("Chinese") Gordon slain at Khartoum, Sudan
1905   Maria A. Trapp, musician and author ("Sound of Music"), born
         The Cullinan diamond, 3,106 carats, found in South Africa
1906   Marriot, in a Stanley Steamer, set a land-speed record of 127.659 mph
1911   Glenn Curtis flew his hydroplane, The Flying Fish
1917   U.S. Army's Tank Corps created
1924   Emperor Hirohito of Japan married Princess Nagako Kuni
1928   Ertha Kitt, singer, born
1932   British M-2 submarine lost off Portland Bill, England
1939   Spanish loyalist government surrendered Barcelona

1947	Prince Carl Gustaf, heir to the throne of Sweden, died in a plane crash
1954	First atomic battery demonstrated
1958	Japanese ferry Nankai Maru vanished in the Inland Sea
1962	Ranger III, lunar probe, launched by U.S.
1964	First American Protestant church dedicated in Moscow, U.S.S.R.
1967	Two days of blizzards in the southern Great Lakes began
1970	Football Jamboree at Easley, South Carolina
1973	Edward G. Robinson, actor, died

January 27th

	Feast of St. John Chrysostom, patron of preachers and invoked against epilepsy
844 AD	Pope Gregory IV died
847	Pope Sergius II died
1166	Prince Henry of Germany married Constance of Sicily
1186	Frederick "Redbeard" crowned ruler of Burgundy
1302	Dante, the writer, was expelled from Florence forever
1540	St. Angela of Brescia died
1614	Imperial proclamation against Christianity in Japan
1629	Abbas the Great, Shah of Persia, died
1662	Lime was first manufactured in America
1689	Czar Peter the Great of Russia married Eudoxia Lopukhina
1756	Wolfgang Mozart, composer, born
1785	University of Georgia became first chartered state university (but it was the second to open)
1788	George Gordon, Lord Byron, the poet, born
1801	Water first flowed through Philadelphia's wooden pipes
1832	Lewis Carroll, author of Alice in Wonderland, born
1850	Samuel Gompers, author and labor leader, born
1851	John James Audubon, artist-ornithologist, died
1856	Two-month armistice signed in the Crimean War
1859	Kaiser William II of Germany was born
1870	Kappa Alpha Theta became the first U.S. sorority
	Cochise's Apache camp destroyed by the U.S. cavalry
1872	Learned Hand, jurist, born
1880	Thomas A. Edison received a patent for his electric lamp
1885	Jerome Kern, composer, born

```
1888      National Geographic Society founded
1900      Adm. Hyman G. Rickover, "father of the atomic
              submarine," born
1901      Verdi, Italian opera composer, died
1914      Civilian government established in Panama
1928      First zeppelin landing on an aircraft carrier
1932      Japanese marines landed in China (excuse was
              the priest killed on the 15th)
1943      U.S. Army Air Force made its first attack in
              Germany
1944      Four submarines launched at U.S.'s Portsmouth
              Naval Yard
1949      Taiping collided with a collier off southern
              China
1958      Brooklyn displayed its county flag, one of
              few in the U.S.
1967      Apollo launching-pad fire killed 3 U.S.
              astronauts
1970      Start of a 600-mile snowmobile race from
              Anchorage to Fairbanks, Alaska
1971      Oriental New Year, the Year of the Pig
1973      Viet Nam war cease-fire signed
```

January 28th

```
          Feast of St. Valerius of Saragossa
814 AD    Charlemagne, Holy Roman Emperor, died of
              pleurisy
893       Charles III, "the Simple," crowned King
              of France
1256      St. Peter Nolesco, patron of midwives, died
              (Feast Day)
          William, King of the Romans, was killed
1457      Henry VII, first Tudor king of England, born
1547      Henry VII, King of England, died
1572      St. Jane Frances Chantal was born
1573      Compact of Warsaw signed, guaranteeing Polish
              religious freedom
1596      Sir Francis Drake, British admiral, buried
              at sea
1611      Johann Hevelius, German astronomer, born
1621      Pope Paul V died of a stroke
1687      Johann Hevelius, German astronomer, died
1712      Jean-Jacques Rousseau, French writer, born
1725      Czar Peter I, "the Great," of Russia died
1807      First streetlights lit (gas; London, England)
1820      Jersey City, New Jersey, incorporated
1840      First modern Egyptian expedition for Nile
              exploration reached its turnabout
1855      The Panama Railroad, coast to coast, completed
1861      South Carolina adopted its state flag
```

1870	City of Boston vanished in the Atlantic with 171 aboard
1871	Paris surrendered to the Germans (Franco-Prussian War)
	H.R. Arthur exploded
1878	First commercial telephone exchange opened (New Haven, Conn.)
1884	Piccard twins, French balloonists, born
1889	Arthur Rubinstein, pianist, born
1902	Carnegie Institute established
1914	Beverly Hills, California, incorporated
1915	Coast Guard created by an Act of Congress
1922	Washington, D.C.'s Knickerbocker movie theater collapsed
1926	U.S. signed for membership in the Permanent Court of International Justice
1933	Adolf Hitler was made Chancellor of Germany
1945	First convoy set out on the Burma Road, retaken from the Japanese
1948	Joo Maru struck a mine off Okayama, Japan
1956	"Tokyo Rose" completed her sentence for treason
1966	Escavation begun at the site of a prehistoric camp near Nice, France
1972	Republic Day in India

January 29th

	St. Francis de Sales Feast Day, patron of writers
	Feast of St. Gildas the Wise
591 AD	St. Sulpicius died (Feast Day)
1118	Pope Paschal II died
1327	King Edward III crowned in England
1535	French edict proclaimed, resulting in emigration of Huguenots
1579	Union of Utrecht (Low Countries alliance against Spain)
1584	William the Silent, governor of the Netherlands, assassinated
1653	French Literary Academy founded
1696	Czar Ivan V of Russia died
1819	Sir Thomas Raffles founded Singapore
1820	King George III of England died, blind and insane
1843	William McKinley, 25th President of the U.S., born
1845	"The Raven," Edgar Allan Poe's poem, first published
1861	Kansas became a state
1863	Cavalry killed 224 Shoshone Indians at their Bear River Camp
1874	John D. Rockefeller, Jr., millionaire, born

1879	City charter of Memphis, Tennessee, repealed
1885	Congress rejected Panama Canal treaty with Nicaragua
1895	Brass tribesmen attacked the Royal Niger Co. station (Africa)
1903	Vina Delmar, novelist, born
1906	King Christian IX of Denmark died
	Port wine officially defined as to where grown, exported, and its alcohol content
1913	Design for the Lincoln Memorial, Washington, D.C. approved
1918	John Forsythe, actor, born
1919	Prohibition Amendment became law, effective January 1920
1920	A meeting was held to organize the American Iris Society
1923	Paddy Chayefsky, playwright, born
1929	"The Seeing Eye," guide-dog foundation, organized
1933	Sara Teasdale, poetess, died
1945	U.S.S. Serpens exploded off Guadalcanal

January 30th

	Feast of 3 Hierarchs (Orthodox; Sts. Basil, Gregory, and John Chrysostom)
	Feast of St. Martina
435 AD	Rome made peace with the Vandals, ending its "fall"
680	St. Bathild, queen to King Clovis II of France, died (Feast Day)
1118	Gelasius II elected Pope
1167	Matilda, Queen of England, died
1328	King Edward III of England remarried Philippa of Hainaut
1349	Guanther of Schwarzburg elected King of Germany
1592	Ippolyto Aldobrandini elected Pope (Clement VIII)
1648	Treaty of Westphalia made Low Countries independent of Spain
1649	Charles I, King of England, beheaded
1730	Peter II, Czar of Russia, died of smallpox on his wedding day
1734	Last dinner meeting of the Calves' Head Club, formed in derision of King Charles I of England
1790	Lifeboats first used
1798	Reps. Lyon and Griswold had the first U.S. Congressional brawl
1836	Betsy Ross, flagmaker, died

```
1853      Napoleon III of France married Eugenie de
                   Montijo
1866      Pere David first got specimens of his deer
          Gelett Burgess, author of "I Never Saw a
                   Purple Cow," born
          Missouri exploded on the Ohio River
1868      Meteorite rain fell near Pultusk, Poland
1870      Blackfoot Indian camp wiped out by a surprise
                   attack
1882      Franklin D. Roosevelt, U.S. President, born
1883      Orion nebula photographed
1894      Boris III, King of Bulgaria, born
1895      Collision of German Elbe and British Crathie
1902      Anglo-Japanese Alliance signed against Russia
1914      S.S. Monroe sunk in a collision off Virginia
1917      First jazz record cut
1934      Frank N. Doubleday, publisher, died
1937      Hitler repudiated "War Guilt" clause of
                   Versailles treaty
1943      U.S. cruiser Chicago torpedoed in the Solomon
                   Islands
1945      German Wilhelm Gustloff, 6000 refugees aboard,
                   sank
1948      Mahatma Gandhi, Indian political-religious
                   leader, assassinated
1959      Danish freighter Hans Hedtoft hit an iceberg
                   off Greenland
1964      Russia's Elektrons I and II launched into space
          Ranger 6, U.S. Moon probe, landed on target
1972      Total eclipse of the moon
1973      Western Mexico was rocked by an earthquake
```

January 31st

```
          Feast of St. Cyrus and John
314 AD    St. Sylvester became Pope
410       St. Marcella died (Feast Day)
626       St. Aidan (or Maedoc) of Ferns died (Feast Day)
1580      Cardinal Henry, King of Portugal, died
1615      Cape Horn, South America, discovered
1616      First trip completed both ways around Cape Horn
1797      Franz Schubert, composer, born
1806      Fletcher Harper, founder of Harper's maga-
                   zine, born
1858      Great Eastern steamship launched
1864      Robert E. Lee appointed Commander in Chief of
                   Confederate forces
1875      Zane Grey, western author, born
1876      All Sioux Indians ordered onto reservations,
                   beginning the Sioux Indian War
1878      Metropolis wrecked off North Carolina
```

1880	The <u>Atlanta</u> with 290 aboard vanished after leaving Bermuda
1881	Alfred Harcourt, publisher, born
1885	Anna Pavlova, ballerina born
1892	Eddie Cantor, comedian, born
1902	Edward Beverly Mann, western novelist, born
1905	John O'Hara, writer, born
1913	Liquor trade forbidden in the Belgian Congo
1915	Gary Moore, television personality, born
1917	Wyoming adopted its state flag
1919	Jackie Robinson, baseball great, born
1923	Norman Mailer, author, born
1925	George Washington Cable, author, died
1933	John Galsworthy, author, died
1938	Princess Beatrix of the Netherlands born
1941	"Jersey Joe" Walcott, boxer, born
1943	Nazi-occupied Stalingrad retaken by the Russians
1945	Battle of the Bulge ended
1951	Atomic Energy Commission authorized to produce hydrogen bomb
1953	Storms and flood tides devastated England and Holland
	<u>Princess Victoria</u> sank in storm off Northern Ireland
1958	First U.S. satellite, <u>Explorer I</u>, was launched
1961	<u>Samos II</u> launched
1968	Nauru, an eight-square-mile country, became independent
1970	Pancake Feed at Arapahoe, Nebraska

FEBRUARY

Full Moon - Snow Moon
Beaver Round-up Month at Dillingham, Alaska
California gray whales migrate to Mexico calving
                    grounds
First weekend - Cordova, Alaska Iceworm Festival
First week - Bears born
2nd Friday - Start of annual Alaskan fur rendezvous
                    at Anchorage
2nd weekend - Dartmouth College Winter Carnival
                    (Hanover, N.H.)
3rd Monday - Washington's Birthday observance
                    (as of 1971)
            Start of British Industries Fair (11 days
                    in London and Birmingham)

February 1st

	St. Brigid (or Bride) Day, Irish abbess
	National Freedom Day (U.S.)
	Feast of St. Ignatius of Antioch/Theophoros, martyred by the lions of Rome

            St. Brigid (or Bride) Day, Irish abbess
            National Freedom Day (U.S.)
            Feast of St. Ignatius of Antioch/Theophoros,
                    martyred by the lions of Rome
 772 AD   Adrian I elected Pope
1328   Charles IV, "the Fair," King of France, died
1553   First fair at Lyme Regis, Dorsetshire,
                    England
1691   Pope Alexander VIII died
1733   Augustus II, "the Strong," King of Poland died
1790   First meeting of the U.S. Supreme Court (New
                    York City)
1793   First fugitive slave law in the U.S. passed
1814   Lord Byron's "The Corsair" published and
                    10,000 sold
1840   First U.S. college of dentistry chartered
                    (Baltimore)

```
1859      Denver's first hoel, The Eldorado, opened
1861      Texas seceded from the Union
1865      Abolishment of slavery bill signed
1887      Harry Scherman, founder of the Book-of-the-
                Month Club, born
1901      Clark Gable, actor, born
1904      S.J. Perelman, author, born
1908      King Carlos I and the Crown Prince of Portugal
                assassinated
1918      French ship LaDive torpedoed in the Mediter-
                ranean
1944      Piet Mondrian, Dutch artist, died
1952      U.S. named Communist China the aggressor in
                Korea
          United Arab Republic (Egypt and Syria)
                formed
1970      Frontier Days and Rodeo at Homestead, Florida
          Swamp-buggy races at St. Petersburg, Florida
1973      Mt. Asama volcano erupted (Japan)
```

February 2nd

```
          Candlemass
          Groundhog Day (especially in Punxsutawney,
                Pennsylvania)
          Purification (Protestant Episcopal)
 962 AD   Otto II, King of the Lombards, crowned Holy
                Roman Emperor
1208      James I, "the Conqueror," King of Aragon, born
1389      Last date for English Guilds to send partic-
                ulars of their organization
                to the Royal Council
1440      Frederick IV crowned German King
1461      King Edward IV of England defeated his Earls
                at Mortimer's Cross (2nd Battle
                of St. Albans)
1494      Columbus founded the West Indian slave trade
1509      Battle of Div (Portuguese destroyed the Moslem
                fleet)
1534      Swabian League expired
1558      Lutheran University of Jena opened
1640      St. Joan of Lestonnac died (Feast Day)
1651      Nell Gwyn, actress and mistress of King
                Charles II of England, born
1653      New Amsterdam became the first American city
                to receive a charter of self-
                government (New York City)
1709      Alexander Selkirk, the real Robinson Crusoe,
                rescued
1769      Pope Clement XIII died of a stroke
1780      France decided to support the American
                Revolution
1801      First Parliament of England and Ireland met
```

1804	George Walton, signer of the Declaration of Independence, died
1831	Mauro Capellari elected Pope Gregory XVI
1848	Treaty of Guadalupe Hidalgo (Mexico and U.S.) gave U.S. Texas, Arizona, and California
1854	Stephen H. Horgan, inventor of half-toning, a means of printing pictures, born
1859	Havelock Ellis, physician-psychologist-writer, born
1876	Baseball's National League formed with 8 teams
1879	Monroe Doctrine invoked to settle a boundary dispute between Venezuela and British Guiana
1882	Geoffery O'Hara, composer of "K-k-k-katy," born
	Knights of Columbus, Catholic fraternal organization, founded
	James Joyce, author, born
1893	First close-up movie taken (of a sneeze) in Thomas Edison's studio
1894	Kearsarge wrecked on Roncatof Reef
1901	Army Nurse Corps organized as part of the medical department
	Jascha Heifetz, violinist, born
1910	Joan Bennett, actress, born
1919	Ann Fogarty, fashion designer, born
1922	James Joyce's novel Ulysses published in Paris
1932	Reconstruction Finance Corp. began operation
1934	Export-Import Bank of Washington created
1939	Japanese submarine, I-36, sank in Bungo Channel
1942	Swedish ship Amerikaland sank off Cape Hatteras
1943	Germans surrendered at the Battle of Stalingrad
1959	Black and white students first shared classrooms in public schools in Virginia
1969	Boris Karloff, actor, died
1970	Underwater Film Festival at Santa Monica, California
	Buffalo Dance at San Filipe Pueblo, New Mexico
	Bertrand Russell, philosopher, died
1971	Start of the Carrot Carnival at Holtville, California
	Natosat II, military communications satellite launched

Feast of St. Werburgh, daughter of King Wulf-
      here of Mercia (england)
Feast of St. Ia

316 AD   St. Blaise martyred (patron of wool weavers
      carvers and builders; invoked
      against wild beasts, coughs,
      goiter, and throat diseases)
      Feast Day

590   Pope Gregory I, "the Great," elected to office
619   St. Lawrence of Canterbury, 2nd bishop, died
      (Feast Day)
1116   Koloman, King of Hungary, died
1468   Johann Gutenberg, pioneer printer, died
1472   York Cathedral reconsecrated (England)
1518   Silence imposed on Augustine monks by the Pope
1521   Magellan discovered Shark Island in the Pacific
1679   Jan Steen, Dutch artist, died
1690   Masachusetts Colony began issuing its own
      bills of credit
1809   Illinois became a U.S. territory
      Felix Mendelssohn, composer, born
1811   Horace Greeley, journalist, born
1821   Elizabeth Blackwell, first woman doctor, born
1831   Revolt of the Papal States began
1848   British claimed Orange Free State, South
      Africa
1853   Hudson Maxim, inventor of smokeless gun-
      powder, born
1865   Hampton Roads Conference (U.S. Civil War)
      David Lawrence Pierson, originator of Con-
      stitution Day (September 17th),
      born
1867   Prince Mutsuhito became Emperor of Japan at
      age 15
1874   Gertrude Stein, author, born
1882   Meteorite rain fell near Mocs, Transylvania
1894   Norman Rockwell, artist, born
1895   Nick Kenny, columnist-lyricist, born
1898   National Biscuit Company incorporated
1907   James A. Michener, author, born
1911   California adopted its state flag
1916   Daljin Maru sank in the Pacific
1917   U.S. severed diplomatic relations with Germany
      Housatanic steamship sunk by a German sub-
      marine
1923   Lassen Peak volcano erupted (Califonria)
1924   Woodrow Wilson, 28th President of the U.S.,
      died
1943   Troopship Dorchester torpedoed and sunk
      (Four Chaplains' Day)
1945   Yalta Conference began
      U.S. forces recaptured Manila, Philippines

```
1947      Snag Airport, Yukon, reported record cold for
              North America of minus 81 de-
              grees
1951      Chapel dedicated to the Four Chaplains at
              Philadelphia
1954      Queen Elizabeth II became the first reigning
              British monarch to visit Aus-
              tralia
1963      Tanker Marine Sulphur Queen vanished in the
              Gulf of Mexico
1965      OSO 2, solar study satellite, launched
1972      Winter Olympics opened in Sapporo, Japan
```

February 4th

```
          Feast of St. Phileas
          Feast of St. Andrew Corsini
          Ceylon Independence Day
  47 BC   Battle of Thapsus
 211 AD   Septimius Severus, Roman military dictator,
              died
  846     St. Joannicius died (Feast Day)
  900     Louis, "the Child," crowned King of Germany
 1189     St. Gilbert of Sempringham  founder of the
              only English order, Gilbertines,
              died (Feast Day)
 1498     Antonio Pollaivolo, sculptor of Papal tombs,
              died
 1505     St. Joan of France, deposed Queen, died
              (Feast Day)
 1693     St/ John de Britto, missionary to India,
              martyred (Feast Day)
 1764     Topsham, Maine, incorporated
 1783     Southern Italy and Sicily rocked by an earth-
              quake
 1797     Peru and Ecuador shaken by an earthquake
 1809     Louis Braille, inventor, born
 1810     Illinois Territorial Seal first used
 1861     Confederate States of America organized
              (Montgomery, Alabama)
 1868     "Greenback" paper money discontinued in the U.S.
 1889     Philippines declared war on the U.S.
          French courts dissolved the bankrupt Panama
              Canal Company
 1897     Ludwig Erhard, German statesman born
 1899     Philippine guerrilla war for independence
              began
 1900     MacKinley Kantor, novelist, born
 1902     Charles Lindbergh, flyer, born
 1916     National Bank of the Philippines  chartered
 1917     U.S. troops withdrew from Mexico (Mexican Revo-
              lution)
```

```
1941    United Service Organizations founded
1943    Solar eclipse
1948    Griffith O. Ellis, publisher, died
1953    Ben Ames Williams, novelist, died
1970    Sert II satellite launched
1971    Rolls-Royce, Ltd., went bankrupt
1973    Start of the Chinese year 4671
```

February 5th ───
───

```
        Constitution Day, national holiday in Mexico
251 AD  St. Agatha died in prison (patron of Catonia,
                Sicily, nurses, and bell-makers;
                invoked against breast disease and
                fire) (Feast Day)
1265    Guy Foulques elected Pope as Clement IV
1597    Christian missionaries in Japan killed by the
                governor at Nagasaki (Feast of
                Martyrs in Japan)
1699    Joseph Ferdinand, ruler of Bavaria, died of
                smallpox
1723    John Witherspoon, signer of the Declaration of
                Independence, born
1725    Bering expedition set out from St. Petersburg,
                Russia
1788    Sir Robert Peel, British statesman, born
1818    Charles XIII, King of Norway and Sweden, died
1826    Millard Fillmore married Abigail Powers
1838    Abram Joseph Ryan, "Poet of the Confederacy,"
                born
1840    John Boyd Dunlop, pioneer of the pneumatic rub-
                ber tire, born
1850    Bishop Rock Lighthouse, almost complete, destroyed
                by a storm (England)
1861    Sellers patented his kinematoscope, a basic
                motion picture device
1870    The Press Association, British news agency,
                began functioning
1873    Maritime Association of the Port of New York
                founded
1884    Grolier Club, organization of New York book-
                lovers, founded
1887    Verdi's Othello first produced
1892    Temperature in Siberia reached 94 degrees be-
                low zero
1906    Allan Seager, author, born
        John Carridine, actor, born
1911    Missouri's 2nd state capitol destroyed by fire
1918    British ship Tusconia torpedoed off Ireland
1931    Campbell set a speed record of 246,086 mph
                in a Napier-Campbell car
1934    Hank Aaron, baseball player, born
```

```
1970        Start of Cambridge, Maryland, Muskrat-skinning
                 Championship
1972        Marianne Moore, poet and baseball fan, died
1913, 1940, 2008  Shrove Tuesday
```

```
            Feast of St. Dorothy, martyr
            Feast of St. Photius, patriarch of Constan-
                 tinople
            Feast of St. Titus, first missionary to Crete
            Feast of St. Vaast (Gaston), patron of child-
                 ren who are slow to walk
            Kannokura ("Where the Gods Live"), festival of
                 the Shinto religion
 337 AD    Julius I became Pope
 679       St. Amand of Maastricht, missionary-bishop,
                 died (Feast Day)
1519       Sir Walter Raleigh left England to explore
                 Guiana, S. America
1564       Christopher Marlowe, English playwright, born
1665       Queen Anne of England born
1670       Frederick III, King of Denmark and Norway, died
1682       LaSalle sighted the Mississippi River
1685       King Charles II of England died
1704       Pope Clement XII died
1756       Aaron Burr, U.S. vice-president, born
1778       French-American treaty signed for aid against
                 England
1788       Massachusetts ratified the Constitution
1833       Otto, German-born king of Greece, arrived
                 in his kingdom
1838       Zulu warriors massacred Dutch settlers in Natal,
                 S. Africa
1862       Fort Henry fell to Union forces
1873       Peru and Bolivia signed a mutual-defense agree-
                 ment
1895       Babe Ruth, baseball great, born
1899       Congress ratified the treaty ending the
                 Spanish-American War
1904       Russo-Japanese War began
1911       Ronald Reagan, actor-politician, born
1922       Limitation of Armaments Conference ended
                 (Washington, D.C.)
1936       Start of Garmisch-Partenkirchen, Germany,
                 Olympics
1951       Train wreck at Woodbridge, New Jersey
1952       King George VI of England died
1954       Kashmir acceded to India
1968       Winter Olympics becan at Grenoble, France
1970       Chinese Year of the Dog, 4668, began
1971       Central Italy rocked by an earthquake
```

1913, 1940, 2008 Ash Wednesday, beginning of
                  Lent
1951. 2035, 2046 Shrove Tuesday

February 7th

              Feast of St. Romuald
              Feast of St. Theodore the General
1478 AD   Sir Thomas More, English statesman, born
1639   French Academy began its great dictionary
                  of the French language
1799   Ch'ing Lung, Chinese emperor, died
1804   John Deere, steel-plow inventor, born
1812   Great North American earthquake
              Charles Dickens, author, born
1837   King Gustavus IV of Sweden died in exile
1863   Orpheus wrecked off New Zealand
1864   Housatanic, (Union) sunk by H.L. Hunley
                  (Confederate), 1st warship sinking
                  by a submarine
1878   Pope Pius IX died
1885   Sinclair Lewis, novelist, born
1894   Mississippi adopted its state flag
1901   Queen Wilhelmina of Holland married Henry,
                  Duke of Mecklenburgh-Schwerin
1904   Baltimore business district fire
1915   First wireless message sent from a moving train
                  to a station
1929   Christina, Queen Regent of Spain, died
1950   U.S. recognized South Viet Nam
1970   Final Day of the Muskrat-skinning Champion-
                  ship at Cambridge, Maryland
1951, 2035, 2046, Ash Wednesday
1967, 1978, 1989, 2062, 2073 Shrove Tuesday

February 8th

              Feast of St. Cuthman
              Feast of St. John Matha
1250 Ad   7th Crusade rested at Mansura, Egypt, and fought
                  a battle
1587   Mary, Queen of Scots, beheaded
1601   Earl of Essex attempted a rebellion against
                  Elizabeth I, Queen of England
1643   Start of the first Fair at Irbit, Russia
1690   French and Indians attacked Schenectady, New
                  York
1693   William and Mary College, 2nd in U.S.,
                  chartered
1792   Mrs. Hannah Snell, a deserter from the army and
                  who was wounded as a sailor,
                  died insane

1793	U.S. Presidential salary set at $25,000 per year
1800	Ceremony held at Church of the Invalides, Paris, to mourn the death of George Washington
1802	Inventor Simon Willard patented the banjo clock
1807	Naopleon defeated the Russians at Eylau
1825	Harriet J. H. Robinson, suffragist, born
1828	Jules Verne, author, born
1837	Alexander Pushkin, Russian poet, wounded in a duel
1849	Roman National Assembly divested the Pope of all governing power and proclaimed a Republic
1853	Children's Aid Society founded
1861	Henry W. Leonard, inventor, born
1863	Nathan Hale, journalist-author, died
1865	Prizefighting made illegal in Missouri
	First black major in the U.S. Army commissioned
1881	First regular skiing tournament held in U.S. (Redwing, Minn.)
1888	Dame Edith Evans, actress, born
1893	Trinacria wrecked off the coast of Spain
1908	$8 million fire destroyed Paterson, New Jersey
1910	Boy Scouts chartered in the U.S.
1915	Movie Birth of a Nation premiered
1920	Lana Turner, actress, born
1921	Peter A. Kropotkin, Russian geographer, died
1931	Riverside Church in New York City dedicated
1937	Spanish insurgents captured Malaga (Spanish Civil War)
1949	Cardinal Mindszenty convicted of treason and espionage (Hungary)
1960	Surname of the English Royal Family became Mountbatten-Windsor
1962	Tiros IV, weather satellite, launched
1971	Sun Pageant at Narvik, Norway, celebrating sun's return

1967, 1978, 1989, 2062, 2073 Ash Wednesday
1910, 1921, 2005, 2084 Shrove Tuesday

February 9th

	Feast of St. Apollonia (patron of dentists; invoked against toothache)
	Feast of St. Nicephorus of Antioch
	Feast of St. Teilo
444 AD	St. Cyril of Alexandria died (Feast Day)
720	Umar II, Moslem caliph, died
1098	Ridwan failed to relieve the Crusader's siege of Antioch
1119	Pope Calixtus II crowned in France
1458	Mathias I, King of Hungary, married Catherine of Bohemia

```
1507    Santa Appollonia Island discovered by Pereira
1588    Dunke of Medina-Sidonia appointed to head the
            Spanish Armada though he was not
            a sailor and was prone to seasick-
            ness
1670    Christian V became King of Norway and Denmark
1674    New Jersey returned to England by treaty with
            Holland
1770    Bostonians organized against drinking tea un-
            til the tax was removed
1773    William Henry Harrison, 9th President of the
            U.S. born
1789    Franz Gabelsberger, calculating-machine inventor,
            born
1797    First white men, shipwrecked, landed in Vic-
            toria, Australia
1814    Samuel Tilden, New York governor and presidential
            candidate, born, (won popular,
            lost by 1 in Electoral College)
1822    American Indian Soceity organized
1865    Robert E. Lee made Commander in Chief of Con-
            federacy
1870    U.S. Weather Bureau established
1874    Amy Lowell, poet, born
1893    Verdi's Falstaff opera first produced
1904    Russian cruisers Variag and Korietz sunk off
            Korea by the Japanese
1909    Dean Rusk, U.S. statesman, born
1910    French Gen. Chanzy wrecked off Minorca
1911    Lincoln Memorial building approved by Congress
1913    Great meteor shower seen over Canada
1914    Gypsy Rose Lee, performer, born
1933    Lowest temperature, 66 degree below zero, in
            the U.S. recorded at Yellowstone
            Park, Wyoming
        Oxford Union voted itself a pacifist group (Eng-
            land)
1942    France's Normandie burned at the pier in New
            York City
        "War Time" effected, setting clocks ahead one
            hour
1955    First subway in Rome, Italy opened
1969    First closing of New York State Thruway due to
            weather
1970    Start of two-day Pike Festival at Hillman,
            Michigan
1971    Southern California rocked by an earthquake
1910, 1921, 2005, 2084,  Ash Wednesday
1932, 1937, 2016, 2027, 2100  Shrove Tuesday
```

	St. Paul's Shipwreck (Holiday in Malta)
543 AD	St. Scholastica, twin sister of St. Benedict, died (Feast Day; invoked against storms)
1471	Frederick II, the "Iron," of Brandenberg died
1480	Japanese Emperor Go-Tsuchimikado, having reigned 12 years, finally occupied his palace in Kyoto
1519	Cortez sailed from Cuba for Mexico
1567	Lord Henry Darnley, husband of Mary, Queen of Scots, was strangled
1675	Lancaster, Massachusetts, sacked by Indians
1696	A plot to assassinate William of Orange, ruler of England, failed
1722	British man-of-war Swallow captured the pirate ship Royal Fortune
1733	James Oglethorpe founded Savannah, Georgia
1763	France ceded Canada to England at the Peace of Paris, ending the French and Indian War
1792	Japan rocked by an earthquake
1829	Pope Leo XII died
1840	Queen Victoria of England married Albert of Saxe-Coburg-Gotha
1849	The Harbinger, a weekly magazine, ceased publication
1854	Millard Fillmore married Caroline C. McIntosh
1855	Biddeford, Maine, incorporated
	Rights of U.S. citizenship granted to offspring born abroad (of citizens)
1863	Tom Thumb married Lavinia Warren
1870	Young Women's Christian Association founded (New York City)
1893	Jimmy Durante, comedian, born
1894	Harold Macmillan, British statesman, born
1890	Boris Pasternak, author, born
1899	Herbert Hoover married Lou Hanry
1912	Dr. Joseph Lister, pioneer English surgeon, died
1913	Merriman Smith, author-journalist, born
1916	Germany classified armed merchantmen as warships
1918	Abdul Hamid II, "the Great Assassin" (of Armenians), Sultan of Turkey, died
1923	Wilhelm Roentgen, X-ray inventor, died
1933	First singing telegram delivered
1939	Pope Pius XI, libertarian and mountain-climber, died
1942	Alice H. Rice, author of Mrs. Wiggs and the Cabbage Patch, died
1947	Italy signed a peace treaty with Britain, U.S., France, and USSR

                    Russia signed a peace treaty with Finland, Hun-
                        gary, Rumania, and Bulgaria
                    U.S. signed a peace treaty with Hungary, Bul-
                        garia, and Rumania
1954   U.S. farm surpluses decreed unsalable to Com-
                        munist countries
1960   Cardinal Stepinac, Primate of Yugoslavia, died
1961   Niagara Falls hydroelectric project began pro-
                        ducing power
1962   Gary Powers, U-2 pilot and convicted spy,
                        traded to U.S. by USSR for Rudolf
                        Abel, their spy
1964   Australian destroyer <u>Voyager</u> involved in a
                        Pacific collision
1971   <u>Apollo 14</u> splashed back from the moon
1973   An earthquake rocked Colima, Mexico
1932, 1937, 2016, 2027, 2100 Ash Wednesday
1948, 1959, 1970, 2032, 2043, 2054, 2065 Shrove
                        Tuesday

February 11th
───

                    Japanese Founding Day
                    Feast of St. Cecilia, a sufferer in Africa
                        during the persecution of Dio-
                        cletian
660 BC   Jimmu became ruler of Japan
731 AD   Pope Gregory II died
821   St. Benedict of Aniane died (Feast Day)
824   St. Paschal I, Pope, died
1115   Holy Roman Empire's army defeated at Welfesholz
1252   Ottakar II, King of Bohemia, married Mar-
                        garet, widow of King Henry VII of
                        Germany
1398   The English translation of <u>De proprietatibus</u>
                        <u>rerum</u> encyclopedia completed
1466   Elizabeth of York, wife and queen of Henry VII,
                        King of England, born
1503   Elizabeth of York, queen to Henry VII of England,
                        died
1531   English clergy henceforth to regard the ruler
                        as the head of the church
1554   Lady Jane Grey, claimant to the English throne,
                        beheaded
1628   Special tax levied in England for a fleet to
                        defend against the French
1802   Lydia Child, novelist-abolitionist, born
1815   News of peace with England reached New York
                        (War of 1812)
1828   DeWitt Clinton, New York governor, died
1847   Thomas A. Edison, inventor, born
1858   Bernadette had her first vision of Our Lady of
                        Lourdes

1879	Honoré Daumier, French artist, died
1881	Phoenix, Arizona, incorporated as a city
1887	The Epoch, a literary magazine, founded in New York
1893	Naronic vanished having left Liverpool for New York
1895	Georgetown became part of Washington, D.C.
1901	Milan Obrenovic IV, deposed king of Serbia, died
1907	Colorado River flow to Salton Sink again closed
1908	Sir Vivian Fuchs, Antarctic explorer, born
1909	Max Baer, boxer, born
1916	Bandelier National Monument established
1920	First business session of the League of Nations met (London)
1922	Naval limits treaty signed by U.S., England, France, Italy, and Japan
1927	Opening of Tutankhamen's mummy began
1929	Vatican City, Rome, became a sovereign state
1945	Yalta Conference ended
1948	Meteorite landed near Norton, Kansas
1965	Titan-3A rocket launched for testing

1948, 1959, 1970, 2032, 2043, 2054, 2065 Ash Wednesday
1902, 1964, 1975, 1986, 1997, 2059, 2070, 2081 Shrove Tuesday

----
February 12th

	Feast of St. Julian the Hospitaller (patron of violinists, jugglers, clowns, shepherds, pilgrims, hotel-keepers, ferrymen, travelers needing lodging)
	Feast of St. Marina, female monk
	Feast of the Seven Founders
1111 AD	Henry V, uncrowned Holy Roman Emperor, kidnapped the Pope
1242	Henry VII, King of Germany, died
1424	King James I of Scotland married Jane Beaufort
1541	Santiago, Chile, founded
1542	Catherine Howard, 5th wife of England's King Henry VIII, beheaded
1736	Maria Theresa of Austria married Francis of Lorraine
1742	Charles VII crowned Holy Roman Emperor
1771	King Adolphus Frederick of Sweden died
1775	Louisa Johnson Adams, wife of John Quincy, 6th President of the U.S., born
1789	Ethan Allen, American patriot, died
	Times and Patowmack Packet, first Washington, D.C. newspaper, founded
1809	Charles Darwin, naturalist, born
	Abraham Lincoln, 16th President, born

```
1832        Ecuador annexed the Galapagos Islands
1834        Bangor, Maine, incorporated as a city
1849        Chicago, Burlington and Quincy Railroad Co.
                 incorporated
1869        Start of a four-day storm that sank fishing
                 fleets off Newfoundland
1873        Gold dollar became the U.S. currency standard
1875        Meteorite rain fell near Homestead, Iowa
1880        John L. Lewis, eyebrowed labor leader, born
1884        Alice Lee Roosevelt Longworth, daughter of
                 Teddy, born
1885        German East Africa Company chartered
1904        Ted Mack, "Original Amateur Hour" host, born
1906        Island of Formosa rocked by an earthquake
1907        Larchmont sank off Long Island, New York
1908        National Association for the Advancement of
                 Colored People formed
1912        Republic of China formed
1915        Cornerstone of Lincoln Memorial laid (Washing-
                 ton, D.C.)
1919        DePalma set a land-speed record of 149.875
                 mph, in a Packard
1929        Lily Langtry, actress, died
1932        Princess Astrid of Norway born
1953        Earthquake rocked eastern Iran
1961        Venus probe launched
            Sputnik 8, Russian satellite, launched
1971        James C. Penney, merchant, died
1902, 1964, 1975, 1986, 1997, 2059, 2070, 2081  Ash
                 Wednesday
1907, 1918, 1929, 1991, 2002, 2013, 2086, 2092, 2097
                 Shrove Tuesday
```

February 13th

```
            Ides of February
1014 AD     King Sweyn I of Denmark died
1476        French laid siege to Granson, Switzerland
1566        St. Augustine, Florida, founded
1570        Ivan the Terrible's massacre of Novgorod,
                 Russia, ended
1590        St. Katherine de'Ricci died (Feast Day)
1619        Peace of Deulina signed by Russia, Sweden,
                 and Poland
1633        Galileo arrived in Rome, as ordered by the
                 Inquisition
1635        First public school in America opened in Boston
1660        King Charles Gustavus of Sweden died
1668        Spain recognized Portugal as an independent
                 country
1683        Giovanni Piazzetta, Italian artist, born
```

1689	William and Mary proclaimed joint rulers of Britain
1692	Massacre of the MacDonalds at Glencoe, Scotland
1741	First magazine in the U.S. published
1772	Desolation Island discovered
1836	Cornplanter, Seneca Indian chief, died
1883	Richard Wagner, composer, died
1885	Bess (Mrs. Harry S.) Truman, First Lady, born
	George M. Johnson, western novelist, born
1895	Lumieres got a French patent on their motion-picture projector
1904	Panama's constitution adopted
1919	"Tennessee Ernie" Ford, humorist, born
1960	France exploded its first atomic device (Sahara desert)

1907, 1918, 1929, 1991, 2002, 2013, 2086, 2092, 2097
Ash Wednesday
1923, 1934, 1945, 2018, 2024, 2029 Shrove Tuesday

February 14th

	Feast of St. Cyril (Orthodox)
	(Ex-St.) Valentine's Day (patron of engaged couples; invoked against plague, epilepsy, and fainting)
27 BC	Beginning of the Augustan Era
270 AD	Roman priest, Valentine, martyred
433	St. Maro, hermit, died (Feast Day)
842	"Strasbourg Oaths" Sworn
1009	St. Bruno of Querfurt and party massacred by the Lithuanian heathens
1014	Henry II, "the Saint," crowned Holy Roman Emperor
1130	Innocent II elected Pope
1432	Henry VI, King of England and France, entered London
1571	Benvenuto Cellini, Italian goldsmith, died
1676	John III crowned King of Poland
1764	Site chosen for trading post, first building at St. Louis, Missouri
1768	Ivan Krylov, Russian fable author, born
1779	Captain Cook killed by the natives in Hawaii
1780	Sir William Blackstone, English jurist, died
1838	Edwin Ginn, founder of Ginn Brothers publishers, born
1844	Alice (Mrs. Theodore) Roosevelt, died
	Fremont's Rocky Mountain expedition reached the Sierra Madre
1846	The National Press home journal founded
1859	Oregon became a state
1876	Elisha Gray filed for a patent on his telephone a few hours after Alexander Graham Bell did

```
1894       Jack Benny, comedian, born
1896       Boris, heir to Bulgaria, received into the
                Orthodox faith
1905       Thelma Ritter, actress, born
1911       Studebaker Corporation incorporated
1912       Arizona became a state
1913       Mel Allen, sportscaster, born
1927       Wyoming state flag again adopted
1929       Gangland massacre in Chicago killed seven
           Puerto Rico's legislature first met in the
                capitol
1933       Michigan's banks ordered closed
1934       Solar eclipse
1939       German warship Bismarck launched
1946       The Bank of England went public
1949       Chaim Weizmann elected first President of
                Israel
1956       20th Communist Party Congress began
1970       Salt Grass Trail Raid at Brenham, Texas
1972       Start of the Chinese Year of the Rat, 4670
1923, 1934, 1945, 2018, 2024, 2029  Ash Wednesday
1956, 1961, 2040, 2051  Shrove Tuesday
```

February 15th


```
           Feast of Lupercalia honoring the Roman god Pan
           Anniversary of the Death of Buddha
           Feast of St. Sigfrid, missionary to Sweden
 494 AD    Roman sacrifices of Lupercalia last held
1145       Pope Lucius II died and Eugenius III elected
1152       Conrad III, King of Germany, died
1288       Jerome Maschi elected Pope as Nicholas IV
1368       Sigismund, King of Hungary and Bohemia, Holy
                Roman Emperor, born
1386       Wladislas II crowned King of Poland
1502       Amerigo Vespucci set sail for South America
1564       Galileo, astronomer, born
1637       Ferdinand II, Holy Roman Emperor, died
1645       British standing army founded
1726       Abram Clark, signer of the Declaration of
                Independence, born
1763       Treaty of Hubertusburg ended Seven Years' War
1809       Cyrus McCormick, harvester inventor, born
1812       Charles L. Tiffany, founder of the jewelry
                company, born
1820       Susan B. Anthony, suffragist, born (Minnesota
                holiday)
           William Ellery, signer of the Declaration of
                Independence, died
1854       Pennsylvania Railroad opened Philadelphia-to-
                Pittsburgh line
1862       Union ship, the ironclad Monitor, completed
```

```
1863        Speke and Grant reached Gondokora sailing down
                the Nile
1869        Chatham, New York, incorporated
1874        Sir Ernest Shackleton, Antarctic explorer, born
1879        Rival princes for Burmese throne massacred, a
                standard practice for the new king
1898        Maine battleship exploded in the harbor at
                Havana, Cuba
1907        Cesar Romero, actor, born
1912        Yuan Shik-K'ai elected first president of the
                Republic of China
1917        Caranza called a constitutional convention
                (Mexico)
1937        American elm became the state tree of Nebraska
1954        Two Frenchmen descended 13,284 feet in the
                Atlantic in a bathyscaph
1956, 1961, 2040, 2051  Ash Wednesday
1972, 1893, 1994, 2056, 2067, 2078, 2089  Shrove Tuesday
```

February 16th
_____

```
 309 AD     St. Elias and companions martyred (Feast Day)
            St. Pamphilus died
1001        Roman barons put the Pope and Holy Roman Emperor
                to flight
1220        Bokhara fell to the Mongols
1486        Maximilian I chosen King of Germany
1579        Gonzalo Jimenez de Quesada, explorer of Colom-
                bia, died
1779        New Jersey Journal founded, first in the state
1786        James Monroe married Elizabeth Kortright
1804        Stephen Decatur burned the U.S. frigate
                        Philadelphia in Tripoli harbor
                        4 months after Tripoli pirates
                        captured it
1805        Octave Henri Marie Mirbeau, French dramatist-
                journalist, born
1812        Henry Wilson, born Jeremiah J. Colbath, Vice-
                President of the U.S., born
1814        King Christian VIII of Denmark elected Regent
                of Norway
1823        Li Hung Chang, Chinese statesman, born
1846        Battle of Sobraon ended First Sikh War in India
1862        Fort Donelson fell to Union forces
1866        Honduras adopted its national flag
1868        The Jolly Corks reorganized, becoming the Bene-
                volent and Protective Order of Elks
1869        The harbor at Boston, Massachusetts, froze over
1878        Silver dollar became legal U.S. money
1895        Alabama adopted its state flag
1898        Katherine Cornell, actress, born
1900        American Samoa officially became American Samoa
```

```
1903        Edgar Bergen, ventriloquist, born
1910        Yucatan struck an iceberg, was beached, and sank
1913        Evidence discovered in South Dakota of an early
                      French try for the Northwest
                      Passage
1917        Octave Henri Marie Mirbeau, French dramatist-
                      journalist, died
1923        First radio-telescope news messages transmitted
                      from U.S. to England
1936        Closing ceremonies ending the Garmisch-
                      Partenkirchen Olympics
1945        Bataan recaptured by American forces
            U.S. reoccupation of Corregidor began
1956        Last of the Third Avenue Elevated Railroad
                      removed in New York City
1958        Great blizzard buried New England
1959        Fidel Castro became Premier of Cuba
1961        Explorer I launched
1965        Pegasus I launched
1966        From now on, Lenten fasting is limited to Ash
                      Wednesday and Good Friday
1972        Islamic year 1392 began
1972, 1983, 1994, 2056, 2067, 2078, 2089  Ash Wednesday
1904, 1915, 1926, 1988, 1999, 2010, 2021, 2083, 2094
                      Shrove Tuesday
```

February 17th

```
            Roman ceremony honoring Mars, God of War
                      (Quirinus)
 364 AD     Jovian, Emperor of the Roman Army, died
 603        St. Fintan of Cloneenagh died (Feast Day)
 661        St. Finan died (Feast Day)
1247        Henry Raspe, King of Germany, died
1317        French Inquisition set against Spirituals, an
                      offshoot of the Franciscan friars
1387        Heathen religions banned in Poland
1400        Richard, deposed king of England, murdered
1405        Tamerlane, Oriental conqueror, died
1461        First Battle of St. Albans in the War of the
                      Roses (England)
1490        Charles, Duke of Bourbon, born
1621        Miles Standish appointed military commander of
                      Plymouth Colony
1673        Molière, French dramatist, died
1692        Charter granted for founding first American
                      postal system
1754        English began a fort of the site of Pittsburgh,
                      Penna.
1771        Bath, Maine became the first town to incorpo-
                      rate under U.S. authority
            Rene Theophile Laennec, stethoscope inventor,
                      born
```

```
1854      Frederick Krupp, arms manufacturer, born
1855      Right to construct a telegraph from the
                    Mississippi to the Pacific
                    granted
1856      Frederick E. Ives, inventor of photographic
                    half-tones, born
1857      Samuel S. McClure, organizer of the first
                    newspaper syndicate, born
1865      Confederates evacuated Columbia and Charles-
                    town, South Carolina
1867      First ship passed through the Suez Canal
1880      An assassin blew up the Czar's dining room
                    (Russia)
1888      First telephone exchange in California opened
                    at San Francisco
1890      British ship Duberg wrecked in the China Sea
1897      National Organization of Mothers, the begin-
                    ning of the Parent-Teachers
                    Association, founded
1908      Red Barber, sportscaster, born
1909      Geronimo, Apache Indian chief, died
1924      Margaret Truman Daniels, daughter of the
                    President, born
1934      King Albert I of Belgium killed while
                    mountain climbing
1936      Jimmy Brown, football player-actor, born
1958      St. Clare of Assissi proclaimed patron of
                    television
1959      Vanguard II launched
1967      Start of 6 days of floods in Rio de Janeiro
          Chemical plant explosion in Hawthorne,
                    New Jersey
1969      Start of the Chinese year of the rooster, 4667
1904, 1915, 1926, 1988, 1999, 2010, 2021, 2083, 2094
                    Ash Wednesday
1931, 1942, 1953, 2015, 2026, 2037  Shrove Tuesday
```

February 18th

```
          Bursting Day in Iceland (when the sea-ice
                    crumbles)
449 AD    St. Flavian of Constantinople died
676       St. Colman of Lindisfarne died (Feast Day)
1386      King Wladislaus II of Poland married Jadwiga
                    of Hungary
1478      George, Duke of Clarence and brother of King
                    Edward IV of England, executed
                    for treason by drowning in a
                    barrel of wine
1493      Columbus reached the Azores
1516      Queen Mary I ("Bloody Mary") of England born
1546      Martin Luther, German religious leader, died
```

```
1562        Huguenot colonists left France for Florida
1564        Michaelangelo, Italian artist, died
1622        English-Persian seige of Portuguese at
                 Hormuz began
1653        English defeated Dutch fleet at Portsmouth
1678        Pilgrim's Progress published
1685        LaSalle made the first white settlement in
                 Texas
1688        First vote against slavery recorded in U.S.
                 (Germantown, Penna.)
1784        Nicolo Paganini, Italian violinist, born
1795        Lewiston, Maine, incorporated
1828        Echigo, Japan, rocked by an earthquake
1849        First scheduled steamship from New York
                 arrived in San Francisco, by way
                 of Cape Horn
1851        Six members of the Oatman family massacred
                 by Arizona Indians
1857        Max Klinger, German artist, born
1861        Jefferson Davis sworn in as President of the
                 Confederacy
1890        Adolphe Menjou, actor, born
1892        Wendell Willkie, Presidential candidate, born
1898        Frances Willard, temperance supporter, died
1902        Charles L. Tiffany, founder of the jewelry
                 company, died
1915        Harry W. Leonard, inventor, died
            Germany began blockading England with
                 submarines
1919        Jack Palance, actor, born
1930        Planet Pluto discovered
1932        Manchuria became Manchukuo, a Japanese
                 puppet state
1939        Golden Gate International Exposition opened
                 (San Francisco)
1942        Albert Payson Terhune, author, died
            U.S. destroyer Truxton and cargo ship Pallus
                 ran aground off Newfoundland
1947        Gallitzin, Pennsylvania, train wreck
1956        First monorail system in the U.S. made a trial
                 run (Houston)
1968        End of the Winter Olympics at Grenoble, France
1972        World Prayer Day
1931, 1942, 1953, 2015, 2026, 2037  Ash Wednesday
1947, 1958, 1969, 2042, 2048, 2053  Shrove Tuesday
```

February 19th

```
 439 AD     St. Mesrop died (Feast Day)
 607        Boniface III became Pope
1473        Copernicus, astronomer, born
1594        Sigismund III, King of Poland, crowned King of
                 Sweden
```

1717	David Garrick, English actor, born
1778	Daniel W. Harmon, author-explorer, born
1797	Peace of Talentino settled differences between France and the Vatican over the Papal States
1803	Ohio became a state
1817	King William III of Holland born
1843	Adeline Patti, singer, born
1861	Emancipation Act freed the Russian serfs
1864	Knights of Pythias, fraternal organization, founded
1865	Sven Hedin, explorer of Asia, born
1873	John H. Fahey, publisher, born
1893	Sir Cedric Hardwick, English actor, born
1912	Ceil Chapman, fashion designer, born Stan Kenton, bandleader, born
1916	Eddie Arcaro, jockey, born
1923	William H. Goodyear, author-archaeologist, died
1936	Billy Mitchell, aviator, died
1945	U.S. invasion of Iwo Jima began
1970	Molniya 1/13, Russian communications satellite, launched

1947, 1958, 1969, 2042, 2048, 2053 Ash Wednesday
1901, 1920, 1980, 1985, 2064, 2075 Shrove Tuesday

February 20th

	Feast of St. Ulrich (or Wulfric) of Haselburg
342 AD	St. Shahdost, Persian bishop, martyred (Feast Day)
1431	Pope Martin V died
1437	James I, King of Scotland, stabbed to death
1500	Charles I, King of Spain, born
1513	Pope Julius II, creator of the Swiss Guard, died
1546	Edward VI crowned King of England
1680	La Voisin, French sorceress, executed North Yarmouth, Maine, incorporated
1777	King Joseph of Portugal died
1790	Joseph II, Emperor of Austria and the Holy Roman Empire, died
1792	U.S. federal post office system established
1808	Honore Daumier, French artist, born
1815	U.S.S. Constitution captured by H.M.S. Cyane and Levant
1854	Livingston's party reached Lake Dilolo, Africa
1857	North German Lloyd Steamship Company founded
1864	Confederates were victorious at Olustee, Florida
1865	Cape Fear River forts captured by the Union forces

```
1872       Metropolitan Museum of Art opened (New York
                City)
1878       Vincenzo Gioacchino Pecci elected Pope,
                Leo XIII
1889       Maritime Canal Company of Nicaragua incorpo-
                rated
1895       Cuban Revolution resumed
1914       John Daly, television personality, born
1915       Panama-Pacific International Exposition
                opened in San Francisco
1920       Robert E. Peary, Arctic explorer, died
1927       Sidney Poitier, actor, born
1943       Paracutin volcano's birth buried all of
                Parangaricutiro, Mexico, except
                the church bell tower
1962       John Glenn made 3 earth orbits in a Mercury
                capsule
1965       Ranger 8 photographed and then landed on
                the Moon
1967       daVinci's "Ginevra de Benci" bought by the
                National Gallery of Art
                (Washington, D.C.)
1970       Lantern Festival, marking the end of the
                Chinese New Year celebrations
1901, 1920, 1980, 1985, 2064, 2075  Ash Wednesday
1912, 1917, 1996, 2007, 2080, 2091  Shrove Tuesday
```

February 21st
```
1198 AD    Pope Innocent III was ordained as a priest
1508       Michelangelo's "Pope Julius" put in place
1598       Boris Godunov elected Czar of Muscovy
1613       Michael Romanov elected Czar of Russia
1630       Rubens, Flemish artist, knighted in England
1728       Peter III, Czar of Russia, born
1730       Pope Benedict XIII died of influenza
1779       Captain Cook was buried at sea
1795       Santa Anna, Mexican revolutionary, born
1807       Martin Van Buren married Hannah Hoes
1808       Russia declared war on Sweden
1851       Mary W. Shelley, author of Frankenstein,
                born
1853       $3 gold pieces authorized in the U.S.
1878       First telephone directory issued (New Haven,
                Connecticut)
1904       National Ski Association of America founded
1907       British ship Berlin sank off the Hook of
                Holland
1916       Battle of Verdun
1919       Worcester, Massachusetts, art museum bought
                a Gainsborough
1924       First official Alaskan air mail flight
1937       Crown Prince Harald of Norway born
```

1940	Federal Hall, New York City, became a national monument
1963	Northeast Libya rocked by an earthquake
1967	Canadian trawler Cape Bonnie wrecked in Halifax harbor
1968	Four British teams set out with dogsleds from Alaska to Norway over the North Pole
1969	Volcano on Deception Island, Antarctica, erupted
1970	Speckled Perch Festival at Okeechobee, Florida
1973	Southern California rocked by an earthquake
1912, 1917, 1996, 2007, 2080, 2091	Ash Wednesday
1928, 1939, 1950, 2012, 2023, 2034, 2045	Shrove Tuesday

February 22nd

	Arbor Day in Texas
	Ancient Romans held family reunions
606 AD	Pope Sabinian died
1072	St. Pietro Damiani died
1276	Pope Innocent V crowned
1297	St. Margaret of Cortona died (Feast Day)
1371	David II, King of Scotland, died
1403	Charles VII, King of France, born
1440	Ladislas, King of Bohemia and Hungary, born
1649	Westminster Assembly first met (London)
1690	Charles Le Brun, French artist, died
1732	George Washington, 1st President, born
1776	Boston Newsletter, first regularly published American newspaper, ceased publication
1778	Rembrandt Peale, artist, born
1784	First U.S. ship to sail to China left New York City
1798	Durham, Connecticut, began the installation of the first public water system
1810	Frederick Chopin, composer, born
1812	Hazard and Caledonia fought a naval battle
1813	British captured Ft. Presentation, New York
1819	Spain ceded Florida to the U.S.
	James Russell Lowell, poet-diplomat, born
1821	First Order of Odd Fellows group in the U.S. formed (Maryland)
1827	Charles Wilson Peale, portrait artist, died
1837	Michigan's state flag first flown
1847	Battle of Buena Vista began (U.S. against Mexico)
1851	Kirkwood ran aground in New Jersey, having mistaken the Smith Hotel for a vessel that wouldn't return its signal

```
1875      Jean-Baptiste Corot, French artist, died
1876      John Hopkins University formally opened
1879      F. W. Woolworth opened his first store
                    (Utica, New York)
1885      Washington Monument dedicated
1888      Washington Monument opened
1889      Dakota Territory made into 2 states
1892      Edna St. Vincent Millay, poet, born
1895      Latham exhibited his motion-picture projector
1901      Rio de Janeiro wrecked at San Francisco
1906      Achilles asteroid discovered
1932      Edward Kennedy, Massachusetts senator, born
1933      Campbell, in a Napier-Campbell, set a land-
                    speed record of 272.109 mph
1947      Harry K. Thaw, slayer of architect Stanford
                    White, died
1963      Northern Libya rocked by earthquake
1965      Felix Frankfurter, Supreme Court Justice, died
1928, 1939, 1950, 2012, 2023, 2034, 2045  Ash Wednesday
1944, 1955, 1966, 1977, 2039, 2050, 2061, 2077  Shrove
                    Tuesday
```

February 23rd

```
          Feast of St. Mildburga
 155 AD   St. Polycarp, bishop of Smyrna, martyred by
                    fire
 687      Pepin of Heristal arrived in France
1011      St. Willigis died (Feast Day)
1072      St. Peter Damian died (Feast Day)
1305      A sermon preached in Italy mentioned spectacles
1421      Catherine, queen to King Henry V of England,
                    crowned
1440      Mathias I, King of Hungary, born
1447      Pope Eugenius IV died
1505      Columbus was granted a license to ride a mule
                    in Spain
1516      Ferdinand, King of Spain, died
1685      George Frederick Handel, composer, born
1781      George Taylor, signer of the Declaration of
                    Independence, died
1784      Rhode Island legislature authorized the free-
                    ing of slaves
1785      New York Morning Post and Daily Advertiser,
                    first New York daily newspaper,
                    founded
1791      John Wesley, founder of Methodism, died
1792      Sir Joshua Reynolds, English artist, died
1799      First U.S. national quarantine legislation
                    passed
1815      Robert Fulton, steamboat inventor, died
1821      Poet John Keats died of consumption
1822      Boston, Massachusetts, incorporated as a city
```

```
1847      U.S. defeated Mexico at Buena Vista
1848      John Quincy Adams, U.S. President, died
1869      The state legislature authorized the building
              of Nevada's capitol
1886      Commercial production method for aluminum
              invented
1887      Importation of opium from China forbidden
              (U.S.)
1905      First Rotary Club founded (Chicago)
          Sally Victor, hat designer, born
1913      Francisco Madero, President of Mexico,
              assassinated
1916      Ministry of Blockade created in England
1917      Federal Board of Vocational Education
              created in U.S.
1920      First wireless telephone broadcast (Chelmsford,
              England)
1927      Federal Radio Commission established in U.S.
1942      A Japanese submarine fired on an oil refinery
              at Santa Barbara, California
1945      U.S. flag raised on Iwo Jima
1946      Gen. T. Yamashita, Japanese commander in the
              Philippines, hanged
1954      Salk polio vaccine first used for mass
              inoculation (Pittsburgh)
1960      Prince Naruhito Hironomiya of Japan born
1965      Stan Laurel, of Laurel and Hardy comedy team,
              died
1967      End of 6 days of flooding in Rio de Janeiro
1968      Fannie Hurst, novelist, died
1969      Saud, deposed king of Arabia, died
1944, 1955, 1966, 1977, 2039, 2050, 2061, 2077  Ash
              Wednesday
1909, 1971, 1982, 1993, 2066, 2072  Shrove Tuesday
```

February 24th

```
          Feast of St. Matthias (patron of carpenters,
              tailors, and reformed drunks;
              invoked against smallpox)
  259 AD  Sts. Montanus and Lucius martyred (Feast Day)
  303     First Roman edict for persecution of Chris-
              tians published
1389      Albert of Mecklenburg, unpopular king of
              Sweden, captured
1446      Lottery drawn in Bruges, Belgium is the
              earliest known
1509      Papal Bull issued against duels
1525      Charles V, Holy Roman Emperor, crushed the
              French at Pavia and captured King
              Francis I
          Richard de la Pole, pretender to the English
              throne, died
```

```
1530        Last imperial coronation of a Holy Roman
                  Emperor
1557        Mathias, Holy Roman Emperor, born (never
                  crowned)
1577        Eric XIV, deposed king of Sweden, died of
                  poison
1582        Gregorian calendar reform completed
1587        Miguel de Cervantes Saavedra, author of Don
                  Quixote, excommunicated
1619        Charles Le Brun, French artist, born
1653        New York's first city hall opened, in a
                  tavern
1827        Augusta chosen the capital of Maine
1836        Winslow Homer, artist, born
1855        Cavalry destroyed a Mescalero Apache village
                  in New Mexico
1863        Arizona became a U.S. Territory
1868        President Andrew Johnson impeached
1903        U.S. acquired the Guantanamo Naval Station
                  in Cuba
1905        Simplon Tunnel completed between Switzerland
                  and Italy
            West Virginia state flag adopted
1907        Imperatrix, an Austrian ship, wrecked
1909        Maine adopted its state flag
            New Hampshire adopted its state flag
1918        Florizel wrecked near Cape Race, Newfoundland
            Flag of Estonia adopted
1922        Chinde, Portuguese East Africa devastated by
                  a cyclone
1932        Campbell, in a Napier-Campbell, set a land
                  speed record of 253.96 mph
1942        First broadcast made of The Voice of America
1949        Israel and Egypt signed a general armistice
                  agreement
1966        Iwame Nkrumah, President of Ghana, overthrown
1970        Flag Day, a national holiday in Mexico
            Start of Holi (Festival of Color) in Nepal
            Conrad Nagel, actor, died
1909, 1971, 1982, 1993, 2066, 2072  Ash Wednesday
1903, 1914, 1925, 1998, 2004, 2009, 2088, 2093, 2099
                  Shrove Tuesday
```

February 25th

```
 138 AD     Antoninus Pius was adopted by Emperor Hadrian
                  as the successor to Rome
 493        Negotiations opened between the Roman army,
                  besieged at Ravenna, and the
                  Osgoths
 616        St. Ethelbert, King of Kent, died (Feast Day)
 779        St. Walburga died (Feast Day)
```

1601	Earl of Essex, leader of a foiled rebellion, beheaded in England
1634	Wallenstein, German noble and general, murdered
1643	The governor of New York started an Indian war with an attempt to remove the tribes on the west bank of the Hudson River
1713	Frederick I, first king of Prussia, died
1723	Sir Christopher Wren, English architect, died
1728	Peter II crowned Czar of Russia
1778	Jose De San Martin, South American liberator, born
1779	Fort Sackville, Indiana, captured by the Americans
	Vincennes, Canada, fell to American forces
1807	Slavery ended in England
1825	Peru adopted its national flag
1836	Samuel Colt got a patent on his revolver
1841	Auguste Renoir, French artist, born
1847	Pennsylvania Railroad got its letters patented
1848	Edward Harriman, financier, born
1862	Congress approved the issuance of "greenbacks"
1863	National Bank Act passed, allowing their free formation
1870	Hiram R. Revels, a black, took the oath as a U.S. senator
1873	Enrico Caruso, singer, born
1881	Phoenix, Arizona, incorporated
1888	John Foster Dulles, U.S. statesman, born
1894	Steele Mackaye, folding theater-seat inventor, died
1901	United States Steel incorporated
1908	Frank G. Slaughter, physician-author, born
1913	Sixteenth Amendment passed, authorizing income tax
1916	Germany captured Fort Dovaumont
1925	Glacier Bay National Monument established (Alaska)
1932	Adolf Hitler became a German citizen
1948	Czechoslovakia joined the Communist bloc
1954	President Adibal-Shishakli of Syria resigned after an army uprising
1956	Communist Party Congress proclaimed peaceful coexistence with the West
1964	Cassius Clay knocked out Sonny Liston for the heavyweight boxing title

1903, 1914, 1925, 1998, 2004, 2009, 2088, 2093, 2099 Ash Wednesday

1936, 1941, 2020, 2031 Shrove Tuesday

	Feast of St. Porphyry of Gaza
747 BC	Beginning of the Era of Nabonasser
364 AD	Valentinian became Emperor of the Roman army at Nicaea
493	Romans in Ravenna surrendered to the Osgoths
1154	Roger II, King of Sicily, died
1266	Battle of Benevento
	Manfred, King of Sicily, died
1361	King Wenceslaus of Germany born
1564	Christopher Marlowe, English playwright, baptized
1802	Zebulon Pike's expedition captured by the Spanish (Western U.S.)
	Victor Hugo, French author-playwright, born
	Esek Hopkins, first commodore of the U.S. Navy, died
1815	Napoleon escaped from Elba
1846	William F. ("Buffalo Bill") Cody born
1848	Second Republic proclaimed in France
1855	First public school system in the South established (Nashville, Tennessee)
1861	Ferdinand, King of Bulgaria, born
1869	Nadezhda Krupskaya, wife of Lenin, born
1870	New York City's first subway supposedly opened, but none really functioned before 1904
1903	Richard Gattling, machine-gun inventor, died
1909	Austro-Hungary and Turkish treaty signed, annexing Bosnia and Herzogovinia
1915	First really successful use of a flamethrower by the Germans at Verdun
1916	Jackie Gleason, comedian, born
	French cruiser _Provence_ sank in the Mediterranean
1917	President requested Congress to order the arming of U.S. merchant ships
1919	Grand Canyon became a national park
1922	Margaret Leighton, actress, born
1925	Oregon state flag adopted
1961	Mohammed V, King of Morocco, died
1970	Eve of Iduladha, a Moslem festival
1971	Islamic year 1391 began
	Start of the Parade of Chariots at Limassol, Cyprus

1936, 1941, 2020, 2031 Ash Wednesday
1952, 1963, 1974, 2036, 2047, 2058, 2069 Shrove Tuesday

	Roman ceremony honoring Mars, god of war
	Feast of St. Leander
288 AD	Constantine born
1458	George of Podebrad chosen King of Bohemia
1545	Scots defeated the English at Ancrum Moor
1776	Battle of Moore's Creek, North Carolina
1807	Henry Wadsworth Longfellow, poet, born
1812	Lord Byron, English poet, made his maiden speech in Parliament
1847	Illinois legislature brought into being the Chicago, Rock Island, and Pacific Railway
1860	Abraham Lincoln gave his "Cooper Union Address"
1862	St. Gabriel Possenti died (Feast Day)
1869	Genealogical and Biographical Society of New York founded
1872	Thanksgiving held at St. Paul's in London for King Edward VII's recovery from typhoid
1881	Battle of Majuba, Dutch victory over the English in the Boer War
1900	England's Labour Party founded
	British forces captured Pieter's Hill, South Africa
1902	Marian Anderson, opera signer, born
	John Steinbeck, novelist, born
1905	Montana adopted its state flag
1906	Samuel Phangley, astronomer, died
1917	Arizona adopted its state flag
	Mount Union, Pennsylvania, train wreck
1921	Porter, Indiana, train wreck
	King George II of Greece married Elizabeth of Rumania
1923	Tanana River railroad bridge completed (Alaska)
1930	George H. Putnam, publisher, died
1932	Elizabeth Taylor, actress, born
1936	Ivan Pavlov, psychologist and dog experimenter, died
1939	Nadezhda Krupskaya, Lenin's wife, died
1972	Statehood Day Celebration (Nevis, St. Kitts, Anquilia, British West Indies)

1952, 1963, 1974, 2036, 2047, 2058, 2069 Ash Wednesday
1906, 1968, 1979, 1990, 2001, 2063, 2074, 2085 Shrove Tuesday

----

Funeral Service for Sardines at Curiepe, Venezuela

Feast of St. Romanus (invoked for cure of
insanity and protection from
drowning)
Kalevala National Day, Finland
Feast of the Martyrs of the Plague at
Alexandria
591 AD Gregory I became Pope
992   St. Oswald of Worcester died (Feast Day)
1258   Tatars burned Baghdad
1476   Beseiged Granson, Switzerland, surrendered
to the French
1572   Catherine of Austria, third wife of Sigismund
II of Poland, died
1638   Battle of the Rheinfelden, Germany
1648   Christian IV, King of Denmark and Norway, died
1704   Deerfield, Massachusetts, attacked by Indians
1781   Richard Stockton, signer of the Declaration of
Independence, died
1785   Horea, self-styled emperor of Rumania, broken
on the wheel for treason
1791   French National Guard turned back the attack
on Vincennes
1824   Blondin, French tightrope-walker, born
1827   Baltimore and Ohio Railroad chartered
1832   Portland, Maine, incorporated
1837   Illinois state capital moved to Springfield
1845   Texas was invited to join the U.S.
1851   Compagnie Des Messageries Maritimes, French
steamship company, founded
1854   U.S. Republican Party formed
1861   Colorado became a U.S. territory
1868   Louis I, King of Bavaria, died
1894   Ben Hecht, novelist-playwright, born
1901   Linus Pauling, biochemist, born
Jupiter's south tropical disturbance first
observed
1911   Elizabeth Tunnel, part of the Los Angeles
aqueduct system, completed
1916   Henry James, novelist, died
1917   Germany tried to get Mexico to declare war on
the U.S.
1941   King Alphonso XIII of Spain died in exile
1942   Japanese landed on Java
1951   Preliminary report made by Kefauver's Senate
Crime Committee
1956   Swampscott, Massachusetts, train wreck
1959   Maxwell Anderson, playwright, died
1961   "Lone Tree" became a Washington State Monument
1969   Scheduled Apollo 9 flight postponed due to
astronauts' colds
1970   Finals of All-Northwest Barbershop Ballad
Contest at Forest Grove, Oregon

End of Festival of the Pines at New Plymouth,
                New Zealand
1973   Kuril, Japan, rocked by an earthquake
          Earth tremor shook midAtlantic U.S. coast
1906, 1968, 1979, 1990, 2001, 2063, 2074, 2085 Ash
                Wednesday
2096   Shrove Tuesday (Leap Year)
1911, 1922, 1933, 1995, 2006, 2017, 2090 Shrove Tuesday

February 29th

          Leap Year Day
 468 AD   Pope St. Hilarus died
 992   Oswald, Archbishop of York, England, died
1288   It was made legal in Scotland for women to
                propose to men
1634   Wallenstein, Austrian general, murdered
1704   40 killed, 100 carried off by Indians from
                Deerfield, Massachusetts
1712   General Montcalm, hero of the French and
                Indian War, born
1756   Christian F. Hansen, Danish architect, born
1804   Orders given for construction of the first
                lighthouse on the Great Lakes
1808   Charles Pritchard, British astronomer, born
1864   Jan Svatopluk Macher, Czech poet, born
1922   Teachers' Registration Council established
                (England)
1944   British and Indian troops drove the Japanese
                from Burma
1960   Agadir, Morocco, hit by an earthquake, tidal
                wave, and fire
1972   Tokyo rocked by an earthquake
2096   Ash Wednesday
2028   Shrove Tuesday

MARCH

Full Moon - Lenten Moon; Worm Moon
            Roman festival of Anna Perrena, goddess of
                the year
First Sunday after Easter - Quasimodo or Low Sunday

March 1st

	Golden Shears International Sheep Shearing Championships at Masterton, New Zealand
	Feast of St. David (or Dewi), patron of Wales
	Town Meeting Day in Vermont
	Tree Festival in Iraq
154 BC	Until now, this was New Year's Day to the Romans
49	Caesar's command in Gaul expired
293 AD	Constantinus the Pale, father of Constantine, named Caesar
1389	St. Antoninus born
1562	French Protestants (Huguenots) massacred at Vessy
1638	First Swedish settlers, inventors of the log cabin, arrived in America
1642	York, Maine, incorporated, first settlement to do so
1780	First U.S. bank, that of Philadelphia, chartered
	First act to abolish slavery passed by Pennsylvania
1790	First U.S. census (recorded 17 states, 3,929,214 people) authorized
1792	Leopold II, Holy Roman Emperor and ruler of Austria, died
1803	Ohio became a state

1927, 1938, 1949, 1960, 2022, 2033, 2044 Shrove Tuesday

```
----------------------------------------------------
March 2nd
----------------------------------------------------
```

672 AD	St. Chad died (Feast Day)
986	Lothair, King of France, died
1127	St. Charles the Good (or the Dane) murdered
1160	Frederick I, Holy Roman Emperor, excommunicated
1316	King Robert II of Scotland born
1476	Swiss defeated Burgundians (French) at Granston
1769	DeWitt Clinton, New York governor, born
1793	Sam Houston, soldier-statesman, born
1806	Benito Juarez, President of Mexico, born (National Holiday)
1810	Pope Leo XIII born
1818	Second pyramid of Gizeh, the tomb of Chephren, opened
1819	Arkansas became a U.S. territory
1834	Horace Greeley founded the New Yorker, a weekly literary newspaper
1835	Francis I, Emperor of Austria and the last Holy Roman Emperor, died
1836	Texas declared its independence from Mexico
1853	Washington became a U.S. territory
1855	Nicholas I, the "Iron Czar" of Russia, died
1861	Nevada and the Dakotas became U.S. territories
1865	Custer and his Union forces defeated the Confederates at Waynesboro, Virginia
1867	First U.S. Board of Education established
1889	National Zoological Park established by Congress
1893	Montana's great seal and state flag adopted
1899	Mt. Rainier National Park established
1904	Theodor Seuss Geisel, author as Dr. Seuss, born
1916	Elizabeth, Queen of Rumania, died
1917	Inhabitants of Puerto Rico became U.S. citizens
1939	Eugene Mary Joseph John Pacelli elected Pope (Pius XII)
1944	521 killed by coal fumes in an Italian railroad tunnel
1949	A U.S. bomber completed a nonstop, around-the-world flight (94 hours, 1 minute)
1955	Norodom Suramarit became King of Cambodia
1956	Morocco became independent of France
1958	Sir Vivian Fuchs and party completed their Antartic crossing
1968	Zond 4, Russian satellite, launched

1927, 1938, 1949, 1960, 2022, 2033, 2044 Ash Wednesday
1954, 1965, 1976, 2049, 2055, 2060 Shrove Tuesday

	Japanese Doll Festival
	Feast of St. Aelred
	Feast of St. Marinus of Caesarea
	Feast of St. Winwaloe (or Guenole)
1033 AD	St. Cunegund, Queen of Bavaria, died (Feast Day)
1431	Gabriel Condulmaro elected Pope (Eugenius IV)
1605	Pope Clement VIII died
1703	Robert Hooke, scientist, died
1778	Royal Pennsylvania Gazette, Philadelphia newspaper, founded
1817	Alabama became a U.S. territory
1820	Missouri Compromise slavery bill passed Congress
1845	Florida became a state
1847	Alexander Graham Bell, telephone inventor, born
1849	"Double Eagle" $20 and $1 gold pieces authorized
	Minnesota became a U.S. territory
	U.S. Department of the Interior established
1857	Congress approved mail service for the far West by coach
1861	Serfdom abolished in Russia
1863	National Academy of Sciences incorporated by an act of Congress
1865	Bureau of Freedmen, Refugees and Abandoned Land created by Congress
1878	Bulgaria liberated from the Turks (Bulgarian National Holiday) by the Treaty of San Stefano
	Pope Leo XIII crowned in the Sistine chapel
1883	U.S. got a postal money order system
1890	"Buffalo Bill" Cody met Pope Leo XIII in St. Peter's Square
1901	National Bureau of Standards established
1911	North Dakota's state flag adopted
1918	Russian Bolshevik government surrendered to German (Brest-Litovsk)
1920	Julius Boros, golfer, born
1924	Caliph Abdul Mejid expelled from Constantinople
1925	Chicago permitted to use Lake Michigan water for the disposal of sewage
1934	Herbert Youngblood and John Dillinger, bank robbers, escaped from jail
1959	Pioneer IV, lunar probe, launched
1969	Feast of Esther
	Apollo 9 and lunar landing craft launched

1954, 1965, 1976, 2049, 2055, 2060 Ash Wednesday
1908, 1981, 1987, 1992, 2071, 2076, 2082 Shrove Tuesday

Firemen's Anniversary (Louisiana)

303 AD	St. Adrian, patron of soldiers, martyred
561	Pelagius I, Pope, died
1394	Portugal's Prince Henry the Navigator born
1461	Edward IV took possession of the English crown
1484	St. Casimir, patron of Poland, died (Feast Day)
1493	Columbus reached Lisbon, Portugal
1519	Cortez landed in Mexico
1675	John Flamsteed, "Father of modern astronomy," appointed Royal Astronomer of England
1681	William Penn granted a charter to found his colony
1789	U.S. Constitution went into effect with the first meeting of Congress (Federal Hall, New York City)
1791	Vermont became a state
1824	Royal National Lifeboat Institution founded (England)
1825	Quincy, Illinois, with 10 residents, became the Adams County seat
1826	First railway charter in the U.S. granted to the Granite Railway Company
1829	Crowds in the White House at Jackson's inauguration broke furniture and china
1837	Chicago incorporated as a city
1849	Battle of Novara (Austria-Italy)
1861	Confederate States adopted "the Stars and Bars" as their flag
1863	Idaho became a U.S. territory
1872	Boston Globe newspaper founded
1880	New York Daily Graphic contained the first newspaper photograph
1888	Knute Rockne, football great, born
1901	Charles H. Goren, bridge player, born
1908	Collingswood, Ohio, school fire and panic killed 176
1913	U.S. Department of Commerce and Labor established
	First hunting law governing bird shooting passed
1917	First woman in Congress (Jeanette Rankin of Montana) began her term
	U.S. Senate killed a bill to arm merchant ships
1918	U.S.S. Cyclops left Barbados and disappeared
1933	Franklin D. Roosevelt became the last President to be inaugurated on this date

```
1937    National Arboretum founded by an act of Congress
1942    U.S. Army Air Force sank 3 Japanese troopships
                at Subic Bay, Philippines
1956    Lt. Colonel Jose Marie Lemus became President
                of El Salvador
1960    Belgian munitions ship exploded in Havana, Cuba
                harbor
1965    A gas pipeline exploded near Natchitoches,
                Alaska
1968    O.G.O. V satellite launched
1969    Holi Festival in Northern India
        Purim (Hebrew Festival of Lots)
1908, 1981, 1987, 1992, 2071, 2076, 2082  Ash Wednesday
1919, 1924, 1930, 2003, 2014, 2025, 2087, 2098  Shrove
                Tuesday
```

March 5th

```
        Annual Fair at Bury, Lancashire, England
        Boys' Day in Japan
        Feast of St. Ciaran of Saighir
        Feast of St. Phocas of Antioch
        Feast of St. Piran
475 AD  St. Gerasimus, who drew a thorn from the paw of
                a lion, died (Feast Day)
1152    Frederick I (Barbarosa) elected King of Germany
1324    David II, King of Scotland, born
1380    Construction began of St. Mary's College,
                Oxford, England
1432    Treaty of Rennes signed between France and
                Brittany
1534    Correggio, Italian artist, died
1658    Antoine de la Mothe Cadillac, explorer, born
1770    Boston Massacre
1824    Britain declared war on Burma
        James Merrit Ives, of Currier and Ives
                lithographers, born
1836    Patent Arms Manufacturing Company formed to
                produce Colt revolvers
1850    Louisville and Nashville Railroad Company
                incorporated
1853    Howard Pyle, American artist-writer, born
1900    Madame Butterfly produced as a play in New York
                City
1908    Rex Harrison, actor, born
1912    Spanish ship Principe de Austrias sank
1913    German destroyer S-178 and cruiser Yorck
                collided near Helgoland
1927    U.S. Marines landed in China to protect
                American property during a civil
                uprising
```

```
1950        Edgar Lee Masters, poet (Spoon River Anthology)
                 died
1953        Joseph Stalin, Russian premier, died
1959        Explorer II launched
1968        Solar Explorer II, sun-study satellite, launched
1969        Purim (Hebrew Festival of Lots)
1919, 1924, 1930, 2003, 2014, 2025, 2087, 2098
                 Ash Wednesday
1935, 1946, 1957, 2019, 2030, 2041, 2052  Shrove Tuesday
```

March 6th

```
            Feast of St. Cyneburga
 203 AD     Sts. Perpetua and Felicity martyred (Feast
                 Day)
 766        St. Chrodegang died (Feast Day)
1405        King John II of Castile born
1447        St. Colette died (Feast Day)
            Tommaso Parentucelli elected Pope (Nicholas V)
1454        Casimir IV added Prussian areas to Poland
1475        Michelangelo, Italian artist, born
1480        Treaty of Alcacovas gave the Canary Islands
                 to Spain
1521        Magellan discovered the Mariana Islands
                 (Magellan Day, Guam)
1604        Charles IX became King of Sweden
1612        A tournament was held in Paris to celebrate the
                 wedding of King Louis XIII
1620        Cyrano de Bergerac born
1622        John Mason chartered to found New Hampshire
1629        Edict of Restitution restored their property to
                 the Catholic churches
1775        First black Masons initiated into an Army
                 Lodge that was stationed near
                 Boston
1806        Elizabeth Barrett Browning, poet, born
1809        Thomas Heyward, signer of the Declaration of
                 Independence, died
1836        Davy Crockett, frontiersman, killed at the fall
                 of the Alamo to Mexican forces
1837        The Seminole Indians agreed to end their war
1857        Dred Scott slavery decision made by the U.S.
                 Supreme Court
1862        Battle of Pea Ridge, Arkansas, began
1885        Ring Lardner, humorist, born
1888        Louisa May Alcott, author of Little Women, died
1889        Emile Zola's novels seized by Canadian customs
                 as obscene
1896        Charles King completed the first Detroit-built
                 car
1906        Lawrence Schoonover, novelist, born
```

1912	Air mail service proposed, to be rejected by Congress
1915	Massachusetts state flag revised
1924	Egyptian government opened Tutankhamen's mummy, officially
1926	Shakespeare Memorial Theater burned (Stratford-on-Avon, England)
1932	John Philip Sousa, composer, died
1933	Presidential order closed all banks in the U.S.
1935	Oliver Wendell Holmes, Jr., jurist-author, died
1938	Spanish insurgent cruiser Baleares sunk by Loyalists off Cartagena
1945	Lippizaner horses removed from Vienna to escape approaching Russian troops
1957	Republic of Ghana established
1964	King Paul I of Greece died
1968	Ellen Price, model for Copenhagen's "Little Mermaid" statue, died
1970	Nassau Cup Race, Bahamas (30 miles for sailboats)
1973	Pearl Buck, writer, died
1935, 1946, 1957, 2019, 2030, 2041, 2052	Ash Wednesday
1962, 1973, 1984, 2057, 2068	Shrove Tuesday

March 7th

	St. Joseph's Day (Patron of Rio Chico, Venezuela)
161 AD	Antoninus Pius, Roman emperor, died
1080	King Henry IV of Germany excommunicated
1138	Conrad III again chosen King of Germany
1274	St. Thomas Aquinas died (patron of all Catholic schools; Feast Day)
1307	King Edward I of England died
1530	The Pope refused King Henry VIII's request for a divorce
1573	Venice recognized the Turkish rule of Cyprus
1693	Pope Clement XIII born
1707	Stephen Hopkins, signer of the Declaration of Independence, born
1714	Peace of Rastatt signed
1724	Pope Innocent XIII died
1782	Start of a two-day massacre of Christian Indians at New Philadelphia, Ohio
1802	Sir Edwin Landseer, English artist, born
1804	First Bible Society founded
1808	Portuguese Royal Family arrived in Brazil
1815	Napoleon acclaimed by soldiers sent to arrest him
1831	England's Royal Astronomical Society incorporated
1849	Luther Burbank, botanist, born

1850	Tomas Masaryk, first president of Czechoslovakia, born
	Daniel Webster made his antisecession speech in the Senate
1870	First male and female Grand Jury impaneled (Wyoming)
1872	Piet Mondrian, Dutch artist, born
1875	Maurice Ravel, French composer, born
1876	Telephone patent granted to Alexander Graham Bell
1889	Ben Ames Williams, novelist, born
1907	Wild prairie rose became the North Dakota state flower
1908	Semblance of peace restored in Nevada gold-miners' strike
1912	Discovery of the South Pole announced by Amundsen
1913	Dynamite explosion killed 55 in Baltimore
1926	First successful radio-telephone call made between New York and London
1927	Tange, Japan, rocked by an earthquake
1936	German troops began to occupy the Rhineland
1938	Spanish insurgents killed 1,000 in Barcelona air raids
1945	U.S. forces crossed the Rhine at Remagen Bridge
1949	First homes at Levittown, Long Island housing development, went on sale
1950	Coplon and Gubicher were found guilty of espionage
1957	Suez Canal opened after four months of closure by Egypt
1962	OSO I satellite launched
1965	Queen Louise of Sweden died
1970	Total eclipse of the sun
1962, 1973, 1984, 2057, 2068	Ash Wednesday
1905, 1916, 2000, 2079	Shrove Tuesday

```
==========================================================
March 8th
==========================================================
```

	Feast of St. Senan of Scattery
648 AD	St. Felix of Dunwich died (Feast Day)
690	St. Julian of Toledo died (Feast Day)
1144	Pope Celestine II died
1198	Philip elected King of Germany
1550	St. John of God, patron of the mortally sick, died (Feast Day)
1556	Charter granted for founding Holy Trinity College at Oxford, England
1618	Johann Kepler discovered the third law of planetary motion
1702	King William III of England died and Anne, his sister-in-law, was proclaimed Queen
1766	Hirosaki, Japan, shaken by an earthquake

1787	Karl von Grafe, "Father of plastic surgery," born
1801	British forces landed in Egypt
1841	Oliver Wendell Holmes, Jr., Supreme Court Justice, born
1844	King Charles XIV of Sweden, born Jean-Baptist Bernadotte of France, died
1845	Commodore Perry's treaty with Japan ratified by the U.S.
1849	Thomas Swing was appointed first U.S. Secretary of Interior
1853	Isaac Winslow filed for a patent on canning corn
1858	Ruggiero Leoncavallo, opera composer, born
1862	Confederates defeated at Pea Ridge, Arkansas
	Confederate ironclad Merrimac sank the Union's Cumberland and Congress
1865	A canal began to connect Amsterdam with the North Sea
1869	Hector Berlioz, composer, died
	University of Deseret organized (Salt Lake City, Utah)
1894	New York state passed a dog-licensing law
1895	The constitutional convention of Utah finished its job
1896	Volunteers of America held its first public meeting
1901	Dust storms began in Algeria that were to deposit almost 2 million tons on Europe
1909	South Dakota adopted its state flag
1916	Germany declared war on Portugal
1917	Count Ferdinand von Zeppelin, inventor, died
1920	Switzerland and Cuba joined the League of Nations
1921	Dato, Premier of Spain, assassinated in Madrid
1930	William Howard Taft, 27th U.S. President, died
1931	Justice Oliver Wendell Holmes spoke to the nation via radio
1942	Japanese landed on New Guinea
1950	First shipment of planes under the NATO agreement landed in France
1954	Japan signed a mutual trade pact with the U.S.
1957	Ghana entered the United Nations
1958	U.S. Navy was without a battleship, the last having been added to a "mothball" fleet
1965	First U.S. ground combat unit landed in Viet Nam
1970	Last day of the World Championship Gold-Panning Contest at Rosamond, California
	Start of the two-day Chingay Procession, the gathering of the Chinese clans, in Malaysia

                   Festival of Teahouses (Okinawa)
1971   Harold Lloyd, comedian of early films, died
1972   Airship (Zeppelin) Europe had its maiden voyage
1905, 1916, 2000, 2079 Ash Wednesday
2011, 2095 Shrove Tuesday

March 9th

                   Feast of St. Gregory of Nyssa
1152 AD   Frederick I ("Barbarosa") crowned King of
                   Germany
1440   St. Frances of Rome died (Feast Day)
1451   Amerigo Vespucci, explorer, born
1463   St. Katherine of Bologua died
1629   Czar Alexis Mikhailovich of Russia born
1661   Jules Mazarin, French cardinal-statesman, died
1793   Imprisonment for debt abolished in France
1796   Napoleon married Josephine
1857   St. Dominic Savio died (Feast Day)
1862   Battle of the "ironclads," the Monitor and the
                   Merrimac
1882   First U.S. patent issued for false teeth
1885   North Carolina state flag adopted
                   Bread treated with carbon dioxide patented
1888   William I, Emperor of Germany, King of Prussia,
                   died
1899   Congress voted $50 million for defense in the
                   Spanish-American war
1902   Edward Durrell Stone, architect, born
1904   Maryland state flag adopted
1911   Utah state flag adopted
1913   Alan Ladd, actor, born
1916   Pancho Villa raided Columbus, New Mexico
                   (Mexican Revolution)
1918   Mickey Spillane, mystery writer, born
1922   New Jersey became the last state to ratify the
                   Prohibition Amendment
1923   A meteorite fell near Ashdon, England
1932   Henry Pu Yi became the ruler of Manchuria as a
                   Japanese puppet state
1933   President granted money control powers by
                   Congress
1944   U.S.S. Leopold torpedoed in the Atlantic
1955   Matthew Henson, black member of Peary's Arctic
                   expedition, died
1961   Russia sent the first dog into space in Sputnik
                   9
1963   Dynamite plant explosion at Madderfontain,
                   South Africa
1970   Islamic New Year 1390
2011, 2095 Ash Wednesday
1943, 2038 Shrove Tuesday

New Hampshire Primary Election Day

241 BC Carthaginian fleet defeated off the Aegates
        Islands by the Romans in the
        First Punic War

320 AD The Forty Martyrs were killed (Feast Day)

1040   Harold I, King of England, died

1302   Dante, author, threatened with burning should
        he return to Florence, Italy

1410   Wire invented

1452   Ferdinand, King of Spain, born

1496   Columbus left Hispaniola to return to Spain

1503   Ferdinand I, Holy Roman Emperor, born

1527   Baber, by victory at Kanwaha, became ruler of
        Northern India

1617   Peace of Stolbova signed by Russia, Poland,
        and Sweden

1628   Marcello Malpighi, discoverer of capillary
        circulation, born

1629   King Charles I of England dissolved
        Parliament, not to recall it for
        11 years

1640   Gardiner's Island, first English settlement in
        New York, founded

1643   End of the first fair at Irbit, Russia

1776   Louise, Queen of Prussia, born

1779   The Potato War over Bavarian succession ended

1785   Thomas Jefferson appointed to replace aging
        Benjamin Franklin as U.S. Minister
        to England

1812   Lord Byron's Childe Harold's Pilgrimage first
        published

1813   The Order of the Iron Cross founded in Prussia

1817   Blanketeers marched on London

1826   King John II of Portugal died

1844   King Edward VII of England married Alexandra
        of Denmark

1845   Alexander III, Czar of Russia, born

1858   Dr. Livingstone left England for Africa, again

1864   Maximilian II, King of Bavaria, died

1867   Lillian D. Wald, founder of the Henry Street
        Settlement House, born

1871   Grand Lodge of the Benevolent and Protective
        Order of Elks incorporated

1876   "Mr. Watson, come here please; I want you."
        (first telephone use)
        Anna Hyatt Huntington, sculptor, born

1880   First Salvation Army Mission to the U.S. landed
        in New York

1889   King John of Abyssinia killed battling the
        dervishes

1896   A hat-tipping device patented in the U.S.

```
1905      Mukden, Manchuria, fell to the Japanese
1906      Carnegie Foundation founded
1915      A German cruiser reported its feat, being the
                     first to deliberately sink a U.S.
                     vessel
1916      Russia invaded Persia
1923      Greek ship Alexander sunk off Peraius
1933      Long Beach, California, rocked by an earthquake
1935      Hitler rejected the Versailles treaty and
                     ordered conscription (draft) in
                     Germany
1947      Western Meadowlark and American Elm chosen as
                     symbols of North Dakota
1948      Jan Masaryk, Czech foreign minister, supposed-
                     ly committed suicide
1949      "Axis Sally" convicted of treason for Nazi
                     propaganda broadcasts
1964      Prince Edward of England born
1970      Mock Peasant Wedding, Thebes, Greece
1971      U.S. Senate approved voting for 18-year-olds
1943, 2038  Ash Wednesday
```

_____

March 11th
_____

```
250 AD    St. Pionius died (Feast Day)
638       St. Sophronius died (Feast Day)
859       St. Eulogius of Cordoba died (Feast Day; patron
                     of carpenters)
1302      Romeo married Juliet
1314      Jacques De Molay, last leader of the Knights
                     Templar, burned at the stake in
                     France
1513      Giovanni de Medici elected Pope (Leo X)
1702      Daily Courant, first British daily newspaper,
                     appeared
1794      Congress authorized the building of 6 warships
1810      Marie Louise of Austria married Napoleon by
                     proxy
1811      First wedding held in the White House
                     (Madison's sister-in-law to a
                     Supreme Court Justice)
1820      Benjamin West, artist, died
1846      Treaty of Lahore signed in the Sikh War
1847      "Johnny Appleseed" died
1861      Confederate States of America adopted their
                     constitution
1868      Ground broken for the capitol of Illinois
1875      Guadalajara, Mexico, rocked by an earthquake
1888      "Blizzard of '88" began, lasting 3 days
1893      New York was authorized to purchase Fire Island
                     as a quarantine center
```

	Wanda Gag, children's author-illustrator, born
1895	Spanish ship <u>Reina Regenta</u> foundered in the Atlantic
1898	U.S. military mobilized for the Spanish-American War
1899	King Frederick XI of Denmark born (King's Birthday holiday)
1913	Utah state flag revised
1917	Beginning of a four-day revolt of the Russian armed forces
1929	Seagrave, in an Irving-Napier car, set a land-speed record of 231.446 mph
1930	William Howard Taft became the first U.S. President to be buried at Arlington
1931	Chinese steamer exploded in the Yangtze River
1932	Spain legalized divorce
1938	Hitler invaded Austria
1941	Bill signed beginning "Lend-lease" aid to our Allies
1952	U Win Maung became President of Burma
1957	Richard E. Byrd, flying explorer, died
1960	<u>Pioneer 5</u> launched
	Roy Chapman Andrews, author, explorer, zoologist, died
1970	Mock Peasant Wedding in Thebes, Greece, continued
	Erle Stanley Gardner, author of "Perry Mason" series, died
1971	Purim (Hebrew Feast of Lots)
	Decoration Day in Liberia

March 12th

	Feast of St. Paul Aurelian (or of Leon)
295 AD	St. Maximilian died (Feast Day)
604	St. Gregory the Great, Pope and patron of singers and scholars, died (Feast Day)
1022	St. Simeon the New Theologian died (Feast Day)
1144	Lucius II elected Pope
1208	St. Peter of Castelnau canonized
1664	New Jersey established as a British Colony by James, Duke of York (later King)
1789	First U.S. Post Office opened
1796	Napoleon set out from France for his Italian campaign
1799	Philadelphia broke ground for a reservoir
1802	First non-Indian child, a black, born in North Dakota
1806	Venezuelan flag first flown

1824	Ross and companions camped in the "Valley of Troubles," Montana
1841	U.S.S. President lost
1851	University of Manchester, England founded
1864	Ulysses S. Grant became Union General-in-Chief
1868	Britain annexed Basutoland
1907	French battleship Jena exploded
	Idaho state flag authorized
1912	Girl Scouts of America founded
1913	Foundation stone of a "commencement column" laid at chosen capitol site (Canberra, Australia)
1914	George Westinghouse, inventor, died
1917	Executive order to arm American merchant ships
	Czarist government ended in Russia
1921	Gordon MacRae, actor-singer, born
1925	Japanese ship Uwajima Maru sank off Takashima
1928	Edward Albee, playwright, born
1933	First "fireside chat" broadcast by President Roosevelt
1934	Japanese ship Tomozurv capsized west of Nagasaki
1940	Finnish-Russian peace treaty signed
1943	Bobby Fischer, chess champion, born
1945	Vienna State Opera house hit and burned by American bombs
1947	President requested $400 million to combat Communism in Turkey and Greece
1956	Dr. Jesus de Galindez, Columbia University instructor, vanished
1961	A German team made the first winter climb of the north face of Mt. Eiger
1968	Mauritus Island became an independent nation within the British Commonwealth

---

March 13th

	Feast of St. Euphrasia
4 BC	Lunar eclipse
732 AD	St. Gerald died (Feast Day)
1138	Conrad III crowned King of Germany
1462	Gutenberg Bible printed
1493	Columbus left Lisbon, Portugal
1613	Michael I became Czar of Russia
1644	Rhode Island became a separate colony
1741	Joseph II, Holy Roman Emperor, born
1781	Herschel discovered the planet Uranus
1784	Two-thirds of Pera, Turkey, was destroyed by fire
1808	Christian VII, ruler of Norway and Denmark, died

```
1809        King Gustavus II of Sweden was kidnapped and
                    Charles XIII named Regent
            George, Lord Byron, poet, took his seat in the
                    House of Lords (English Parliament)
1852        New York Lantern published the first Uncle Sam
                    picture
1881        Czar Alexander II of Russia assassinated
1884        Standard Time established in the U.S.
            Basutoland became a British African colony
1903        Hawaii adopted its territorial flag
1921        Mongolian Peoples' Republic (Communist)
                    proclaimed
1928        St. Francis Dam collapsed, killing 450 near
                    Los Angeles
1937        Elihu Thomson, inventor, died
            British, French, Italian, and German warships
                    began patrolling the Spanish coast
                    (Spanish Civil War)
1938        Political and geographical union of Germany and
                    Austria proclaimed
1943        Stephen Vincent Benet, poet-novelist, died
1955        Mahendra Bir Bikram Shah became King of Nepal
1969        Apollo 9 splashed down in the Atlantic
1970        Start of annual 3-day Rattlesnake Roundup at
                    Sweetwater, Texas
1971        Explorer 43 satellite launched
```

March 14th

```
            Ancient Roman ceremony benefitting war horses
            Annual fair at Sutton Coldfield, Warwickshire,
                    England
 378 AD     Palm Sunday in France
 968        St. Matilda, Queen of Germany, died (Feast Day)
1009        St. Boniface or Bruno of Querfurt died
1794        Eli Whitney granted a patent on his cotton gin
1800        Barnabo Chiaramonti was elected Pope Pius VII
1804        Johann Strauss, composer, born
1812        First U.S. war bonds were sold
1820        Victor Emmanuel II, King of Italy, was born
1844        Umberto, King of Italy, was born
1862        General Pope and his Union army captured New
                    Madrid, Missouri
1864        The Bakers discovered Lake Albert, part of the
                    Nile
1869        Dr. Livingstone reached Ujiji to pick up
                    supplies (Africa)
            Neville Chamberlain, English statesman, born
1879        Albert Einstein, scientist, born
1883        Karl Marx, founder of Communism, died
1888        The 3-day "Blizzard of '88" ended
1891        Idaho's great seal adopted
1903        First U.S. game preserve founded
```

1913	Spring wildfowl shooting and the sale of wild game birds outlawed in the U.S.
1915	German cruiser <u>Dresden</u> blown up by its crew
1919	Max Shulman, author, born
1920	Hank Ketcham, creator of "Dennis the Menace," born
1927	Jan Tschakste, first President of Latvia, died
1932	George Eastman, founder of Kodak Camera Company, died
1939	Republic of Czechoslovakia dissolved
	Hungarian troops seized Carpatho-Ukraine, USSR
1950	FBI's "10 most wanted" list begun
1958	Prince Albert Alexander Louis Pierre, heir to Monaco, born
1960	Bakersfield, California, train wreck
1968	<u>Cosmos 206</u>, Russian satellite, launched
1971	End of the Water Drawing Festival at Todaiji, Japan

March 15th

	Ides of March
	Turkey buzzards return to Hinkley, Ohio
	Ancient Romans sacrificed a 6-year-old bull to Cybele
45 BC	Pompey camped at Munda, Spain
44	Julius Caesar was assassinated
493 AD	Odoacer the Barbarian, King of Italy, slain by Theodoric the Osgoth
933	King Henry V of Germany defeated the Magyars
1147	Alphonso I, King of Portugal, stormed the Moorish fortress of Santarem
1493	Columbus returned to Spain from Hispaniola
1521	Magellan sighted the Philippine Islands
1607	Charles IX crowned King of Sweden
1660	England's "Long Parliament" ended
	St. Louise de Marillac, founder of the Sisters of Charity of St. Vincent de Paul, died (Feast Day)
1767	Andrew Jackson, U.S. President, born
1781	British victory at Guilford Courthouse, North Carolina
1798	Oneida County, New York, founded
1820	Maine became a state
	St. Clement Hofbauer died (Feast Day)
1832	New York Institute for the Blind, first in the U.S., opened with three pupils
1848	Gold discovery first announced in a California newspaper, San Francisco's <u>Californian</u>
1858	Liberty Hyde Bailey, horticulturalist-author, born

```
1871    Philadelphia got a paid fire department
1875    Archbishop John McClosky made first American
            Cardinal
1898    Sir Henry Bessemer, steel-making inventor, died
1909    Edward P. Weston, aged 71, left New York to walk
            to San Francisco
1915    David Schoenbrun, news correspondent, born
1916    Harry James, bandleader, born
        General Pershing entered Mexico
1917    End of a four-day revolt by Russia's armed
                forces when Czar Nicholas II
                abdicated
1919    American Legion organized in Paris
1942    Rachel Field, author, died
1943    Empress of Canada torpedoed off Freetown, West
                Africa
1970    Expo '70 opened at Osaka, Japan
```

March 16th

```
        Start of a 3-day fair at Preston, Lancashire,
                England
        Feast of St. Julian of Antioch
        Feast of St. Paul the Simple
        Feast of the Martyrs of North America (Jesuit
                missionaries killed by the
                Indians)
  45 BC Caesar arrived at Munda, Spain
1021 AD St. Heribert of Cologne died (Feast Day)
1285    King Alexander III of Scotland died after a
                fall from his horse
1452    Frederick IV, King of Germany, married Leonora
                of Portugal
1494    Maximilian I, Holy Roman Emperor, married Bianca
                Sforza
1561    Portuguese Jesuit missionaries in East Africa
                killed
1713    Asiento Treaty signed, a slave trade agreement
                among Britain, France, and Spain
1739    George Clymer, signer of the Declaration of
                Independence, born
1751    James Madison, 4th U.S. President, born
1778    New York State coat of arms adopted
1792    King Gustavus III of Sweden shot at a
                masquerade
1802    U.S. Military Academy founded at West Point
1833    Parley's Magazine, a children's illustrated,
                founded
1889    Two U.S. and two German warships wrecked by a
                typhoon in the Samoan Islands
1898    Aubrey Beardsley, illustrator, died
1903    Senator Mike Mansfield born
1906    Florence, Colorado, train wreck
```

1910	Barney Oldfield, in a Benz car, set a land-speed record of 131.724 mph
1922	Fuad I was proclaimed King of Egypt
1923	Hawthorne became the Missouri state flower
1926	Goldenrod proclaimed the state flower of Kentucky
	First liquid-fuel rocket flown
1928	Presbyterian Medican Center Hospital opened in New York City
1939	Bohemia and Moravia became German protectorates
1945	U.S. captire of Iwo Jima completed
1971	Thomas E. Dewey, New York governor and presidential candidate, died
1976	Purim (Hebrew Feast of Lots)
1913, 2008	Palm Sunday

March 17th

	Ancient Roman festival honoring all the gods
	Feast of St. Joseph of Arimathaea
180 AD	Marcus Aurelius, Roman Emperor, died
461?	St. Patrick, patron of Ireland, died
659	St. Gertrude of Nivelles died (Feast Day)
1190	Passover
1336	Edward, son of King Edward III of England, became the first to bear the title of Duke
1473	James IV, King of Scotland, born
1649	The English Parliament abolished the office of king
1763	First St. Patrick's Day parade held in New York City
1776	British troops evacuated Boston, Massachusetts (Evacuation Day, a state holiday)
1805	Napoleon created the Kingdom of Italy
1808	Ferdinand VII became King of Spain
1849	King William II of Holland died
1861	Victor Emmanuel declared King of Italy
1870	Wellesley College chartered (Massachusetts)
1876	U.S. Cavalry captured and burned a Sioux camp at the Little Powder River, but the Indians drove them out
1882	Frank Buck, animal collector, born
1891	Utopia involved in a collision off Gibraltar
1894	Paul Green, writer-educator, born
1897	Bob Fitzsimmons won the heavyweight boxing title from James C. Corbett
1898	The first practical submarine submerged for 2 hours
1902	Bobby Jones, golfer, born
1905	Franklin D. Roosevelt married Anna Eleanor Roosevelt, a cousin

```
1912      First Japanese cherry tree in Washington, D.C.,
                 planted by Mrs. William Howard
                 Taft (officially)
1919      Nat King Cole, singer, born
          First meeting of the American Legion ended
                 (Paris)
1929      First air passenger from the U.S. arrived in
                 Alaska
1941      National Gallery of Art opened (Washington,
                 D.C.)
1942      General MacArthur reached Australia from the
                 Philippines
1945      Remagen Bridge over the Rhine collapsed, but a
                 temporary span had been built
1958      Vanguard I launched
1973, 1976  Purim (Hebrew Feast of Lots)
```

```
============================================================
March 18th
============================================================
```

```
          Feast of St. Frigidian, patron of Lucca, Italy
 386  AD  St. Cyril of Jerusalem died (Feast Day)
 731      Gregory III consecrated Pope
 971      St. Edward the Martyr, King of England,
                 assassinated to make Ethelred,
                 "the Unready," king
1227      Pope Honorius III died
1229      Frederick II crowned himself King of
                 Jerusalem
1314      39 Knights Templar ordered burned at the
                 stake (France)
1567      St. Salvator of Horta died (Feast Day)
1584      Ivan IV, "the Terrible," Czar of Russia, died
1609      Frederick III, King of Norway and Denmark,
                 born
1612      Bartholomew Legate became last person burned
                 in England for his religious
                 opinions
1662      Public bus service began in Paris
1673      Lord Berkley sold his half of New Jersey to the
                 Quakers
1745      Sir Robert Walpole, English statesman, died
1766      Britain repealed the Stamp Act
1777      New Jersey's Committee of Safety organized
1782      John C. Calhoun, statesman-orator, born
1796      John Fitch was granted a 14-year monopoly to
                 build and operate steamboats in
                 New Jersey's waters
1801      Aboukir, Egypt, surrendered to British forces
1837      Grover Cleveland, 22nd U.S. President, born
1844      Nikolai Rimsky-Korsakov, composer, born
1845      New England Historical Genealogical Society
                 formed
```

1858	Rudolf Diesel, engine inventor, born
1861	Neville Chamberlain, English statesman, born
1870	Lake Meritt (Oakland, California) became the first U.S. National Wildlife Refuge
1896	The Founders and Patriots of America incorporated
1911	All persons over 21 empowered to vote in Portugal
	Roosevelt Dam in Arizona opened
1913	King George I of Greece assassinated
1915	British battleships Irresistible and Ocean were torpedoed in the Dardanelles
1920	Danzig adopted its national flag
1921	1,000 lost when Hong Kong hit a rock near Swatow, China
1925	Married Danish women granted legal equality with their husbands
1926	Women allowed to practice law in Turkey
1932	Chauncey Olcott, author of "My Wild Irish Rose," died
1937	New London, Texas school explosion killed 294
1938	Mexico nationalized its oil industry
1949	North Atlantic Defense Pact (NATO) adopted
1953	Northwest Turkey was rocked by an earthquake
1956	Louis Bromfield, novelist, died
1959	Hawaii admitted into the United States
1962	Truce ended Moslem revolt against the French in Algeria
1965	Boatload of Indian pilgrims sank in a storm in Gobindseger Lake, India
	Russia launched Voskhod II and had the first space walk
	Farouk, deposed King of Egypt, died
1973	Purim
1951, 2035	Palm Sunday

March 19th

	St. Joseph's Day (patron of carpenters, wheelwrights, and combatants against Communism)
	Swallows return to Capistrano (California)
	Ancient Romans rededicated Minerva's temple
235 AD	Maximinus proclaimed Emperor by the Roman army
387	Good Friday in France
624	Mohammed proclaimed the "Day of Deliverance"
1148	The 2nd Crusade reached Antioch
1227	Ugolini Conti elected Pope Gregory IX
1307	Douglas Castle, Scotland, while held by the English, was destroyed by Black Douglas, the owner

1452	Frederick III became the last Holy Roman emperor crowned in Rome
1603	John IV, "the Fortunate," King of Portugal, born
1649	House of Lords abolished in England (Reformation)
1687	Robert Cavalier, Sieur de LaSalle, explorer of the Ohio and Missippi valleys, shot to death
1721	Pope Clement XI died
1734	Thomas McKean, signer of the Declaration of Independence, born
1793	Royalists outlawed in France by the French Convention
1813	David Livingstone, African missionary-explorer, born
1821	Sir Richard Burton, explorer, born
1823	Augustin de Iturbide, Emperor of Mexico, abdicated
1835	James E. Scripps, newspaper publisher, born
1859	Faust opera first produced (Paris
1860	William Jennings Bryan, author-statesman, born
1864	Charles M. Russell, artist, born
1882	Gaston Lachaise, French sculptor, born
1883	"Vinegar Joe" Stillwell, Army officer, born
1891	Georges Seurat, French artist, died
	Earl Warren, California governor and Supreme Court Justice, born
1902	Foaud Chehab, President of Lebanon, born
1915	Austrian stronghold of Przemysl temporarily fell to Russia
1918	Daylight Savings Time first used in New York City
1920	U.S. Senate again rejected Versailles peace treaty
1924	Japanese submarine number 43 involved in a collision off Sasebo
1925	New Mexico state flag adopted
	U.S. Patent Office transferred to the Department of Commerce from the Department of the Interior
1928	Charles Lindbergh received the Woodrow Wilson Foundation Peace Award
1932	Mt. McKinley National Park enlarged to include almost 2 million acres of Alaska
1944	Lynda Bird Johnson (Robb), daughter of the President, born
1945	U.S. aircraft carrier Franklin damaged, but made it into port
1950	Edgar Rice Burroughs, creator of "Tarzan," died
1951	Willow Goldfinch became Washington's state bird
1967	Rio de Janeiro struck by floods

```
1969      Islamic New Year (1389)
1967, 1978, 1989, 2046, 2062, 2073, 2084  Palm Sunday
```

March 20th

```
  43 BC  Ovid, Roman poet, born
  71 AD  Solar eclipse
 526     Antioch, Syria, rocked by an earthquake
 580     St. Martin of Braga died (Feast Day)
 687     St. Cuthbert died (Feast Day)
         St. Herbert died (Feast Day)
1239     Frederick II, Holy Roman Emperor,
                 excommunicated again
1393     St. John of Nepomuk died
1413     King Henry IV of England died
1565     Contract made by King Philip of Spain for
                 settlement of Florida
1602     Dutch East India Company chartered
1619     Mathias, Holy Roman Emperor, died
1697     Peter "the Great," Czar of Russia, began his
                 European tour
1727     Sir Isaac Newton, observer of gravity, died
1810     John McClosky, first U.S. Cardinal, born
         Napoleon's only son, King of Rome, born
1815     Napoleon's "100 Days" return began
1820     Edward Judson, dime novelist as Ned Buntline,
                 born
1828     Henrik Ibsen, Norwegian writer, born
1848     Louis I, King of Bavaria, abdicated
1852     Uncle Tom's Cabin first published (in two
                 volumes)
1861     Mendoza, Argentina, destroyed by an earthquake
                 and fire
1882     Dr. Urho Kekkonen, President of Finland, born
1883     International patent-protection convention
                 signed
1890     General Federation of Women's Clubs organized
         Lauritz Melchior, opera singer, born
1898     "Open Door Policy" of trade with China began
1901     "Open Door Policy" announced in the U.S.
1908     Sir Michael Redgrave, English actor, born
1919     Sankey Commission on British coalmining
                 presented an interim report
1927     Mrs. Snyder and her corset-salesman lover
                 murdered Mr. Snyder
1954     Samuel Shellabarger, author, died
1961     Republic of Togo adopted a U.S.-style
                 constitution
1970     Natosat communications satellite launched
         Tunisian Independence Day
1910, 1921, 1932, 2005, 2016  Palm Sunday
```

```
           Farmers' Day in Afghanistan ushers in the New
                   Year
           Bird Day in Iowa
           Feast of St. Benedict (invoked against the
                   Devil, fever, and inflammatory
                   and kidney diseases
           Feast of St. Edna
           Feast of St. Serapion of Thmius
5507 BC    The World was created, according to Chronicum
  47       Caesar defeated Ptolemy, Cleopatra's rival, at
                   Alexandria
 387 AD    Easter in France
1146       Bernard of Clairvaux preached the Second
                   Crusade and King Louis VII of
                   France took the Cross
1152       Marriage of King Louis VII of France and
                   Eleanor of Aquitaine was annulled
1241       Valdemar II, King of Denmark, died
1282       Start of the final struggle between England
                   and Wales
1487       St. Nicholas von Flue died (Feast Day)
1556       Archbishop Cranmer burned during Queen Mary's
                   efforts to restore England to
                   Catholicism
1685       Johann Sebastian Bach, composer, born
1800       Barnabo Chiaramonti crowned as Pope Pius VII
1814       Austrian, Russian, and Prussian troops entered
                   Paris
1857       William Scoresby, Arctic explorer, died
1866       First National Soldiers' Home authorized
                   (Dayton, Ohio)
1871       Henry Morton Stanley began exploring Africa
1880       Hans Hoffmann, artist, born
1895       Ismail, Khedive of Egypt, died
1898       U.S. blamed the explosion of the Maine on
                   sabotage
1903       Mark Hellinger, journalist-author, born
1905       Phyllis McGinley, children's author, born
1906       John D. Rockefeller III born
1910       Green Mountain, Iowa train wreck
1918       Battle of the Somme began
1919       Communist government seized power in
                   Czechoslovakia
           Frick purchased Gilbert Stuart's portrait of
                   Washington
1921       Poland became an independent republic
1929       Olav V, King of Norway, married Martha of
                   Sweden
1959       Only 4 of 34 starters finished the Grand
                   National Steeplechase at Aintree,
                   England
```

1965   Ranger 9 launched
            Beginning of the Selma-Montgomery civil rights
                    march in Alabama
1970   Skin Divers' Holiday and Treasure Hunt at Port
                    Townsend, Washington
1971   Carnivals at Fosses and Stavelot, Belgium
1913, 2008 Good Friday
1937, 1948, 2027, 2032, 2100 Palm Sunday

March 22nd

            Ancient Roman Procession of the Sacred Pine
 752 AD   St. Zacharius, last of the Greek Popes, died
1221   Robert of Courtenay crowned King of Rumania
1459   Maximilian I, Holy Roman Emperor, born
1471   King George Podiebrad died
1594   Paris surrendered to King Henry IV of France
1599   Sir Anthony VanDyck, artist, born
1621   Plymouth Colony made a treaty with the
                    neighboring Indians that was kept
                    on both sides for 50 years
1622   First massacre of whites by Indians (350 died
                    in Virginia)
1719   Serfs on Prussian royal lands freed
1757   Battle of Plassey, India
1765   Stamp Act became law in England and its colonies
1794   U.S. passed an act prohibiting U.S. vessels
                    from supplying slaves to other
                    countries
1797   King William I of Germany and Prussia born
1820   Stephen Decatur, Jr., naval hero, killed in
                    a duel
1822   Rosa Bonheur, French artist, born
1837   Slaves in Puerto Rico freed
1848   Uprising in Milan, Italy, crushed by Austrian
                    troops
1861   First American nursing school chartered
                    (Philadelphia)
1887   Interstate Commerce Commission appointed
1891   Chico Marx, comedian, born
1895   Lumieres exhibited their motion-picture
                    projector (Paris)
1899   Excavation begun at the ancient city of
                    Babylon
1903   Soufriere volcano on St. Vincent Island
                    erupted
1913   Missouri state flag adopted
1917   U.S. recognized Russia's provisional government
1929   Western Meadowlark became the state bird of
                    Nebraska
1939   Hitler annexed Memel to Germany
1945   League of Arab States formed

```
1970        Start of Easter Weddings, a Norwegian Lapp
                  ceremony
            Purim (Hebrew Feast of Lots)
1940        Good Friday
1959, 1964, 1970, 2043, 2054, 2065  Palm Sunday
```

March 23rd

```
            Roman military ceremony honoring Mars, god of
                  war
            Feast of St. Gwinear
1169 AD     Shirguh, Caliph of Egypt, died of indigestion
1281        Simon de Brie crowned Pope (Martin IV)
1324        Louis IV, Holy Roman Emperor, excommunicated
1369        Pedro (Peter) "the Cruel," King of Castile,
                  assassinated
1430        Margaret of Anjou, Queen of England, born
1534        Henry VIII, King of England, was declared
                       truly married to Catherine of
                       Aragon by the Pope
1555        Pope Julius II died
1606        St. Toribio of Lima died
1685        Johann Sebastian Bach, composer, baptized
1729        William Hogarth, British artist, eloped with
                  Jane Thornhill
1775        "...give me Liberty or give me death!"  (Patrick
                  Henry)
1777        Peekskill, New York, burned by the British
1786        George Washington planted 4,000 chestnut trees
                  at his Mount Vernon home
1815        U.S.S. Hornet captured H.M.S. Penguin
1823        Schuyler Colfax, U.S. Vice President, born
1840        First photograph of the moon, a daguerreotype,
                  taken
1857        Fannie Farmer, famed cook and candy-maker, born
1862        Battle of the Shenandoah Valley began (Virginia)
1868        University of California founded at Oakland
1887        Juan Gris, Spanish artist, born
1901        War for Philippine Independence ended
1903        The Wright brothers applied for a patent on
                  their airplane
1907        Colton, California, train wreck
1908        Japanese  ship Matsu Maru sank after a collision
                  near Hakodate
            Joan Crawford, actress, born
1912        Wernher von Braun, rocket expert, born
1921        Donald Campbell, speed-record setter, born
1927        Kansas state flag adopted
1939        Roger Bannister, first man to run a mile in
                  less than 4 minutes, born
1949        Burton Hendrick, editor-author, died
```

```
1956      Pakistan ("Land of the Pure") became a republic
                    (Pakistan Day, a national holiday)
1965      Gemini 3 launched
1970      Holi Festival in Northern India
1902, 1975, 1986, 1997, 2059, 2070, 2081, 2092  Palm
                    Sunday
1951, 2035, 2046  Good Friday
1913, 2008  Easter
```

March 24th
```
          St. Gabriel the Archangel Day
          Start of Clitheroe, Lancashire, England fair
          Ancient Roman day of mourning and abstinence
1267      St. Louis IX, King of France, decided to under-
                    take the 7th Crusade
1381      St. Catherine of Sweden died (Feast Day;
                    invoked against miscarriages)
1455      One of Prince Henry the Navigator's expedi-
                    tions set sail for southern
                    waters
          Pope Nicholas V died
1490      George Agricola, "Father of minerology," born
1558      Ferdinand I crowned Holy Roman Emperor
1580      First bombs thrown (Holland)
1603      Queen Elizabeth I of England died
1613      Michael Romanov, Czar of Russia, found
1680      William Penn asked for permission to found
                    the colony of Pennsylvania
1783      Spain recognized U.S. independence
1784      Massachusetts Centinel, a Boston newspaper,
                    founded
1794      Uprising in Cracow, Poland, against its
                    occupying nations
1801      As of this date, duties had to be paid on
                    paper products in England
          Paul I, Czar of Russia, strangled to death
1812      Jean-Baptiste Bernadotte, Swedish king by
                    Napoleon's appointment, broke
                    off relations with France
1814      Shelley, English poet, remarried his wife,
                    Harriet Westbrook
1828      Pennsylvania agreed to expenditure for rail-
                    road construction
1834      John Wesley Powell, explorer of Grand Canyon,
                    born
1855      Andrew Mellon, financier, born
1866      Marie Amelie Therese, Queen to Louis Philippe,
                    the last King of France, died
1878      Euridice foundered at sea off the Isle of
                    Wight
1880      Society of American Taxidermists formed
```

```
1882       Tuberculosis germ discovery announced by
                 Dr. Robert Koch
           Henry Wadsworth Longfellow, poet, died
1898       First American-made gas carriage (automobile)
                 sold
1900       Work begun on New York City's subway system
1902       New York governor and Presidential candidate,
                 Thomas E. Dewey, born
1903       Bankers' Trust Company of New York City
                 incorporated
1905       Jules Verne, author, died
1916       Steamer Sussex torpedoed in the English
                 Channel
1919       King Charles I of Austro-Hungary exiled
1927       U.S. and British consulates in China were
                 looted
1934       Philippine Islands granted independence,
                 effective 1945
1937       National Gallery of Art established by an Act
                 of Congress
1938       Paul L. Haworth, historian-educator, died
1939       Madrid, Spain, surrendered to the insurgents
1953       Queen Mary, wife of King George V of England,
                 died
1955       San Francisco Mint turned out its last coin,
                 a penny
1956       Woolly bear caterpillars gave up weather
                 predicting
1959       Ferry service ended between New York City and
                 Weehawken, New Jersey
1964       First U.S. John F. Kennedy 50¢-pieces issued
1918, 1929, 1991, 2002, 2013, 2024, 2086, 2097  Palm
                 Sunday
1967, 1978, 1989, 2046, 2062, 2073, 2084  Good Friday
1940  Easter
```

March 25th

```
           Annunciation or Lady Day (Protestant and
                 Eastern Orthodox)
           Feast of the Virgin (Greece)
           English Quarter Day - rents due; move in or
                 out
           New Year's Day for Medieval Christians
 708 AD    Constantine elected Pope
1133       King Henry II of England born
1252       Conrad the Younger, King of Jerusalem and
                 Sicily, born
1255       Manfred, self-appointed King of Sicily,
                 excommunicated
1347       St. Catherine of Siena born
1555       Valencia, Venezuela, founded
```

```
1584      First American colonists set sail from England
1634      Lord Calvert's colonists landed in Maryland
                (Maryland Day)
1668      First recorded horse race in America
                (Hempstead, N.Y.)
1687      Episcopal Church established in Boston's Old
                South Meeting House
1700      Second Partition Treaty of the Spanish Empire
                signed
1751      Last time this date started the legal year in
                England
1861      Savage's party, chasing Indians, were first to
                enter the Yosemite Valley,
                California
1863      Philadelphia Public Leger, newspaper, founded
1867      Arturo Toscanini, orchestra conductor, born
1898      Hillsdale, New Jersey, incorporated
1899      Baron de Reuter, founder of the news agency,
                died
1911      Triangle Shirtwaist factory fire, New York
                City
1914      Aline Saarinen, television newswoman, born
1915      U.S. submarine F-4 sank off Honolulu harbor
1921      Queen Alexandra of Yugoslavia born
1924      Greek Assembly exiled its royalty (Greek
                Independence Day)
1950      Frank Buck, animal collector, died
1951      MacArthur threatened China with naval and
                air attacks (Korean War)
1954      From Here to Eternity won the Oscar for Best
                Picture
1957      "Euromarket" began
1961      U.S. launched Explorer 10
          Russia launched Sputnik 10 with a dog aboard
1965      Four-day civil rights march reached Montgomery
                from Selma, Alabama
1969      Waffle Day in Sweden
1970      Start of Holiday for Everybody exhibit at
                Herning, Denmark
1971      Civil war erupted in East Pakistan
1923, 1934, 1945, 1956, 2018, 2029, 2040  Palm Sunday
1910, 1921, 1932, 1005, 2016  Good Friday
1951, 2035, 2046  Easter
```

==
March 26th
==

```
          Kuhio Day, holiday in Hawaii
          Last day of Clitheroe, Lancashire, England, fair
 651 AD   St. Braulio died (Feast Day)
 809      St. Ludger died (Feast Day)
1027      Conrad II crowned Holy Roman Emperor
1144      St. William of Norwich died (Feast Day)
```

```
1388          Construction of St. Mary's College, Oxford,
                  England, begun
1649 OS       John Winthrop, first governor of Massachusetts
                  colony, died
1804          Louisiana became a U.S. territory
1812          La Guaira, Venezuela, destroyed by an earthquake
1821          Northwest Company merged with the Hudson's
                  Bay Company
1826          John VI, King of Portugal, died
1827          Ludwig von Beethoven, composer, died
1845          Daniel W. Harmon, author-explorer, died
1856          First trolley line, Boston to Cambridge,
                  opened in New England
              Yakima Indian attackers held at bay by 9 men
                  in a blockhouse (Washington)
1863          Daniel W. Harmon, author-explorer, died
              The Bakers set out from Gondokoro to explore
                  the Nile
1868          Fuad I, King of Egypt, born
1874          Conde Nast, publisher, born
1875          Robert Frost, poet, born
1881          Carol proclaimed King of Rumania
1892          Walt Whitman, poet, died
1896          New Jersey state flag adopted
1902          Cecil Rhodes, African administrator, died
1908          Betty MacDonald, author The Egg and I, born
1914          General William Westmoreland born
1917          Joseph Stalin returned to Petrograd after 3
                  years of exile in Siberia
1918          Foch became Supreme Allied Commander
              Kentucky state flag adopted
              Claude Debussy, French composer, died
1923          Vermont state flag adopted
              Sarah Bernhardt, actress, died
1928          Pennsylvania Art Museum opened
1929          Nevada state flag adopted
1930          "Wild Mary Sudik" oil well came in (Oklahoma)
1953          Height of the Mau Mau violence in Kenya,
                  Africa
              Salk polio vaccine announced
1954          Russia declared East Germany a sovereign state
              Spanish ship Guadalete sank in a Mediterranean
                  storm
1961          Sputnik 10 and its dog passenger recovered
1961, 1972, 2051, 2056  Palm Sunday
1932, 1937, 1948, 2027, 2032, 2100  Good Friday
1967, 1978, 1989, 2046, 2062, 2073, 2084  Easter
```

March 27th

Frankmason Day (Venezuela)
Ancient Roman procession honoring Cybele,
    mother of all the gods

```
              Feast of St. John of Damascus
              Feast of St. Rupert of Salzburg
  394 AD      St. John the Egyptian died (Feast Day)
 1077         Rudolph crowned King of Germany
 1306         Robert I, "the Bruce," crowned King of
                         Scotland at Scone
 1378         Pope Gregory XI died
 1482         Mary of Burgundy, heiress to northern France
                         and the wife of Holy Roman
                         Emperor Maximilian I, died
 1513         Ponce de Leon discovered Florida
 1559         Earl of Essex sent to put down a rebellion
                         in Ireland
 1615         Marguerite of Valois, Queen of Navarre, died
 1625         King James I of England and Ireland and IV of
                         Scotland died
 1712         Zuytdorp, a Dutch East Indiaman, vanished
                         after passing the Cape of Good
                         Hope
 1785         Louis XVII, nonreigning King of France, born
 1794         U.S. Navy created
 1802         Treaty of Amiens signed by England and France
 1804         U.S. Navy Yard established at Washington, D.C.
 1813         Nathaniel Currier, of Currier and Ives
                         lithographers, born
 1821         Austrian troops reoccupied Naples, Italy
 1845         Wilhelm Roentgen, X-ray inventor, born
 1846         General Winfield Scott took Vera Cruz, Mexico
 1852         Code Napoleon again became the name of the
                         French laws
 1855         Kerosene gas patented
 1879         Edward Steichen, photographer, born
 1886         Geronimo, Apache Indian leader, agreed to
                         surrender but didn't
 1899         Gloria Swanson, actress, born
 1922         Barnaby Conrad, bull-fighting author, born
 1927         Bluebird became the official state bird
                         of Missouri
 1955         First coast-to-coast color television
                         broadcast (Cal.-N.Y.
 1964         Ariel 2 launched
              Severe earthquake in Alaska
 1968         Yuri Gagarin, a Russian and the first man
                         to orbit the Earth in space,
                         died in a plane crash
 1969         Mariner VII launched toward Mars
 1970         Monkey God Festival in Singapore
              Procession of the Weeping Virgins in Romont,
                         Switzerland
 1975         Passover begins
 1904, 1983, 1988, 1994, 2067, 2078, 2089  Palm Sunday
 1959, 1964, 1970, 2043, 2054, 2065  Good Friday
 1910, 1921, 1932, 2005, 2016  Easter
```

	Feast of St. John of Capestrano
193 AD	Pertinax, Roman Emperor, assassinated
1255	Pope Martin IV died
1394	St. Mary's College, Winchester, England, opene opened
1483	Raphael, Italian artist, born
1515	St. Theresa born
1797	First washing machine granted a U.S. patent
1802	Pallas asteroid discovered
1814	U.S.S. Essex defeated off Valpariso, Chile
1886	Geronimo, Apache Indian leader, escaped after a day of surrender
1889	"King Alfred" daffodil introduced to the Royal Horticultural Society (England)
1891	Paul Whitman, bandleader, born
1898	Spanish blamed explosion of the Maine on an internal problem, not sabotage
1912	British ship Yongala sank in a storm off Australia
1915	Fabala was sunk by the Germans
1925	Nebraska state flag adopted
1930	Constantinople became Istanbul
1938	Charles M. Flandrau, essayist, died
1942	Devastating British air raid on Lubeck, Germany
1943	Sergei Rachmaninoff, composer, died
1957	Christopher Morley, poet-novelist, died
1958	W. C. Handy, blues composer, died
1967	King Saud of Arabia dethroned
1969	Dwight D. Eisenhower, 34th President, died
1970	Governor's 4th Annual Frog-Jumping Contest at Springfield, South Carolina
	Oxford-Cambridge Crew Race on the Thames (England)
	Gediz, Turkey, shattered by an earthquake
	Start of 3-day rattlesnake hunt at Waurika, Oklahoma

1915, 1920, 1926, 1999, 2010, 2021, 2083, 2094 Palm Sunday

1902, 1975, 1986, 1997, 2059, 2070, 2081, 2092 Good Friday

1932, 1937, 1948, 2027, 2032, 2100 Easter

	Feast of St. Mark of Arethusa
49 BC	Caesar entered Rome to attack Pompey
327 AD	Sts. Jonah and Berikjesu died (Feast Day)
403	Battle of Pollentia began the Goths' invasion of Italy
1058	Pope Steven X died

```
1134       St. Stephen Harding died
1198       St. Berthold died (Feast Day)
1461       Reign of Henry VI, King of England, ended with
                     the Yorkists victory at Towton
                     (War of the Roses)
1464       Mathias I crowned King of Hungary
1565       Turks sailed to attack Malta
1638       First Swedish expedition to the New World
                     landed in Delaware
1790       John Tyler, U.S. President, born
1792       Gustavus III, King of Sweden, assassinated
1809       King Gustavus IV of Sweden abdicated
1813       John Tyler married Letitia Christian
1814       Andrew Jackson defeated the Creek Indians
1848       John Jacob Astor, fur millionaire, died
1853       Elihu Thomson, inventor, born
1857       Start of the Sepoy mutiny in India
1867       Lincoln Memorial approved by Congress
1875       Lou Henry (Mrs. Herbert) Hoover born
1882       Knights of Columbus chartered
1889       Howard Lindsay, playwright-producer, born
1891       Georges Seurat, French artist, died
1913       Tennessee River floods killed 467
1916       Amherst, Ohio, train wreck
           Eugene McCarthy, senator and presidential can-
                     didate, born
1918       Pearl Bailey, singer, born
1921       Iowa state flag adopted
1927       Seagrave, in a Sunbeam car, set the first land-
                     speed record over 200 mph,
                     203.790 mph
1939       Spanish civil war ended
1951       Rosenbergs and Sobell found guilty of wartime
                     sabotage
1970       Youth Day in Taiwan
           Explosion of the Cart Festival in Florence,
                     Italy
1971       Gangaur Festival, India
1931, 1942, 1953, 2015, 2026, 2037, 2048  Palm
                     Sunday
1907, 1918, 1929, 1991, 2002, 2013, 2024, 2086, 2097
                     Good Friday
1282, 1959, 1964, 1970, 2043, 2054, 2065  Easter
```

March 30th
```
           Feast of St. John Climacus
           Feast of St. Osburga
1135 AD    Maimonides, Jewish philosopher, born
1191       Hyacinth Bobo became Pope (Celestine III)
1282       Sicilian revolt against French rule began
1533       King Henry VIII of England divorced Catherine
                     of Aragon
```

```
1536    Ibrahim, Grand Vizier of Turkey, strangled on
            Sultan's order
1595    Fisherman landed on Monhegan Island, Maine,
                to stay for the summer season
1791    Maryland ceded the District of Columbia to
                the federal government
1806    Code Napoleon became law in Italy
1822    Florida became a U.S. territory
1840    "Beau" Brimmel, English man of fashion, died
1842    Drs. Crawford and Long performed the first
                surgery under ether but didn't pub-
                lish the results
1848    Don Carlos VII, claimant to the Spanish throne,
                born
1854    A mail coach and its cavalry escort were
                attacked by Jicarilla Apaches
                (New Mexico)
1856    Crimean War ended by the Treaty of Paris
1867    U.S. purchase of Alaska from Russia (Seward
                Day state holiday)
1899    United Fruit Company incorporated
1909    Queensboro Bridge opened to traffic (New
                York City)
1913    Franklin Lane, singer, born
1920    Julliard Music Foundation incorporated
        Czechoslovakian national flag adopted
1956    Mt. Nameless, extinct Siberian volcano,
                erupted
1970    L'Emaischen (Young Lover's Day) in Luxembourg
1972    Beginning of Passover
1947, 1958, 1969, 1980, 2042, 2053, 2064  Palm Sunday
1923, 1924, 1945, 1956, 2018, 2029, 2040  Good Friday
1902, 1975, 1986, 1997, 2059, 2070, 2081, 2092  Easter
1420, 1913, 2008 Quasimodo or Low Sunday
```

March 31st

```
1492 AD Jews expelled from Spain by royal edict
1547    King Francis I of France died
1561    San Cristobal, Venezuela, founded
1571    British seized fortress of Dumbarton, Scot-
                land
1594    Tintoretto, Italian artist, died
1621    King Philip III of Spain died
1671    Ann Hyde, wife of King James II of England,
                died
1732    Joseph Haydn, composer, born
1764    British evacuated Manila, Philippines
1809    Edward Fitzgerald, translator of Omar
                Khayyam, born
1811    Robert W. Bunsen, burner inventor, born
1814    Allies against Napoleon marched into Paris
1820    First U.S. missionaries arrived in Hawaii
```

```
1821        Bethany, Pennsylvania, incorporated
1823        Charter granted for a railroad between Phila-
                 delphia and Columbia, Pennsylvania
1829        Francis Xavier Castigtrone elected Pope
                 (Pius VIII)
1837        John Constable, English artist, died
1848        William Waldorf Astor, viscount and author,
                 born
1850        John C. Calhoun, statesman-orator, died
1854        First treaty signed between Japan and
                 the U.S.
1865        Union forces won the battle at Dinwiddie
                 Courthouse, Virginia
1868        Refrigerated railroad car patented
1870        First black voted in a municipal election
                 (Perth Amboy, N.J.)
1876        First title-guarantee insurance company in the
                 U.S. was organized
1885        Woman's College (now Goucher College) founded
                 (Baltimore)
1895        Vardis Fisher, novelist, born
1896        Whitcomb L. Judson received a patent on his
                 hookless fastener (forerunner of the
                 zipper)
1909        Last U.S. troops left Cuba
1913        John Pierpont Morgan, financier, died
1914        Southern Cross wrecked in Belle Isle Strait
1915        Henry Morgan, television personality, born
1917        U.S. purchased Virgin Islands from Denmark
                 (Transfer Day)
            Emil von Behring, discoverer of diphtheria
                 antitoxin, died
1918        Daylight Savings Time first used in the U.S.
1921        Great coal workers' strike in Britain began
1931        Knute Rockne, football great, killed in a
                 plane crash
1932        Ford introduced its V-8 engine
1936        National Recovery Act activities ended
1938        Clarence Darrow, famed lawyer, died
1948        The Cold War began
1970        Goat and Crab Races held at Buccoo Village,
                 Tobago
1971        ISIS-2, U.S.-Canadian satellite, launched
1972        Feast of Holi in India
1901, 1912, 1985, 1996, 2075, 2080  Palm Sunday
1961, 1972, 2051, 2056  Good Friday
1918, 1929, 1991, 2002, 2013, 2024, 2086, 2097  Easter
1940  Quasimodo or Low Sunday
```

APRIL

Full Moon - Pink Moon or Egg Moon
First Monday - Tater Day in Benton, Kentucky, honoring
sweet potato
Second Sunday - Mother-in-law's Day
Third Tuesday - Arbor Day in Montana
Last Friday - Arbor Day in Utah
Sunday nearest the 26th - Order of Cape Henry obser-
vances at Colonial National
Historic Park, Virginia

April 1st

	April Fool's Day
	Intolerance Day in Houston, Texas
	Feast of St. Lazarus
568 AD	Lombards assembled to cross the Alps to Italy
1132	St. Hugh of Grenoble died (Feast Day)
1204	Eleanor of Aquitaine, Queen of France and of England, died
1548	Sigismund I, King of Poland, died
	Parliament ordered the Book of Common Prayer printed in English
1578	William Harvey, first observer of blood circulation, born
1672	Archibald Armstrong, jester to 2 English kings, buried
1748	New excavations begun at Pompeii
1799	Pope Pius IV set out to escape from Napoleon, unsuccessfully
1815	Otto von Bismarck, German statesman, born
1834	James Fisk, financier, born
1841	Brook Farm, a transcendental colony, founded at West Roxbury, Mass.

1848	Report of California gold discovery mailed to New York
1852	Final installment of the serialization of Uncle Tom's Cabin appeared in the National Era
1853	Cincinnati, Ohio, got the first paid fire department in U.S.
1867	International Exhibition opened at Paris, France
1868	Canada established the Post Office Savings Bank
1869	Pere David became the first white man to record seeing a live giant panda
1873	British ship Atlantic wrecked off Nova Scotia
1889	Wallace Beery, actor, born
1891	Commonwealth of Australia adopted this title
1894	Henri LeCaron, British spy, died
1898	First sale of an automobile transacted
1900	William Benton, publisher of Encyclopaedia Britannica, born
1901	Turkish ship, Asian, wrecked in the Red Sea
1911	First British military flying group organized
1912	Metric system became official for weights and measures in Denmark
1914	Permanent government for the Panama Canal Zone effected
1918	Royal Air Force founded in England
1919	Nevada restored capital punishment
1922	William Manchester, author, born
1925	Hebrew University, Jerusalem, opened
1928	Town of Hochst, Germany incorporated with Frankfort-on-Main
1930	First New York-to-Bermuda airplane flight completed
1937	Burma and India made separate British colonies
1940	British Overseas Airways Corporation formed
1945	U.S. forces invaded Okinawa (final land campaign of World War II)
1947	King George II of Greece died
1948	Tsavo National Park created in Kenya, Africa Communist blockade of Berlin, Germany began
1954	Five U.S. Congressmen shot on the House floor
1960	Tiros I, a weather satellite, launched
1970	Olive Festival at Crus del Eje, Argentina

1917, 1928, 2007, 2012, 2091 Palm Sunday
1904, 1983, 1988, 1994, 2067, 2078, 2089 Good Friday
1923, 1934, 1945, 1956, 2018, 1019, 1040 Easter
1951, 2035 Quasimodo or Low Sunday

April 2nd
===

	Feast of St. Mary of Egypt (patron of penitent women who formerly lived in sin)
742 AD	Charlemagne, first Holy Roman Emperor, born
999	Sylvester II elected Pope

1250	Seventh Crusade surrendered to the Moslems
1272	Richard, King of the Romans, died
1305	Louis X became King of Navarre
1416	Ferdinand I, King of Aragon, died
1501	St. Francis of Paola, died
1502	Arthur, Prince of Wales, elder brother of King Henry VIII of England, died
1559	King Philip II of Spain married Isabella of France
1595	A Dutch fleet sailed for the East Indies
1657	Ferdinand III, Holy Roman Emperor, died
1768	Bouganville, French explorer, landed on Tahiti
1770	All British duties, excepting the tea tax, revoked in the colonies
1792	First U.S. mint established and the coinage of dimes was authorized; also the "Eagle" ($10.00), "Half-eagle" ($5.00) and "Quarter-eagle" ($2.50) gold pieces, and the silver dollar
1794	First balloon company created by French decree
1796	Vortigern, supposedly a Shakespeare play, opened at Drury Lane Theater, London
1805	Hans Christian Andersen, author, born
1840	Emile Zola, French novelist, born
1844	George H. Putnam, publisher, born
1849	Punjab was annexed to British India
1862	Nicholas M. Butler, founder of the first U.S. school of journalism, born
1865	Confederate evacuation of Petersburg and Richmond, Virginia began
1870	Punchinello, New York comic magazine, founded
	Ground-breaking for the Nevada capitol held
1872	Sergei Rachmaninoff, Russian composer, born
1879	British defeated Zulu tribesmen at Ginghilono
1889	Patent issued to Charles M. Hall for the commercial production of aluminium
1891	Max Ernst, artist, born
1896	Barnum and Bailey's Circus opened in New York with a car leading the parade
1917	German zeppelins staged an air raid on Edinburgh, Scotland
	President Wilson requested a declaration of war against Germany
	Russian Jews emancipated
1918	University of Capetown founded (South Africa)
1925	Oklahoma adopted its state flag
1930	Emperess Zauditu of Ethiopia, died
1945	U.S. troops captured airfields at Legaspi, Philippines
1947	United Nations placed former Japanese islands under U.S. trusteeship
1963	Explorer 17 launched
1964	Zond II, solar orbiter, launched

1970   Schmeckfest (German food fair) at Freeman,
               South Dakota
       Wine Fair at Greuenmacher, Luxembourg
1939, 1944, 1950, 2023, 2034, 2045 Palm Sunday
1915, 1920, 1926, 1999, 2010, 2021, 2083, 2094 Good
               Friday
1961, 1972, 2051, 2056 Easter
1967, 1978, 1989, 2046, 2062, 2073, 2084 Quasimodo or
               Low Sunday

April 3rd

Feast of St. Burgundofara
304 AD St. Pancras of Taormina, died (Feast Day)
1245   King Philip III, "the Bold," of France, born
1253   St. Richard of Chichester, died (Feast Day)
1279   Kublai Khan defeated the Sung Chinese in a sea
            battle
1287   Pope Honorius IV, died
1367   King Henry IV of England, born
1559   Peace of Chateau Cambresis ended French claims
            to Italy
1682   Murillo, Spanish artist, fell to his death
               while illustrating the ceiling of
               a convent in Cadiz
1755   Simon Kenton, frontiersman, born
1778   Pierre Bretonneau, first doctor to perform a
            tracheotomy for croup, born
1783   Washington Irving, author, born
1800   Gustavus IV crowned King of Sweden
1822   Edward Everett Hale, author of Man Without a
             Country, born
1860   Pony Express' first riders left Sacramento,
             California, and St. Joseph, Missouri
1861   Reginald de Koven, composer ("Oh, Promise Me"),
             born
1862   James Clark Ross, polar explorer, died
        Reginald Heber, hymn-writer, died
1865   Hong Kong and Shanghai Banking Corporation
            offices opened
        Confederate evacuation of Richmond and Petersburg,
        Virginia completed
1882   Jesse James, outlaw, shot by his own gang for
            the reward
1884   Daniel Steinman wrecked off Nova Scotia
1897   Johannas Brahms, composer, died
1898   George Jessel, "Toastmaster General," born
        Henry R. Luce, founder of Time magazine, born
1907   Standard Oil of Indiana fined for accepting
            freight rebates
1912   Hungarian government suspended the Croatian
            constitution
1924   Marlon Brando, actor, born

1936   Hauptmann, kidnapper of the Lindbergh baby,
                electrocuted
1946   Lt. General Homma, Japanese commander of the
                Bataan death march, executed
1965   SNAP-10A launched
1969   Beginning of Passover
1970   Schmeckfest (German food fair) at Freeman, South
                Dakota
            Maple Festivals began at St. Albans, Vermont
                and Chardon, Ohio
1971   Mt. Etna, Sicily, erupted again
1972   Start of Holy Week in Greece
            Lover's Market in Luxembourg
1955, 1966, 1977, 2039, 2050, 2061, 2072 Palm Sunday
1931, 1942, 1953, 2015, 2026, 2037, 2048 Good Friday
1904, 1983, 1988, 1994, 2067, 2078, 2089 Easter
1910, 1921, 1932, 2005, 2016 Quasimodo or Low Sunday

April 4th ───

            Ancient Roman games honoring Cybele, mother of
                all the gods
 431 BC   Peloponnesian War began
 186 AD   Caracalla, Roman Emperor, born
 304   Sts. Agape, Chionia, and Irene, died (Feast Day)
 397   St. Ambrose, church statesman, died (Feast Day)
 636   St. Isidore of Seville, died (Feast Day)
 896   Pope Formosus, died
1292   Pope Nicholas IV, died
1305   Joan, Queen to King Philip the Fair of France,
                died
1406   King Robert III of Scotland, died
1490   Mathias, King of Hungary, died
1581   Queen Elizabeth I knighted explorer Francis
                Drake
1588   King Frederick II of Denmark and Norway, died
1589   St. Benedict the Black, died (Feast Day)
1617   John Napier, inventor of logarithms, died
1802   Dorthea Dix, educator-poet, born
1841   President William Henry Harrison died after a
                month in office
1850   Los Angeles incorporated as a city
1870   California legislature passed the act creating
                Golden Gate Park
1895   Nebraska's legislature adopted the Goldenrod
                        as the state flower and the nick-
                        name "Tree-planter state"
1896   Robert Sherwood, playwright, born
1905   Kangra, India, rocked by an earthquake
1912   Isaac K. Funk, Wagnalls' publishing partner, died
1920   Nebraska completed its first test on tractors
1924   Gil Hodges, baseball player, born
1932   Tony Perkins, actor, born

```
1933        Elizabeth B. Custer, wife of the general, died
1949        North Atlantic Treaty signed
1953        Turkish submarine Dumiupinar collided with the
                Swedish Naboland in the Dardanelles
1968        Unmanned Apollo VI launched
            Martin Luther King, Jr., civil rights leader,
                assassinated
1970        South Carolina's Tricentennial Celebration at
                Charleston
            Independence Day Celebration in Senegal, Africa
            Start of the Jeep Safari at Moab, Utah
1909, 1971, 1982, 1993, 2004, 2066, 2077, 2088,  Palm
                Sunday
1947, 1958, 1969, 1980, 2042, 2053  Good Friday
1915, 1920, 1926, 1999, 2010, 2021, 2083, 2094  Easter
```

April 5th
```

            Feast of St. Kazurus (Bulgaria)
            Arbor Day in Korea
            Chin Ming Festival (Chinese visit graves)
            End of the British government's fiscal year
2348 BC     Noah's ark grounded on Mt. Ararat
 823 AD     Lothair I crowned Holy Roman Emperor
1355        Charles IV crowned Holy Roman Emperor
1419        St. Vincent Ferrer, patron of brick and tile
                manufacturers, plumbers and pavement
                workers, died (Feast Day)
1494        Lightning struck Santa Maria del Fiore church
                in Florence
1605        Stephen Bocskay elected Prince of Transylvania
1614        Pocahontas married colonist John Rolfe
1649        Elihu Yale, godfather of the University, born
1697        King Charles XI of Sweden, died
1726        Benjamin Harrison, signer of the Declaration
                of Independence, born
1753        British Museum founded (London)
1764        British Parliament passed the Sugar Act,,
                affecting the "triangle trade" of
                slavery
1768        First American Chamber of Commerce founded (New
                York City)
1792        First U.S. Presidential veto exercised
1793        Original plans for the U.S. Capitol accepted
1822        Theodore R. Timby, inventor, born
1827        James Henry Hackett became the first American
                actor to appear abroad on the stage
            Joseph Lister, surgeon, born
1829        Pope Pius VIII, crowned
1837        Algernon Swinburne, poet, born
1842        Shah Shuja, King of Afghanistan, assassinated
1856        Booker T. Washington, educator-author, born
1879        Peru and Chile declared war on each other
```

```
1900        Spencer Tracy, actor, born
1901        Chester Bowles, author-statesman, born
1902        "Battling Nelson" knocked out Willie Rossler
                   with1 punch, the total fight
                   lasting 12 seconds
1915        Jess Willard knocked out Jack Johnson in 26
                   seconds for the heavyweight boxing
                   title
1930        Mahatma Gandhi began his march to the sea (India)
1933        First successful lung removal by surgery
                   performed
1942        British cruisers Dorsetshire and Cornwall sunk
                   by Japanese planes off Ceylon
1954        Princess Martha of Sweden, wife of King Olav V
                   of Norway, died
1965        Pyrgos, Greece rocked by an earthquake
1969        Oxford-Cambrdige Boat races on the Thames,
                   England
            Explosion of the Cart Spectale at Florence,
                   Italy
1903, 1914, 1935, 1936, 1998, 2009, 2020, 2093  Palm
                   Sunday
1901, 1912, 1985, 1996, 2075, 2080  Good Friday
1931, 1942, 1953, 2015, 2026, 2037, 2048  Easter
1959, 1964, 1970, 2043, 2054, 2065  Quasimodo or Low
                   Sunday
```

April 6th

```
            Annunciation Day (Russian Orthodox)
            Han Sik (Cold Food Day) Korea
  64 BC     Solar eclipse
  46        Caesar defeated sons and allies of assassinated
                   Pompey at Thapsus, North Africa
 121 AD     Marcus Aurelius, Roman Emperor, born (or 21st,
                   or 26th depending on which
                   historian)
1199        Richard I, "the Lionhearted," King of England,
                   died of a cross-bow wound
1203        St. William of Aebelholt, died (Feast Day)
1249        St. Louis IX, King of France, taken prisoner by
                   the Moslems
1327        Petrarch, Italian poet, first saw Laura, his
                   inspiration
1348        Laura, inspiration of the poet Petrarch, died
                   of plague
1483        Raphael, Italian artist, born
1520        Raphael, Italian artist, died
1528        Albrecht Durer, German artist, died
1712        Slaves in New York revolted
1748        Pompeii ruins discovered
1773        First court west of the Alleghenies opened at
                   Hanna's Town, Pennsylvania
```

```
1793        Committee of Public Safety extablished in France
1810        Edmund H. Sears, author ("It Came Upon A
                 Midnight Clear"), born
1830        Church of Jesus Christ of Latter-Day Saints
                 (Mormons) founded
1862        Battle of Shiloh or Pittsburg Landing, Tennessee
1866        First post of the Grand Army of the Republic
                 founded (Decatur, Illinois)
1869        Celluloid, the first plastic, patented
1886        Declaration of Berlin, an English-German treaty,
                 signed
1890        Anthony Fokker, airplane builder, born
1892        Lowell Thomas, traveling author, born
1896        Benjamin Harrison married Mary S. L. Dimmick
            Start of first Modern Olympic Games (Athens,
                 Greece)
1897        Slavery abolished in Zanzibar
1903        Charles R. Jackson, author (The Lost Weekend),
                 born
1909        Peary and company reached the North Pole on
                 their 6th attempt
1915        The Turks sank the British battleship Lord
                 Nelson
1917        U.S. entered World War I, declaring war on
                 Germany
1918        Battle of the Somme ended
1939        Canton and Enderbury Islands placed under U.S.-
                 British protection
1965        Early Bird, a commercial communications
                 satellite, launched
1968        Satellites OV-1-13 and OV-1-14 launched by one
                 rocket
            Hemisfair opened in San Antonio, Texas
1971        Igor Stravinsky, composer, died
1941, 1952, 2031, 2036  Palm Sunday
1917, 1928, 2007, 2012, 2091  Good Friday
1947, 1958, 1969, 1980, 2042, 2053, 2064  Easter
1902, 1975, 1986, 1997, 2059, 2070, 2081, 2092  Quasimodo
                 or Low Sunday
```

April 7th

```
            World Health Day
  30 AD     Jesus Christ crucified
   451      Attila the Hun plundered Metz, France
  1321      The Four Martyrs of Tana, missionary-explorers,
                 killed in Moslem India
  1459      University of Ingolstadt, Germany, founded
  1506      St. Francis Xavier, Jesuit missionary, born
  1508      St. Nilus of Sora, died (Feast Day; Russian
                 Orthodox)
  1521      Magellan landed at Cebu, Philippines
  1537      Furness Abbey surrendered to the English king
```

```
1614      Domenico Theotocopuli, El Greco the artist,
               died
1652      First permanent white settlement in South
               Africa founded by the Dutch
1719      St. John-Baptist de la Salle died
1739      Dick Turpin, English robber, hanged
1768      Paris catacombs consecrated as cemeteries
1770      William Wordsworth, poet, born
1788      Marietta, Ohio, settlement established
1798      Mississippi became a U.S. Territory
1827      First friction matches sold (England)
1831      Pedro I, emperor of Brazil, abdicated in favor
               of his 6-year-old son
1832      An English farmer sold his wife for 20 shillings
               and a Newfoundland dog
1862      Confederates surrendered Island 10 to the
               Union forces
1880      American Society of Mechanical Engineers
               founded
1891      P. T. Barnum, showman, died
1897      Walter Winchell, columnist, born
1900      Frederick Church, artist, died
1914      Canada's Grand Trunk Pacific Railroad completed
1927      First public demonstration of television
1933      Beer and wine became legal beverages in the U.S.
               after 13 years of prohibition
1937      Pennsylvania farmers threw strikers out of a
               chocolate factory so they wouldn't
               lose any more milk sales
1945      Japanese battleship Yamato sunk by U.S. planes
               off Kyushu Islands
1947      Henry Ford, inventor, died
1954      Turkish oil resources denationalized
1955      West Germany granted sovereignty
1959      First atomic-generated electricity produced
               (Los Alamos, New Mexico)
          Oklahoma repealed Prohibition
1968      Luna 14, Russian moon orbiter, launched
1970      Start of the National Cherry Blossom Festival,
               Washington D.C.
1974      Beginning of Passover
1963, 1968, 1974, 2047, 2058, 2069  Palm Sunday
1939, 1944, 1950, 2023, 2034, 2045  Good Friday
1901, 1912, 1985, 1996, 2075, 2080  Easter
1907, 1918, 1929, 1991, 2002, 2013, 2024, 2086, 2097
               Quasimodo or Low Sunday
```

April 8th

          Festival of the Virgin of the Valley at
               Catamarca, Argentina
          Korean and Japanese celebrations of Buddha's
               birthday

```
217 AD   Caracalla, Roman dictator, murdered by the
              Praetorian Guard
1143     John II, "the Good," Eastern Roman Emperor,
              killed on a wild boar hunt
1341     Petrarch crowned Rome's Poet Laureate
1364     John II, "the Good," King of France, died in
              England, unable to ransom himself
1378     Bartolomeo Prignano elected Pope Urban VI
1455     Alfonso Borgia elected Pope Calixtus III
1492     Lorenzo de Medici, ruler of Florence, Italy,
              died
1498     King Charles VIII of France died
1513     Ponce de Leon landed in Florida, claiming it
              for Spain
1546     Roman Catholic Church accepted the Apocrypha
              at the Council of Trent
1605     King Philip IV of Spain born
1681     Pennsylvania colonists promised peace,
              prosperity, and happiness by
              William Penn
1730     First Jewish synagogue in New York City
              consecrated
1795     King George IV of England married Caroline of
              Brunswick
1805     Hugo von Mohl, botanist and originator of the
              cell theory, born
1812     Louisiana became the 18th state
1818     King Christian IX of Denmark died
1826     Henry Clay dueled with John Randolph over a
              Congressional debate
1830     Mexican laws passed forbidding slavery and
              American settlement in Texas
1838     Great Western steamship sailed from Bristol,
              England, for New York
1842     Elizabeth, wife of General George Custer, born
1875     King Albert I of Belgium born
1893     Mary Pickford, actress, born
1895     U.S. Supreme Court declared the 1894 income tax
              unconstitutional and the monies
              were returned
1896     New York state flag adopted
1902     Mt. Santa Maria in Guatemala erupted
1904     Entente cordiale between France and Britain
              established
         Los Islands off the coast of Africa ceded to
              France
         Longacre Square changed to Times Square (New
              York City)
1905     Ilka Chase, actress-author, born
1912     Nile steamers collided near Cairo
1913     Sonja Henie, ice skater, born
1918     First air squadron of the U.S. Army assigned to
              observation duty at the front
1919     Frank Woolworth, merchant, died
```

```
1939      Albainian King Zog I went to exile
1942      Japanese sank British carrier Hermes and
                    destroyer Vampire in the Indian
                    Ocean
          Greek Enderania sank off Turkey
          Bataan fell to the Japanese (Philippines)
1952      U.S. government seized steel mills to prevent
                    a strike
1953      Jomo Kenyatta found guilty of Mau Mau activities
                    (Kenya)
1954      DEW line radar network announced
1956      Six U.S. Marine recruits drowned during training
                    at Parris Island, South Carolina
1961      British liner Dara burned in the Persian Gulf
1970      Nimbus IV, weather satellite, launched
1471, 1759, 1906, 1979, 1990, 2001, 2063, 2074, 2085,
                    2096  Palm Sunday
1195, 1955, 1966, 1977, 2039, 2050, 2061, 2072  Good
                    Friday
1917, 1928, 2007, 2012, 2091  Easter
1923, 1934, 1945, 1956, 2018, 2029, 2040  Quasimodo or
                    Low Sunday
```

April 9th

```
          Feast of St. Waudru (patron of Mons, Belgium)
  ? BC    Israelites marched into Egypt
 751 AD   Pope Constantine died
1217      Peter of Courtenay consecrated Emperor of
                    Rumania
1241      Mongols defeated Polish and German knights at
                    the battle of Liegnitz
1483      King Edward IV of England died
1486      Maximilian I crowned King of Germany
1555      Marcellus Cervini elected Pope (Marcellus II)
1585      First English colonists sailed for North Carolina
1626      Sir Francis Bacon, philosopher-statesman, died
1682      LaSalle claimed the Mississippi River Valley
                    for France
1738 OS   Rufus Putnam, "father of Ohio," born
1747      Simon, Lord Lovat, became last person beheaded
                    in England
1756      Suraj-ud-Dowlah became Nawab of Bengal
1806      Isambard Kingdom Brunel, English civil engineer,
                    born
1813      Molly Pitcher, Revolutionary War heroine, died
1816      Congress repealed the tax on furniture and
                    gold and silver watches
1833      First free public library in U.S. established
                    (Peterboro, N.H.)
1835      King Leopold II of Belgium born
1852      John Howard Payne, composer of "Home, Sweet
                    Home," died
```

1864	Maximilian accepted the Imperial crown of Mexico
1865	Confederates surrendered at Appomattox
	Last Confederate cavalry charge (Farmville, Virginia)
	Charles Steinmetz, electrical engineer, born
1868	Sea Bird burned on Lake Michigan
1869	American Museum of Natural History opened (New York City)
1870	Nikolai Lenin, Russian revolutionary leader, born
1881	Billy the Kid convicted of murder
1883	Frank O. King, creator of "Gasoline Alley," born
1886	Civil Rights Act passed by Congress over Presidential veto
1888	Sol Hurok, impresario, born
1889	Efrem Zimbalist, violinist, born (Russia)
1894	Tommy Manville, millionaire-marrier, born
1898	Spain granted armistice in Cuba (Spanish-American War)
1905	Senator J. William Fullbright born
1914	Americans arrested at Tampico, Mexico (Mexican Revolution)
1917	U.S. flag first carried in World War I by an American who served with the Canadians at Vimy Ridge
1933	Peruvian constitution established
1934	Zephyr, first diesel-powered streamliner, put into service
1938	Boundary settled between El Salvador and Guatemala
1940	Germany invaded Denmark and Norway
1941	Greenland became a U.S. protectorate
1945	U.S. Liberty ship explosion at Bari, Italy, killed 360
	British planes sank German battleship Adm. Schier at Kiel
1949	Last Army Day Parade held (New York City)
1953	Grand Duke Jean, ruler of Luxembourg, married Princess Josephine-Charlotte of Belgium
1959	Frank Lloyd Wright, architect, died
1970	Martyrs Day in Tunisia
1971	Buddha's Birthday celebrations in India
1911, 1922, 1933, 1965, 2006, 2017, 2028, 2090	Palm Sunday
1148, 1490, 1521, 1909, 1971, 1982, 1993, 2004, 2066, 2077, 2088	Good Friday
1939, 1944, 1950, 2023, 2034, 2045	Easter
1961, 1972, 2051, 2056	Quasimodo or Low Sunday

```
1257      Aibex, Caliph of Egype, murdered by his wife
1512      King James V of Scotland born
1585      Pope Gregory XIII died
1599      Gabrielle D'Estrees, mistress of King Henry IV
               of France, died
1606      Sir Walter Raleigh sold his interest in the
               colony at Jamestown, Virginia
1727      Samuel Heinicke, educator of the deaf and dumb,
               born
1783      Queen Hortense of Holland, Napoleon'a step-
               daughter, born
1794      Admiral Matthew Perry, U.S. naval hero, born
1829      William Booth, founder of the Salvation Army,
               born
          Lucifer match invented
1841      Horace Greely founded The New York Tribune
1847      Joseph Pulitzer, publisher, born
1849      Walter Hunt received a patent on the safety
               pin
1865      Last Confederate Cabinet meeting held (Charlotte,
               N.C.)
1868      British defeated the Abysinnians at Arogre
1871      P. T. Barnum's Great Traveling Moral Exposition
               of the Wonder World first opened
               in Brooklyn, New York
1872      Arbor Day first observed (Nebraska)
1903      Clare Booth Luce, author-playwright, born
1904      Queen Isabella II of Spain died
1909      Algernon Swinburne, poet, died
1916      First professional golf tournament held
1917      Munitions plant explosion at Eddystone,
               Pennsylvania
1919      Emiliano Zapata, Mexican General, ambushed
               (Revolution)
1924      Arkansas state flag adopted
1938      Austrian popular vote ratified union with
               Germany
1941      Britain's women's army auxilary given full
               military status
1958      Morocco became independent of Spain
1959      Crown Prince Akihito of Japan married Michiko
               Shoda
          A World War II bomb exploded in the Philippines
1963      U.S. nuclear submarine Thresher sank
1971      Beginning of Passover
          Fourth Annual Frog-jumping Contest at Springfield,
               S.C.
          U.S. Ping-Pong team arrived in Red China
1927, 1938, 1949, 1960, 2022, 2033, 2044  Palm Sunday
1903, 1914, 1925, 1936, 1998, 2009, 2020, 2093, 2099
               Good Friday
```

1904, 1983, 1988, 1994, 2067, 2078, 2089   Quasimodo or
                                            Low Sunday

April 11th

         Feast of Pope St. Leo the Great
         Feast of St. Tiburtius, martyr
421 BC   Technical peace between Athens and Sparta
                    interrupted the Peloponnesian War
146 AD   Severus, Roman Emperor, born
678   Pope Donus died
714   St. Guthlac died (Feast Day)
1241   Mongols defeated Hungarians and Crusaders at
                    Miskoic, Russia
1242   Mongols defeated Hungarian army under King
                    Bela IV on the Mohi Plain
1492   Marguerite d'Angouleme, Queen of Navarre, born
1506   Construction begun on a new Vatican basilica,
                    to continue until 1626
1521   Battle of Ravenna, Italy
1555   Joanna, "the Mad," Queen of Spain, died
1689   Mary II and William III crowned rulers of
                    England
1713   Treaty of Utrecht ended the War of Spanish
                    Succession
1755   Dr. James Parkinson, first researcher on
                    "shaking palsy," (Parkinson's
                    Disease), born
1805   Treaty of Alliance between England and Russia
                    against France
1814   Napoleon abdicated
1834   British deposed rajah of Coorg province, India
1845   Large part of Pittsburgh, Pennsylvania,
                    destroyed by fire
1862   Charles Evans Hughes, jurist-author, born
1873   Modoc Indians turned a peace conference into a
                    massacre (Oregon)
1893   Dean Acheson, statesman, born
1898   President asked Congress for authority to
                    intervene in Cuba
1899   Spanish-American War ended
1902   Quentin Reynolds, author, born
1903   St. Gemma Galgani died (Feast Day)
         King Edward VII of England reviewed the garrison
                    at Gibralter
1913   Oleg Cassini, designer, born
1921   German national flag adopted
1926   Luther Burbank, botanist, died
1951   General Ridgeway replaced MacArthur in Korea
1970   Mountain Folk Festival at Berea, Kentucky
         International Plowing Match at Lynden,
                    Washington
         John O'Hara, novelist, died

```
                  Apollo 13, manned lunar flight (troubled),
                       launched
1971          Explosion of the Cart Festival at Florence,
                  Italy
1954, 1965, 1976, 2049, 2055, 2060  Palm Sunday
1941, 1952, 2031, 2036  Good Friday
1909, 1971, 1982, 1993, 2004, 2066, 2077, 2088  Easter
1915, 1920, 1926, 1999, 2010, 2021, 2083, 2094  Quasimodo
                  or Low Sunday
```

April 12th

```
              Feast of St. Zeno of Verona
352 AD        St. Julius I, Pope, died
372           St. Sabas the Goth died (Feast Day)
1204          Fourth Crusade took Constantinople
1577          Christian IV, King of Denmark and Norway, born
1660          British periodical Mercurius Politicus ended
                  publication
1689          Pope Innocent XI died
1693          First printing press arrived in New York City
1723          Last French legislation passed to supress duels
1724          Lyman Hall, signer of the Declaration of
                  Independence, born
1755          The Connecticut Gazette founded in New Haven
1776          Halifax, North Carolina made its declaration of
                  independence from England (state
                  holiday)
1777          Henry Clay, statesman, born
1811          John Jacob Astor's colonists arrived at Cape
                  Dissappointment, Washington
1842          Mutual Life Insurance Company of New York
                  chartered
1853          United States Trust Company incorporated
1858          First American billiards championship played
                  (Detroit)
1861          Confederate attack on Fort Sumter began
              "The Great Locomotive Chase" took place
1864          Confederate forces captured Fort Pillow,
                  Tennessee
1877          Britain annexed Transvaal
1878          "Boss" Tweed, New York City politician, died in
                  jail
1892          First portable typewriter patented
1893          American Railway Union organized
1896          End of the first modern Olympic games (Athens,
                  Greece)
1900          Congress granted civil government to Puerto Rico
1904          Lily Pons, opera singer, born
1905          First performance given at the New York
                  Hippodrome
1908          Chelsea, Massachusetts, devastated by fire
1912          Clara Barton, Red Cross founder, died
```

```
1916      Pershing battled Pancho Villa at Parral
                (Mexican Revolution)
1918      Solote Tubou became Queen of Tonga
1924      Tubular steel golf-club shafts approved for
                championship U.S. play
1934      231-mph wind recorded at Mt. Washington, New
                Hampshire
1945      President Franklin D. Roosevelt died
1946      Franklin D. Roosevelt's birthplace in Hyde Park,
                New York became a national shrine
1949      First televised total eclipse of the moon
1955      Salk antipolio vaccine approved
1961      Yuri Gagarin made the first Russian space flight
1964      Polyot II, Russian satellite, launched
1970      Hampton-Preston Historical Museum at Columbia,
                South Carolina dedicated
1971      L'Emaischeu (Young Lovers' Day) in Luxembourg
1908, 1981, 1987, 1992, 2071, 2076, 2082  Palm Sunday
1963, 1968, 1974, 2047, 2058, 2069  Good Friday
1903, 1914, 1925, 1936, 1998, 2009, 2020, 2093, 2099
                Easter
1931, 1942, 1953, 2015, 2026, 2037, 2048  Quasimodo or
                Low Sunday
```

April 13th

```
          Ides of April
          Feast of Sts. Carpus and Papylus, martyrs
1087 AD   Travelers of Chaucer's Canterbury Tales began
                their journey
1401      Tsuchimikado-den, Japan's Imperial palace,
                burned to the ground
1436      French drove English out of Paris (100 Years'
                War)
1523      Christian II, King of Denmark, went into exile
1598      Edict of Nantes ended persecution of Huguenots
                (French Protestants)
1605      Theodore II proclaimed Czar of Russia when
                Boris Godunovy of Muscovy died
1743      Thomas Jefferson, U.S. President, born
1759      George Frederick Handel, composer, died
1769      Captain Cook anchored at Tahiti
1846      Pennsylvania legislature incorporated the
                Pennsylvania Railroad
1852      Frank Woolworth, merchant, born
1868      British captured Magdala, Ethiopia
1904      Russian battleship Petropavlovsk hit a mine off
                Port Arthur
1907      Harold Stassen, presidential candidate, born
1912      A naval branch of England's flying corps was
                formed and a flying school founded
1914      Thug-murderers of gambler Herman Rosenthal
                executed at Sing Sing (New York)
```

```
1925      Theater Guild Theater opened in New York City
1928      Teddy Roosevelt shot a giant panda for the
              Chicago Museum
1943      Thomas Jefferson Memorial, Washington, D.C.,
              dedicated
1960      Transit 1B, navigational satellite, launched
1970      Songkrant Day (Throwing Water Festival) in
              Singapore
1919, 1924, 1930, 2003, 2014, 2025, 2087, 2098  Palm
              Sunday
1906, 1979, 1990, 2001, 2063, 2074, 2085, 2096  Good
              Friday
1941, 1952, 2031, 2036  Easter
1947, 1958, 1969, 1980, 2042, 2053, 2064  Quasimodo or
              Low Sunday
```

April 14th

```
          Feast of St. Justin
          Feast of St. Tiburtius
 972 AD   Otto II, Holy Roman Emperor, married Theophano,
              princess of the Eastern Roman Empire
1028      Henry III, "the Black," Holy Roman Emperor,
              crowned King of Germany
1199      Henry VI crowned Holy Roman Emperor
1386      St. Mary's College, Oxford, England, opened
1578      King Philip III of Spain born
1582      College of Edinburgh, Scotland, founded
1775      Ben Franklin and the Quakers organized the first
              abolitionist society
1791      First life insurance company is U.S. chartered
1792      Law establishing U.S. consular service passed
1818      Surgeon General established as head of the
              Army Medical Department
1828      First edition of Noah Webster's American
              Dictionary of the English Language
              published
1860      Franklin, first permanent settlement in Idaho,
              founded
1861      Fort Sumter surrendered to the Confederates
1865      President Abraham Lincoln assassinated
1887      President Lincoln reburied at Springfield,
              Illinois
1890      Pan American Union established (Pan American Day)
          Maury H. B. Paul, original "Cholly Knickerbocker"
              journalist, born
1894      Edison's vending-machine peep show opened in
              New York City
1896      Fresno, California, got electricity
1905      Grave of John Paul Jones discovered in Paris
1906      Cornerstone laid for House of Representatives
              Office Building in Washington, D.C.
```

```
1910      William Howard Taft started the custom of the
                      President's throwing the first
                      baseball of the season
1917      Switzerland declared its neutrality in World
                      War I
1918      First U.S.-German air battle of World War I
1924      Louis Sullivan, architect credited with
                      originating skyscrapers, died
1925      Rod Steiger, actor, born
1931      Alfonso XIII, King of Spain, forced into exile
1944      Explosion in Bombay, India harbor killed 700
1948      Theater television first demonstrated (New York
                      City)
1961      First live broadcast from Russia carried by the
                      British Broadcasting Company
1968      Cosmos 212, Russian linking space vehicle,
                      launched
1970      Basque Festival, Maccachin, Argentina
1935, 1946, 1957, 2019, 2030, 2041, 2052  Palm Sunday
1911, 1922, 1933, 1965, 2006, 2017, 2028, 2090   Good
                      Friday
1675, 1963, 1968, 1974, 2047, 2058, 2069  Easter
1901, 1012, 1985, 1996, 2075, 2080  Quasimodo or Low
                      Sunday
```

April 15th

```
          United States income taxes due
1491 BC   Israelites arrived in the wilderness
   43     Antonius attacked Pansa at Forum Gallorum
   69 AD  Marcus Slavius Otho, Roman Emperor, committed
                      suicide
  911     Pope Sergius III died
 1053     Godwine, Earl of the West-Saxons, died (England)
 1205     Baldwin I of Rumania captured by Bulgarians at
                      Adrianople
 1450     French defeated English at Formigny (100 Years'
                      War)
 1452     Leonardo da Vinci, artist-inventor, born
 1646     King Christian V of Denmark and Norway born
 1719     Marquise de Maintenon, second wife of King
                      Louis XIV of France, died
 1741     Charles Wilson Peale, American portrait painter,
                      born
 1764     Marquise de Pompadour, mistress of King Louis
                      XV of France, died
 1789     Gazette of the United States, first news
                      journal of government affairs,
                      founded
 1800     Sir James Clark Ross, Polar explorer, born
 1812     Indian massacre at Fort Dearborn (Chicago,
                      Illinois)
          Pierre Etienne Rousseau, French artist, born
```

```
1817       First permanent school for the deaf opened
                    (Hartford, Conn.)
1843       Henry James, novelist, born
1850       San Francisco incorporated
           John L. Stevens got permission to build a
                    railroad across the Isthmus of
                    Panama from Colombia
1857       Clarence Darrow, lawyer, born
1861       President Lincoln called up the 75,000 militia
1862       Westernmost Civil War skirmish took place at
                    Picacho Pass, Arizona
1865       President Lincoln, shot day before, died
1867       Stevens Institute of Technology founded
                    (Hoboken, N.J.)
1873       Ecole Polytechnique, French military academy,
                    reorganized
1874       Compulsory education law passed by New York
                    legislature
1875       James J. Jeffries, boxer, born
1886       New building for the Library of Congress
                    authorized
1889       Thomas Hart Benton, artist-author, born
1900       International Exposition opened in Paris
1904       Andrew Carnegie established a hero-award fund
                    of $6 million
1912       Titanic struck an iceberg and sank
1916       Gregory Peck, actor, born
1920       Sacco and Vanzetti accused of murder in
                    Braintree, Mass.
1937       House of Representatives passed an anti-lynching
                    bill
1938       Spanish insurgents divided loyalist Spain
1968       Cosmos 213, Russian space vehicle, launched
                    then linked up with Cosmos 212
1969       Former Queen Victoria-Eugenie of Spain died
1972       National Ramp Festival, Richwood, West Virginia
                    (wild onion harvest)
1976       Passover begins
1962, 1973, 1984, 2057, 2068  Palm Sunday
1927, 1938, 1949, 1960, 2022, 2033, 2044  Good Friday
1906, 1979, 1990, 2001, 2063, 2074, 2085, 2096  Easter
1917, 1928, 2007, 2012, 2091  Quasimodo or Low Sunday
```

April 16th

```
           De Deigo's Birthday (Puerto Rican Holiday)
           New Year's Day in Burma
1178 BC    Solar eclipse
 556 AD    Pelagius crowned Pope
1116       St. Magnus of Orkney died (Feast Day)
1189       St. Druon died (Feast Day; invoked against
                    ruptures, hernias, unpleasant
                    births)
```

1291	Rudolph Hapsburg bought the rights to govern Lucerne, Switz.
1746	England defeated Scotland and "Bonnie Prince Charles" at Culloden
1783	St. Benedict Labre died (Feast Day; patron of displaced persons)
1787	First American comedy, The Contrast, opened in New York City
1789	George Washington left Mount Vernon to be inaugurated
1827	The Youth's Companion, juvenile publication, founded
1828	Francisco Goya, Spanish artist, died
1834	Self-lighting cigars, locofocos, patented by John Marck
1844	Anatole France, French author and critic, born
1850	Marie Tussaud of the waxworks, Paris, died
1862	Slavery abolished in the District of Columbia by Congress
1867	Wilbur Wright, airplane inventor, born
1879	St. Bernadette died (Feast Day; visionary of Lourdes)
1889	Charlie Chaplin, actor, born
1902	Last Philippine guerilla forces surrendered
1905	Tennessee adopted its state flag
1906	Chile rocked by an earthquake
1915	Robert Paul Smith, author, born
1916	George W. Peck, "Peck's Bad Boy," died
1917	Lenin, after 10 years in exile, returned to Russia
1940	Bob Feller pitched an opening-day no-hitter (Cleveland beat Chicago, 1 to 0)
	Princess Margrethe of Denmark born
1945	British planes sank German battleship Leutzow
1947	French Grandchamp exploded in Texas City harbor
1955	Prince Henri, heir to Duchy of Luxembourg, born
1966	Abu Simbel removal completed, saving this temple from inundation by Aswan Dam waters (Egypt)
1968	Edna Ferber, novelist, died
1970	Last Day of the Summer Festival in Iceland
1972	Two giant pandas arrived in the U.S. from China

1856, 1905, 1916, 2000, 2079 Palm Sunday
1824, 1954, 1965, 1976, 2049, 2055, 2060 Good Friday
1865, 1911, 1922, 1933, 2006, 2017, 2028, 2090 Easter
1939, 1944, 1950, 2023, 2034, 2045 Quasimodo or Low Sunday

April 17th

Flag Day in American Samoa
Feast of St. Stephen Harding

| 617 AD | St. Donnan died (Feast Day) |
| 744 | Walid II, Caliph of Baghdad, murdered |

```
 858      Pope Benedict III died
1087      St. Robert of Chaise-Dieu died (Feast Day)
1421      100,000 people drowned in Dort Floods
1524      Giovanni da Verrazano discovered the Narrows
                   and New York Harbor (Verrazano Day
                   in New York)
1535      Antonio de Mendoza appointed first Spanish
                   viceroy in Mexico
1605      Pope Leo XI crowned
1610      Henry Hudson began the voyage that discovered
                   Hudson's Bay
1702      East and West New Jersey consolidated into one
                   colony
1711      Joseph I, King of Austria and Germany and the
                   Holy Roman Emperor, died of smallpox
1741      Samuel Chase, signer of the Declaration of
                   Independence, born
1754      French and Indian drove the English from the
                   area around Pittsburgh, Pennsylvania
1790      Benjamin Franklin, statesman, died
1794      Warsaw, Poland, uprising against the occupying
                   Russians
1837      John Pierpont Morgan, financier, born
1851      Monot Ledge light tower collapsed in a storm
                   (Massachusetts)
1861      Virginia seceded from the Union
1868      United Kingdom vanished with 80 aboard
1885      William H. Ireland, forger of Shakespearian
                   plays, died
1895      Treaty of Shimonoseki ended Sino-Japanese War
1897      Thornton Wilder, novelist-playwright, born
1918      William Holden, actor, born
1920      Military aviation school chartered for Maracay,
                   Venezuela
1921      First oil well came in at Larado, Texas
1946      Last French occupation troops left Syria
1961      Bay of Pigs invasion by Cuban exiles crushed
1970      Safe Driving Rodeo at Baxley, Georgia
          Pooram in Kerala, India (all-night temple
                   festival)
          Troubled Apollo 13 landed in the Pacific
1971      Maple sugar season ended
1973      Beginning of Passover
2011, 2095  Palm Sunday
1908, 1981, 1987, 1992, 2071, 2076, 2082  Good Friday
1927, 1938, 1949, 1960, 2022, 2033, 2044  Easter
1955, 1966, 1977, 2039, 2050, 2061, 2072  Quasimodo or
                   Low Sunday
```

April 18th

```
          Hepatica and bloodroot bloom
 387 AD   Palm Sunday in Egypt
```

1417	Frederick of Hohenzollern invested as Elector of Brandenberg
1479	Reconstruction of the Japanese imperial palace begun after city of Kyoto was destroyed by a civil war
1506	Foundation stone for new St. Peter's Basilica laid in theVatican (Rome)
1636	Sir Julius Caesar, English barrister, died
1775	Paul Revere rode
1797	Napoleon and the French signed an armistice with Austria
	British attacked San Juan, Puerto Rico
1861	Union troops evacuated Harper's Ferry, Virginia
1864	Dybbol, Denmark, fell to the Prussians
1865	Confederates surrendered at Durham Station, N.C.
1882	Leopold Stokowski, symphony conductor, born
1884	Pomona collided with the State of Florida
1902	Solona, Guatemala, wrecked by an earthquake
1906	San Francisco devastated by earthquake and fire
1907	Stephen Longstreet, author, born
1917	Queen Mother Frederika of Greece, born
1932	Ford Model B, last of the original 4-cylinder cars, introduced
1942	General Doolittle and company bombed Japanese cities
1945	Ernie Pyle, journalist, killed in World War II
1946	League of Nations ended, giving its physical assets to the United Nations
1949	Ireland established as a republic
1954	Gamal Abdul Nasser became Premier of Egypt
1955	Albert Einstein, physicist, died
1956	Prince Rainier III, ruler of Monaco, married actress Grace Kelly
1958	A sunken munitions ship exploded at Okinawa
1970	World Clam-Gulping Championship at Port Townsend, Wash.
	Palm Sunday in Greece
1971	Easter (Greek Orthodox)
	Festival of the Heavenly Queen (Hong Kong fishermen's goddess)

1943, 2038 Palm Sunday
1919, 1924, 1930, 2003, 2014, 2025, 2087, 2098 Good
            Friday
1954, 1965, 1976, 2049, 2055, 2060 Easter
1490, 1521, 1909, 1971 1982, 1993, 2004, 2066, 2077,
            2088 Quasimodo or Low Sunday

April 19th_____

            Patriots Day in Maine and Massachusetts
            Primrose Day in England

Feast of St. Expeditus (invoked in pressing
                emergencies)
49 BC   Caesar, enroute to Spain, attacked Marseilles
1012 AD St. Alphege, Archbishop of Canterbury,
                murdered (Feast Day)
1054   Pope St. Leo IX, originator of the Crusades,
                died (Feast Day)
1127   St. Felix of Valois born
1588   Veronese, Italian painter, died
1689   Former Queen Christina of Sweden died
1721   Roger Sherman, signer of the Declaration of
                Independence, born
1775   Battle of Concord, Massachusetts
1793   Ferdinand I, Emperor of Austria, born
1813   Benjamin Rush, signer of the Declaration of
                Independence, died
1819   Fort Wayne in Indiana abandoned
1824   George Gordon, Lord Byron the poet, died in
                Greece of malaria
1827   Rene Caillie, French African explorer, began
                his trek to Timbuktoo
1839   Treaty of London made Belgium and Holland
                separate countries
1850   Clayton-Bulwer Treaty signed (Panama Canal)
1857   Main building of the University of Northern
                Pennsylvania at Bethany burned
                to the ground
1861   Blockade of Confederate ports declared
        Massachusetts troops attacked in Baltimore on
                their way to Washington
1871   Traders Deposit Company bank founded
1882   Charles Darwin, naturalist, died
1892   Charles Duryea claimed to have driven his car
1906   Pierre Curie, scientist, died
1916   Germany agreed to U.S. demands concerning
                submarine warfare
1937   Franco set up the Spanish government on a
                one-party system
1939   French ship Paris burned at Le Havre
1940   Little Falls, New York, train wreck
1948   Burma joined the United Nations
1968   Remnants of the snowmobile expedition reached
                the North Pole
        Cosmos 215 launched for Russian astronomy
                studies
1969   Declaration of Independence Day in Venezuela
1971   Salyut, Russian orbiting space station,
                launched
1935, 1946, 1957, 2019, 2030, 2041, 2052 Good Friday
1908, 1981, 1987, 1992, 2071, 2076, 2082 Easter
1903, 1914, 1925, 1936, 1998, 2009, 2020, 2093, 2099
                Quasimodo or Low Sunday

April 20th

	Feast of St. Agnes of Montepulciano
1314 AD	Pope Clement V died
1534	Jacques Cartier left France on his first voyage of Canadian exploration
1627	Spanish fleet burned by the English at Santa Cruz
1648	Future King James II of England escaped the Parliamentarians by sailing to Holland
1741	Frederick the Great and the Prussians defeated the Austrians at Mollwitz
1768	Canaletto, Italian artist famed for his architectural scenes, died
1777	First New York state constitution adopted
1792	France declared war on Austrian Empire
1828	Rene Caillie, French African explorer, entered Timbuktoo
1836	Wisconsin became a U.S. territory
1839	Charles (or Carol), King of Rumania, born
1861	Robert E. Lee resigned from the U.S. Army
1866	Charles elected Prince of Rumania
1871	Overhead steam rail service began in New York City
1883	Edouard Manet, French artist, died
1889	Adolf Hitler born
1893	Joan Miro, Spanish artist, born
	King Ferdinand of Bulgaria married Marie Louise de Bourbon
1894	Harold Lloyd, movie comedian, born
1902	The Curies discovered radium
1904	Louisiana Purchase Exposition opened (St. Louis, Missouri)
1910	Robert F. Wagner, New York City mayor-diplomat, born
1911	Roman Catholicism ceased being the state religion of Portugal
1913	Lionel Hampton, musician, born
1931	Welland Canal, connecting Lakes Erie and Ontario, opened to traffic
1939	New York World's Fair opened
1944	U.S.S. Paul Hamilton torpedoed off Algiers
1947	King Christian X of Denmark died
1962	Russia-China pact signed
1967	Peking Municipal Revolutionary Committee established its authority (China)
1970	Beginning of Passover
1971	"Cuckoo Day"

1962, 1973, 1984, 2047, 2068 Good Friday
1919, 1924, 1930, 2003, 2014, 2025, 2087, 2098 Easter
1941, 1952, 2031, 2036 Quasimodo or Low Sunday

		Feast of St. Beuno
		Roman herdsmen leaped 3 times over bonfires to honor Pales
		Last year's wine first tested in Ancient Rome
?	BC	Israelites saved by the quail
753		Rome, Italy, founded
121	AD	Marcus Aurelius, Roman emperor, born (or 6th or 26th depending on which historian)
341		St. Simeon Barsabba'e died (Feast Day)
586		Leovigild, King of the Visgoths, died
1073		Pope Alexander II, supporter of Norman invasion of England, died
1109		St. Anselem, Archbishop of Canterbury, died (Feast Day)
1393		John Capgrave, English historian, born
1526		Battle of Panipat, India
1757		Prussians defeated Austrians at Reichenberg
1775		Retreat from Concord, Massachusetts
1782		Construction began on the Presidio of Santa Barbara (Calif.)
1783		Reginald Heber, hymn-writer, born
1798		British Mars defeated French Hercule
1818		Henry Wheeler Shaw, humorist as "Josh Billings," born
1823		First steamboat started up the Mississippi River
1835		Samuel Slater, "father of American manufacturing," died
1836		Mexicans defeated at San Jacinto (Texas State Holiday)
1838		John Muir, scientist-naturalist, born
1846		United Order of True Sisters founded
		William H. Goodyear, archaeologist-author, born
1849		Henry R. Elliot, editor-novelist, born
1856		First train crossed the Mississippi River (Rock Island, Ill.)
		Johnson Oatman, composer of "Count Your Blessings," born
1868		Umberto, King of Italy, married Margherita Teresa of Savoy
1870		President Grant gave the island of Bolma to Portugal, not Britain
1875		"Cave of the Winds" discovered at Manitou Springs, Colorado
1892		Francis P. Gaines, educator-author, born
1894		George Bernard Shaw's Arms and the Man first produced (London)
1898		U.S. delcared a state of war with Spain
1910		Samuel Clemens, writer as Mark Twain, died
1915		Anthony Quinn, actor, born
1925		Albert National Park established (Congo)
1926		Sir Henry Mance, English scientist-inventor, died

	Queen Elizabeth II of England born
1930	Robert Bridges, England's Poet Laureate, died
	Fire struck the penitentiary at Columbus, Ohio
1952	Granville Fortescue, soldier-playwright, died
	U.S. cruiser St. Paul damaged off Korea
1955	U.S. ratified the treaty giving sovereignty to West Germany
1956	Charles MacArthur, playwright, died
1960	Brasilia declared the new capital city of Brazil
1962	Century 21 Exposition opened at Seattle, Washington
1965	Paul Jung, clown, died
	New York City's World's Fair opened for the second season
1967	Kastraki hydoelectric project begun on the Acheloos River, Greece
1968	Molniya 1-H, Russian communications satellite, launched
1969	Bruce Tulloh of England left Los Angeles to break the transcontinental run record
1971	Independence Day celebration at Riobamba, Ecuador
	"Papa Doc" Duvalier, Haiti's president for life, died

1905, 1916, 2000, 2079   Good Friday
1935, 1946, 1957, 2019, 2030, 2041, 2052   Easter
1963, 1968, 1974, 2047, 2058, 2069   Quasimodo or Low Sunday

April 22nd

	Arbor Day in Nebraska
	Feast of St. Conrad of Parzham
	Feast of St. Theodore of Sykeon
536 AD	St. Agapetus, Pope, died
960	Basil II crowned Emperor of the Eastern Roman Empire
1370	Construction of the Bastille, Paris fortress and prison, begun
1418	Council of Constance, reuniting the Roman Catholic Church after the Great Schism, ended
1451	Queen Isabella of Spain, backer of Columbus, Born
1500	Pedro Alverez de Cabral landed in Brazil and claimed it for Portugal
1541	St. Ignatius of Loyala, founder of the Society of Jesus (Jesuits), elected its first general
1707	Henry Fielding, English novelist, born

1711	Eleazar Wheelock, founder of Moor's Indian Charity School (now Dartmouth College), born
1774	New York Tea Party
1793	U.S. declared neutrality in the war between Britain and France
1796	French-Austrian battle at Mondovi, Italy
1827	Thomas Rowlandson, English artist, died
1832	Julius S. Morton, originator of Arbor Day, born
1834	St. Helena Island became English crown property
1861	Robert E. Lee left home to take charge of Virginia's troops
1864	"In God We Trust" became the U.S. motto
1870	Lenin, Russian revolutionary, born (national holiday)
1879	Assassination attempt failed on King Umberto of Italy
	The Forward, world's largest Jewish daily newspaper, first published
1884	Colchester, England, rocked by an earthquake
1886	Abram Joseph Ryan, "Poet of the Confederacy," died
1889	Oklahoma Territory land rush for homesteaders (state holiday)
1891	Blanco Encalada exploded in Caldera Bay
1892	First U.S. anatomy school, Wistar Institute, incorporated
1904	Robert J. Oppenheimer, physicist, born
1908	Eddie Albert, actor, born
1915	Second battle of Ypres began and gas was first used as a weapon
1916	Yehudi Menuhin, violinist, born
1928	Keech, in a White-Triplex car, set a land speed record of 207.552 mph
1929	Japan's Toyo Kuni Maru wrecked on Rocky Cape Erino
1930	Naval reduction treaty of London signed by U.S., Britain, France, Italy, and Japan
1964	New York World's Fair opened for the first season
1969	Bermuda Peppercorn Ceremony in St. George held
1970	Intelstat III F7, communications satellite, launched
1971	Start of Summer (Holiday in Iceland)
	Soyus 10, Russian manned space orbiter, launched
2011, 2095	Good Friday
1962, 1973, 1984, 2057, 2068	Easter
1906, 1979, 1990, 2001, 2063, 2074, 2085, 2096	Quasimodo or Low Sunday

---

April 23rd

Beginning of a two-day fair at Dover, England

	Start of a week-long fair at Lincoln, England
	Day of Shepherds in Bulgaria
	Fair at one time at Guilford, Surry, England
290 AD	St. George executed (Feast Day; patron of England and Portugal, soldiers and Boy Scouts; invoked against skin diseases)
997	St. Adalbert of Prague died (Feast Day)
1014	King Brian Boru of Ireland defeated the Danes near Dublin
1016	Ethelred the Unready, King of England, died
1349	King Edward III of England began the Order of the Garter
1445	King Henry VI of England married Margaret of Anjou
1616	William Shakespeare, English playwright, died
	Cervantes, Spanish author, died ("Don Quixote")
1661	Charles II crowned King of England, "The Merry Monarch"
1723	Mrs. Hannah Snellborn, a deserting soldier, wounded as a sailor
1731	William Williams, signer of the Declaration of Independence, born
1775	J. M. W. Turner, English artist, born
1791	James Buchanan, 15th U.S. President, born
1823	Delaware and Hudson Company chartered for canals and railroads
1838	Great Western steamship completed her maiden voyage (Bristol, England to New York)
1850	William Wordsworth, poet, died
1859	First issue of The Rocky Mountain News published (Denver, Colorado)
1860	Stuart's expedition reached the middle of Australia
1861	Robert E. Lee took command of Virginia's troops
	"Maryland, My Maryland," state song, written
1879	Talbot Mundy, novelist, born
1884	France given the right to purchase the Congo Free State
1896	First public showing of a motion picture (New York City)
1910	International Exhibition, Brussels, Belgium opened
1911	Burman, in a Benz automobile, set a land speed record of 141.732 mph
1921	Warren Spahn, baseball pitcher, born
1925	Royal Commission of English food prices made its report
1928	Shirley Temple, actress-diplomat, born
1941	Greece surrendered to Italy and Germany
	British ship Rajputana torpedoed
1946	Ed Head pitched a no-hitter and Brooklyn beat Boston 5-0

Mussolini's body stolen from a pauper's grave
in Milan
1964   Ken Johnson pitched a no-hitter but lost the
game on errors (Cincinnati 1,
Houston 0)
1965   Molniya I, Russian communications satellite,
launched
1943, 2038 Good Friday
1905, 1916, 2000, 2079 Easter
1911, 1922, 1933, 2006, 2017, 2028, 2090 Quasimodo or
Low Sunday

April 24th---

Arbor Day in Maine
Procession of Epitaph (Cyprus)
Feast of St. Ivo (patron of St. Ives, England)
753 BC Beginning of the Roman Era
624 AD St. Mellitus died (Feast Day)
709 or
710   St. Wilfrid died
858   Nicholas I "the Great" elected Pope
1505   Amerigo Vespucci, Italian mapmaker, became a
citizen of Spain
1546   English Navy Board chartered by King Henry VIII
1547   Charles V, Holy Roman Emperor, defeated the
Protestants at Muhlberg
1576   St. Vincent de Paul, French founder of Lazarite
Missionaries and Sisters of
Charity, born
1585   Felice Peretti elected Pope (Sixtus V; rebuilt
Lateran Palace)
1629   Peace signed between England and France
1704   Boston News Letter, first regular American
newspaper, founded
1743   Edmund Cartwright, inventor of the power loom,
born
1766   Robert Bailey Thomas, founder of Farmers'
Almanac, born
1792   "La Marseillaise," French national anthem,
composed by Claude P. Rouget
de Lisle
1800   Library of Congress established
1827   Baltimore and Ohio Railroad incorporated
1832   Erie Railroad Company incorporated by New York
legislature
1854   Emperor Francis Joseph of Austro-Hungary
married Elizabeth of Wittelsbach
1868   St. Euphrasia Pelletier died (Feast Day)
1877   Russia declared war on Turkey
1890   General Federation of Womens' Clubs organized
1895   Joshua Slocum sailed alone from Boston in a 36-
foot boat to circle the globe

```
1898        Spain declared war on the U.S. (Spanish-
                          American War)
1904        Willem de Kooning, artist, born
1905        Robert Penn Warren, author, born
1916        Ireland's Easter Rebellion began
1934        Shirley McLaine, actress, born
1947        Willa Cather, novelist-poet, died
1965        Military coup in Santo Domingo
1968        Mauritius joined the United Nations
1970        Start of Captain Cook Festival at Kailua-Kona,
                          Hawaii
            Beethoven's Bicentennial Birthday Celebration
                          in Luxembourg
1972        San Marco 3, U.S.-Italian satellite, launched
2011, 2095  Easter
1927, 1938, 1949, 1960, 2022, 2033, 2044  Quasimodo or
                          Low Sunday
```

April 25th

```
            Our Lady of Coromoto in Venezuela
            Feast of St. Mark the Evangelist (patron of
                          Venice, Italy, lawyers, and
                          glaziers)
            Ancient Romans invoked Robigus, Spirit of
                          Mildew, to spare the corn
            Anzac Day - Australians honor their war dead
 404 BC     Later Peloponnesian war ended with Athens'
                          surrender to Sparta
 799 AD     Pope Leo III kidnapped
1142        St. William of Monte Vergine died (Feast Day)
1214        St. Louis XI, King of France, born
1284        King Edward II of England, first to be named
                          Prince of Wales, born
1342        Pope Benedict XII, 3rd Avignon Pope, died
1482        Margaret of Anjou, wife of King Henry VI of
                          England, died
1533        William the Silent, governing prince of the
                          Spanish Netherlands, born
1599        Oliver Cromwell, English soldier-statesman, born
1607        Dutch defeated Spanish fleet at Gibraltar Bay
1661        Alcoholic beverage sellers first licensed in
                          England
1719        First edition of Daniel Defoe's Robinson Crusoe
                          was published
1792        First person, a highwayman, executed by
                          guillotine (Paris)
            "La Marseillaise," French national anthem, first
                          sung
1805        Lewis and Clark reached the junction of the
                          Missouri and Yellowstone Rivers
1809        Ratisbonne (or Regensberg) captured by Napoleon
```

```
1819      Independent Order of Odd Fellows founded
                (Baltimore)
1859      Digging of the Suez Canal began
1862      New Orleans surrendered to Admiral Farragut
1864      du Hauron applied for a French patent for a
                motion picture machine
1866      First Decoration Day celebrated (Columbia,
                Mississippi)
1873      Walter de la Mare, English poet and novelist,
                born
          Howard R. Garis, creator of Uncle Wiggily,
                born
1874      Guglielmo Marconi, wireless inventor, born
1896      Royal Victorian Order instituted in England
1904      George Schreiber, Belgian artist, born
1915      Allies landed at Gallipoli
1918      Ella Fitzgerald, "First Lady of Song," born
          Chinese ship Kiang-Kwan in a collision off
                Hankow
1926      Riza Khan Pahlavi crowned Shah of Iran
1932      New Shakespeare Memorial Theater opened at
                Stratford-on-Avon (England)
1934      2 1/2-mile bridge completed connecting Venice
                with Italy
1935      Oregon's capitol destroyed by fire
1945      U.S. and Russian troops met at the Elbe River,
                Germany
          United Nations Conference on International
                Organization opened at San
                Francisco
1946      Naperville, Illinois, train wreck
1959      St. Lawrence Seaway opened
1960      Lar, Iran rocked by an earthquake
1962      Ranger IV landed on the moon
1968      Cosmos 218, Russian satellite, launched
1943, 2038  Easter
1954, 1965, 1976, 2049, 2055, 2060  Quasimodo or Low
                Sunday
```

April 26th
_____

```
          Feast of St. Cletus, the third Pope
 121 AD   Marcus Aurelius, Roman Emperor, born (or 6th,
                or 21st depending on which
                authority you read)
 757      Pope Stephen III died
1228      Conrad IV, King of Germany, born
1396      St. Stephen of Perm died (Feast Day)
1521      Magellan killed by the natives on Mactan Island
1564      William Shakespeare, poet-playwright, baptized
1573      Maria de' Medici, Queen of France, born
1607      Jamestown solonists sighted Virginia
```

```
1689      Peter the Great, Czar of Russia, clipped the
                beards and moustaches off his court
1718      Esek Hopkins, first Commodore of the U.S. Navy,
                born
1731      Daniel Defoe, novelist, died
1768      First art exhibit at England's Royal Academy
                opened
1771      Vassalboro and Winslow, Maine, incorporated
1782      Marie Amelie Therese, wife of King Louis
                Philippe of France, born
1785      John James Audubon, artist-naturalist, born
1798      Eugene Delacroix, French artist, born
1803      Meteorite rain fell on L'Aigle, France
1812      Alfred Krupp, German metallurgist, born
1822      Frederick Law Olmstead, landscape architect,
                born
1872      Mt. Vesuvius volcano erupted suddenly
1875      Syngman Rhee, Korean statesman, born
1882      Charles Darwin, naturalist, buried in West-
                minster Abbey
1893      Anita Loos, author, born
1907      Tercentenary Exposition of Jamestown, Virginia
                opened
1913      Wisconsin state flag adopted
          International Exposition, Ghent, Belgium,
                opened
1915      Italy declared war on Austro-Hungarian Empire
1923      George VI, King of England, married Lady
                Elizabeth Bowes-Lyon
1949      Transjordan changed its name to Jordan
1951      William N. Oatis, Associated Press correspon-
                dent, arrested in Czechoslovakia
                as a spy
1952      U.S. destroyer Hobson and carrier Wasp collided
                in the Atlantic
1954      Geneva Conference on Far Eastern Affairs opened
1957      Opening of Jamestown, Virginia's, 350th
                Anniversary Festival
1962      Ariel I satellite launched
1964      Tanzania (Tanganyika-Zanzibar) joined the United
                Nations (Union Day)
1908, 1981, 1987, 1992, 2071, 2076, 2082  Quasimodo or
                Low Sunday
```

April 27th

```
          Feast of St. Maughold
          Feast of St. Peter Canisius
          Feast of St. Toribio of Lima
1124 AD   King Alexander I of Scotland died
1172      King Henry II of England left Ireland
1278      St. Zita died (Feast Day; patron of maidservants
                and housekeepers)
```

1509	City of Venice, Italy, excommunicated by Pope Julius II
1605	Pope Leo XI died, 10 days after his coronation
1667	John Milton sold _Paradise Lost_ copyright for 10 English pounds
1682	Theodore III, Czar of Russia, died
1686	First charter granted for New York City
1737	Edward Gibbon, author of _Decline and Fall of the Roman Empire_, born
1798	U.S. Navy established
1813	Zebulon Pike, explorer, died
	U.S. forces captured Toronto, Canada
1816	First U.S. protective tariff law passed
1822	Ulysses Simpson Grant, U.S. President, born
1846	Christy Minstrels first appeared in New York City
1850	First American-owned steamship began commercial Atlantic crossings
1852	"Telegram" replaced "telegraphic dispatch"
1863	_Anglo-Saxon_ wrecked off Cape Race
1865	Cornell University (New York) incorporated
	Sultana, packed with Union prisoners, exploded on the Mississippi
1882	Ralph Waldo Emerson, philosopher-poet, died
1891	Ground broken for Grant's tomb in New York City
1892	Cornerstone for Grant's tomb laid
1893	Prototype of the modern typewriter patented
1897	Grant's tomb dedicated (New York City)
1898	Ludwig Bemelmans, creator of "Madeline," born
1914	American troops sent to Mexico (Mexican Revolution)
1920	Milton, in a Dusenberg, set a land-speed record of 156.046 mph
1926	_Chichibu_ ran aground off Horomushiro, Japan
1937	First Social Security payment made
1938	Zog I, King of Albania, married Geraldine, a Hungarian countess
1944	Jim Tobin pitched a no-hitter and Boston beat Brooklyn, 2-0
1960	Republic of Togo became independent
1961	Sierra Leone became an independent part of the British Commonwealth
	Explorer II satellite launched
1965	Edward R. Morrow, broadcaster, died
1967	First male heir to the Dutch throne in 3 generations, Willem-Alexander, born
1968	Tom Phoebus pitched a no-hitter and Baltimore beat Boston, 6-0
1970	Gypsy Rose Lee, entertainer, died
1971	Capt. Samuel L. Gravely, Jr. became the first black U.S. Admiral
1919, 1924, 1930, 2003, 2014, 2025, 2087, 2098	Quasimodo or Low Sunday

	Mars, Roman god of war, conceived
	Start of 6-day festival for Flora, Roman goddess of flowers
	Feast of St. Paul of the Cross
32 AD	Marcus Salvius Otho, Roman emperor, born
1180	King Philip II of France married Isabella of Hainaut
1220	Salisbury Cathdral construction began (England)
1442	Edward IV, King of England, born
1656	Vergulde Draeck, Dutch East Indiaman, sank off Australia
1708	Half of Kyoto, Japan, including the imperial palace, burned
1753	Franch Achard, discoverer of sugar-beet extraction, born
1754	Giovanni Piazzetta, Italian artist, born
1758	James Monroe, 5th U.S. President, born
1770	Captain Cook landed on Australia
1788	Maryland ratified the U.S. Constitution
1789	Mutiny took place on the Bounty
	Reveillon's wallpaper factory destroyed (Paris)
1817	Rush-Botot Treaty limited naval arms on the Great Lakes
1841	St. Peter Chanel, missionary to the South Seas, martyred (Feast Day)
1855	California imposed a $50 tax on every entering Chinese
1865	Sir Samuel Cunard, steamship line founder, died
	University Club founded in New York City
1881	Billy the Kid escaped his makeshift jail
1892	John Jacob Niles, folksinger, born
1894	The Iconoclast magazine founded by O. Henry in Texas
1910	Daily Mail's air context began, 15 miles 1 stop (England)
1913	Ken Purdy, writer, born
1921	Philadelphia construction wages reduced $1.16 to 88¢ per hour
1926	Parry-Thomas, in a Thomas-Special car, set a land-speed record of 170.624 mph
1942	Coffee rationing went into effect in the U.S.
1945	Mussolini, captured while trying to get to Switzerland, hanged
1947	Kon-Tiki sailed from Peru
1951	Robert Volger, U.S. businessman accused of spying, released by Hungary
1952	Truman ended national emergencies declared for World War II
1956	New York Coliseum, exhibition hall, opened (New York City)

```
1961      Warren Spahn pitched a no-hitter and Milwaukee
               beat San Francisco, 1-0
1965      U.S. Marines landed in the Dominican Republic
               to prevent a Communist coup
1967      Universal and International Exhibition (Expo
               '67) opened at Montreal
          South Streat Seaport Museum chartered (New York
               City
1969      Charles de Gaulle resigned as President of France
1970      McComb Area Feeder Pig Sale in Mississippi
          Festival of the Heavenly Queen (Hong Kong
               fishermen's goddess)
          Meteor 4, USSR weather satellite, launched
1971      Red Trillium bloomed in Massachusetts
          Goddess A-Ma Festival in Macao
1935, 1946, 1957, 2019, 2030, 2041, 2052  Quasimodo or
               Low Sunday


-------------------------------------------------------
April 29th
-------------------------------------------------------

          Focsani, Rumania's annual fair
 998 AD   Otto III, Holy Roman Emperor, took the Palace
               of St. Angelo, Italy
1109      St. Hugh of Cluny (Feast Day; invoked against
               fevers)
1111      St. Robert of Molesme died (Feast Day)
1307      Marmaduke de Tweng's first fair opened at
               Kendal, England
1430      Joan of Arc entered besieged Orleans (100
               Years' War)
1769      Arthur Wellesley, Duke of Wellington, victor at
               Waterloo, born
1792      Matthew Vassar, brewer, merchant, and college-
               founder, born
1818      Czar Alexander II of Russia born
1836      Simon Kenton, frontiersman, died
1842      Zipper patented
1853      Santa Anna resumed presidency of Mexico for the
               5th and last time
1857      First electric locomotive ran on the Baltimore
               and Ohio rail lines at 19 mph
1861      Maryland voted not to secede from the Union,
               52 to 13
1863      William Randolph Hearst, newspaper publisher,
               born
1878      First Gilbert elevated train ran in New York
               City
1881      Tararua wrecked off New Zealand
1889      Jenatzy, in a Jamais Contente Jenatzy car, set
               a land-speed record of 65.79 mph
1894      Unemployed persons marched on Washington
1899      "Duke" Ellington, musician-composer, born
1900      Casey Jones had his train wreck
```

```
1901        Emperor Hirohito, 12th to rule Japan, born
                      (National Holiday)
1905        Maloney's glider, launched from a hot-air
                      balloon, flew 20 minutes
1920        Contract awarded for grain elevator construc-
                      tion at Grand Forks, North Dakota
1925        First woman member, Dr. Florence Sabin,
                      elected to the National Academy
                      of Science
1926        General strike called for in England
1927        New Orleans saved from flooding by the
                      destruction of a levee below the
                      city
1947        Jim Ryun, runner, born
1954        Tibet recognized as part of Red China by India
1965        Explorer 27 launched to study Earth's gravity
1971        Israeli Independence Day
1962, 1973, 1984, 2057, 2068  Quasimodo or Low Sunday
```

April 30th

```
            Walpurgis Night Festival in Finland and Sweden
 463 BC     Solar eclipse
 259 AD     Sts. Marian and James martyred (Feast Day)
1380        St. Catherine of Siena, patron of Italian
                      nurses, died (Feast Day)
1450        Frederick of Hohenzollern invested as Elector
                      of Brandenberg
1492        Columbus got his commission of exploration
                      from Spain
1555        Marcellus Cervini, Pope Marcellus II, died of
                      a stroke after 3 weeks in office
1662        Mary II, Queen of England, born
1748        Jacques Louis-David, French artist, born
1778        Philips Academy, Andover, Massachusetts,
                      opened
1790        Samuel Heinicke, educator of the deaf and dumb,
                      died
1798        Congress created the U.S. Navy Department
1803        U.S. bought Louisiana  from Spain
1812        Louisiana became a state
1813        Astor's expedition of western exploration
                      returned to St. Louis, Missouri
1821        College of Detroit became the University of
                      Michigan
1827        Foundation stone of the University of London
                      laid
1832        Portland, Maine, got its city charter
1842        St. Joseph Cottolengo died (Feast Day
1853        First successful American-built clipper ship
                      launched
1861        Virginia state flag adopted
```

1871	Massacre of Apache Indians at Fort Grant, Arizona
1879	Sarah J. B. Hale, author of "Mary Had a Little Lamb," died
1883	Edouard Manet, French artist, died
1889	Washington Square Arch, New York City, dedicated
1900	Hawaii became a U.S. Territory
1908	Japanese ship Matsu Shima exploded off the Pescadores
1909	Juliana, Queen of the Netherlands, born (National Holiday in Holland and Surinam)
1915	Germans torpedoed U.S. tanker Gulflight
1918	Exile of Russian Imperial Family to Ekaterinburg
1923	Mossamedes ran aground at Cape Frio, Africa
1936	New Hampshire got its first legal sweepstakes lottery since 1894
1939	Public television broadcasts in the U.S. began
1940	Tex Carleton pitched a no-hitter and Brooklyn beat Cincinnati 3-0
1945	Adolf Hitler committed suicide
1946	Bob Feller pitched a no-hitter and Cleveland beat New York, 1-0
1947	Boulder Dam renamed Hoover Dam
1948	Organization of the American States charter signed
1952	U.N. forces stopped a massive Chinese offensive in Korea
1965	Brooklyn Heights, settled in 1634, became a National Landmark
1967	Barber and Miller pitched a no-hitter but Baltimore lost to Detroit, 1-0 on errors
1972	Last run made by the Brighton Belle, famous English train
1905, 1916, 2000, 2079	Quasimodo or Low Sunday

Full Moon - Flower Moon, Milk Moon
First Monday - Wool and Cattle Fair at Tenterden, Kent,
                England
First Friday - Arbor Day in Rhode Island
First Friday after May 1st - Arbor Day in Idaho
First Saturday - Kentucky Derby Horse Race at
                  Churchill Downs
First Sunday (of every year ending in 0 - First of the
                  season's Passion Plays at Oberam-
                  mergau, Germany
2nd Sunday - Mother's Day
              Diaper Day at Jacksonville Beach, Florida
Third Saturday - Armed Forces Day
Last Monday - Memorial Day observances (as of 1971)
First week - Bangtail Muster Festival at Alice Springs,
                Australia

May 1st
_____

              International Worker's Day in Venezuela
              May Day (Political celebrations in Communist
                        countries; Morris Dancers in Eng-
                        land)
              Feast of St. Joseph the Worker (Malta)
              Feast of Sts. Philip and James
              Loyalty Day in U.S.
              Start of Festival of St. Efisio at Pula, Sardinia
              Dedication Day of the Good Goddess's temple on
                        the Avantine in Rome
              Tivoli Gardens, Copenhagen, opens for the sea-
                        son
              St. George's Day in Greece
              Race of the Old Man in Arachova, Greece

```
            Fair at Penryn, Cornwall, England
            Feast of St. Brieuc
            Lei Day in Hawaii
            Labor Day in Aruba, Bulgaria, Burundi, Costa
                    Rica, Dahomey, Honduras, Iceland,
                    Kenya, Malagasy Republic, Philip-
                    pines, Poland, Uganda, Yugoslavia
  305 AD   Roman Emperor Diocletian abdicated
  686      St. Ultan died (Feast Day)
  1308     King Albert of Germany murdered by his disin-
                    herited nephew
  1316     Edward Bruce crowned King of Ireland
  1345     St. Peregrine Laziosi died (Feast Day)
  1572     Pope Pius V died
  1625     King Charles I of England married Henrietta
                    Marie of France by proxy
  1693     Weekly postal service begun between Portsmouth,
                    N.H. and Virginia
  1703     Czar Peter the Great founded St. Petersburg
                    (Leningrad), Russia
  1704     First American newspaper advertisement ap-
                    peared (Boston News-letter)
  1778     Third and unbreakable chain strung across the
                    Hudson River at West Point
  1784     New York University established
  1792     Rufus Porter, founder of Scientific American
                    magazine, born
  1795     U.S. flag changed to 13 red and white stripes
                    plus 15 white stars on a blue field
  1815     Georgetown University, Washington, D.C.,
                    founded
  1841     First emigrant train for California left
                    Independence, Mo.
  1851     Great Exposiiton, Crystal Palace, opened in
                    London
  1854     Construction of Great Eastern steamship began
  1860     First patent issued for a shaving mug to
                    Thomas E. Hughes
  1861     Erie Railroad began operating a ferry between
                    New York and New Jersey
  1862     General Butler, Union, took control of New
                    Orleans
  1867     Treaty of London guaranteed neutrality of
                    Luxembourg
  1871     First U.S. postal card issued
  1873     International Exposition opened in Vienna
            David Livingstone, African explorer, died
  1885     First skyscraper, 10 stories, with a steel
                    skeleton, begun (Chicago)
  1893     Columbian Exposition, Chicago, opened
  1896     Nasr-ed-Din, Shah of Iran, assassinated
  1898     Admiral Dewey was victorious at Manila Bay,
                    sinking 7 Spanish ships
```

```
1901       Pan-American Exposition opened (Buffalo, New
                York)
1904       Anton Dvorak, composer, died
1909       Kate Smith, singer, born
1912       Winthrop Rockefeller, Arkansas governor, born
1915       German ads in American newspapers warned that
                ships flying the British flag were
                subject to being sunk
1916       Irish revolt leaders imprisoned
1917       Glenn Ford, actor, born
           Carranza became legal president of Mexico
1918       City of Athens involved in a collision off
                Delaware
           Jack Parr, television personality, born
1920       Princess Margaret of Sweden died
1931       Empire State Building completed and dedicated
1936       Haile Selassie, Ethiopian emperor, escaped
                Italian advance
1941       Howard Johnson, songwriter ("When the Moon Comes
                Over the Mountain"), died
1948       People's Republic of Korea formed (Communist
                North Korea)
1958       Memorial to the People's Heroes completed in
                Peking, China
1960       U.S. U-2 reconnaisance plane shot down by the
                USSR
1963       James W. Whittaker became the first American
                to reach the top of Mt. Everest
2011, 2095  Quasimodo or Low Sunday
```

May 2nd
```
           Adoration of the Cross (Venezuela)
373 AD     St. Athanasius died (Feast Day)
903        Boris I, Tsar of Bulgaria and Orthodox Saint,
                died
1459       St. Antoninus died
1519       Leonardo da Vinci, artist-inventor, died
1670       Hudson Bay Fur Company chartered
1729       Catherine the Great, Russian Empress, born
1740       Transit of Mercury
1780       French set sail to support the Americans
                in the Revolution
1791       British man-of-war Alligator became the first
                British ship to salute the U.S.
                flag
1813       Battle of Lutzen (Prussia and Russia against
                Napoleon)
1814       King Louis XVIII entered Paris, his capital
1840       The Log Cabin, weekly campaign paper for
                William Henry Harrison, begun
```

```
1842      Fremont set out on his expedition to the Rocky
                Mountains
1863      Gen. "Stonewall" Jackson shot at Chancellors-
                ville, Va.
1865      $100,000 reward offered for the capture of
                Jefferson Davis
1880      Columbia became the first steamboat with
                electricity (San Francisco to
                Portland, Oregon)
1885      Good Housekeeping magazine first published
1890      Oklahoma became a U.S. territory
1903      Dr. Benjamin Spock, pediatrician-writer,
                born
1904      Bing Crosby, singing actor, born
1917      First Liberty Loan subscriptions started
1923      First non-stop transcontinental flight made
1926      "Man-eating leopard of Rudraprayag," credited
                with 125 deaths, killed
1927      Alaskan territorial flag adopted
1931      First televised wedding performed
1932      Congress accepted Theodore Roosevelt Island
1935      King Faisal III of Iraq born
1945      Russian troops captured Berlin
1952      First jet plane passenger service began (London
                to Johannesburg, South Africa)
1960      Caryl Chessman executed, 12 years after being
                convicted of robbery and
                kidnapping
1964      Mt. Gosaintham in Tibet climbed by a Chinese
                team who set a bust of Mao Tse
                Tung on the mountaintop
1965      Early Bird television satellite first used
1969      Israeli Independence Day
          Wawona Tunnel Tree, a sequoia in Yosemite
                National Park, was discovered to
                have fallen
1970      Labor Day in the Cameroons
          San Gennaro Festival in Naples, Italy
1971      Buddha's Birthday in Hong Kong
1972      J. Edgar Hoover, head of the FBI since its
                inception, died
1943, 2038  Quasimodo or Low Sunday
```

May 3rd

```
          Japanese Constitution Day
          Feast of St. Alexander
          Bury, Lancashire, England fair
          Invention of the Holy Cross
          Beginning of 3 days of kite battles at Hama-
                matsu, Japan
          Girls' Festival (Doll Displays) in Japan
```

```
328 AD   St. Helena for the Cross of Christ at Jerusalem
         died          died (Feast Day)
1074     St. Theodosius of the Caves died (Feast Day)
1270     King Bela IV of Hungary died
1469     Mathias I, King of Hungary, elected
                         King of Bohemia
         Machiavelli, Italian statesman-writer, born
1471     Battle of Tewkesbury ended the War of the
                         Roses (England)
1679     James Sharp, Scotch Episcopalian archbishop,
                         beaten to death
1772     Christian Indians, founders of the New Phila-
                         delphia, Ohio, arrived there
1786     Transit of Mercury
1810     Lord Byron, the poet, swam the Hellespont
1814     King Louis XVIII installed on the French throne
1826     Beginning of a general strike in England
1833     Mormons adopted the name Latter-day Saints
1851     America's Cup yacht America christened in East
                         Boothbay, Maine
1887     Tombstone, Arizona, rocked by an earthquake
1895     Rhodesia named by proclamation
1898     Golda Meir, Israeli Prime Minister, born
1907     Earl Wilson, columnist, born
1913     William Inge, playwright, born
1919     Airplane passenger service began
1921     "Sugar Ray" Robinson, boxer, born
1926     Beginning of a general strike in England
1933     Nellie Taylor Ross named first woman director
                         of the U.S. Mint
1952     First commercial jet plane went into service
         First plane landed at the geographic North Pole
1965     El Salvador rocked by an earthquake
1967     Replica of the America's Cup yacht America
                         christened in East Boothbay, Maine
1970     Corn Dance at Cochiti Pueblo, New Mexico
         Ceremonial races and corn dance at Taos Pueblo,
                         New Mexico
         Third Annual Flowering Crabapple Festival at
                         Canfield, Ohio
         Tenth anniversary of Brasilia celebrated
                         (Brazil)
         Old Dover Day, Dover, Delaware
         Florida Folk Festival at White Springs
         Santa Cruz Feast, Peumo, Chile
```

May 4th

```
         Primary Election Day in Ohio
         Rhode Island Independence Day (1776; declared
                         itself free from England)
         Youth Festival in Communist China
```

        End of the 6-day festival honoring Flora,
            Roman goddess
        Feast of St. Florian (patron of Austria;
            invoked against fire)
 387 AD St. Monica died (Feast Day)
1038   St. Gothard died (Feast Day)
1244   Catholic hierarchy captured by Pisa in a dis-
            pute between Pope Gregory IX
            and the Holy Roman Emperor
1483   King Edward V of England arrived in London
1493   Columbus was given a Spanish coat of arms
1626   Peter Minuit, purchaser, landed on Manhattan
            Island
1769   Sir Thomas Lawrence, English artist, born
1780   First English Derby horse race run at Epsom
            Downs
1796   Horace Mann, educational reformer, born
1800   Napoleon proclaimed Emperor of France
1803   John H. B. Latrobe, artist-philanthropist,
            born
1807   Russia defeated by France at the battle of
            Friedland
1824   Rufus Putnam, "father of Ohio," died
1826   Frederick Church, artist, born
1827   John Speke, discoverer of the source of the
            Nile, born
        Georges Karaiskakis, Greek independence leader,
            killed in action
1849   Battle of Mestre (Austria-Hungary)
1850   Part of San Francisco destroyed by fire
1851   Start of a fire that destroyed 3/4 of San
            Francisco
        3/4 of St. Louis, Missouri destroyed by fire
1873   William H. McGuffey, educator and founder of
            the Eclectic Reader, died
1886   Haymarket labor rioting broke out in Chicago
1889   Francis, Cardinal Spellman, born
        Maritime Canal Company of Nicaragua organized
1896   The Daily Mail, London newspaper, founded
1897   Disastrous fire in a Paris motion-picture
            theater
1927   Academy of Motion Picture Arts and Sciences
            formed
1930   Roberta Peters, opera singer, born
1945   German troops began to surrender
1969   Clam Prix at Ocean Shores, Washington
1970   Labor Day on Antigua

May 5th

        Children's Day, a Japanese Holiday Feast of
            Banners for boys

```
                   Boys' Day in Communist China (reed-wrapped
                             cumplings eaten)
                   Korean Festival of Tano (youth activities)
   449 AD          St. Hilary of Arles died (Feast Day)
   884             Pope Marinus I died (Feast Day)
  1045             Gregory VI elected Pope
  1260             St. Jutta died (Feast Day)
  1292             Adolph of Nassau became King of Germany
  1352             Rupert, King of Germany, born
  1474             Cornerstone laid for Magdalen College,
                             Oxford, England
  1572             Pope St. Pius V died (Feast Day)
  1606             Jean Nicot, French diplomat who brought
                             tobacco back to his country,
                             died
  1617             Nicholas Hilliard named English royal artist
  1673             England recaptured St. Helena Island
  1705             Leopold I, Holy Roman Emperor and King of
                             Germany, died
 1707, 1753, 1832, 1957  Transits of Mercury
  1747             Leopold II, Holy Roman Emperor, born
  1760             Earl of Ferrer hanged for murder, the last
                             English nobleman to die a felon
  1778             George Washington announced France's alliance
                             with the U.S.
  1818             Karl Marx, founder of Communism, born
  1821             Napoleon Bonaparte died on St. Helena Island
  1826             Eugenie, wife of Napoleon III of France, born
  1827             Andrew Johnson, U.S. President, married
                             Eliza McCardle
  1831             Detroit Free Press newspaper founded
  1842             Great fire burned in Hamburg, Germany
  1846             National Medical Association founded (U.S.)
  1847             American Medical Association founded out of
                             the National Medical Association
  1851             San Francisco's fire put out, but 3/4 of the
                             city destroyed
  1862             Battle of Williamsburg, Virginia
  1864             Battle of the Wilderness
                   Confederate ironclad Albemarle defeated Union
                             sidewheeler Sassacus
  1868             Memorial Day established for May 30 by the Grand
                             Army of the Republic
  1871             Cochise and the Apaches defeated the 3rd Cavalry
                             at Bear Springs
  1883             Rev. Josiah Henson, the original Uncle Tom, died
  1884             Start of two days of financial panic in New
                             York City
  1890             Christopher Morley, poet-novelist, born
  1902             Bret Harte, author, died
  1906             Freer Gallery of Art given to the Smithsonian
                             Institution
  1912             Pravda, Russian newspaper, first published
  1914             Tyrone Power, actor, died
```

```
1925      John Scopes arrested for teaching theory of
              evolution
1936      Italian Premier Mussolini announced annexation
              of Ethiopia
1938      French Lafayette burned in drydock at Le Havre
1941      Haile Selassie returned to Addis Ababa, Ethio-
              pia (Liberation Day National
              Holiday)
1954      Netherlands Carillon installed in a temporary
              tower in Washington, D.C.
1955      West Germany became a sovereign state
1960      Netherlands Carillon permanently installed and
              dedicated
1961      Alan B. Shepherd in Mercury's Freedom 7 made the
              first U.S. manned space flight
1962      "Bo" Belinsky pitched a no-hitter and Los
              Angeles beat Baltimore 2-0
1967      New York World Journal Telegram ceased
              publication
1970      Coronation Anniversary in Thailand
```

```
==========================================================
May 6th
==========================================================
```

```
          Fair at Walsall, Staffordshire, England
          Feast of St. John of Damascus
2348 BC   Noah's ark grounded on Mt. Ararat, according to
              Blair and Usher
1491      Moses climbed Mt. Sinai
 973 AD   Henry II "the Saint," Holy Roman Emperor, born
1092      Lincoln, England, cathedral consecrated
1210      Rheims, France, cathedral destroyed by fire
1211      New Rheims cathedral begun
1501      British brig Speedy captured Spanish frigate
              El Gamo
1527      Duke of Bourbon killed after sacking Rome with
              the Lutheran Army
1536      Jacques Cartier's third expedition left Canada
              for France
1542      St. Francis Xavier arrived in Goa, India
1545      King Henry VIII's Primer henceforth to be used
              in all English churches
1634      Beacon set on Beacon Hill, Boston
1682      King Louis XIV of France moved into Versailles
1697      Trinity Church founded in New York City
1758      Robespierre, French politician, born
1781      Battle of Newport, Rhode Island
1808      First ocean-going steamboat completed its
              maiden voyage (Hoboken, New
              Jersey, to Philadelphia)
1835      New York Herald began publication
1840      First postage stamp, "black penny," issued in
              England with adhesive on it
```

	Father Gallitzin, "apostle of the Alleghanies," died
1851	John Gorrie received the patent for basic modern refrigeration method
1856	Sigmund Freud, psychologist, born
	Robert E. Peary, Arctic explorer, born
1859	Gregory gold mine discovered in Colorado
	Alexander von Humboldt, explorer, died
1861	Arkansas seceded from the Union
1862	Henry David Thoreau, naturalist-philosopher, died
1870	Sir James Young Simpson, anesthesia pioneer, died
1877	Crazy Horse, Sioux Indian, surrendered
1878, 2003	Transits of Mercury
1882	William, last Crown Prince of Germany, born
1884	New York Produce Exchange opened
1889	Universal Exposition at Paris, with the Eiffel Tower, opened
1895	Rudolph Valentino, actor, born
1896	Samuel P. Langley tried to fly his experimental plane
1908	Manoel became King of Poland
1910	King Edward VII of England died
1915	Orson Wells, actor, born
	Theodore H. White, journalist-author, born
1916	First telephone conversation with a ship at sea took place
1919	Frank Baum, creator of <u>The Wizard of Oz</u>, died
1931	Willy Mays, baseball great, born
1937	<u>Hindenberg</u> zeppelin exploded and burned (Lakehurst, N.J.)
1941	Stalin succeeded Molotov as Premier of USSR
	Igor Sikorsky first showed his helicopter
1942	Corregidor surrendered to the Japanese
1951	Cliff Chambers pitched a no-hitter and Pittsburgh beat Boston 3-0
1953	"Bobo" Holloman pitched a no-hitter and St. Louis beat Philadelphia 2-0
1954	Roger Bannister ran the first sub-4-minute mile (3:59.4)
1960	Princess Margaret Rose of England married Anthony Armstrong Jones, photographer
1970	Procession of St. Martin de Porres, first black saint, in Peru
	Coronation Day Anniversary, holiday in Thailand
1972	Start of a weekend of Turtle Races at Joshua Tree, Calif.

```
685 AD   Marwan, Moslem caliph, died
721      St. John of Beverly died (Feast Day)
973      Otto I, "the Great," Holy Roman Emperor,
            died
1577     Queen Elizabeth I forbade Puritan meetings in
            England
1655     England took the island of Jamaica from Spain
1665     Great festival held at Versailles, France
1718     Mary of Modena, widow of King James II of
            England, died
1724     Catherine I crowned Empress-consort of Russia
1777     U.S.S. Suprise captured H.M.S. Prince of Orange
            in the English Channel
1739     First U.P. Presidential inaugural ball held
            (New York City)
1799, 1924   Transits of Mercury
1800     Indiana became a U.S. Territory separate from
            the Ohio Territory
1812     Robert Browning, poet, born
1826     Varina (Mrs. Jefferson) Davis, first lady of
            the Confederacy, born
1833     Johannes Brahms, composer, born
1834     Coorg Province of India annexed to the terri-
            tory of the British East India
            Company
1840     Peter I. Tchaikovsky, composer, born
1842     Disastrous fire in Hamburg, Germany, finally
            put out
1847     City College of New York chartered
1873     Salmon P. Chase, U.S. statesman, died
1875     Schiller wrecked off the Scilly Islands
1884     End of two days of financial panic in New
            York City
1891     First successful photographs of solar flares
            taken
1892     Archibald MacLeish, poet, born
1901     Gary Cooper, actor, born
1915     Lusitania sunk off Ireland by a German sub-
            marine; 1,198 died
1919     Japan was given control of former German Paci-
            fic Islands north of the Equator
1923     Anne Baxter, actress, born
1933     Johnny Unitas, football player, born
1939     Italy and Germany announced their military
            and political alliance
1945     Germany surrendered unconditionally to the
            Allies at Reims, France
1963     Telstar II, communications satellite, launched
1969     Cunard liner, Queen Elizabeth II, sailed
            into New York
1970     Holy Blood Procession at Bruges, Belgium
```

                    Ascension Day in Dahomey
                    Sardinian Cavalcade (Folk Festival) held at
                         Sassari (& 1971)
       1971   Mohammed's Birthday in Malaysia

May 8th
_____

                    Helston, Cornwall, England holiday
                    Fair at Sherborne, England
                    Feast of St. Victor
       615 AD   Pope Boniface IV died
       1147   St. Peter of Tarentaise died (Feast Day)
       1222   Henry VII crowned King of Germany
       1429   Seige of Orleans, France, raised (100 Years'
                         War)
       1444   St. Michael, one of the Azores Islands,
                         discovered
       1521   St. Peter Canisius born
       1541   Hernando DeSoto discovered the Mississippi
                         River
       1559   Act of Supremacy made the Anglican (Episco-
                         palian) Church the state religion
                         of England with the ruler as head
                         of the Church
       1660   Monarchy restored in England with proclamation
                         of Charles II as King
       1758   Pope Benedict XIV died
       1769   New York Chronicle newspaper founded
       1806   Robert Morris, signer of the Declaration of
                         Independence, died
       1819   Kamehameha, King of Hawaii, died
       1820   Act of Congress created the U.S. Botanical
                         Gardens
       1823   "Home, Sweet Home" first heard, in the produc-
                         tion of Clari, or the Maid of
                         Milan opera
       1828   Jean Henri Dunant, Swiss philanthropist and
                         founder of the Red Cross, born
                         (Red Cross Day)
       1844   Echigo, Japan, rocked by an earthquake
       1845, 1970   Transits of Mercury
       1861   Richmond, Virginia, became the capital of the
                         Confederacy
       1862   Confederate forces evacuated Pensacola,
                         Florida
       1869   Religious freedom proclaimed in Spain
       1879   George B. Selden applied for the first
                         U.S. automobile patent
       1884   Harry S. Truman, 33rd U.S. President, born
       1895   Thomas B. Costain, author, born
                    Fulton J. Sheen, Roman Catholic clergyman
                         and writer, born

```
1899      Boundary between Mexico and Guatemala set
1902      Mt. Peelee volcano on the island of Martinique
                    erupted, wiping out St. Pierre
                    and 30,000 people
1905      First U.S. transcontinental auto race began
1906      Roberto Rossellini, filmmaker, born
1929      Jan Mayen, Arctic island, annexed to Norway
1942      U.S. carrier Lexington sunk in the Battle of
                    the Coral Sea but the Japanese
                    were defeated
1945      Germany surrendered (V-E Day)
1954      Dien Bien Phu, Vietnam fell to the Communist
                    forces
1968      Jim Hunter pitched a perfect game and Oakland
                    beat Minnesota, 4-0
1970      Last Day of week-long Bangtail Muster Festival
                    at Alice Springs, Australia
          Inferno Slalom Ski race held at Tuckerman's
                    Ravine, N.H.
```

May 9th
_____

```
          National Liberation Day (Czechoslovakia)
          Feast of St. Christopher (Orthodox)
 389 AD   St. Gregory of Nazianzus died (Feast Day)
1204      Baldwin I elected Emperor of Rumania
1216      Droitwich, England fair held
1386      Treaty of Windsor allied England and Portugal
1476      Charles, Duke of Burgundy, reviewed his troops
                    near Lausanne, Switzerland
1502      Columbus left Spain on his last voyage
1598      King Henry IV of France entered Rennes,
                    Brittany in state
1671      England's royal jewels stolen from the Tower
                    of London
1689      Free government restored in Connecticut with the
                    recovery of the Oak Tree Charter
1754      First newspaper cartoon appeared (Philadelphia
                    Gazette)
1763      Pontiac and the Ottowa Indians attacked Detroit
1781      Pensacola, Florida, captured by the Spanish and
                    French from the British
1791      Francis Hopkinson, signer of the Declaration of
                    Independence, died
1800      John Brown, abolitionist-raider, born
1859      First mail coach of the Leavenworth and Pike's
                    Peak Express Line reached Denver,
                    Colorado
1865      Jefferson Davis was captured by the U.S.
                    Cavalry
1879      Fort Assinniboine established in Montana
1881      Phoenix, Arizona, adopted its seal
```

1882	Henry J. Kaiser, industrialist, born
1891	Transit of Mercury
1902	Ohio state flag adopted
1903	Paul Gaugain, French artist, died
1908	U.S. Senate voted against establishing Mothers' Day
1914	Mothers' Day established by Presidential proclamation
1923	King and Queen of England received by the Pope
1926	Admiral Byrd flew over the North Pole
1927	First Australian Parliament met at Canberra
1928	Pancho Gonzales, tennis player, born
1929	Solar eclipse
1945	Date set for end of U.S. operations in Europe with respect to World War II
1946	Victor Emmanuel III, King of Italy, abdicated
1949	Prince Louis II, ruler of Monaco, died
1951	European Coal and Steel Plan proposed
1961	East Pakistan hit by typhoon and tidal waves
1965	Luna IV, Russian moon shot, launched
1970	Feast of the goddess A-Ma held in Macao
1971	Cats' Festival at Ypres, Belgium
	Buddha's Birthday of Wesak Day in Ceylon, Korea, and Malaysia
1972	Lilac Festival at Ponoare, Rumania

May 10th

	Skunks born
	Confederate Memorial Day (North and South Carolina
1130 AD	St. Isidore the Farm-servant died (Feast Day)
1291	Angels carried the home of Mary and Joseph to Dalmatia
1459	St. Antonino died (Feast Day)
1501	An expedition left Europe to explore Brazil
1510	Botticelli, Italian artist, died
1534	Jacques Cartier sighted Newfoundland
1730	George Ross, signer of the Declaration of Independence, born
1774	King Louis XV died
1775	Queen Caroline Matilda of Denmark died
	Americans captured Fort Ticonderoga from the British
	Second Continental Congress first met
1796	French battled Austrians at Lodi, Italy
1801	Tripoli declared war on the U.S. over tribute
1818	Paul Revere, riding silversmith, died
1823	First steamboat up the Mississippi River arrived at Fort Snelling, Minnesota

1845   New World, a New York fiction weekly, ceased
                   publication
1849   Astor Place riots in New York City (revenge for
                   treatment of an American actor
                   in England)
           Hokusai Katsushuka, Japanese artist, died
1857   Sepoy Rebellion began in India
1863   General "Stonewall" Jackson, shot at Chancel-
                   lorsville, died
1864   Union victory at the second Battle of the
                   Wilderness or Spotsylvania
                   Courthouse
1865   Jefferson Davis, captured, charged with treason
1869   Transcontinental railroad completed at Promon-
                   tory Point, Utah
1871   Treaty of Frankfurt ended Franco-Prussian War
1873   Final defeat of the Modoc Indian War in Calif.-
                   Oregon
1879   A meteor fell near Estherville, Iowa
1899   Fred Astaire, dancing actor, born
1900   Yoshihito, Japanese crown prince, married
                   Princess Sadako
1902   David O. Selznick, film producer, born
1904   Henry Morton Stanley, African explorer, died
1905   First session of the Duma, Russian parliament,
                   opened
1908   Mothers' Day first celebrated
1918   British ship Santa Anna torpedoed in the
                   Mediterranean
1919   Victory Liberty Loan, the fifth and last,
                   ended
1924   J. Edgar Hoover named director of new Federal
                   Bureau of Investigation
1930   Edward L. Stratmeyer, author of Rover Boys,
                   Tom Swift, Bobbsey Twins, etc.,
                   died
1940   Germany invaded Holland, Luxembourg, and
                   Belgium
1943   Peru's National Library destroyed by fire
1945   A U.S. airplane accepted the first post-war
                   surrender of a German submarine
1970   Lilac Festival at Ponoare, Rumania
           Cat Festival at Ypres, Belgium

May 11th
_____

           Feast of St. Asaph
           Feast of Sts. Philip and St. James the Less
           Feast of St. Methodius
  14 AD   Census of Roman citizens completed
   330   Constantinople dedicated to the Blessed Virgin
                   Mary and inaugurated as the Roman
                   capital of the East

433	Justinian I, "the Great," eastern Roman Emperor, born
603	St. Comgall died (Feast Day)
994	St. Mayeul died (Feast Day)
1509	Louis II crowned King of Bohemia
1625	Henrietta Marie of France married by proxy to King Charles I of England
1643	Mercurius Civicus, first regular illustrated periodical in London, appeared
1647	Peter Stuyvesant arrived in New Amsterdam (New York City)
1706	Solar eclipse
1745	British and Germans defeated by French at Fontenoy in the war over Austrian Succession
1751	Pennsylvania Hospital, Philadelphia, chartered
1779	John Hart, signer of the Declaration of Independence, died
1844	Littell's Living Age magazine founded in Boston
1852	Charles W. Fairbanks, U.S. vice-president, born
1858	Minnesota became a state (Minnesota Day holiday)
1860	Garabaldi landed at Marsala (struggle for Italian unification)
1862	Confederates scuttled their ironclad Merrimack
1864	Union cavalry victory at Yellow Tavern, Virginia
1865	Kukule discovered the benzene theory
1866	"Black Friday," financial panic in London
1888	Irving Berlin, composer, born
1892	Margaret Rutherford, actress, born
1898	U.S. Marines landed at Guantanomo Bay, Cuba
	Battle of Manila Bay began
1904	Salvador Dali, Spanish artist, born
1910	Glacier National Park created
1915	American College of Physicians chartered
1939	Six-month border dispute began between Japanese Manchuria and Russian Mongolia
1940	New York World's Fair opened for the second season
1944	Frederick Faust, author as "Max Brand," died
1945	373 killed when the U.S. carrier Bunker Hill was damaged
1949	Israel joined the United Nations (Official Israeli Independence Day holiday)
1955	Japanese ferry Shian Maru involved in a collision in the Inland Sea
1963	Sandy Koufax pitched a no-hitter and Los Angeles beat San Francisco 8-0
1970	Decoration Day in Liberia

	Feast of Sts. Pankratus, Liberatus, and Servatius
	Fatima Pilgrimage in Portugal
	Feast of St. Germanus of Constantinople
	Feast of Sts. Nereus and Achilleus, martyrs
20 BC	Treaty between Rome and Parthia returned to Rome standards that had been captured 33 years before
403 AD	St. Epiphanius of Salamis died (Feast Day)
1003	Pope Sylvester II died
1310	54 Knights Templar burned as relapsed heretics in France
1349	Fourth new vicar appointed to Shaftsbury, England, church when predecessors died of the plague
1364	First University endowed in Cracow, Poland
1539	DeSoto left Cuba searching for the 7 Cities of Gold
1588	Day of the Barricades in Paris, France
1621	Edward Winslow married Susanna White, the first such to take place in Plymouth Colony (Massachusetts)
1641	William II, Prince of Orange, married Princess Mary of England
1653	Construction began on the Wall Street wall (New York City)
1670	Augustus II "the Strong," King of Poland, born
1768	Dolly Madison, First Lady, born
1780	Charleston, South Carolina, fell to the British
1781	St. Ignatius of Laconi died (Feast Day)
1789	First meeting of the Society of Tammany (New York City)
1803	Justin Liebig, discoverer of chloroform, born
1812	Edward Lear, English artist-writer, born
1814	Robert Paine, signer of the Declaration of Independence, died
1820	Florence Nightingale, nurse, born
1864	Third Battle of the Wilderness
1875	First shut-out in a baseball game, Chicago over St. Louis, 1-0
1880	Lincoln Ellsworth, explorer-author, born
1881	Tunesia became a French Protectorate
1914	First national observance of Mothers' Day
1921	Farley Mowat, author, born
1925	Amy Lowell, poet, died
	Yogi Berra, baseball player, born
1926	End of a paralyzing general strike in England

	Amundsen, Ellsworth, and party flew over the North Pole in a dirigible
1937	King George VI and Queen Elizabeth of England crowned in Westminster Abbey
1949	Berlin blockade lifted
1955	Last train of New York City's Third Avenue El ran
	Sam Jones pitched a no-hitter and Chicago beat Pittsburgh, 4-0
1956	Carl Erskin pitched a no-hitter and Brooklyn beat New York 3-0
1958	Body of unknown soldier from World War II chosen in Paris
1965	Barisal in East Pakistan struck by cyclone and tidal waves
1970	Buddha's Birthday celebration in Hong Kong
1971	Southwestern Turkey rocked by earthquakes

May 13th

	Second day of Fatima Pilgrimage in Portugal and Macao
	Feast of St. Erconwald
	Feast of St. Robert Bellarmine
	Start of 24 hours of sunlight, daily at Hammerfest, Norway
	Walrus calves born
	Feast of St. Servatius (invoked against rodents and leg diseases and for success of enterprises)
	Fair at Lowestoft, Suffolk, England
	Fair at Lymington, Hampshire, England
1028 AD	St. Euthymius the Enlightener died (Feast Day)
1390	King Robert II of Scotland died
1515	Mary, sister of King Henry VIII of England, widow of King Louis XII of France, married Charles, Duke of Suffolk against her brother's wishes, this time in England
1572	Hugo Buoncompagne elected Pope (Gregory XIII)
1607	Jamestown, Virginia colony founded by 105 Englishmen
1645	Venice defeated Turkey at the Battle of the Dardanelles
1717	"The Potato War" over Bavarian Succession ended with the Treaty of Teschen
1769	John VI, King of Portugal, born
1779	Marie Theresa, Archduchess of Austria and Queen of Hungary and Bohemia, born
1783	Society of the Cincinnati, first U.S. veterans' organization, formed

1830	Ecuador became a republic and independent of Colombia
1834	St. Andrew Fournet died (Feast Day)
1842	Sir Arthur Sullivan, British composer of operettas, born
1846	U.S. declared war on Mexico
1857	Michigan opened the first state agricultural college
1859	Queensland, Australia, became a separate state from New South Wales
1865	Last engagement of the Civil War, the Confederate victory at Palo Pinto, Texas
1871	Italy declared the Pope sovereign only in the Vatican, Castel Gondolfa, and the Lateran
1882	Georges Braque, French artist, born
1883	James Young, pioneer in the petroleum industry, died
1884	Cyrus McCormick, harvester inventor, born
1885	Juliana Ewing, children's author, died
1886	New York State created a commission to report on the humane and practical methods of executing the death sentence
1890	Louisiana Lottery Co. offered the state $1 million annually for the privilege of operating
1907	Daphne DuMaurier, novelist, born
1914	Joe Louis, boxer, born
1915	British ship Goliath torpedoed by a Turkish destroyer
1916	"Preparedness Parade" held in New York City
1918	First U.S. airmail postage stamps issued
1927	Juan Gris, Spanish artist, died
1936	Baker Island in the Pacific placed under the control of the U.S. Department of Interior
1940	"Blood, Tears, Toil, and Sweat" speech made in Parliament by Winston Churchill
1947	U.S. Senate approved the Taft-Hartley Act
1949	Thomas Clark Hinkle, children's author, died
1954	U.S. and Canada joined for construction of the St. Lawrence Seaway
1960	Mt. Dhaulagirl, 26,810 feet tall in Nepal, climbed by a Swiss team
1970	Peter Stuyvesant Day on Curaco

May 14th

Feast of St. Michael Garicoits
Feast of St. Pachomius
Unification Day in Liberia
Fair at Newark, Nottinghamshire, England
| 637 AD | St. Carthage died (Feast Day) |

964	Pope John XII died, unshriven
1264	Battle of Lewes, England (Henry III against the Earl of Leicester)
1316	Charles IV, King of Bohemia and Holy Roman Emperor, born
1491	Modern-day Passover observances began
1494	Columbus discovered Jamaica
1553	Marguerite de Valois, queen of Navarre, born
1608	Charles the Great, King of Lorraine, died
1609	Henry Hudson began the voyage that sent him up the Hudson River
1610	King Henry IV of France and Navarre stabbed
1643	King Louis XIII of France died
1675	Warrant issued for rebuilding St. Paul's Cathedral, London
1686	Gabriel D. Fahrenheit, German physicist, born
1710	King Adolphus Frederick of Sweden born
1764	St. Paul's Chapel begun in New York City
1771	King Louis XVIII of France married Louise Marie Josephine of Savoy
1775	William Penn Academy became the College of Pennsylvania (now the University of Pennsylvania)
1780	Louisville, Kentucky, incorporated
1787	A convention met in Philadelphia to draft the Constitution
1796	First smallpox injection given by Edward Jenner
1804	Lewis and Clark expedition left St. Louis, Missouri
1842	Illustrated London News first appeared
1851	Erie Railroad opened from Piermont to Dunkirk, New York
1856	Stock for the U.S. Army's first and only camel corps, 34 of them, arrived in Texas
1861	Robert E. Lee became a Confederate Brigadier General
	George B. McClellan became a Union Major General
1863	Union forces captured Jackson, Mississippi
1879	Art Institute of Chicago incorporated
1881	St. Mary Mazzarello died (Feast Day)
1902	Donald Barr Chidsey, author, born
1912	King Frederick VIII of Denmark died
1916	Start of the Battle of Asiago, Austrian defeat on the Italian front
1917	First Liberty Loan offered to the U.S. public
1923	Flogging abolished in Florida labor camps
1925	Patrice Munsel, singer, born
1929	First airmail service between North and South America began
1930	White House Police Force joined the Secret Service

```
              Constitution of Syria adopted
              Carlsbad Caverns National Park established
                 (New Mexico)
1940          Totem pole on Washington State Office Campus
                 dedicated
              Rotterdam, Holland devastated by German bombs
1942          Congress authorized the Women's Army Corps
1945          German submarine, U-858, surrendered 44 miles
                 off New Jersey
1948          State of Israel proclaimed and recognized by
                 the U.S.
1955          Warsaw Treaty Organization formed
1959          Ground-breaking ceremony for the Lincoln Center
                 of the Performing Arts (New York
                 City)
1963          Kuwait joined the United Nations
1965          John F. Kennedy Memorial dedicated at Runny-
                 mede, England
1970          Midnight sun returned to North Cape, Norway
              Start of 2-day Independence Day celebrations
                 in Paraguay
```

May 15th

```
              Roman festival honoring Mercury
              Straw Hat Day
              Feast of St. Dympna, patron of the insane
              Feast of St. John-Baptist de la Salle
              Japanese Hollyhock Festival
1043 AD       St. Hallvard died, (Feast Day; patron of Oslo,
                 Norway)
1092          King Philip I of France kidnapped Bertrada
                 de Montfort
1464          Final victory of York over Lancaster in the
                 War of the Roses at Hexham,
                 England
1602          Cape Cod discovered by Bartholomew Gosnold
                 of England
1773          Prince Metternich, Austrian statesman, born
1796          Napoleon and his army entered Milan, Italy
1800          Start of Napoleon and the French Consular
                 Guard's 5-day crossing of the
                 St. Bernard Pass to Italy
1812          New York City's city hall dedicated
1848          First hospital in New Jersey opened, a mental
                 institution in Trenton
1850          U.S. Botanical Garden re-established by
                 Congress
1854          United States Magazine founded
1856          Frank Baum, creator of the Wizard of Oz, born
1858          Royal Opera House, Covent Garden, opened in
                 London
```

	Dr. Livingstone's party reached the mouth of the Zambesi River
1859	Pierre Curie, scientist, born
1860	Garibaldi defeated the Neopolitans at Calatafimi, Sicily
1862	U.S. Department of Agriculture established
1864	Gen. Sherman and the Union victorious at Resaca, Georgia
1874	Harvard and McGill Universities played football for their only game, but the rules were the basis for the modern game
1883	Geronimo's Mexican camp captured by the U.S. Army
1894	Katherine Anne Porter, author, born
1904	Clifton Fadiman, author-editor, born Japanese battleships Hatsuse and Yashima hit mines
1905	Las Vegas, Nevada, founded
1909	James Mason, actor, born
1916	Entertainment Tax effected in England
1918	Military planes began the first regular airmail service between New York City and Washington, D.C.
1920	Tomb of the Unknown Soldier dedicated at Arlington National Cemetery, Washington, D.C.
1923	Richard Avedon, photographer, born
1940	First nylon stockings sold
1944	Clyde Shoun pitched a no-hitter and Cincinnati beat Boston, 1-0
1947	$400 million expenditure approved by Congress to fight Communism in Greece and Turkey
1952	Virgil Trucks pitched a no-hitter and Detroit beat Washington, 1-0
1957	Britain's first hydrogen bomb tested
1958	Sputnik 3 launched by the Russians
1960	Sputnik 4, Russian satellite, launched Don Cardwell's no-hitter let Chicago beat St. Louis 4-0
1963	Gordon Cooper orbited the World in a Mercury capsule, Faith 7
1964	First stage of the Aswan High Dam completed in Egypt
1965	Avalanche struck Garmisch-Partenkirchen, Germany
1967	Edward Hopper, artist, died
1968	Northern Japan struck by an earthquake
1969	Abe Fortas became the first U.S. Supreme Court Justice to retire under outside pressure
1971	Hollyhock Festival at Kyoto, Japan Donald F. Duncan, Yo-Yo inventor, died

	Feast of St. John of Nepomucene (patron of bridges; invoked against disaster)
	Feast of St. Andrew Bobola
	Feast of St. Fructuosus of Braga
	Feast of St. Honorius of Amiens
218 AD	Marcus Aurelius Antoninus proclaimed Emperor of Rome
578	St. Brendan the Voyager died (Feast Day)
1160	St. Ubaldo died (Feast Day)
1265	St. Simon Stock died (Feast Day)
1364	French victory over England at Cocherel, France
1568	Mary, Queen of Scots, took refuge in England
1605	Camillo Borghese elected Pope (Paul V)
1620	William Adams, first Englishman in Japan, died
1681	First female dancers appeared on the stage
1691	Jacob Leisler became first American colonist hanged for treason
1727	Catherine I, Empress of Russia, died in Paris
1763	Indians burned the fort at Sandusky, Ohio
1770	Marie Antoinette of Austria married King Louis XVI of France
1771	Regulators defeated in North Carolina
1799	Honore de Balzac, French novelist, born
1801	William Henry Seward, U.S. statesman and purchaser of Alaska, born
1804	Elizabeth P. Peabody, founder of the first U.S. kindergarten, born
1825	Bolivia declared its independence from Spain
1831	David E. Hughes, inventor of the type-printing telegraph, born
1861	Kentucky House of Representatives voted to remain neutral in the Civil War
1864	Platt Rogers Spencer, handwriting expert, died
1866	Congress authorized the 5¢ piece, called the half-dime
1868	Impeachment proceedings against President Andrew Johnson failed
1875	Earthquake shook Venezuela and Colombia
1886	Emily Dickinson, poet, died
1905	Henry Fonda, actor, born
1919	Liberace, pianist, born
	3 U.S. Navy seaplanes left Trepassy, Newfoundland to fly across the Atlantic
1920	Joan of Arc canonized as a saint
1928	Royal Tweed Road Bridge in Scotland opened
1929	First motion-picture "Oscars" awarded
1935	Czechoslovakia and Russia concluded a mutual defense pact
1953	William N. Oatis, Associated Press correspondent, released on spy charges in Czechoslovakia

```
1961      British team climbed Mt. Nuptse on the Nepal-
                    Tibet border
1969      A Russian space vehicle landed on Venus
```

May 17th

```
 352 AD   Liberius became Pope
 885      Stephen VI elected Pope
1164      St. Heloise died
1198      Frederick II, aged 4, crowned King of Sicily
1215      English barons marched on King John in London
1242      Henry III, King of England, landed in France
                    to assert his claim to the French
                    throne
1592      St. Paschal Baylon died (Feast Day; patron of
                    eucharistic congresses and
                    organizations)
1606      The Czar-pretender to the Russian throne died,
                    after ruling a year, in a revolt
                    against his and his predecessors'
                    policies
1642      Montreal founded in Quebec, Canada
1648      Battle of Zusmarshausen (30 Years' War)
1741      John Penn, signer of the Declaration of
                    Independence, born
1768      Caroline, wife of King George IV of England,
                    born
1784      George Washington purchased an ice cream
                    machine and recorded that fact
1792      New York Stock Exchange founded
1814      Christian VII elected King of Norway
          Norway's constitution promulgated (Norway
                    Independence Day)
1829      John Jay, statesman-jurist, died
1838      Tallyrand, French statesman, died
1840      Nicolo Paganini, Italian violinist, died
1848      Ferdinand I escaped Vienna for Innsbruck,
                    Austria
1849      15 blocks of St. Louis, Missouri burned along
                    with several steamboats at
                    their wharves
1855      Geronimo, Apache Indian leader, escaped the
                    reservation
1858      U.S. Army defeated by 1,200 Washington state
                    Indians
1875      First Kentucky Derby horserace run
1876      Whole 7th Cavalry  left Fort Abraham to battle
                    the Sioux
1877      First telephone exchange, with 6 subscribers,
                    began operation (Boston)
1884      Congress granted Alaska a civil government
1886      King Alphonso XIII of Spain born
```

```
1894      Europeans first witnessed an eruption of Mt.
                Nyiragongo volcano in the Congo
1905      John Patrick Goggan, playwright, born
1910      Hotel Adams, Phoenix, Arizona burned to the
                ground
1912      El Salvador adopted its national flag
1913      First "Be Kind to Animals Week" began
1914      Stewart Alsop, columnist, born
1916      Daylight Savings Time bill passed in England
1917      Leon Trotsky, revolutionist, returned to
                Russia
1919      First of 3 U.S. Navy seaplanes, flying the
                Atlantic, arrived at the Azores
                Islands
1920      Regular air service begun between Amsterdam
                and London
1933      Spain disestablished the Roman Catholic Church
                by Parliamentary edict
1937      Spanish loyalists set up a new government
1945      Start of the Battle of Bessang Pass, Philip-
                pines
1948      USSR recognized Israel
1951      French LST Adour exploded at Nhatrong,
                Indonesia
1954      U.S. Supreme Court ruled against school
                segregation
1955      Illinois became "The Land of Lincoln"
1958      F. Hugh Herbert, playwright-novelist, died
1963      Don Nottebart pitched a no-hitter and Houston
                beat Philadelphia, 4-1
1968      ESRO 2B launched, the first so to be a success
                for the European Space Research
                Organization
1970      Thor Heyerdahl and Ra II sailed from Morocco
                to cross the Atlantic on a
                reed raft
          World Championship Pirogue Races at Lafitte,
                Louisiana
1971      Mohammed's Birthday celebration in Malaysia
                and Singapore
1972      1100th Anniversary of the Kingdom of Norway
                (national holiday)
```

May 18th
```
          Feast of St. Eric, patron of Sweden
603 BC    Solar eclipse
562 AD    Pope St. John I died in prison, put there by
                the Holy Roman Emperor (Feast Day)
872       Louis II crowned Holy Roman Emperor
1152      King Henry II of England married Eleanor of
                Aquitaine
```

1291	Acre, last Christian hold in the Holy Land, fell to the Sultan of Egypt
1410	King Rupert of Germany died
1514	King Francis I of France married Claude
1587	St. Felix of Cantalice died (Feast Day)
1588	The Armada sailed from Spain for England
1643	English royal warrant issued, authorizing King Charles I medals
1675	Jacques Marquette, missionary-explorer, died
1727	Peter II proclaimed Emperor of Russia
1756	Britain declared war on France (French and Indian War)
1804	France proclaimed an empire with Napoleon as emperor
1852	School attendance in U.S. made compulsory
1866	Nova Coronae, temporary star, discovered to be covered with blazing hydrogen
1868	Nicholas II, last Czar of Russia, born
1872	Bertrand Russell, British philosopher, born
1882	First light shown from new Eddystone Lighthouse (England)
1888	Samuel Shellabarger, author, born
1897	Frank Capra, filmmaker, born
1904	Western Union cut off service to pool rooms Jacob K. Javits, U.S. Senator, born
1913	Perry Como, singer, born
1914	Pierre Balmain, fashion designer, born
1917	Selective conscription (draft) adopted in U.S.
1919	Margot Fonteyn, ballerina, born
1921	Edward Everett Tanner III, author as Virginia Rowans and Patrick Dennis, born
1933	Tennessee Valley Authority created
1940	Antwerp, Belgium, surrendered to the Germans
1951	Jacob S. Coxey, leader of the 1894 march of the unemployed on Washington, died
	United Nations General Assembly voted for arms embargo against Red China
1956	Swiss team climbed Lhotse I, 27,923 feet, on the Tibet-Nepal border
1969	Peace Day
1970	Mohammed's Birthday celebrations in Ceylon

May 19th

715 AD	Gregory II elected Pope
988	St. Dunstan died (Feast Day)
1214	London granted a charter authorizing the election of city officials
1217	Battle of Lincoln Fair, England
1218	Otto IV, Holy Roman Emperor, died

1296	Peter Moronne, Pope St. Celestine V, died (Feast Day)
1303	St. Ives or Ivo of Brittany died (Feast Day; patron of lawyers, jurists, notaries, bailiffs, and orphans)
1342	Pierre Roger crowned Pope Clement VI
1364	Charles V, "the Wise," crowned King of France
1535	Jacques Cartier began his second voyage to Canada
1536	Anne Boleyn, second wife of King Henry VIII of England, beheaded
1579	Peace of Arras gave Spain control of the Low Countries
1607	University of Gressen, Germany, chartered
1643	Spanish Army lost to the French at Rocrou, France
	United Colonies of New England formed
1653	Rhode Island decreed that there be no slaves in that colony for 10 years
1769	Giovanni Vincenzo Antonio Ganganelli elected Pope Clement XIV
1777	Button Gwinnett, signer of the Declaration of Independence, died
1780	New England's "Dark Day"
1795	Josiah Bartlett, signer of the Declaration of Independence, died
	John Hopkins, philanthropist, born
1802	French Legion of Honor founded
1846	Robert Bailey Thomas, founder of The Farmers' Almanac, died
1848	U.S. war with Mexico ended
1857	Patent granted for first electical fire alarm system
1879	Lady Astor, first woman to sit in England's House of Commons, born
1896	Dimple-producing machine patented
1897	Rhode Island state flag adopted
1898	Spanish Admiral Cervera reached Santiago, Cuba
1918	Last German air raid on Britain for World War I
1946	Booth Tarkington, author, died
1950	Munitions barges exploded at South Amboy, New Jersey
1970	Billy Goat Auction at Deidesheim, Germany
	Wesak Day or Buddha's Birthday celebration in Ceylon, Korea, and Malaysia
	Echternach, Luxembourg Dancing Procession
1971	Ogden Nash, poet, died
1972	Start of Rooster Days Rodeo Weekend at Broken Arrow, Okla.

```
526 AD    Antioch, Syria rocked by an earthquake
685       King Ecgfrith of England died
794       St. Ethelbert of the East Angles murdered
              (Feast Day)
1259      King Henry III of England ceded Normandy to
              France
1277      Pope John XXI died of injuries sustained when
              his palace collapsed on him
1293      Kamakura, Japan, rocked by an earthquake
1306      King Edward I of England gave the Duchy of
              Aquitaine to his son
1444      St. Bernardine of Siena died (Feast Day)
1498      Vasco da Gama arrived in India
1506      Christopher Columbus, explorer, died poverty-
              stricken
1514      Corporation of Trinity House, organization of
              English mariners, chartered
1536      Henry VIII, King of England, married Jane
              Seymour
1553      Three British ships sailed in search of the
              Northwest Passage
1631      Swedish victory at Magdeburg, Germany, in the
              30 Years' War
1648      Wladislaus IV, King of Poland, died
1663      William Bradford, first printer in New York
              City, born
1727      Sir Isaac Newton, discoverer of gravity, died
1751      Echigo, Japan rocked by earthquake
1775      Mecklenberg Declaration of Independence framed
              at Charlotte, North Carolina
1777      Cherokee Indians ceded part of South Carolina
              to the U.S.
1785      First survey of the Northwest Territories of
              the U.S. authorized by Congress
1800      Napoleon and the French Consular Guard
              completed their crossing of the
              St. Bernard Pass to Italy
1813      Battle of Bautzen (Russia and Prussia against
              Napoleon)
1818      William G. Fargo of Wells Fargo born
1825      New York Courier, first Sunday paper in the
              city founded, lasting one year
1843      Lafayette, Revolutionary War hero, died
1855      First printing telegraph-type ticker patented
1856      Dr. Livingstone completed the crossing of
              Africa, west to east
          "The Crime Against Kansas" speech given in the
              Senate by Charles Sumner
1861      Homestead Act passed
1886      Congress provided for a study of the effects of
              alcohol on drinkers
```

```
1895      Latham's motion-picture projector publicly
              exhibited
1902      American occupation of Cuba ended
1908      James Stewart, actor, born
1922      British ship Egypt involved in a collision
              off France
1927      Lindbergh's non-stop flight to Paris began
1930      First flight of an airplane released from a
              dirigible completed
1932      Amelia Earhart began first trans-Atlantic
              flight by a woman
1941      U.S. Office of Civil Defense created
1947      Solar eclipse
1950      First Annual Armed Forces Day parade held
              (Washington, D.C.)
1958      Van Cliburn, pianist, became first musician
              given a New York ticker-tape
              parade
1963      U.S. Supreme Court legalized desegregation
              sit-ins
1967      Prince Paul of Greece born
1970      Visak Bauja, or Buddha's Birthday, in Cambodia
          Armed Forces Day on Guam
```

May 21st

```
          Feast of Sts. Constantine and Helen (Greek
              Orthodox)
          Ancient Roman festival honoring all the gods
          Holy Trinity Day in Venezuela
 427 BC   Plato, Greek philosopher, born
 996 AD   Otto III crowned Holy Roman Emperor
1170      St. Godric died (Feast Day)
1254      Conrad IV, King of Germany, died
1388      University of Cologne, Germany, chartered
1420      Henry V, King of England, betrothed to
              Catherine de Valois of France
1424      James I crowned King of Scotland
1471      Albrecht Durer, German artist, born
          Henry VI, deposed King of England, murdered
              in the Tower
1502      St. Helena Island discovered
1527      King Philip II of Spain born
1542      Hernando deSoto, explorer, died
1565      Turkish troops attacked Malta
1674      John III elected King of Poland
1688      Alexander Pope, English poet, born
1799      Napoleon, having failed to take Acre after
              12 assaults, retired
1819      Burlington Arcade, a London shopping mall,
              opened
1832      First national Democratic convention met
              (Baltimore)
```

1856	John Brown raided Lawrence, Kansas
1861	North Carolina seceded from the Union
	First cog railway in Europe, Viznau-Rigi, opened
1862	Act of Congress provided for the education of black children in Washington, D.C.
1875	Edmund Heller, naturalist-explorer, born
1878	Glenn Curtis, aviation pioneer, born
1881	Clara Barton, founder of the American Red Cross, born
	U.S. Lawn Tennis Association formed
1894	Manchester, England, ship canal opened
1897	Bust of Sir Walter Scott unveiled in Westminster Abbey
1904	Robert Montgomery, actor, born
1912	Harold Robbins, novelist, born
1913	Irving Shulman, author, born
1916	Daylight Savings Time effected in England
1919	Women's suffrage bill passed the House of Representatives
1927	Lindbergh completed his New York-to-Paris flight
1932	Amelia Earhart completed the first woman's trans-Atlantic flight
1948	First telephone exchange established in Kodiak, Alaska's oldest settlement
1952	Queen Juliana of Holland opened a new canal, connecting Europe with the North Sea
	Brooklyn Dodgers beat the New York Giants 19-1, scoring 15 runs in the first inning
	Gen. Dwight Eisenhower presented with Medaille Militaire, France's highest award
1956	First U.S. hydrogen bomb dropped from a plane exploded over Bikini Atoll
1960	Nine days of earthquakes and tidal waves began in Chile
1965	First block of Abu Simbel temple moved to higher ground to protect it from the rising Nile River
1970	Buddha's Birthday in India
	Navy Day, the opening of Congress in Chile
	Mohammed's Birthday in Tunesia
1971	Anastenaria Feast (Byzantine church celebrations in Greece)

May 22nd

National Maritime Day (U.S.A.)
Feast of St. Paul (Greek Orthodox)

```
                Annual pilgrimage to Trinity Church, Kolpino,
                    Russia
   415 BC    Hermae busts in Athens mysteriously mutilated
   337 AD    Constantine the Great, Roman Emperor, died
  1200       Treaty of LeGoulet signed by England and France
  1216       French invasion troops landed in England
  1246       Henry Raspe elected King of Germany
  1455       First Battle of St. Albans, England (York
                    defeated Lancaster in the War
                    of the Roses)
  1457       St. Rita, patron of the impossible, died
                    (Feast Day)
  1499       Swiss victory at Battle of Calven Gorge
  1509       Henry VII, first Tudor King of England, died
  1526       Holy League of Cognac made between France
                    and the Pope
  1667       Pope Alexander VII died
  1670       Secret Treaty of Dover signed between England
                    and the Pope
  1764       Bolivar City, Venezuela founded
  1795       First newspaper in Washington, D.C. Impartial
                    Observer and Advertiser began
                    publication
  1807       Aaron Burr went on trial for treason
  1813       Richard Wagner, composer, born
  1819       Start of first successful trans-Atlantic
                    voyage under steam propulsion
                    (S.S. Savannah)
  1837       National University of Athens, Greece, founded
  1843       1,000 people left the Missouri River on the
                    "Great Migration" to Oregon
  1849       Patent issued to Abraham Lincoln for a method
                    to lift ships over shoals (never
                    got further than the model stage
                    in development)
  1856       Preston Brooks assaulted Charles Sumner in the
                    U.S. Senate
  1859       Ferdinand II Bomba, King of Sicily, died
             Sir Arthur Conan Doyle, creator of Sherlock
                    Holmes, born
             Francis II, last Bourbon King of Naples,
                    ascended to the throne
  1881       King Carol of Rumania crowned
  1882       Korea opened to U.S. trade
  1885       Victor Hugo, author, died
  1892       A British warship sank in the LaPlata River
  1900       Patent issued to Edwin S. Votey for first
                    practical pneumatic player piano
  1906       Wright brothers granted a patent on their
                    airplane
  1907       Sir Lawrence Olivier, actor, born
  1912       U.S. Marine Corps Aviation instituted, with
                    one pilot who had had less than 3
                    hours flight instruction
```

```
1914    Vance Packard, author, born
1915    George Baker, cartoonist ("Sad Sack"), born
1919    A food plant exploded at Cedar Rapids, Iowa
1920    Congress adopted the Civil Service pension
            plan
1929    First aerial police patrol begun (Teterboro,
            New Jersey)
1930    First television feature act shown in a
            theater (Schenectady, New York)
1931    Russian submarine Number 9 sank in the Gulf
            of Finland
1939    Italy and Germany signed a 10-year military
            pact
1943    Helen H. (Mrs. William Howard) Taft, First
            Lady, died
1946    Karl Frank, Nazi governor of Czechoslovakia,
            hanged for the massacre at Lidice
1953    Bill signed giving states title to their off-
            shore lands for oil drilling
1971    Eastern Turkey badly shaken by an earthquake
```

May 23rd
_____

```
        Feast of St. William of Rochester
 34 AD  Holy Ghost descended
  607   St. Desiderius died (Feast Day)
 1059   Philip I crowned King of France
 1116   St. Ivo of Chartres died (Feast Day)
 1125   Henry V, Holy Roman Emperor, died
 1173   St. Euphrosyme of Polotsk died (Feast Day)
 1430   Joan of Arc captured by the Burgundians
 1480   Turks arrived at Rhodes prepared to beseige it
 1498   Savonarola, a heretic, burned
 1533   King Henry VIII's marriage to Catherine of
            Aragon declared null by Cranmer
            (England)
 1541   Jacques Cartier began his third voyage to
            Canada
 1688   Protestant-Catholic clash in Prague began
            30 Years' War
 1701   Captain Kidd, New York citizen, hanged as
            a pirate and murderer in London
 1706   Battle of Ramilles, English-Dutch defeat of
            France, cost France her claims
            to Belgium
 1707   Carolus Linnaeus, botanist, born
 1752   William Bradford, first printer in New York
            City, died
 1785   Benjamin Franklin invented bifocals
 1788   South Carolina ratified the Constitution
 1842   First stockholders' meeting of Cincinnati,
            Ohio's observatory held
 1846   Mexico declared war on the U.S.
```

```
1868      "Kit" Carson, frontiersman, died
1871      Treaty of Frankfurt ended Franco-Prussian
               War
1872      First National Convention of Workingmen
               political party met
1883      Douglas Fairbanks, actor, born
1895      New York City Public Library established
1903      First cross-country auto trip began in
               San Francisco
1911      New York City Public Library dedicated
1915      Italy declared war on Austro-Hungarian Empire
1918      British ship Moldavia torpedoed in the Atlantic
1925      Tajima, Japan, rocked by an earthquake
1927      Charles Lindbergh, flyer, was awarded the Cross
               of the Legion of Honor in Paris
1934      Bonnie, of Bonnie and Clyde, died
1938      Time, Inc., acquired the Literary Digest
               magazine
1939      U.S. submarine Squalus sunk off Portsmouth,
               New Hampshire
1943      Delair, New Jersey train wreck
1951      Communists took over Tibet
1952      Nationalized railroads were returned to their
               owners by the U.S. government
               after seizure over 1950 labor
               dispute and threatened strike
1960      Israel caught Adolf Eichmann, Nazi war criminal
1965      Organization of American States peace-keeping
               force established in the Domini-
               can Republic
1967      Greek tanker Circe exploded in the Mediter-
               ranean
1969      Five U.S. satellites launched with one
               rocket
          Scotch Broom Festival, Bainbridge Island,
               Washington
          Hebrew  Shevuoth
```

May 24th

```
 592 AD   St. Simeon Stylites the Younger, a pillar-
               dwelling Ascetic, died (Feast
               Day)
1089      LaFranc, Archbishop of Canterbury, died
1153      St. David I, King of Scotland, died (Feast
               Day)
1487      Lambert Simnel, posing as King Edward VI
               of England, crowned in Ireland
               (Henry VII recognized him as a
               Yorkist dupe and made him Royal
               Falconer)
1543      Copernicus, Polish astronomer, died
```

1658	French and English forces battled at Dunkirk
1689	Toleration Act passed (English toleration of all but Roman Catholic dissenters)
1819	Queen Victoria of England born
1830	First 14 miles of Baltimore and Ohio railroad opened to horsedrawn traffic
1833	John Randolph, statesman-orator, died
1844	First public telegraph message sent: "What has God wrought?"
1856	Marshal Henri Petain, French soldier, born
1869	Powell's expedition began its sail through the Grand Canyon
1871	Reading Railroad incorporated
1875	National Bankers' Association founded (U.S.)
1879	William Lloyd Garrison, abolitionist, died
1881	Victoria capsized in the Thames River, Canada
1883	Brooklyn Bridge opened to traffic
	Elsa Maxwell, hostess, born
1885	First steel railroad rails manufactured, experimentally
1893	Anti-saloon League founded
1899	First auto-repair shop opened (Boston)
1916	British government began conscription
1917	Duke of Bedford born
1928	Dirigible Italia crossed the North Pole
1929	Ground-breaking in lower Manhattan for construction of the West Side Highway
1935	First night major-league ball game played (Cincinnati)
	James W. Blake, composer of "Sidewalks of New York," died
1941	President Roosevelt declared a national emergency
	British battleship Hood sunk by German battleship Bismarck
1956	Delaware Turnpike Bridge, connecting New Jersey and Pennsylvania toll roads, opened
1959	John Foster Dulles, U.S. statesman, died
1960	Midas 2 launched
1962	Scott Carpenter made his orbits in Mercury Aurora 7
1967	Dime a Dip Supper at Bristol, Vermont
1968	"Chief," last U.S. Army cavalry horse, died
1969	One-room school, reconstructed at Kansas State Teachers' College, dedicated
1970	Sacred Furrow Day in Cambodia (Royal plowing to increase the harvest)
	Youth Day in Zambia
1972	Start of 2-day pilgrimage of the gypsies at Stes. Maries de la Mar, France

          Feast of the Three Marys
          African Freedom Day in Zambia, Continental
               Liberation Day in Chad

709 AD St. Aldhelm died (Feast Day)
1085   Pope St. Gregory VII died (Feast Day)
1184   Glastonbury, England, monastery destroyed by
               fire
1201   Start of first 15-day fair at Great Grimsby,
               Lincolnshire, England
1261   Pope Alexander IV died
1315   Edward Bruce invaded Ireland
1555   King Henry II of Navarre died without ever
               ruling
1559   First Protestant synod in France met in Paris
1571   Stephen Bathory elected Prince of Transylvania
1577   Barinas, Venezuela, founded
1787   Constitutional Convention opened in the U.S.
1803   Ralph Waldo Emerson, poet-philosopher, born
1810   Argentina became independent of Spain
               (national holiday)
1838   Last Congressional appropriation for the
               National (Cumberland) Road made
1852   Springfield, Massachusetts, organized as a city
1853   Argentina constitution completed
1862   Union forces crossed the Chickahominey River
1863   Vicksburg, Mississippi, surrendered to the
               Union
1864   Union victory at New Hope Church, Georgia
1865   St. Madeleine Sophie died (Feast Day)
1869   U.S. Cabinet took up a discussion of the 8-hour
               workday
          Vienna State Opera House opened as Imperial
               Royal Court Opera Theater
1887   Opera Comique, Paris, burned
1888   Banquet Theater fire in Oporto, Portugal
1889   Rosa Bonheur, French artist, died
          Igor Sikorsky, helicopter inventor, born
1894   Dashiel Hammett, creator of "Sam Spade," born
1895   Nicholas II had last Russian Czarist coronation
1897   Gene Tunney, boxer, born
1898   Bennet Cerf, author-publisher and punster,
               born
1908   Central American Court of Justice established
1911   Porfirio Diaz, president of revolutionary
               Mexico, resigned
1915   British battleship Triumph torpedoed
1916   Austrians defeated on the Italian front at
               Asiago
1919   Fuad I, King of Egypt, married Princess Nazli
1928   Dirigible Italia crashed on the Arctic ice

1935	Olympian Jesse Owens broke 5 world records and tied a 6th
1954	Haile Selassie, Ethiopian Emperor, visited the U.S.
1955	Mt. Kanchenjunga, 28,208 feet tall on the Nepal-Sikkim border, scaled, except for the last 6 feet
1963	Organization of African Unity formed
1969	Thor Heyerdahl set sail in Ra, a reed boat, in an attempt to prove that the ancient Egyptians could have sailed to the Americas
1970	Commonwealth Day in the Bahamas honoring Queen Victoria

May 26th

	International Theater Day in Venezuela
	Feast of St. Augustine or Austin of Canterbury
17 AD	Roman Triumph held for Germanicus Caesar
1232	The Pope sent the first Inquisition team to Aragon, Spain
1445	King Charles VII of France added 15 new companies to his army
1577	Frobisher and a new expedition set out for Northern Canada
1583	Susanna, first child of William and Ann Shakespeare, baptized
1595	St. Philip Neri died (Feast Day)
1645	St. Mariana of Quinto died (Feast Day)
1660	King Charles II landed in England to reclaim his kingdom
1668	First New Jersey colonial assembly met at Elizabethtown
1781	Bank of North America incorporated in Philadelphia
1799	Alexander Pushkin, Russian poet, born
1805	Napoleon crowned King of Italy
1816	Solar eclipse
1846	Sir George D. T. Goldie, founder of Nigeria, born
1857	Dred Scott and his family were freed from slavery
1862	Isaac Babbitt, alloy inventor, died
1864	Montana became a U.S. territory
1865	Last of the Confederate Army, 18,000 strong, surrendered at Brazos, Texas
1867	Princess Victoria Mary of Teck, future wife of King George V of England, born
1868	Andrew Johnson, U.S. President, was not impeached
	Last public execution in England performed
1874	Forerunner of the Brooklyn Elevated Railway chartered

```
1886      Al Jolson, entertainer, born
1895      Paul Lucas, actor, born
1902      Statue of Rochambeau, French soldier of the
                    American Revolution, unveiled in
                    Washington, D.C.
1906      Henrik Ibsen, Norwegian writer, died
1907      Ida S. (Mrs. William) McKinley, First Lady,
                    died
1908      Robert Morley, actor, born
1910      Artie Shaw, bandleader, born
          Laurence S. Rockefeller born
1913      New York City actors union formed as Actors'
                    Equity
1918      Leasowe Castle torpedoed in the Mediterranean
          Georgia, USSR, declared itself a republic
1920      Peggy Lee, singer, born
1926      Banca d'Italia became the sole issuer of
                    currency in Italy
1927      15-millionth Model T left the Ford assembly
                    line
1934      Century of Progress Exposition opened for the
                    second season in Chicago
1940      Retreat from Dunkirk began
1951      Lincoln Ellsworth, explorer-author, died
1952      Peace contract signed among West Germany, U.S.,
                    Britain, and France
1954      Solar ship of Cheops, Egyptian pharaoh, found
          Aircraft carrier Bennington damaged off Rhode
                    Island
1959      Harvey Haddix pitched 12 perfect innings, but
                    1 hit in the 13th let Milwaukee
                    beat Pittsburgh, 2-0
1960      First real wedding held onstage at the
                    Metropolitan Opera
1966      Guyana, formerly British Guiana, became
                    independent
1968      Prince Frederick Andre Henrik Christian of
                    Denmark born
```

May 27th

```
          Feast of St. Eleuterius, patron of Barinitas,
                    Venezuela
          Feast of St. Julius of Durostorum
735 AD    St. Bede died (Feast Day)
1471      Vadislau elected King of Bohemia
1562      First white settlement on North America founded
                    on Parris Island, South Carolina
1564      John  Calvin, French-Swiss religious leader,
                    died
1626      William II, Prince of Orange, born
1652      Patent issued for founding Flatbush, New York
                    (Brooklyn) by Peter Stuyvesant
```

1679	Habeas corpus became part of English Common Law
1703	Construction of St. Petersburg (Leningrad), Russia, began
1707	Marquise de Montespan, mistress of King Louis XIV of France, died
1755	First city water pumping station founded in America in Bethlehem, Pennsylvania
1756	Maximilian I, King of Bavaria, born
1777	Button Gwinnett, signer of the Declaration of Independence, died of dueling wounds
1782	George Washington recorded that he refused to be addressed as King
1818	Amelia J. Bloomer, suffragist, temperance advocate, and fashion setter, born
1819	King George V of Hanover born
	Julia Ward Howe, composer ("Battle Hymn of the Republic"), born
1836	Jay Gould, financier, born
1844	Polk's became the first Presidential nomination reported by telegraph
1867	Thomas Bulfinch, author of Bulfinch's Mythology, died
1878	Isadora Duncan, ballerina, born
1892	First elevated railroad in Chicago opened
1893	Oklahoma Historical Society founded
1905	Japan destroyed the Russian fleet (8 battle-ships, 12 cruisers, 6 destroyers) in Tsushima Strait
1907	Rachel Carson, naturalist-author, born
1910	Sam Snead, golfer, born
1911	Vincent Price, actor, art expert, and cook, born
	Hubert H. Humphrey, statesman, born
1915	Herman Wouk, author, born
	British battleship Majestic torpedoed
1918	Battle of the Aisne began
1919	One of 3 U.S. seaplanes flying the Atlantic reached Portugal
1929	Charles Lindbergh, flyer, married Ann Morrow, author
1933	Century of Progress Exposition opened in Chicago
1935	National Industrial Recovery Act (NRA) declared unconstitutional
1936	Cunard's Queen Mary began its trans-Atlantic maiden voyage
1941	German battleship Bismarck sunk by the British
	Unlimited national emergency in U.S. proclaimed by the President
1945	20 convoy ships involved in iceberg-caused collisions
1949	Robert Ripley, founder of "Believe It or Not," died
1960	The Negro American Labor Council founded

1970   Constitution and Freedom Day in Turkey
1971   Pink ladyslippers bloom (New England)

May 28th

```
            Dragon Boat Festival in Hong Kong
  585 BC   Solar eclipse ended the Battle of Lydians
               against Persians
    82     Caelius, Roman politician, born
  567 AD   St. Germanus of Paris died (Feast Day)
   640     Severinus elected Pope
  1081?    St. Bernard of Montjoux died (Feast Day; patron
               of mountaineers)
  1156     Sicilians defeated the Greeks at Brindisi
  1262     Philip III, King of France, married Isabella
               of Aragon
  1698     Old Swede's Church in Wilmington, Delaware,
               begun
  1738     Joseph Guillotin, inventor, born
  1754     Battle of Great Meadows, Pennsylvania, first
               engagement of the French and
               Indian War
  1759     William Pitt, English statesman, born
  1837     Tony Pastor, discoverer of performer Lillian
               Russell, born
  1843     Noah Webster, dictionary writer, died
  1854     British and French declared war on Russia
               (Crimean War)
  1863     First black regiment in the Civil War left
               Boston for the front
  1864     Maximilian, Emperor of Mexico, arrived in Vera
               Cruz
  1892     Sierra Club, conservationist organization,
               founded
  1897     Destruction of Santiago Gate in San Juan,
               Puerto Rico, began
  1900     British annexed the Orange Free State in
               South Africa
            Solar eclipse
  1918     Americans captured and held Cantigny, France
  1929     First color movie premiered ("On With the
               Show")
  1934     Dionne quintuplets born
  1937     Golden Gate Bridge opened to traffic (San
               Francisco)
  1940     Belgium surrendered to Germany
  1942     Sugar rationing began in the U.S.
  1959     Able and Baker, monkey astronauts, recovered
               from their space flights
  1971     Medieval Archery Contest held at Gubbio, Italy
            Mars 3, USSR Martian probe, launched
  1972     Duke of Windsor, formerly King Edward VIII of
               England, died
```

1176 AD	Holy Roman Army defeated at Legnano, Italy
1180	Isabella of Hainaut, wife of the King, crowned Queen of France
1282	Glastonbury, England, granted an annual fair on this date
1289	Charles of Salerno crowned King of Sicily
1328	Philip IV crowned King of France
1418	Burgundian troops entered Paris (100 Years' War)
1453	Constantinople fell to the Turks, becoming capital of their Ottoman Empire
1607	St. Mary Magdalen dei Pazzi died (Feast Day)
1613	King Charles II of England born
1724	Pietro Francesco Orsini elected Pope (Benedict XIII)
1736	Patrick Henry, Revolutionary War hero, born
1766	The New York Journal or General Advertiser founded
1790	Last of the original 13 colonies, Rhode Island, ratified the constitution
1814	Empress Josephine, divorced wife of Napoleon, died
1848	Wisconsin became a state
	The Californian suspended publications because most of its subscribers had gone to the goldfields
1860	Queensland, Australia Parliament first met
1865	New Republican party formed against slavery
1877	Fletcher Harper, founder of the magazine chain, died
1888	Massachusetts adopted the Australian ballot system
1892	Frederick Faust, author as Max Brand, born
	The New York Herald began giving free ice to tenement-dwelling families
1898	Beatrice Lillie, comedienne, born
1903	Bob Hope, comedian, born
1910	Glenn Curtis won $10,000 for the first nonstop flight between Albany and New York City
1911	Sir William Gilbert of the Gilbert and Sullivan operettas, drowned
1914	Canadian ship Empress of Ireland sank after a collision in the St. Lawrence River
1916	U.S. presidential flag adopted
1917	John F. Kennedy, U.S. President, born
1918	Finland adopted its national flag
1920	Solar eclipse
1932	Bonus March on Washington began
1937	Matupi and Vulcan volcanoes in the Bismarck Islands erupted

```
1939    Bronx-Whitestone Bridge opened to traffic
1942    John Barrymore, actor, died
1944    U.S. aircraft carrier Block Island torpedoed in
             the Atlantic
1953    Hillary's party reached the summit of Mt.
             Everest
1959    Council of the Entente formed (economic
                 alliance among Niger, Dahomey,
                 Ivory Coast, and Upper Volta)
1960    Nine days of earthquakes and tidal waves ended
             in Chile
1970    Mila Dunnabi - Mohammed's Birthday celebrations
             in Surinam
        Old Fiddlers' Reunion in Athens, Texas
```

May 30th

```
 727 AD  St. Herbert died
1252     St. Ferdinand of Castile died (Feast Day)
1431     St. Joan of Arc burned as a witch (Patron of
              France; Feast Day)
1498     Columbus set out from Spain on  his third
              voyage
1527     University of Marburg, Germany, founded
1539     DeSoto landed in Florida
1574     King Charles IX of France died
1593     Christopher Marlowe, English playwright,
              killed in a quarrel
1635     Treaty of Prague ended 30 Years' War
1640     Peter Paul Rubens, artist, died
1672     Czar Peter the Great of Russia born
1744     Alexander Pope, English poet, died
1778     Voltaire, French philosopher, died
1814     Treaty of Paris put King Louis XVIII on the
              French throne
1854     Kansas and Nebraska became U.S. territories
1862     Union victory at the Battle of Fair Oaks or
              Seven Pines
1883     Twelve trampled to death in a panic on the
              Brooklyn Bridge
1888     James A. Farley, statesman, born
1896     First automobile accident took place (New
              York City)
1901     Cornelia Otis Skinner, actress-author, born
1909     Benny Goodman, "King of Swing" bandleader,
              born
1912     New York Observer, Presbyterian literary
                   magazine, folded
         Wilber Wright, airplane inventor, died
1914     Mt. Lassen volcano erupted (California)
1922     Lincoln Memorial, Washington, D.C.
                   dedicated
```

1934	Metropolitan Police College opened at Hendon, England
	Celebration in Baltimore to observe Maryland's 300th anniversary
1938	Olympia, Washington, war memorial unveiled
1942	British bombs fell on Cologne, Germany
1958	Unknown soldiers from World War II and Korea buried at Arlington National Cemetery
1961	Rafael L. Trujillo, Dominican dictator, assassinated
1967	Eastern Nigeria proclaimed itself the Republic of Biafra
1971	Procession of the Giant Candle held in Bogen, Germany
	Mariner 9, U.S. Martian probe, launched

May 31st

1433 AD	Sigismund crowned Holy Roman Emperor
1529	Papal legates met to discuss King Henry VIII's marriage to Catherine of Aragon (England)
1584	Boris Godunov crowned Czar of Muscovy
1594	Tintoretto, Italian artist, died
1678	Godiva Procession, celebrating Lady Godiva's ride, first held
1740	Frederick William I, second king of Prussia, died
1790	First U.S. copyright law passed
1793	France's "Reign of Terror" began
1809	Franz Joseph Haydn, composer, died
1818	Guadalajara, Mexico, rocked by an earthquake
1819	Walt Whitman, poet-author, died
1843	Fort Laramie, Wyoming foundations laid
1848	Congress voted money to purchase the unpublished papers of President James Madison
1885	Victor Hugo, French writer, buried
1889	Johnstown, Pennsylvania, flood
1895	Emily Faithful, English philanthropist, died
	Norman Vincent Peale, clergyman-author, born
1902	Boer War ended with the Peace of Vereeniging
1907	Herve Alphand, French statesman, born
1910	Elizabeth Blackwell, first woman doctor, died
	Union of South Africa formed
1913	Popular vote for senators became U.S. law
1916	14 British and 11 German ships sunk in the Battle of Jutland
1917	Indiana state flag adopted
1918	U.S. troopship *President Lincoln* torpedoed

1919	One U.S. Navy seaplane reached Plymouth, England, having left with 2 others, on a trans-Atlantic flight on the 16th
1923	Prince Rainier of Monaco born
1926	Sesquicentennial Exposition, Philadelphia, opened
1928	Union of South Africa adopted its national flag
1935	Quella in Baluchistan State, India, rocked by an earthquake
1943	Joe Namath, football player, born
1961	Union of South Africa became independent of Britain
1962	Adolf Eichmann hanged by Israel for his World War II crimes against humanity
1970	Peru hit by terrible earthquakes and floods
1971	Royal Malay Regiment's birthday celebration held in Brunei

Full Moon - Honey Moon
Second Friday - Queen's Official Birthday and trooping
                    of the colors in London, England
Second weekend - Polish Days in Loup City, Nebraska
Third Sunday - Fathers' Day
                    Magna Carta Day
Weekend closest to the 25th - Reenactment of Custer's
                    Last Stand at Little Big Horn,
                    Montana

June 1st

```
             Beluga whale hunting season opens in Alaska
             Biloxi, Mississippi, Shrimp Festival
             Feast of St. Angela of Brescia
             Feast of St. Pamphilus
1217 AD      Pope Innocent III called for a Fifth Crusade
1792         Kentucky became a State
1796         Tennessee became a State
1801         Brigham Young, Mormon Church leader, born
1813         "Don't give up the ship," said Capt. James
                    Lawrence as the U.S.S. Chesa-
                    peake was captured by H.M.S.
                    Shannon
1815         Otto, King of Greece, born
1831         James Ross planted the British flag on the
                    magnetic North Pole
1834         Ground-breaking ceremonies for the London-to-
                    Birmingham Railroad held in England
1846         Pope Gregory XXI died of cancer
1860         The New York World began as a religious daily
                    newspaper
1868         James Buchanan, U.S. President, died
             U.S. signed the eighth and last peace treaty
                    with the Navajo Indians
```

1878	John Masefield, poet, born
1886	Tuxedo Park, New York, opened
1898	Trans-Mississippi International Exposition opened in Omaha, Nebraska
1905	Lewis and Clark Centennial Exposition opened in Portland, Oregon
1909	Alaska-Yukon-Pacific Exposition opened in Seattle, Washington
1916	Battle of Jutland ended
1920	American Iris Society founded
1926	Marilyn Monroe, actress, born
1939	British submarine Thetis sunk in the Irish Sea
1946	Marshal Ian Antonescu, dictator of Rumania, hanged
1958	Charles de Gaulle became Premier of France
1963	Madaraka (Independence) granted to Kenya, Africa (National Holiday)
1968	Helen Keller, blind and deaf writer-lecturer, died
1969	New York City weather bureau's rain measuring device was damaged by 2-1/3 inches of rain that fell in 2 hours
1970	Soyez 9, manned Russian orbiter, launched

June 2nd

	Feast of Sts. Marcellinus and Peter
177 AD	St. Blandina died (Feast Day)
	The Martyrs of Lyons died (Feast Day)
303?	St. Erasmus (or Elmo), patron of sailors, died (Feast Day)
657	Pope Eugenius died
828	St. Nicephorus of Constantinople died (Feast Day)
1070	Peterborough Abbey in England sacked by the Danes
1192	Geoffrey Plantagenet, Court of Anjou, married Queen Matilda of England
1320	War between France and Flanders ended
1420	Henry V, King of England, married Catherine of France
1635	First Italian immigrant arrived in New York City
	Poet John Milton joined the Honorable Artillery Company of England
1732	Martha Washington, first First Lady, born
1740	Marquis de Sade, writer, born
1773	John Randolph, statesman-orator, born
1784	New Hampshire's temporary government ceased to exist
1835	P. T. Barnum and his circus began their first tour
1837	Seminole Indians fled into the Everglades
1840	Thomas Hardy, English poet-novelist, born

1851	Maine became the first "dry" state
1858	Donati discovered his comet
1860	Paiute Indians of Nevada routed for attacks on the Pony Express
1874	Cornerstone laid for the American Museum of Natural History (New York City)
1875	Quanah Parker, Comanche Indian chief, surrendered
	Castalia, a channel-crossing twin-hulled ship, launched in England
1883	First night baseball game played (Fort Waye, Indiana)
1886	Grover Cleveland married Frances Folsom, becoming the first President to be married while in office
1890	Hedda Hopper, actress-columnist, born
1894	Field Museum of Natural History opened in Chicago
1896	Britain gave Marconi the first patent on his wireless
1915	Austria recaptured the stronghold of Przemysl from Russia
1916	Third Battle of Ypres
1921	U.S. Immigration Act went into effect
1924	President Coolidge signed the Income Tax bill
	American Indians granted citizenship by Congress
1940	King Constantine of Greece born
1946	Italy, in its first election in which women could vote, chose to become a republic (National Holiday)
1952	U.S. Supreme Court ruled seizure of steel mills to prevent an illegal strike
1953	Elizabeth II crowned Queen of England
	Hillary's conquest of Mt. Everest announced in the London Times
1959	A gas truck exploded on the Pennsylvania Turnpike
1961	George S. Kaufman, playwright, born
1964	First nuclear-powered merchant ship, S. S. Savannah, arrived in New York

---

June 3rd

	Feast of the Martrys of Uganda
48 BC	Pompey set out for Heraclea
545 AD	St. Clotilda died (Feast Day)
618	St. Kevin died (Feast Day)
1098	First Crusade captured Antioch, Syria
1596	English expedition to attack Cadiz, Spain, set sail
1621	Dutch West India Company chartered
1657	William Harvey, first observer of blood circulation, struck by paralysis

```
1745      Prussians defeated Austrians and Saxons at
                    Hohenfriedberg
1770      Mission of San Carlos (or Carmel) founded at
                    Monterey, California
1808      Jefferson Davis, president of the Confederacy,
                    born
1834      Garibaldi, Italian nationalist leader, condemned
                    to death but sentence was never
                    carried out
1843      King Frederick VIII of Denmark born
1844      Last great auk captured (last seen in the wild
                    in 1853)
          Gerlad A. Hobart, U.S. vice-president, born
1849      Five Cayuse Indians attacked a Washington mis-
                    sion school
1851      Clipper ship Flying Cloud left New York for
                    California on her maiden voyage
1861      First field use of telegraph system in a war
1862      U.S. recognized Liberia
1864      Confederate victory at the Battle of Cold Harbor
1865      George V, King of England, born
1875      George Bizet, composer of opera Carmen, born
1894      Lake Kivy discovered in the Congo
1898      Coal barge Merrimac sunk at the mouth of
                    Santiago harbor
1899      Johann Strauss, composer, died
1925      Tony Curtis, actor, born
1937      Duke of Windsor, formerly England's King Edward
                    VII, married Wallis Warfield Simpson
1942      First day of the Battle of Midway Island
1950      Mt. Annapurna in Nepal climed by the French
1952      Steel workers strike began in the U.S.
1960      New York City Police Department got "meter
                    maids"
1963      Pope John XXIII died
1965      Ed White made his space walk from Gemini IV
1969      U.S. destroyer Frank E. Evans cut in half by
                    Australian Melbourne
```

June 4th --

```
          Old Maids' Day
          Feast of St. Petroc
          Feast of St. Anthony in Margarita, Venezuela
          Annual Celebration Day at Eton School, England
1039 AD   Conrad II, Holy Roman Emperor, died
1133      Lothair II crowned Holy Roman Emperor
1260      Kublai made Khan, Mongol leader
1365      Charles IV crowned King of Burgundy
1508      Louis II crowned King of Hungary
1608      St. Francis Caracciolo died (Feast Day)
1639      New Haven, Connecticut's government by plan-
                    tation covenant ended
```

```
1717        "Rob Roy" Macgregor captured
1726        New England Courant, Boston newspaper, expired
1738        King George III of England born
1781        Jack Jovette rode to warn Thomas Jefferson of
                    impending capture by the British
1789        Louis XVII became heir to France
1800        French at Genoa surrendered to Austria (Italy)
1805        U.S. made peace with Tripoli
1812        Missouri became a U.S. territory
1831        Leopold I elected King of Belgium
1853        Ground broken for a canal between Lakes Superior
                    and Huron
1878        Turkey gave Cyprus to England
1901        City of Erie beat Tashmoo in a passenger ship
                    race on Lake Erie
1904        Panama national flag adopted
1911        Rosalind Russell, actress, born
1919        Robert Merrill, opera singer, born
            Women's Suffrage bill passed in the U.S. Senate
1929        Cardinal chosen state bird of Illinois
1940        Dunkirk evacuation ended
1941        William II, last emperor of Germany, died
1942        Four Japanese carriers sunk at the Battle of
                    Midway
1947        Taft-Hartley Act approved by the House of
                    Representatives
1949        Theodore Roosevelt National Park dedicated
1956        U.S. published Khrushchev's "peaceful coexis-
                    tence" speech (made in February)
1962        Sandy Koufax pitched a no-hitter and Los
                    Angeles beat Philadelphia 3-0
1966        Sttart of 6 days of Hurricane Alma in southeast
                    U.S.
1970        Sonny Tufts, actor, died
```

===
June 5th
===

```
468 BC      Socrates, Greek philosopher, born
754 AD      Abul'-Abbas, Caliph of Bagdad, died
754 or 755  Boniface and party murded by German heathens
                    (Feast Day)
1249        Seventh Crusade captured Damietta
1288        Battle of Woeringen
1316        Louis X, King of France, died
1510        Michaelangelo was commissioned to make 15
                    statues of saints for the Duomo
                    of Siena, Italy
1594        Four Dutch ships sailed in search of the North-
                    west Passage
1602        First expedition of British East Indian Company
                    reached Achin, Sumatra
1637        600 Pequot Indians killed at Mystic, Connecticut,
                    by the English colonists
```

```
1718    Thomas Chippendale, cabinetmaker, baptized
1723    Adam Smith, British economist, born
1781    Jack Jovette reached Thomas Jefferson to warn
             him of the British attack
1783    First balloon ride, upheld by hot air (France)
1806    Bernadotte, future King of Sweden, named Prince
             of Ponte Corvo by Napoleon
1830    Boston and Maine Railroad incorporated
1837    First meeting held that evolved into the Uni-
             versity of Michigan
1851    First installment of serialized Uncle Tom's
             Cabin appeared in the National Era
1870    Pera, a suburb of Constantinople, ravaged by
             fire
1873    Export of slaves from Zanzibar prohibited
1882    Bombay, India, hit by cyclone and tidal waves
        Igor Stravinsky, composer, born
1898    William Boyd, actor ("Hopalong Cassidy"), born
1900    Stephen Crane, author of Red Badge of Courage,
             died
        Pretoria, South Africa, captured (Boer War)
1901    First hot-air baloon races at Indianapolis,
             India
1911    Colorado state flag adopted
1915    New Danish constitution gave women the vote
1916    British cruiser Hampshire struck a mine in the
             Orkney Islands
1917    Start of register of U.S. men, age 21 to 30,
             for possible draft
1918    Battle of the Aisne ended
1933    Gold standard abolished in U.S.
1936    Green Springs site joined Colonial National
             Historic Park
1942    Ordnance plant explosion in Elwood, Illinois
        U.S. declared war on Bulgaria, Hungary and
             Rumania
1947    European Recovery Program proposed by the Sec-
             retary of State, evolving into the
             Marshall Plan
1967    Beginning of the Arab-Israeli 6-Day War
```

June 6th

```
        Memorial Day, Korean National Holiday
1134    St. Norbert died (Feast Day)
1502    John III, King of Portugal, born
1523    Gustavus I Eriksson crowned King of Sweden
1557    King John III of Portugal died
1599    Velasquez, Spanish artist, baptized
1654    Queen Christine of Sweden abdicated
1755    Nathan Hale, Revolutionary War hero, born
1756    John Trumbull, English artist, born
1799    Patrick Henry, statesman-orator, died
```

1799	Alexander Pushkin, Russian poet, born
1804	Louis A. Godey, Lady's Book publisher, born
1806	Louis Bonaparte proclaimed King of Holland
1809	Sweden got its constitution (Flag Day, national holiday)
1840	New York weekly fiction paper, New World, founded
1842	Steele Mackaye, folding theater-seat inventor, born
1846	England's Corn Laws repealed
1863	Election of King George I of Greece recognized by the world
1872	Alexandra, last Empress of Russia, born
1884	International Convention for the Protection of Patents ratified by the U.S.
1890	Dorothy Heyward, playwright-novelist, born
1891	Sir John MacDonald, first Premier of Canada, died
1893	International Mercantile Marine Company incorporated
1912	Mt. Katmai, Alaska, erupted, creating the Valley of 10,000 Smokes
1925	Chrysler Corporation formed
1933	First drive-in movie opened (Camden, New Jersey)
1935	14th Dalai Lama, Buddhist religious leader, born
1942	U.S. finally defeated Japan at the Battle of Midway Island
1944	Invasion of Normandy began (D-Day)
1968	Randolph Churchill, journalist and only son of Sir Winston, died
1971	Robert F. Kennedy, statesman, assassinated
1971	Seaman's Day holiday in Iceland
	Soyuz II, ill-fated Russian manned orbital flight, launched
1972	Old Bohemian Country Fair held at Chomutov, Czechoslovakia
2012	Transit of Venus

June 7th

	Feast of St. Colman of Dromore
	Feast of St. Meriadoc
	Flag Day in Norway
555 AD	Pope Vigilius died
632	Mohammed died of a stroke
1002	Henry II elected King of Germany
1099	First Crusade reached the walls of Jerusalem
1159	St. Robert of Newminster died (Feast Day)
1329	Robert I, "the Bruce," King of Scotland, died of leprosy
1394	Anne of Bohemia, queen to King Richard II of England, died
1520	King Henry VIII of England and King Francis I of France met on the Field of the Cloth of Gold

1537	Madeleine of France, wife of King James of Scotland, died
1576	Frobisher sailed in search of the Northwest Passage
1631	Mumtax Mahal, wife of Shah Jahan of India, died (Taj Mahal is her tomb)
1692	Port Royal, Jamaica destroyed by an earthquake
1755	Northern Persia rocked by an earthquake
1758	English forces attacked Louisbourg, French Canadian stronghold
1775	First meeting of the Connecticut Committee of Safety
1776	Richard Henry Lee called for a congress of the colonies
1778	Beau Brummel, English man of fashion, born
1811	Sir James Young Simpson, anesthetic pionner, born
1814	Caroline, estranged wife of King George IV, arrived in London, England
1839	Hawaii's "Magna Carta" delivered to the people
1840	King Frederick William III of Prussia died
	Charlotte, Empress of Mexico, born
1848	Paul Gauguin, French artist, born
1864	Abraham Lincoln was nominated for President
1893	Edwin Booth, actor, died
1902	First Game Laws for the district of Alaska established
	Green Tree Saloon dedicated in Council, Alaska
1903	French ship Libau sank after a Mediterranean collision
1905	Union of Norway and Sweden dissolved
1906	James J. Braddock, boxer, born
1909	Jessica Tandy, actress, born
1929	Papal States, extinct since 1870, became State of Vatican City in Rome
1942	U.S. carrier Yorktown sank at Midway Island
1944	British troops captured Bayeux, France
1946	British Broadcasting Corporation television went back on the air
1948	Communists took over Czechoslovakia
1970	E. M. Forster, British novelist, died
1972	Start of a week of Oiled Wrestling Games at Kirkpinar, Turkey

June 8th

410 AD	St. Melania the Elder died (Feast Day)
1042	Hardicanute, nonruling heir to England, died
1154	St. William of York died (Feast Day)
1191	Richard the Lionhearted arrived at beseiged Acre (3rd Crusade)
1492	Elizabeth, wife of King Edward IV of England, died

1504	Michaelangelo's "David" set in place in the Palazzo in Florence, Italy
1783	Thomas Sully, English artist, born
1795	Louis XVII, French king who never reigned, died in prison
1806	George Wythe, signer of the Declaration of Independence, died
1809	Phoenix, first sea-going steamboat, left New York for Philadelphia
1810	Robert Schumann, German composer, born
1845	Andrew Jackson, U.S. President, died
1861	Tennessee seceded from the Union
1867	Seven months of isolation by Indians ended at Fort C. F. Smith, Montana
	Gold discovered (Carissa lode) at South Pass, Wyoming
1869	Frank Lloyd Wright, architect, born
1876	George Sand, author, died
1886	Ludwig II, King of Bavaria, declared insane
1903	Ralph Yarborough, U.S. Senator, born
	Figig, Algeria, bombarded
1915	William Jennings Bryan resigned as Secretary of State over the sinking of the Lusitania
1918	Solar eclipse
1930	Carol II proclaimed King of Rumania
1937	Solar eclipse
1940	British carrier Glorious sunk off Narvik
1943	Japanese battleship Mutsu exploded off Japan
1949	St. Croix National Monument established (Maine)
1955	Mt. Istoro Nal in West Pakistan climbed by an American team
1965	Luna 6, Russian moon shot, launched
1969	Border-crossing between Spain and Gibralter closed
1970	Dragon Boat Festival in Hong Kong, Singapore, and Malaysia
2004	Transit of Venus

===
June 9th
===

	Senior Citizens' Day in Oklahoma
	Feast of St. Pelagia of Antioch
	Feast of Sts. Primus and Felician
	Ancient Roman festival honoring Vesta, goddess of hearths
53 BC	Crassus, Roman general, died battling the Persians
38	Pacorus, Parthian general, died in the Battle of Gindarus against Rome
68 AD	Nero, fiddling Roman emperor, committed suicide
597	St. Columba (or Colmcille), patron of Scotland, died (Feast Day)

```
1075    Henry VI, King of France, defeated the Saxons
            at Homburg
1156    Frederick, "Redbeard," King of Germany, married
            Beatrix of Burgundy
1198    Otto IV chosen King of Germany
1201    Last day of 15-day fair at Great Grimsby,
            Lincolnshire, England
1247    Carpini, papal legate returning from Mongolia,
            reached Kiev, Russia
1480    Turks assaulted Malta
1534    Jacques Cartier sailed into the mouth of the
            St. Lawrence River
1640    Leopold I, Holy Roman Emperor, born
1672    Czar Peter the Great of Russia born
1704    25 pirates sentenced to hang in Boston
1768    Samuel Slater, "father of American manufacturing,"
            born
1772    Newport, Rhode Island, merchants, angered over
            high taxes, burned the revenue-
            cutter Gaspee
1775    Trinidad Bay, California, discovered and claimed
            by Spain
1781    George Stephenson, English locomotive pioneer,
            born
1784    Founding of the Roman Catholic Church in the
            U.S.
1785    Sylvanus Thayer, father of the U.S. Military
            Academy, born
1791    John Howard Payne, composer of "Home, Sweet
            Home," born
1851    Vigilance Committee begun in San Francisco
1855    London Illustrated Times first published
1860    First "dime novel" published, Maleska, or the
            Indian Wife of the White Hunter
1862    Campaign of the Shenendoah Valley ended
1864    First experimental railway post office opened
            (Chicago)
1866    Meteorite fell near Knyahinya, Czechoslovakia
1870    Cornerstone of the capitol of Nevis laid
1890    "Oh, Promise Me" first publicly sung in the
            operetta, Robin Hood
1893    Ford's Theater collapsed (Washington, D.C.)
        Cole Porter, composer, born
1897    Connecticut state flag adopted
1899    James J. Jefferies took the heavyweight boxing
            title from Bob Fitzsimmons
1900    Fred Waring, conductor, born
1902    First Horn and Hardart Automat Restaurant
            opened (Philadelphia)
1909    First U.S. transcontinental women's auto trip
            completed
1911    Carrie Nation, temperance agitator, died
1916    Robert S. McNamara, statesman, born
1922    George Axelrod, author-playwright, born
```

```
1935       Jonkers Diamond, 726 carats, arrived in New York
                  City from England for 35¢ postage
                  registered mail
1940       First Peruvian census since 1876 completed
1948       First woman to do so offered the prayer in the
                  House of Representatives
1959       First ballistic-missile submarine, George
                  Washington, launched
1969       All Indian Rodeo held at White Swan, Washington
1970       Goat Show held at Northampton, Massachusetts
           Queen Elizabeth's birthday observed in Australia
```

June 10th

```
1190 AD    Frederick "Barbarosa," King of Burgundy,
                  Germany and Holy Roman Emperor,
                  drowned
1194       Much of Chartres, France, destroyed by fire
1248       Bergen, Norway, destroyed by fire
1376       Wenceslaus elected King of Germany
1610       First Dutch settlers landed on Manhattan
                  Island
1673       Marquette's party arrived at a Mississippi
                  River tributary
1682       First recorded tornado in America hit New
                  Haven, Connecticut
1800       First log house built at Bethany, Pennsylvania
1801       Tripoli declared war on the U.S.
1826       Janissaries, elite Turkish troops, were wiped
                  out when they attacked the Sultan's
                  palace
1837       Magnetic-needle telegraph patented
           Versailles Palace became a museum (France)
1842       Henry Morton Stanley, African explorer, born
1865       Wagner's opera Tristan und Isolde first produced
1868       Michael Obrenovic III, ruler of Serbia,
                  assassinated
1889       Sessue Hayakawa, actor, born
1898       U.S. Marines invaded Cuba
1909       Edward Everett Hale, author (Man Without a
                  Country), died
1921       Prince Philip Mountbatten, husband of Queen
                  Elizabeth II of England, born
1922       Judy Garland, singer-actress, born
1938       Pandora, a giant panda, arrived at the Bronx
                  Zoo (New York)
1940       Italy declared war on Britain and France
1942       Lidice, Czechoslovakia, destroyed by the Germans
1943       Income-tax withholding bill signed
1945       Gen. Eisenhower received the Jeweled Order of
                  Victory, Russia's highest award
1946       Italy again became a Republic
1956       A week of earthquakes in northern Afghanistan
                  began
```

```
1966        End of 6 days of Hurricane Alma in southeastern
                U.S.
            Sonny Siebert pitched a no-hitter and Cleveland
                beat Washington 2-0
1967        End of the Arab-Israeli 6-Day War
            Princess Margrethe of Denmark married Count
                    Henri de Laborde de Monpezat of
                    France
            First Lady, Ladybird Johnson, attended a clam-
                    bake
1970        Poson Commemoration in Ceylon
```

<u>June IIth</u> ---

```
            Feast of St. Barnabas
            Ancient Roman Festival honoring Mater Matuta
1216 AD     Henry, Emperor of Rumania, died, supposedly
                    poisoned by his wife
1258        Provisions of Oxford reform proposed by Parlia-
                    ment (England)
1488        James III, King of Scotland, murdered
1496        Columbus returned to Spain
1509        King Henry VIII of England married Catherine of
                    Aragon
1514        Christian II crowned King of Norway and Denmark
1560        Mary of Guise, widow of King James V of Scot-
                    land, died
1578        Sir Humphrey Gilbert granted a charter to
                    search for the Northwest Passage
1727        King George I of England died riding in his
                    carriage
1758        Kamehameha, first Hawaiian King, born
                    (Kamehameha Day holiday)
1764        Sandy Hook lighthouse first illuminated (New
                    York harbor)
1770        Captain Cook discovered the Great Barrier Reef,
                    Australia by grounding the
                    Endeavour on it
1776        John Constable, English artist, born
1829        King William I of Prussia married Augusta of
                    Saxe-Weimar
1859        Prince Metternich, Austrian statesman, died
            Comstock Lode claim filed for silver find in
                    Nevada
1861        Convention met at Wheeling to form the state
                    of West Virginia
1864        A ranch family was massacred by the Cheyenne
                    Indians
            Richard Strauss, composer, born
1881        National Theater in Prague, Czechoslovakia
                    opened
1895        Nicolai A. Bulganin, Russian statesman, born
            Duryea granted a patent on his automobile
```

```
1903      Alexander and Draga, rulers of Serbia, assassi-
                nated
1907      Paul Mellon, oil millionaire, born
1913      Rise Stevens, opera singer, born
          Norwegian women received the right to vote
1938      Johnny Vander Meer pitched a no-hitter and Cin-
                cinnati beat Boston 3-0
1940      Britain and France declared war on Italy
1943      Allies seized Pantelleria Island, beginning the
                Italian campaign
1948      Danish ship Kobennaun struck a mine in Kattagat
                Sound
1957      Vroman, Colorado, train wreck
1959      First hovercraft unveiled in England
```

June 12th

```
          Dorohoi, Rumania fair
          St. Anthony's Day in San Antonio, Venezuela
          Feast of St. Eskil
 816 AD   Pope St. Leo III died (Feast Day)
 918      Ethelfleda, daughter of King Alfred the Great
                of England, died
1458      College of St. Mary Magdalen founded at Oxford,
                England
1479      St. John of Sahagun died (Feast Day)
1672      France attacked Holland
1683      "Rye House Plot" to assassinate King Charles II
                discovered in England
1720      Isaac Pinto, translator of the first Jewish
                prayerbook published in America,
                born
1733      King Frederick II of Prussia married Elizabeth
                Christina of Brunswick-Bevern
1775      American sloop Unity captured schooner H.M.S.
                Margaretta
1778      Philip Livingston, signer of the Declaration of
                Independence, died
1792      New York Morning Post and Daily Advertiser,
                first daily newspaper in the city,
                founded
1838      Iowa became a U.S. territory
1839      Abner Doubleday invented baseball
1864      Emperor Maximilian arrived in Mexico City
1870      Sophia Smith, founder of Smith College, died
1876      Thomas Clark Hinkle, children's author, born
1878      William Cullen Bryant, editor-poet, died
          King George V of Hanover died
1882      Union Pacific rails reached Idaho
1897      Sir Anthony Eden, British statesman, born
          Assam, India, rocked by an earthquake
1915      David Rockefeller born
1917      Secret Service protection granted to the Presi-
                dent's family
```

```
1939      Baseball Hall of Fame established at Coopers-
               town, New York
1951      Destroyer Walke sunk off Korea
1954      Jim Wilson pitched a no-hitter and Milwaukee
               beat Philadelphia 2-0
1968      Cosmos 226, Russian satellite, launched
          World of Darkness exhibit opened at the Bronx
               Zoo in New York City
1971      Helsinki Day in Finland
          Miaoulis Naval Feast in Hydra, Greece
```

June 13th
──

```
          Ides of June
          Start of Ancient Rome's 2-day festival of
               Minerva, celebrated by flute-
               players
 323 BC   Alexander the Great died of a fever in Babylon
  40 AD   Virgin Mary, mother of Jesus, died
1231      St. Anthony of Padua died (Feast Day; patron
               of the poor, the illiterate,
               horses and donkeys; invoked to
               find lost objects)
1650      Mercurius Politicus, British periodical,
               first appeared
1777      Lafayette landed in America at Georgetown,
               South Carolina
1865      William Butler Yeats, author, born
1881      Jeanette, Arctic exploration ship, sank 2
               years after having been caught
               in the polar ice
1886      Ludwig II, insane King of Bavaria, drowned
1892      Basil Rathbone, actor, born
1897      John Spivak, author, born
1898      Yukon Territory of Canada organized
1904      Red Grange, football player, born
1907      Pennsylvania state flag adopted
1924      Dominican Republic got a constitition
1927      750,000 pounds of paper showered onto Charles
               Lindberg during his New York
               ticker-tape parade
1943      U.S. Coast Guard ship Escanaba exploded in the
               Atlantic
1944      Corenton, France, fell to the Allies
1956      British occupation of the Seuz Canal ended
1961      Treaty of the Antarctic, guaranteeing research
               by 12 countries, signed by U.S.
1964      West Pakistan devastated by winds and floods
1968      IDSCS 19-26, eight satellites, launched with
               one booster rocket
1970      Feast Day and Corn Dance at Sandia Pueblo,
               New Mexico
```

Feast of St. Basil the Great

510 BC Rome became a republic

847 AD St. Methodius of Constantinople died (Feast
Day)

1170 Henry III crowned King of England to rule
alongside his father, Henry II

1272 Gouda, Holland, founded

1381 Wat Tyler's Rebellion ended with his death
(England)

1497 Duke of Gandia, illegitimate son of Pope
Alexander VI, murdered

1574 Henry of Valois, King of Poland, fled his
kingdom

1645 Battle of Baseby in England's Parliamentary War

1777 "Stars and Stripes" adopted as the U.S. flag
(Flag Day)

1800 First military balloon used in French victory
at Marengo, Italy

Jean Baptiste Kleber, French general, assassinated by a Turk in Cairo

1805 Merriweather Lewis discovered the Great Falls
of the Missouri River

1807 Napoleon defeated the Russians at Friedland

1811 Harriet Beecher Stowe, author, born

1820 John Bartlett, compiler of Familiar Quotations,
born

1825 Pierre L'Enfant, designer of Washington, D.C.,
died

1827 Carpenters in Philadelphia demanded a reduction
to a 10-hour day (granted 1860)

1845 The Harbinger, a weekly magazine, founded

1846 Republic of California flag first raised
(Sonoma)

1850 Big fire in San Francisco, California

1861 Robert E. Lee became a full general of the
Confederate forces

1870 First defeat for Cincinnati's professional baseball team since the beginning of
the 1869 season

1876 Abdul Aziz, Ottoman Sultan, assassinated

1900 Hawaii became a U.S. territory

1902 Twentieth-Century Limited train began its first
run

1906 Margaret Bourke-White, photographer, born

1909 Burl Ives, actor-singer, born

1931 French St. Philbert sank in a storm off St.
Nazaire

1934 Max Baer took the heavyweight boxing title from
Primo Connera by a knockout

1940 German occupation of Paris began

1945 End of the Battle of Bessang Pass, Philippines

1963	Vostok V, Russian manned space flight, launched
1964	West Pakistan struck by high winds and floods
1969	Prospectors' Day in Republic, Washington
1970	Start of the week-long Fiesta de Amancaes of Inca pagentry in Peru
	Lions Lumbermen Day in Catawba, Washington
1971	Rice-planting Day in Osaka, Japan

June 15th

Annual cleaning day of Roman shrines to Vesta

Koreans wash their hair in a stream to ward off ill fortune on Farmers' Day, time for rice transplantings

Feast of St. Vitus (patron of actors and dancers; invoked against rabies, epilepsy, sleeping sickness and shaking diseases)

763 BC	Solar eclipse
844 AD	Louis II crowned King of Italy
923	Robert I, usurper of France, killed in battle with the real king
960	St. Edburga of Winchester died (Feast Day)
1094	Spanish troops under El Cid took Valencia from the Moors
1215	Magna Carta signed
1219	Danes defeated Estonians at the Battle of Reval
1246	Leopold VI, last Babenberg ruler of Austro-Hungary, killed in battle
1301	Charles I enthroned as King of Hungary
1330	Edward, the Black Prince of England, born
1601	St. Germaine of Pibrac died (Feast Day)
1728	Shah Alam, Mogol ruler of India, born
1752	Benjamin Franklin flew his kite in a thunderstorm
1775	George Washington was appointed first U.S. General
1776	Colony of New Hampshire elected to become independent of England
1836	Arkansas became a state
1843	Edvard Grieg, composer, born
1844	Charles Goodyear applied for a patent on vulcanized rubber
1846	Treaty with England set Oregon Territorial boundary at 49th Parallel ("54-40 or fight")
1849	James K. Polk, 11th U.S. President, died
1864	Start on the three-day seige of Petersburg, Russia
	Arlington National Cemetery established (Washington, D.C.)
1867	Nebraska state seal adopted
	Atlantic Cable Quartz Lode, a gold vein, discovered in Montana

1869	Start of the National Peace Jubilee, Boston
1888	Frederick III, King of Germany and Prussia, died after ruling 99 days
1896	Sanriku, Japan, rocked by an earthquake
1904	Saul Steinberg, artist, born
1905	Gustav VI, King of Sweden, married Princess Margaret
1914	Steamer General Slocum burned in the East River of New York City
1938	Johnny Vander Meer pitched his second no-hitter in five days and Cincinnati beat Brooklyn 6-0
1939	French submarine Phenix sank off Indo-China
1963	Juan Marichal pitched a no-hitter and San Francisco beat Houston 1-0
1969	Fort Simcoe Flag Day at Fort Simco, Washington
1970	Grieg's birthday celebrated at Lofthus, Norway

June 16th

	Feast of St. John Regis
	Feast of Sts. Cyricus and Julitta, mother and son martyrs
	Feast of St. Tikhon of Amathus
408 BC	Alcibiates triumphantly entered Athens after a seven-year absence
632 AD	Persian Era of Yazdegerd began
1246	St. Lutgard died (Feast Day)
1456	Twenty-five-year-old judgment of heresy against Joan of Arc annulled
1464	Rogier Vander Weyden, painter, died
1483	Edward, boy king of England, and his brother imprisoned, to be murdered
1657	Christian Huygens, its inventor, presented a pendulum clock to the Dutch government
1673	Governor's Island, off Manhattan, bought for 2 axes, some beads and nails
1755	Bostonians captured French forts in Nova Scotia
1775	George Washington accepted his commission as the General of the American Army
1809	Calais, Maine, incorporated
1812	British rescinded the blockade of the U.S. to avert the War of 1812
1845	Texas Congress agreed to annexation by the U.S.
1846	Giovanni-Maria Mastai-Forretti elected Pope (Pius IX)
1858	Abraham Lincoln accepted the presidential nomination and made his "house divided" speech
	Gustavus V, King of Sweeden, born
1862	Northern Overland Expedition left St. Paul, Minnesota

```
1874       Act of Congress established the standing army
               at 25,000 men
1888       Casper, Wyoming, founded with the arrival of
               the first train at Fort Casper
1897       Alaskan gold rush began when miners returned
               from there to San Francisco
           Treaty signed for U.S. annexation of Hawaii
1903       Ford Motor Company incorporated, and sold its
               first car
1925       Hackettstown, New Jersey, train wreck
1927       U.S.S. Constitution, nicknamed "Old Ironsides,"
               sent to dry-dock for her 4th
               reconstruction
1930       Elmer A. Sperry, gyro-compass inventor, died
1940       Du Bose Heyward, playwright-author, died
           French ship Champlain sank in port
1941       U.S. submarine 0-9 sank during a test dive
1944       Germans began firing jet-propelled bombs at
               England
1952       European Coal and Steel Plan treaty signed
1955       British submarine Sidon exploded at Portland,
               England
           A military revolution began in Argentina
           Juan Peron, President of Argentina, excommu-
               nicated
1960       Last section of the lower deck on the George
               Washington Bridge completed (New
               York City)
1963       Start of three days of orbits by Russian woman
               astronaut
1966       U.S. tanker Texaco Massachusetts and British
               tanker Alva collided at New York
1970       Birthday of the City God, Taipei, Formosa
```

June 17th

```
           Feast of St. Botolph or Botulf
           Feast of St. Harvey
           Feast of St. Alban (Episcopal)
 900 AD    Fulk, archbishop of Reims, killed by the Count
               of Flanders
 956       Hugh the Great, kingmaker of France, died
1239       Edward I, King of England, born
1397       Eric crowned King of Norway, Denmark and Sweden
1442       Frederick IV crowned King of Germany
1596       Spitzbergen, Norway, settled
1673       Marquette's canoes sailed into the Mississippi
               River
1682       King Charles XII of Sweden born
1696       John III, King of Poland, died
1703 OS    John Wesley, founder of Methodism, born
1745       Siege of Louisburg, Canada, ended in the French
               surrender
```

1767	Lebanon, Maine, incorporated
1775	Battle of Bunker (or Breed's) Hill, beginning Revolutionary War
1783	<u>Pennsylvania Evening Post and Daily Advertiser</u>, first U.S. daily paper, began publishing and lasted 16 months
1789	French National Assembly formed
1794	54 people guillotined in Paris's "Reign of Terror"
1816	Rembrandt Peale got a permit to make gas in Baltimore
	New England struck by a snowstorm
1818	Charles Gounod, composer of <u>Faust</u>, born
1825	Cornerstone of Bunker Hill Monument laid
1832	Steamboat <u>Yellowstone</u> arrived at Fort Union from St. Louis
1837	Charles Goodyear got a patent for unsticky rubber
1843	Bunker Hill Monument dedicated
1849	Henry Clay Frick, millionaire, born
1856	First Republican National Convention held (Philadelphia)
1861	Confederates driven from Booneville and Jefferson City in Missouri
1876	Battle of the Rosebud (U.S. Army defeated by Sioux and Cheyenne Indians)
1877	Nez Perce Indians routed U.S. Cavalry attackers in Idaho (Battle of the White Bird)
1895	Harlem River Ship Canal connecting the Hudson River and Long Island Sound opened
1896	Nansen's met Jackson's Arctic expedition when their paths crossed
	<u>Drummond Castle</u> wrecked off the French coast
1914	John Hersey, author, born
1915	Ferry service begun between New York City and Englewood, New Jersey
1917	Dean Martin, singer-actor, born
1925	International agreement banning poison gas and germ warfare signed
1937	Cornerstone of Oregon's new capitol laid
1939	Cunard liner <u>Mauritania</u> began her maiden voyage (Liverpool, England to New York)
1940	British <u>Lancastria</u> torpedoed off St. Nazaire, 2,500 died
1941	U.S. credits in Italy frozen by the Italian government
1944	Republic of Iceland founded (National Independence Day)
1947	First commercial plane flight around the world left New York City
1950	Intercollegiate regatta first rowed on the Ohio River at Marietta
1953	Anti-Communist workers rioted in East Berlin, Germany

```
1955      John Golden, playwright and songwriter, died
1956      Week of earthquakes in Northern Afghanistan
             ended
1971      U.S. returned control of Okinawa to Japan
```

June 18th

```
          Feast of Sts. Mark and Marcellian
 373 AD   St. Ephraem died (Feast Day)
1155      Frederick "Barbarosa," King of Germany, crowned
             Holy Roman Emperor
1164      St. Elizabeth of Schonau died (Feast Day)
1464      Pope Pius II began a crusade
1541      Hernando deSoto crossed the Mississippi River
1621      First duel in New England fought
1633      Charles I, King of England, crowned King of
             Scotland
1750      Prussians defeated Austrians at Kolin, Bohemia
1778      British evacuated Philadelphia
1812      Congress declared war on Britain because they
             hadn't heard the blockade had ended
1815      Napoleon defeated at Waterloo
1855      Sault St. Marie Canal, connecting Lakes Huron
             and Superior, opened
1864      End of the three-day siege of Petersburg,
             Russia
1873      Susan B. Anthony, suffragist, fined $100 for
             having voted
1880      John A. Sutter, colonizer of California, died
1908      University of the Philippines authorized
1945      General Dwight D. Eisenhower returned from
             Europe
1947      Ewell Blackwell pitched a no-hitter and Cin-
             cinnati beat Boston 6-0
1953      Egypt proclaimed a republic
1965      Titan 3C launched with a dummy satellite
1967      Don Wilson pitched a no-hitter and Houston beat
             Atlanta 2-0
1970      First of 3 days of Salusalu Festival in the
             Fiji Islands
```

June 19th

```
          Feast of St. Boniface or Bruno of Querfurt
          Feast of Sts. Gervase and Protase
 221 BC   Chu Yuan drowned himself, protesting the Hong
             Kong government
 325 AD   First Council of Nice opened, ending with the
             adoption of the Nicene Creed
 936      Louis IV crowned King of France
1312      Piers Gaveston, Earl of Cornwall, beheaded
1341      St. Juliana Falconieri died (Feast Day)
```

```
1566    King James V of Scotland, to be James I of
                Britain, born
1586    English colonists from North Carolina left to
                return to England
1605    Czar-pretender entered Moscow, Russia
1706    "The Giant," great bell of Russia weighing
                288,000 lbs., fell for the second
                time, having been recast after the
                first mishap
1778    Gray, Maine, incorporated
1794    Richard Henry Lee, signer of the Declaration of
                Independence, died
1811    Samuel Chase, signer of the Declaration of
                Independence, died
1846    First formal baseball game played (Hoboken,
                New Jersey)
1849    Mann grain harvester patented
1850    King Charles XV of Sweden married Louisa of the
                Netherlands
1858    Bremen began North German-Lloyd Lines trans-
                atlantic service
1864    Kearsarge, a Union ship sank the Confederate
                Alabama off France
1867    Maximilian, former Emperor, executed in Mexico
1886    William Howard Taft married Helen Herron
1887    Charles Coburn, actor, born
1896    Wallis Warfield Simpson, Duchess of Windsor and
                wife of former King Edward VIII
                of England, born
1902    Guy Lombardo, bandleader, born
1910    Abe Fortas, Supreme Court jurist, born
        Fathers' Day first observed
1911    Portugal abolished its monarchy
1915    Battleship Arizona launched
        Icelandic national flag adopted
1934    National Archives created by an Act of Congress
        Federal Communications Commission established
1936    Solar eclipse
1938    Saugres, Montana, train wreck
1944    Two Japanese aircraft carriers sunk by U.S. sub-
                marines in the first Battle of the
                Philippine Sea
1950    British ship Indian Enterprise exploded in the
                Red Sea
1952    Carl Erskine pitched a no-hitter and Brooklyn
                beat Chicago 5-0
1953    Julius and Ethel Rosenberg executed for wartime
                espionage
1961    Kuwait became independent of Britain
1962    Tiros 5, weather satellite, launched
1963    Russia's woman astronaut returned to earth
        Tiros 7, weather satellite, launched
1969    Dragon Boat Festival in Hong Kong
1970    Midsummer Night Festival in Finland
```

Feast of St. Faelan

National Fair at San Pedro Sula, Honduras

840 AD   Louis I, "the Pious," Holy Roman Emperor, died

981   St. Adalbert of Magdeburg died (Feast Day)

1367   Geoffrey Chaucer granted a royal pension for service

1389   John Plantagenet, 3rd son of King Henry IV of England, born

1529   Peace of Barcelona ended Lutheran attacks on Rome

1596   Cadiz, Spain, sacked again by the English

1632   Lord Baltimore received the charter to found the colony of Maryland

1743   British captured Nuestra Senora de Covadonga, a Spanish treasure ship

1756   "Black Hole of Calcutta" (Indian attack on the British East India Company)

1782   Great Seal of the United States adopted by Congress

1789   French Revolution began

1791   King Louis XVI and his family attempted to escape France

1836   New York Evening Express founded, to become part of the Evening Mail 45 years later

1837   King William IV of England died

1863   West Virginia became a state (West Virginia Day)

1869   End of National Peace Jubilee in Boston, Massachusetts

1876   Santa Anna, Mexican revolutionist, died

1900   German minister to China killed in the Boxer Rebellion

1904   Russian submarine Dolphin sunk

1905   Lillian Hellman, playwright, born

1907   Swiss National Bank opened

1908   Rimski-Korsakov, Russian composer, died

1909   Errol Flynn, actor, born

1924   Audie Murphy, war hero-actor, born

1940   Supplies for China via the Hai-Phong railway ceased

1947   Presidential veto of the Taft-Hartley Act over-ridden by U.S. Congress

1948   Ed Sullivan's television variety hour debuted

1954   Alfred Harcourt, publishing partner, died

1960   Ingemar Johansson was knocked out by Floyd Patterson for the heavyweight boxing crown

1965   Bernard M. Baruch, philanthropist, died

1970   National Hollerin' Contest held at Spivey's Corner, North Carolina

Swiss Cheese Festival held at Middlefield, Ohio

		Merchant Marine Day in Venezuela
		Feast of St. Meen
400	BC	Solar eclipse
168		Lunar eclipse
451	AD	Aetius, Roman general, fought the Huns at Chalons, France

Merchant Marine Day in Venezuela
Feast of St. Meen

400 BC   Solar eclipse
168   Lunar eclipse
451 AD   Aetius, Roman general, fought the Huns at
         Chalons, France
1002   Pope St. Leo IX born
1208   Philip, King of Germany, murdered by his
         daughter's rejected suitor
1377   King Edward III of England died
1591   St. Aloysius died (Feast Day; patron of
         youth)
1598   British captured El Morro, the fort at San
         Juan, Puerto Rico
1631   John Smith, Virginia colonist, died
1633   Galileo questioned by the Inquisition
1672   French captured Doesburg, Holland
1678   Cornerstone of new St. Paul's Cathedral laid
         in London
1756   Of 146 British prisoners locked in "The Black
         Hole of Calcutta," 23 were still
         alive
1777   British captured Fort Ticonderoga
         First volume of the second edition of the
         Encyclopaedia Britannica pub-
         lished
1788   New Hampshire ratified the Constitution
1791   French royal family arrested by revolution-
         aries
1798   Battle of Vinegar Hill in Ireland
1810   Zachary Taylor married Margaret M. Smith
1846   Giovanni-Maria Mastai-Ferretti crowned Pope
         Pius IX
1882   Rockwell Kent, artist-author, born
1905   Jean-Paul Sartre, author, born
         Dwight B. Huss won the first transcontinental
         U.S. auto race, arriving at Port-
         land, Oregon from New York City
1921   Jane Russell, actress, born
         Sulgave Manor, English home of George Washing-
         ton's ancestors, opened as a
         museum
1942   Rommel captured Tobruk, North Africa
1943   Detroit race riots left 34 dead
1963   Giovanni Battista Cardinal Montini became Pope
         as Paul VI
1970   Shrimp Festival at Oostduinkerke, Belgium

Organic Act Day in the Virgin Islands

```
1960        Transit 2A launched
            Greb 1, piggyback satellite, launched
1969        Judy Garland, actress-singer, found dead
1970        National Tree Day in El Salvador
```

```
========================================================
June 23rd
========================================================
```

```
            Viking Festival of Balder, Lord of Life
            Traditionally coldest day of the year in
                        Bolivia
            Eve of the Feast of St. John celebrated as
                        Midsummer Eve in Scandinavia
   79 AD    Vespasian, Roman Emperor, died
  679       St. Etheldreda or Audrey died (Feast Day)
  930       First meeting of the Icelandic Parliament
                        opened
 1097       Turkish army surrendered to Crusaders at Nicaea
 1650       King Charles II of England landed in Scotland
 1661       England given Tangier and Bombay in the
                        marriage contract between King
                        Charles II and Catherine of
                        Portugal
 1664       Duke of York sold New Jersey to Lord Berkley
                        and Sir George Carteret
 1683       William Penn signed a treaty of peace and
                        friendship with the Pennsylvania
                        Indians
 1703       Marie Leszezynska, wife of King Louis XV of
                        France, born
 1743       British and German troops fought the French at
                        Dettingen over the Austrian
                        Succession
 1757       British recaptured Calcutta from the Nawab of
                        Bengal
 1763       Empress Josephine, wife of Napoleon, born in
                        Martinique
            Indian attack on a ship in the Detroit River
                        repulsed
 1784       Machias, Maine, incorporated
 1812       Napoleon, entering Russia, was thrown from his
                        horse when it shied at a rabbit
 1836       The 26 United States divided a $28 million
                        treasury surplus
 1860       U.S. Secret Service established
            St. Joseph Cafasso died (Feast Day)
 1865       Last Confederate General surrendered, Cherokee
                        Chief Stand Watie
 1868       First practical typewriter invention patented
 1870       First passenger train arrived at Denver,
                        Colorado
 1876       Irvin S. Cobb, humorist and writer, born
 1878       Bannock Indians attacked by U.S. Cavalry at
                        Silver Creek, Oregon
```

```
            Feast of St. Albans (Roman Catholic)
            Feast of St. Nicetas of Remesiana
  168 BC   Romans battled Macedonians at Pydna
  431 AD   St. Paulinus of Nola died (Feast Day)
 1101      Roger I, ruler of Sicily, died
 1276      Pope Innocent V died
 1476      Charles, Duke of Burgundy, defeated by the
                   Swiss at Morat
 1535      St. John of Rochester executed
 1559      King Philip II of Spain married Elizabeth of
                   Valois
 1611      Henry Hudson and part of his crew abandoned in
                   Canada by mutineers
 1633      Galileo again questioned by the Inquisition
 1772      Slavery abolished in England
 1774      Ohio Territory annexed to Quebec by England
 1830      Pillory last used in England, in a perjury
                   case
 1832      Paterson and Hudson Railroad began their
                   horse-drawn service in New Jersey
 1840      Hobson claimed New Zealand for England as part
                   of Australia
 1844      Margaret Sidney, author (The Five Little
                   Peppers and How They Grew), born
 1846      Antoine Joseph Sax got a patent on his saxo-
                   phone
 1851      Part of San Francisco, California, destroyed
                   by fire
 1870      U.S. Department of Justice created
 1888      Alan Seeger, poet, born
 1893      British battleship Victoria involved in a
                   collision off Syria
 1894      First auto race, Paris to Rouen, France, run
 1897      Queen Victoria's Diamond Jubilee celebrated
 1898      Erich Maria Remarque, novelist, born
 1911      King George V and Queen Mary crowned in
                   England
 1918      Ivanhoe, Indiana, tran wreck
 1921      First Parliament of Northern Ireland opened
 1922      New tennis stadium opened at Wimbledon, England
           Start of a violent coal-miners' strike in
                   Herrin, Illinois
 1936      Harmon Killebrew, baseball player, born
 1937      Joe Louis took the heavyweight boxing title
                   from James J. Braddock in 8 rounds
 1940      Occupied France signed an armistice with Germany
 1941      Russia invaded by Germany and Rumania
 1944      G.I. Bill signed into law
 1946      First two jet air mail flights flew
 1948      James G. MacDonald appointed first U.S. Ambas-
                   sador to Israel
 1949      Ezzard Charles defeated "Jersey Joe" Walcott
                   for the heavyweight boxing title
 1954      Studebaker Corporation merged with the Packard
                   Motor Car Company
```

```
1887    First infants' hospital, Babies' in New York
                City, founded
1891    U.S. Department of Agriculture began rain-
                making experiments in Texas
1894    King Edward VIII of England born
1895    Norman R. Raine, creator of "Tugboat Annie,"
                born
1898    Emilio Aquinaldo proclaimed himself dictator
                of the Philippines
1903    U.S. Army adopted the Springfield rifle
1910    King Edward VIII titled Prince of Wales
1913    Secret Service protection granted to the
                president-elect
1922    End of violent coal-miners  strike in Herrin,
                Illinois
1928    U.S. proposed the outlawing of war
1931    Wiley Post and Harold Gatty left New York to
                establish a round-the-world flight
                record
1936    Queen Mary became the first woman member of the
                Grand Cross of the Victorian
                Order (England)
1944    Tornadoes struck in Ohio, Pennsylvania, West
                Virginia, and Maryland
1946    William S. Hart, actor-author, died
1947    Taft-Hartley Act passed by the Senate over the
                President's veto
1949    First 12 women graduated from the Harvard
                Medical School
1959    Klaus Fuchs, convicted spy, was returned to
                East Germany
1967    President Johnson met Russia's Premier
                Kosygin at Glassboro, New Jersey
1969    Warren Burger sworn in as Chief Justice of
                the U.S. Supreme Court
1970    Meteor V, Russian weather satellite, launched
        Wainiki holiday celebrated in Poland
        Sun Easter of the Incas at Cuzco, Peru
```

June 24th

```
        Procession to St. John's Cemetery in Laren,
                Holland
        Halifax, Yorkshire, England  fair day
        Midsummer Eve in Italy
        Midsummer Day in England, a quarter-day when
                rents are due and people move in
                or out
        Trees have finished their annual growth
```

```
  ? BC  St. John the Baptist born (Feast Day; patron of
                  bird dealers, invoked against hail,
                  epilepsy, convulsions and spasm,
                  and for the protection of lambs)
 541 AD  Attila the Hun raised his seige of Orleans,
                  France
1065    Ferdinand I, "the Great," King of Castile,
                  died
1314    Scots defeated the English at Bannockburn
1340    Battle of Sluys (England defeated the French
                  invasion fleet)
1371    John of Gaunt, England, unhorsed Sieur de
                  Puissances, France, in a tournament
                  held at Bordeaux, France, ending
                  his term as governor of Aquitaine
1497    John Cabot sighted Cape Breton Islands, Canada
1519    Lucrezia Borgia died
1533    Former Queen Mary of France died
1537    St. Francis Xavier ordained a priest
1540    King Henry VIII of England divorced Anne of
                  Cleves
1542    St. John of the Cross born
1603    Date picked for the abdication of King James I
                  of England by the members of the
                  "Watson plot"
1633    Inquisition finally released Galileo
1680    William Penn asked the King of England for
                  Pennsylvania
1717    Grand Lodge of Freemasons inaugurated in London
1761    Battle of Wilhelmsthal in the Seven Years' War
1768    Marie Leszczynska, wife of King Louis XV of
                  France, died
1771    E. I. DuPont, corporation founder, born
1803    Matthew Thornton, signer of the Declaration of
                  Independence, died
1866    Custer's 7th Cavalry camp attacked by and
                  repulsed the Sioux Indians
        Italians crushed by the Austrians at Custozza
1871    Cornerstone laid for New York State capitol
        Thomas McKean, signer of the Declaration of
                  Independence, died
1885    Woodrow Wilson married Ellen L. Axson
        First black, Samuel D. Ferguson, consecrated as
                  a bishop of the Protestant
                  Episcopal Church of America
1895    Jack Dempsey, boxer, born
1908    Grover Cleveland, U.S. President, died
1917    McNary, Arizona, a logging town, founded
1922    Leslie's Weekly, New York City paper since 1855,
                  expired
1924    New York Mirror, a daily tabloid, founded
1928    A treaty idea that would outlaw war was
                  announced
```

1931	Billy Casper, golfer, born
1932	Siam became a constitutional monarchy by revolution
1941	President announced U.S. aid to Russia
1950	Friendship International Airport, Baltimore, dedicated
1954	First 114 miles of the New York State Thruway opened
1956	Dean Martin and Jerry Lewis broke up their comedy team

June 25th

	Feast of St. Pontius Pilate (Abyssinian Church)
	Feast of St. Febronia
	Feast of St. Prosper of Reggio
841 AD	Emperor Lothair and the Holy Roman Army defeated by German-French allies at Fontenoy-en-Puisaye
930	Hucbald, Benedictine monk and muscle expert, died
1080	Guibert elected antipope as Clement III
1291	Queen Eleanor, widow of King Henry III of England, died
1483	Duke of Gloucester named himself King Richard III of England
1503	Catherine of Aragon, widow of Arthur, Prince of Wales, betrothed to his brother, who would become King Henry VIII of England
1513	Augsburg Confession, distinct break between Catholicism and Protestantism, took place
1635	Island of Martinique became the property of France
1744	First Methodist Conference convened (London)
1770	Boston Chronicle, newspaper, ceased publication
1778	Virginia ratified the Constitution
1807	Czar Alexander I of Russia and Napoleon met on a raft on the Nieman River and swore eternal friendship
1864	William I, King of Wurttemberg, died
1865	First Italian Civil Code promulgated
1870	Queen Isabella II of Spain abdicated
1876	"Custer's Last Stand" at the Little Big Horn, Montana
1906	Stanford White, architect, murdered
1916	Thomas Eakins, artist, died
1921	Latvian National Flag became official
1938	Mary H. Foote, author-illustrator, died
1941	Finland declared war on Russia
1945	United Nations began

```
1950        Korean War began
1957        Hurricane Audrey hit the U.S. Gulf Coast
1962        U.S. Supreme Court ruled prayer in schools
                unconstitutional
1967        Johnson and Kosygin again met at Glassboro,
                New Jersey
1969        Bruce Tulloh of England reached New York City,
                besting the old continental run
                record by 8 days
1972        Blessing of the Sea held at Ostend, Belgium
```

```
            Feast of Sts. John and Paul
   4 AD     Tiberius, step-son of Caesar Augustus, named
                his heir
    363     Julian, Roman Emperor, wounded in battle and
                died
   1097     First Crusade occupied Nicaea
   1178     St. Anthelm died (Feast Day)
   1541     Pizzaro, Spanish conqueror of the Incas,
                assassinated in Peru
   1742     Arthur Middleton, signer of the Declaration of
                Independence, born
   1794     A military balloon was used in the battle of
                Fleurus
   1819     Abner Doubleday, baseball inventor, born
   1824     William Thomson, Lord Kelvin, inventor of the
                submarine cable, born
   1827     Samuel Compton, spinning-mule inventor, died
   1830     King George IV of England died
   1844     John Tyler married Julia Gardiner
   1862     Seven-day battle at Mechanicsville, Virginia,
                began
   1866     500 Indians attacked a Cavalry-escorted wagon
                train in Western Kansas
   1870     The boardwalk in Atlantic City, New Jersey,
                opened
   1879     Ismail, Khedive of Egypt, removed from office
   1892     Pearl Buck, author, born
   1894     Clarence Lovejoy, founder of the college guides,
                born
   1900     Walter Reed began the campaign to wipe out
                yellow fever in Cuba
   1902     Imperial Service Order instituted in England
   1904     Peter Lorre, actor, born
   1917     U.S. expeditionary forces landed in France
   1919     The New York Daily News first appeared on the
                newsstands
   1927     Pons-Winnecke Comet passed within 3-1/2 million
                miles of Earth
   1934     Evangelical and Reformed Church founded in U.S.
```

1934   Congress approved the idea for a Jefferson
              Memorial
1937   Last display by the Royal Air Force held at
              England's Hendon Field
1945   United Nations Charter signed in San Francisco
1959   Official opening and dedication of the St.
              Lawrence Seaway held
         Ingemar Johansson knocked out by Floyd Patterson
              for the heavyweight boxing crown
1960   Malagasy Republic (Madagascar) granted
              independence from France
              (Independence Day)
1970   Final Day of the National Marble Tournament
              at Wildwood, New Jersey
         Trout Festival held at Flin Flon, Manitoba,
              Canada
         Molniya 1/14, Russian communications satellite,
              launched

June 27th

992 AD Battle of Conquereuil
1095   St. Ladislas I, King of Hungary, died (Feast
              Day)
1352   Zug and Aeusser Amt joined the Swiss
              Confederation
1574   Giorgio Vasari, Florentine artist, died
1756   First naval engagement of the French and
              Indian War took place on the Great
              Lakes
1786   George Hellplewhite, furniture-maker, willed
              all to his wife
1787   Gibbon finished writing The Decline and Fall of
              the Roman Empire
1818   El Correo del Orinoco newspaper first published
              in Venezuela
1844   Joseph Smith, founder of the Mormon Church,
              killed
1847   Telepgraph wires were completed between New York
              City and Boston
1861   Central Pacific Railroad of California
              incorporated
1862   Battle of Gaines Mill or Cold Harbor, Virginia
1863   Confederates under General Early invaded York,
              Pennsylvania
1864   Confederate victory at Kenesaw Mountain, Georgia
1874   John Golden, playwright-songwriter, born
         Battle of Adobe Walls (Comanche Indian attack
              on a trading post)
1880   Helen Keller, blind and deaf writer-lecturer,
              born
1882   Idea for England's Manchester Ship Canal
              formulated
         Bank of Japan established

```
1918      British ship Llandovery Castle torpedoed
1944      U.S. forces took Cherbourg, France
1946      Wanda Gag, children's author-illustrator, died
1950      U.S. President ordered intervention in Korean
                War
1969      Start of Sagebrush Olympics at Ephrata,
                Washington
1971      Dragon Boat Festival in Malaysia
```

```
June 28th ===============================================
          ===============================================

          Our Lady of Pilar celebrated in Margerita,
                Venezuela
          Start of Malta's two-day Folk Festival
          Fair Day at Langport, Somerset, England
          Feast of St. Austol
          Feast of St. Potamiaena
 767 AD   St. Paul, Pope died
 930      Icelandic Parliament's first meeting ended
1243      Sinisbaldo Fieschi crowned Pope as Innocent IV
1245      Council of Lyons convened to discuss
                excommunicating the Holy Roman
                Emperor
1491      King Henry VIII of England born
1559      Start of a three-day tournament in Paris in
                which King Henry of France was
                mortally wounded
1672      Albanel reached Hudson's Bay, overland
1703      John Wesley, founder of Methodism, born
1709      Charles XII, King of Sweden, wounded in the
                foot at Poltava
1712      Jean Jacques Rousseau, French philosopher,
                born
1744      Empress Catherine the Great received into the
                Russian Orthodox Church
1754      French and Indians captured Fort Necessity in
                Virginia Territory
1776      British sea attack repulsed at Charlestown,
                South Carolina
1778      Battle of Monmouth, New Jersey
1809      First large boat set sail on Lake Champlain
1838      Victoria crowned Queen of England
1847      St. Vincentia Gerosa died (Feast Day)
1863      James Madison, U.S. President, died
          George G. Meade became Union Commander-in-Chief
1902      U.S. purchased unfinished Panama Canal from
                France
          Richard Rogers, composer, born
1904      Norge wrecked on Rockall Reef
1905      Ashley Montagu, anthropologist-author, born
1906      The Griswold Hotel in Groton, Connecticut,
                opened for business
```

```
1914        Archduke Francis Ferdinand of Austro-Hungary
                was assassinated in Bosnia
1919        Germany and the Allies signed the Treaty of
                Versailles
            Harry S. Truman married Elizabeth V. Wallace
1921        Yugoslavian national flag adopted
1948        Communists meeting in Prague denounced Yugo-
                slavia for not following the
                Marxist doctrine
            Japan struck by earthquakes and resulting fires
1956        Poznan, Poland workers revolted against the
                Communist government
1958        Mackinac Bridge opened, crossing the 5-mile
                straits between U.S. and Canada
1959        Railroad tank car explosion at Mildrin,
                Georgia
1963        Geophysical Research Satellite launched
1965        Pecos National Monument establisned
1969        Lower level of the Verrazano-Narrows Bridge
                opened, connecting Brooklyn and
                Staten Island
            Replica of Columbus's ship, Santa Maria, a St.
                Louis tourist attraction, sank
                in a storm on the Mississippi
            Lummi Stommish at Marietta, Washington
1970        Blessing of the Fishing Fleet performed at
                Provincetown, Massachusetts
1972        St. Paul's Feast or Kato Paphos in Cyprus,
                celebrated by a parade of the
                icons
```

June 29th

```
            Martyrdom of Sts. Peter and Paul, apostles
                (Peter, patron of locksmiths,
                cobblers, and French harvesters;
                Paul, patron of ropemakers,
                invoked against hail and snake-
                bite)
            Start of an 8-day fair at Wolverhampton,
                Staffordshire, England
            Festival Day in Mexcaltitan, Mexico
  48 BC     Caesar defeated Pompey at Pharsalus
 548 AD     Theodora, wife of Emperor Justinian of
                Byzantium, died of cancer
 922        Robert I crowned King of France
1312        Henry VII crowned Holy Roman Emperor
1397        John II, King of Aragon, born
1440        Battle of Anghiari, Italy, saw Milan defeated
                by an alliance of Florence, Genoa,
                Venice, and the Papal States
```

1545	Founding of a Botanical Garden decreed at Padua, Italy
1577	Peter Paul Rubens, artist, born
1613	Globe Theater, London, burned down during a performance of Shakespeare's King Henry VIII
1643	English Royalists defeated the Parliamentarians at Alderton Moor
1767	El Pilar (Margarita), Venezuela, founded
1784	Caesar Rodney, signer of the Declaration of Independence, died
1831	Kingdom of Belgium recognized and Leopold of Saxe-Coburg elected King
1844	Peter I, ruler of Serbia, born
1852	Henry Clay, statesman-orator, died
1855	Daily Telegraph, a London newspaper, first published
1858	Joseph B. Gilder, editor-author, born
1862	Union victory at Savage Station, Virginia
1867	St. Paul of the Cross canonized
1882	Joseph A. Hansom, cab inventor, died
1901	Nelson Eddy, actor-singer, born
1911	Prince Bernhard, husband of Queen Juliana of Holland, born
1916	Western Pacific Railroad incorporated
1925	Santa Barbara, California, rocked by an earthquake
1927	Solar eclipse
1928	Outerbridge Crossing opened, connecting Staten Island, New York, with New Jersey
1938	Congress established Olympic National Park
1941	Ignace Paderewski, Polish composer-statesman, died
1950	North Korean forces captured Seoul, capital of the South
1961	Transit 4A launched
1969	Chung Festival held in Singapore

===
June 30th
===

Feast of the 12 Apostles
Feast of St. Martial of Limoges
Tom Sawyer Day
End of U.S. Government's fiscal year
"Serving the Seasons" to drive out devils in Japan

1139 AD	St. Otto of Bamberg died (Feast Day)
1559	Henry II, King of France, mortally wounded on the last day of a tournament in Paris
1775	Benjamin Franklin was given charge of U.S. postal works

1777	British under Gen. Howe left New Jersey for Staten Island
1815	Stephen Decatur anchored off Algiers and dictated the U.S. peace terms
1841	First passenger train travel on the Erie Railroad
1855	First cross born aloft through Jerusalem's streets since the Crusades
1861	Lola Montez, actress-adventuress, died
	Elizabeth Barrett Browning, poet, died
1862	Union victory at Froyser's Farm, Virginia
	"Stonewall" Jackson stopped by Union forces at White Oak Swamp
1864	U.S. raised the tariff on silk 60 percent
	Yosemite Valley and Mariposa Big Tree Grove granted to California for a park
1870	First U.S. woman graduated from law school
	Steamboat race began between Robert E. Lee and the Natchez on the Mississippi River
1876	First Yale-Harvard Regatta held on the Connecticut River
1891	First passenger train ascended Pike's Peak
1893	Walter Ulbricht, East German statesman, born
1894	London's Tower Bridge reopened
1900	Santa Fe Railroad completed from Chicago to San Francisco
	Maine, Bremen, and Saale burned at Hoboken, New Jersey
1906	U.S. Food and Drug Acts passed
1908	"Great Tunguska Catastrophe" (meteor hit in Russia)
1917	Oklahoma's capitol completed
1927	First woman was granted a pilot's license by the U.S. Department of Commerce
1932	U.S. Botanical Gardens ceased being a source of table flowers for government officials
1940	Paul Klee, Swiss artist, died
1944	U.S. severed diplomatic relations with Finland
1946	Oil from Kuwait began to flow into tankers
	Third atomic bomb test dropped over Bimini Island
1948	Bob Lemon pitched a no-hitter and Cleveland beat Detroit 2-0
1949	"Missouri Waltz" became the Missouri state song
1950	U.S. ground forces entered Korea
	Federal tax on oleomargarine expired
1954	First televised eclipse of the sun in the U.S.
1955	Camp Kilmer, New Jersey, closed as a military installation
1958	Senate approved Alaska's becoming a state

1960	Belgian Congo became the Democratic Republic of the Congo on receiving independence
1962	Sandy Koufax pitched a no-hitter and Los Angeles beat New York 5-0
1963	Pope Paul VI became 262nd to be crowned
1965	Fairleigh Dickinson University Campus at Wroxton Abbey, England, dedicated
1967	U.S. Postal Savings System ended.

Full Moon - Buck Moon, Hay Moon
Weekend closest to the 25th - Taos, New Mexico, Indian
          Festival
Last weekend - Nordic Festival at Decorah, Iowa
Last Thursday - Annual Pony Roundup at Assateague Island,
          Virginia

July 1st

          Gathering of the Clans and Fishermen's Regatta
                    at Pugwash, Nova Scotia, Canada
          Independence Day in Burundi
          Traffic Police Day in Venezuela
          Surinam Freedom Day (observing the abolishment
                    of slavery)
          Feast of St. Simeon Salus
          Feast of St. Serf
 776 BC   Beginning of the Era of the Olympiads
  69 AD   Vespasian proclaimed Roman Emperor
1270   St. Louis IX, King of France, left on his
                    second Crusade
1506   King Louis II of Hungary and Bohemia born
1534   Frederick II, King of Denmark and Norway, born
1552   Antonio de Mendoza, first viceroy of New Spain
                    (Mexico), died
1643   Westminster Assembly first met (London, England)
1676   East and West Jersey divided into New Jersey
                    and Pennsylvania
1690   King James II's defeat by King William of
                    Orange in Ireland cost the Stuarts
                    the English throne
          League of Augsburg army, trying to reach Paris,
                    defeated by the French at Fleurs
1804   George Sand, author, born

1807	Spanish released explorer Zebulon Pike
1823	First Central American Union formed
1847	First adhesive postage stamps in U.S. sold (New York City)
1851	James McNeill Whistler, artist, admitted to West Point
1859	First intercollegiate baseball game played with a final score of Amherst 66, Williams 32, had 13 men per team and went 26 innings
1861	L'Osservatore Romano, Vatican newspaper, first published
1862	Union victory and withdrawal at Malvern Hill, Virginia
	Congress passed the transcontinental railroad bill, creating the Union Pacific
1863	Confederates defeated Union cavalry at Gettysburg, Virginia
1867	Dominion of Canada established (Dominion Day, legal holiday)
1873	Prince Edward Island joined the Dominion of Canada as the smallest province
1874	Philadelphia Zoological Gardens, first in the U.S., opened
	Charles Ross, age 4, kidnapped in Germantown, Pennsylvania
1881	American Red Cross incorporated with Clara Barton as president
1884	Allan Pinkerton, founder of the first U.S. detective agency, died
1896	Harriet Beecher Stowe, author of Uncle Tom's Cabin, died
1898	Teddy Roosevelt and his "Rough Riders" captured San Juan Hill, Puerto Rico
1899	The Gideons, Bible distributors, organized
1901	Philadelphia's public building commission abolished
1905	John M. Hay, statesman-writer, died
1907	Bill Stern, sportscaster, born
1912	Louisiana state flag officially adopted
1916	Start of the 10-day Battle of the Somme
	Dwight D. Eisenhower married Mary (Mamie) G. Dowd
1919	Bethlehem Steel Corporation incorporated
	Construction of the Holland Tunnel under the Hudson River began
1921	University of Dacca, India, opened
1924	First U.S. airmail route established
1925	Long-distance airmail service bagan (New Brunswick, New Jersey, to Chicago, Illinois)
1926	Philadelphia-Camden bridge opened
1931	New Jersey State Tax Department created
	U.S. Plant Patent Law went into effect

```
              First trans-African railway completed
1939          U.S. Lighthouse Service merged with the Coast
                   Guard
              Puerto Rico and the Virgin Islands became a
                   Military Department of the U.S.
                   Army
1942          U.S. Army adopted its 24-hour clock system
1943          "Pay as you go" income tax withholding went
                   into effect
1948          Idlewild Airport officially ópened in New York
                   City (now John F. Kennedy)
1949          South Viet Nam established
1951          Bob Feller pitched a no-hitter and Cleveland
                   beat Detroit, 2-1
1960          Ghana (Gold Coast) gained its independence
                   from Britain, remaining a member
                   of the Commonwealth
1962          Algeria voted for independence from France
              Rwanda became independent of its Belgian
                   trusteeship
1963          Mandatory death penalty for premeditated murder
                   abolished in New York
1965          Robert Ruark, author, died
1966          Medicare went into effect (U.S.)
1967          North Dakota named the Teredo petrified wood
                   its state fossil
1969          Charles of England invested as Prince of Wales
1972          World Championship Watermelon Seed-spitting
                   Contest held at Pauls Valley,
                   Oklahoma
              Start of the International Frisbee Tournament
                   at Houghton, Michigan
```

July 2nd

```
  311 AD     St. Miltiades became Pope
  936        Henry I, "the Fowler," King of Germany, died
 1214        Battle of LaRocheaux-Moines, France
 1298        Battle of Goellheim, in which King Adolph of
                  Germany died
 1439        Portuguese royal permission given for settlement
                  of the Azores Islands
 1468        Charles the Bold, Duke of Burgundy, married
                  Margaret of York
 1566        Nostradamus, French astronomer, died
 1627        Lord Carlisle given all the Caribbean islands
                  by the King of England
 1644        Parliamentarians defeated King Charles I of
                  England at Marston Moor
 1704        Stanislaus I elected King of Poland
 1717        First U.S. book auction held (Boston)
 1747        Allies defeated by the French at Lawfeld in
                  the War of Austrian Succession
```

```
1776    First New Jersey state constitution adopted
1778    Jean Jacques Rousseau, French writer, died
1798    John Fitch, steamboat pioneer, died
1809    Lord Byron sailed from England on Childe
            Harold's Pilgrimage
1836    Dubuque, Iowa, establishment authorized by
            Congress
1849    Rome, Italy fell to the French
1850    Sir Robert Peel, English statesman, died
1855    Start of first territorial legislature meeting
            at Pawnee, Kansas
1859    Discovery of Nevada's Comstock Lode announced
            in the Nevada City Journal
1862    Land Grant Act, basis of many state colleges,
            passed by Congress
1863    Confederate advance at Gettysburg, Pennsylvania,
            stopped
1864    Federal approval granted for the Northern
            Pacific Railroad
1865    Salvation Army founded
1881    President Garfield shot
1883    Bismarck became the capital of the Dakota
            Territories
1903    King Olav V of Norway born
1904    Anton Chekhov, Russian author, died
1908    Thurgood Marshall, first black U.S. Supreme
            Court Justice, born
1912    Voting machine patented
1918    Split Rock, New York, rocked by an explosives
            explosion
1921    President signed Congressional Resolution of
            Peace with Austria and Germany
1926    Agricultural Co-operative Marketing Act
            approved
1932    Manoel II, former King of Portugal, died
1937    Amelia Earhart and her co-pilot lost in the
            Pacific
1957    Iran rocked by an earthquake
1961    Ernest Hemingway, novelist, died of a gunshot
1965    Tiros 10, weather satellite, launched
1970    Start of National Dump Week in Kennebunkport,
            Maine
1972    Stone-skipping and Ge-plunking Open Tournament
            at Sault Ste. Marie, Michigan
```

July 3rd
──

```
        Feast of Sts. Aaron and Julius
        Feast of St. Irenaeus of Lyons
 683 AD St. Leo II, Pope died (Feast Day)
1423    Louis XI, King of France, born
1608    Champlain founded the city of Quebec, Canada
1616    St. Bernardine Realino died (Feast Day)
1642    Marie de'Medici, widow of King Henri IV of
            France, died
```

1731	Samuel Huntington, signer of the Declaration of Independence, born
1738	John Singleton Copley, artist, born
1741	Neustra Senora de la Concepcion, treasure ship, left Vera Cruz but never reached Spain
1754	Washington abandoned Ft. Necessity (French and Indian War)
1775	Washington took command of the colonial troops at Cambridge, Massachusetts
1776	24,000 British and Hessian troops began to disembark on Staten Island, New York
	Maryland declared its independence from England
1778	Indians massacred 300 settlers at Wyoming, Pennsylvania
	Start of the "Potato War" over the Bavarian throne
1863	Pickett's charge at Gettysburg, Pennsylvania, repulsed by Union forces
1869	Mt. Washington's cog railway opened (New Hampshire)
1877	U.S. Army patrol ambushed and killed by Nez Perce Indians
1883	Daphne capsized in the Clyde
1890	Idaho became a state
1898	Cervera's fleet destroyed off Santiago, Cuba
1901	Kid Curry robbed the Great Northern passenger train near Malta, Montana
1905	Philippine coat of arms adopted
1906	George Sanders, actor, born
1908	Joel Chandler Harris, creator of "Uncle Remus," etc., died
1909	Stavros Niarchos, shipping magnate, born
1913	Dorothy Kilgallen, journalist, born
1918	Mohammed V, Sultan of Turkey, died
1920	First Royal Air Force display held at Hendon Field, England
1926	Congress enlarged Sequoia National Park
1935	Japanese ship Midori Maru involved in a collision in the Inland Sea
1940	French battleships Bretagne and Provence sunk
1954	British food rationing ended, completely
1962	Algeria declared its independence from France
1969	Dog Days began
1970	Frances Parkinson Keyes, author, died
	Independence Day celebrated in Guam
	Oaxaca Fair held in Mexico
1972	Start of 2-day Deer Hunt Festival at Winneba, Ghana

		Tom Sawyer Day in Hannibal, Missouri
		All States Picnic in Ontario, California, featuring a table 2 miles long
		Feast of St. Martin of Tours (Episcopal)
740	AD	St. Andrew of Crete died (Feast Day)
959		St. Odo the Good died (Feast Day)
973		St. Ulric of Augsburg died (Feast Day)
1187		Saracens defeated Crusaders at Hittin and captured King Guy of Jerusalem
1567		Mary, Queen of Scots, abdicated
1687		First European description of a typhoon written
1754		Washington surrendered Ft. Necessity to French and Indians
1776		Declaration of Independence signed (U.S. Independence Day)
1802		U.S. Military Academy at West Point opened
1804		Nathaniel Hawthorne, author, born
1817		Construction of the Erie Canal begun (New York)
1821		Slavery abolished in New York State
1826		Stephen Foster, composer, born
		John Adams, 2nd U.S. President, died
		Thomas Jefferson, 3rd U.S. President, died
1828		Chesapeake and Ohio Canal begun
		Baltimore and Ohio Railroad construction begun
1829		"Bus" service begun in London, England
		Cornerstone of the statehouse laid at Augusta, Maine
1831		James Monroe, 5th U.S. President, died
1836		U.S. Patent Office established
1840		First Cunard steamship, Britannia, sailed from Liverpool, England
		Dr. Karl von Grafe, father of plastic surgery, died
1845		Texans voted for annexation to the United States
1848		Cornerstone of the Washington Monument laid
		Chateaubriand, French author, died
1851		Cornerstones of new U.S. Capitol wings laid
		First railroad construction west of the Mississippi begun
1863		Fort Boise established in Idaho
		Vicksburg, Mississippi, surrendered to the U.S. Army
		Vanity Fair, New York City comic weekly, ceased publication
1866		Half of Portland, Maine, destroyed by a fire
1869		First skirmish between U.S. Cavalry and Cochise's Apache Indians in the Burro Mountains
1870		Robert E. Lee steamboat beat the Natchez into St. Louis from New Orleans

1872	Calvin Coolidge, U.S. President, born
1873	Cornerstone of new state capitol laid at Springfield, Illinois
1876	Flagstaff, Arizona settlement named for a lumberjack stunt
	M. S. Harsha patented his barbed wire
1878	George M. Cohan, composer, born
1879	British defeated the Zulus at Ulunidi, South Africa
1883	First silver train left Helena, Montana, carrying 500 tons
	Rube Goldberg, cartoonist, born
	First public rodeo for prizes held (Pecos, Texas)
1884	Statue of Liberty presented to the U.S. by France
1888	First public rodeo at which admission was charged (Prescott, Arizona)
1891	A gold vein, named Independence, discovered at Cripple Creek, Colorado
	Hannibal Hamlin, U.S. Vice-President, died
1898	French La Bourgoyne collided with British Cromartyshire
	Spanish ship Reina Mercedes scuttled at Santiago, Cuba
1900	Louis Armstrong, trumpeter, born
1903	"Big Brother" organization begun
1904	George Murphy, actor-senator, born
1907	Howard Taubman, drama critic, born
1911	Mitch Miller, bandleader, born
1912	East Corning, New York, train wreck
1916	Alan Seeger, poet, died
1917	"Lafayette, we are here" (General Pershing on the arrival of American forces in Paris)
1918	Abigail Van Buren, "Dear Abby" columnist, born
	Thirteen stripes became official on the U.S. flag
1919	Jack Dempsey knocked out Jess Willard for the heavyweight title
1925	Pickwick Club in Boston collapsed
1934	Marie Curie, scientist, died
1937	Comet Finsler discovered
1946	Philippines granted their independence from the U.S.
1953	Mt. Nanga Parbat in Kashmir climbed by an Austrian team
1956	Independence Hall, Philadelphia, became Independence National Historic Park
1968	Radio Astronomy Explorer, an X-shaped satellite, launched
1970	Fighters' Day celebrations held in Yugoslavia

	Alewives return to the sea
	Feast of St. Athanasius the Athonite
	Feast of St. Modwenna
	Feast of St. Philomena of San Severino
907 AD	Bavarians defeated by the Hungarians
1044	Germans defeated the Magyars at Menfo
1100	Godfrey of Boulogne elected King of Jerusalem
1539	St. Antony Zaccaria died (Feast Day)
1632	Sir Anthony Van Dyck, artist, knighted
1653	Wells, Maine incorporated
1764	Ivan VI, Czar of Russia who ruled only as a baby, murdered
1776	Virginia state seal adopted
1779	British sacked New Haven, Connecticut
1799	Sierra Leone became a separate British African Colony
1809	Venezuela declared its independence from Spain (Independence Day)
1810	P.T. Barnum, circus owner, born
1811	Venezuela became a republic
1841	First advertised excursion train ran in England, to a temperance meeting
1853	Cecil Rhodes, British explorer-administrator, born
1861	Franz Segil and his troops were driven from Carthage, Missouri
1865	U.S. Secret Service founded
1881	Mummy of Sethos I of Egypt found
1884	Togoland founded
1898	Spanish warship Alfonso XII sank off Cuba
1902	Henry Cabot Lodge, Jr., statesman, born
1903	Disastrous fire in Nome, Alaska
1910	William S. Porter, short-story writer O. Henry, died
1912	Ligonier, Pennsylvania train wreck
1958	Mt. Gasherbrum I, Kashmir, climbed by an Austrian team
1965	Porfirio Rubirosa, playboy, died
1968	Molniya 1-I, Russian communications satellite, launched
1970	Church boat race across Lake Siljan, Sweden, to services in Leksand
	Swamp-Buggy Races held at Pinellas, Florida
	Antique bottle show and sale held at Laconia, New Hampshire

	Old Milwaukee Day in Wisconsin
	Feast of St. Moninne
699 AD	St. Sexburga died (Feast Day)

1070	St. Godelive died (Feast Day)
1189	King Henry II of England, first of the Planta- genets, died
1266	Norway gave Man and Hebrides Islands to Scotland
1274	Greek and Roman Catholic faiths united, but only for 7 years
1376	Wenceslaus crowned King of Germany
1415	John Hus, Czech church reformer, burned as a heretic
1483	Richard III crowned King of England
1502	Imperial decree founded the University of Wit- tenberg, Germany
1553	King Edward VI of England died, 16 year-old son of Henry VIII
1572	Sigismund II, King of Poland, died
1648	Frederick III acknowledged as King of Denmark and Norway
1699	Capt. Kidd, pirate, arrested in Boston, Mas- sachusetts
1747	John Paul Jones, U.S. naval hero, born
1785	Dollar became the official U.S. monetary unit
1796	Nicholas I, Czar of Russia, born
1806	Pope Pius VII left Rome for 5 years of exile in Napoleon's France
1809	Napoleon defeated the Austrians at Wagram
1816	First expedition to explore the Congo River arrived at its mouth (Africa)
1832	Maximilian, Emperor of Mexico, born
1854	Republican Party formed
	Japan rocked by an earthquake
1865	The Nation, a liberal weekly magazine, founded in New York
1885	Louis Pasteur administered his first success- ful treatment with rabies vaccine
1892	Riots at strikebound Carnegie steel mills in Pittsburgh
1893	King George V of England married Victoria Mary of Teck
1902	St. Mary Goretti died (Feast Day)
1911	Devil's Postpile National Monument created
1915	Illinois state flag adopted
1919	Dorothy Kirsten, opera singer, born
1928	First all-talking picture, Lights of New York, opened in that city
1933	Container opened holding the bodies of Edward IV, and his brother, both murdered
1944	Hartford, Connecticut, circus tent fire
	High Bluff, Tennessee, train wreck
1960	Arkansas Post became a National Memorial
1962	William Faulkner, writer, died
1964	Nyasaland, now Malawi, granted full independence from England

1970	Heroes' Day celebrated in Zambia
	Constitution Day celebration in the Cayman Islands
1971	Louis Armstrong, trumpeter, died

```
July 7th ==========================================================
          ==========================================================
```

	Korean spinsters hope to see Altair and Vega stars and to become proficient seamstresses
	Festival for pilgrims journeying to Canterbury, England
	Fair at Penryn, Cornwall, England
	Feast of St. Fermin, patron of Pamplona, Spain (week-long festival includes running of the bulls)
	Feast of Sts. Cyril and Methodius
	Feast of St. Prosper of Aquitaine
578 BC	Jerusalem destroyed
552 AD	Beginning of the Era of the Armenians
665	St. Ethelburga of Faremoutiers-en-Brie died (Feast Day)
705	St. Hedda died (Feast Day)
755	First Star Festival ordered by Empress-regent Koken of Japan (children hang poems in bamboo trees)
786	St. Willibald died (Feast Day)
1124	Crusaders captured Tyre
1304	Pope Benedict XI died
1307	King Edward I of England died
1348	Ship-borne Black Plague arrived in England at Weymouth
1520	Cortez defeated the Aztecs at Otumba (Mexico)
1623	Virginia colonists began unsuccessful reprisals against Indian attackers
1647	Thomas Hooker, a founder of Connecticut, died
	Rioting in Naples, Italy, over the fruit tax
1683	Turkish seige of Vienna began
1752	Joseph Jacquard, loom inventor, born
1786	Turner, Maine, founded
1807	Treaty of Tilsit (Napoleon, Russia, and Prussia) effected
1828	Miguel took the oath as King of Portugal
1846	Monterey, California captured and annexed to the U.S.
1864	Frontier Scout, first newspaper in North Dakota, began
1865	Conspirators in the assassination of Lincoln hanged
1884	Lion Feuchtwanger, author, born
1887	Marc Chagall, artist, born
	Ferdinand elected Prince of Bulgaria

```
1890      Louisiana state lottery bill vetoed
1909      Andrei Gromyko, Russian statesman, born
1910      Strike against sweatshops in New York City
                    began the International Ladies'
                    Garment Workers Union
1921      Ezzard Charles, prizefighter, born
1923      Gasoline tax effected in Maine
          Warren G. Harding became the first U.S. Pres-
                    ident to visit Alaska
          Committee on the Use of Preservatives and
                    Coloring Matters appointed in
                    England
1928      Chilean ship Angames sank in a storm in
                    Araunco Bay
1930      Air Arthur Conan Doyle, author of Sherlock
                    Holmes series, died
          Construction of Hoover Dam begun
1935      Sir Thomas More made a saint
1937      Minor clash began the Sino-Japanese War
          British proposed a partition of Palestine,
                    establishing the state of Israel
1941      U.S. Marines occupied Iceland
1946      Mother Frances Xavier Cabrini became first
                    sainted U.S. citizen
1952      Breeding grounds of the whooping crane finally
                    discovered
1958      Alaskan statehood bill signed
1965      Annapolis, Maryland, designated a Registered
                    National Historic District
1969      Heroes Day celebrated in Zambia
1970      Saba Saba Day observed in Tanzania
          First of 2 Dairy Days at Mora, Minnesota
```

July 8th

```
          Feast of St. Kilian
          Unity Day in Zambia
303 AD    St. Procopius died (Feast Day)
810       Pepin III, King of France, died
1153      Pope St. Eugenius III died
1173      Eleanor of Aquitaine, wife of King Henry II,
                    sailed from France to England as
                    his prisoner
1249      King Alexander II of Scotland died
1336      St. Elizabeth, Queen of Portugal, died
                    (Feast Day)
1376      Edward, the Black Prince, heir to the English
                    throne, died
1545      Don Carlos, mad prince of Spain, born
1621      La Fontaine, French fable-writer, born
1623      Pope Gregory XV died
1663      Rhode Island Colony chartered
```

1685	Corporation of Trinity House, English mariner's organization, rechartered
1721	Elihu Yale, godfather of Yale University, died
1726	John Ker, Scottish spy, died in debtor's prison
1757	French repulsed British and colonists at Ft. Ticonderoga
1779	Fairfield, Connecticut, burned by the British
1790	Fritz-Greene Halleck, poet, born
1796	First recorded U.S. passport issued
1810	French surrendered Reunion Island to England
1814	King Louis XVIII chased out of France by Napoleon's return
1822	Poet Percy Bysshe Shelley died at sea
1835	Liberty Bell cracked
1838	Ferdinanand von Zeppelin, airship inventor, born
1839	John D. Rockefeller, organizer of the Standard Oil Company, born
1854	Saybrook, became Old Saybrook, and Deep River became Saybrook, Connecticut
1855	Sir William Parry, Arctic explorer, died
1859	King Oscar I of Norway and Sweden died
1862	Turret gun patented
1863	Union capture of Port Hudson gave them control of the Mississippi River
1864	Santee and Teton Sioux Indians defeated by the U.S. Army at Killdeer Mt., South Dakota
1889	John L. Sullivan won the last bare-knuckle heavy weight fight over Jake Kilrain in 75 rounds
	New York's Polo Grounds baseball stadium opened and the home team won
1891	Warren G. Harding married Florence K. DeWolfe
1896	William Jennings Bryan made his "Cross of Gold" speech
1907	First "Ziegfeld Follies" opened
	George Romney, statesman, born
1908	Nelson A. Rockefeller, millionaire and N.Y. governor, born
1913	Walter Kerr, critic-playwright, born
1914	Billy Eckstine, singer, born
1939	Havelock Ellis, physician-psychologist-author, died
1945	Brazilian cruiser Baia exploded in the Atlantic
1948	First women sworn into the U.S. Regular Army
1950	Gen. MacArthur named commander in Korea
1957	Grace (Mrs. Calvin) Coolidge died
1959	First U.S. troops died in combat in Viet Nam
1961	U.S.S. Abraham Lincoln, a polaris submarine, completed

1970   Boardwalk Centennial Parade held in Atlantic
                City, New Jersey
1971   Central Chile rocked by an earthquake
            Explorer 44, U.S. sun-study satellite,
                launched

July 9th

            Feast of St. John Fisher of Rochester
            Feast of St. Thomas More
 518 AD   Anastasius I, Roman emperor, died
 551   Beirut, Syria, destroyed by an earthquake
1386   Swiss defeated Austrians at Sempach
1497   Vasco Da Gama set sail to find a sea route to
                India
1552   Treaty of Passau signed
1575   Queen Elizabeth I of England arrived at Kenil-
                    worth Castle for a very expensive 19-day visit
1578   Ferdinand II, Holy Roman Emperor, born
1584   Prince William the Silent of Orange assas-
                sinated (Holland)
1706   Pierre d'Iberville, colonizer of Louisiana,
                died
1727   St. Veronica Giuliani died (Feast Day)
1755   Braddock and his troops ambushed by French
                and Indians at the Battle of the
                Monongahela
1764   Rhode Islanders at Newport seized Ft. George
                and fired on H.M.S. Squirrel
1776   Declaration of Independence read to colonial
                troops at New York; they tore down
                a statue of King George III in
                celebration
1778   Ratification of the U.S. Articles of Confed-
                eration began
1797   Edmund Burke, English statesman, died
1807   Treaty of Tilsit completed (France, Russia,
                and Prussia)
1816   Argentina proclaimed its independence from
                Spain (Argentine National Day)
1819   Elias Howe, sewing-machine inventor, born
1828   Gilbert Stuart, artist, died
1832   First Commissioner of Indian Affairs appointed
1835   Tomas Palma, first President of Cuba, born
1850   Zachary Taylor, U.S. President, died
            400 buildings in Philadelphia destroyed by fire
1874   Abraham Lincoln Memorial Tower of Westminster
                    Bridge Road foundation laid
                    (London)
1878   Corncob pipe patented by Henry Tibble
            H.V. Kaltenborn, broadcaster, born
1893   Boundary between Guatemala and Honduras set

1900	Commonwealth Constitution Act established the Australian capital at Canberra
1917	British warship Vanguard exploded at Scarpa Flow
1918	Nashville, Tennessee, train wreck
	Congress authorized the Distinguished Service Medal
1921	Hawaii National Park dedicated
1940	Duke of Windsor, formerly King Edward VII of England, appointed Governor of the Bahamas
1947	Princess Elizabeth's engagement to Philip Mountbatten announced (England)
1948	First regularly scheduled airline flight landed at Idlewild (New York City)
1951	War with Germany formally ended by Britain, Fra France, New Zealand, and Australia
1968	Vardis Fisher, novelist, died
	Grand Bee Market held at Veeneudall, Holland
1969	First rhinoceros born in Ireland
1970	Eskimo Olympics opened at Fairbanks, Alaska

July 10th

	Feast of St. Felicitas of Rome, invoked for the birth of male children
	Feast of St. Januarius, Roman martyr
	Feast of St. Alexander, and the 6 other sons of St. Felicity
	Feast of St. Amalburga
138 AD	Hadrian, Roman emperor, died
419	Ostrogoths defeated Romans outside Ravenna
1073	St. Anthony of the Caves died (Feast Day)
1086	King Canute IV of Denmark killed
1290	King Ladislaus IV of Hungary murdered
1451	James III, King of Scotland, born
1460	King Henry VI of England captured in the War of the Roses
1480	Rene I, King of Naples, Sicily and Jerusalem, died
1509	John Calvin, French-Swiss religious leader, born
1559	Henry II, King of France, died of a wound received in a tournament
1605	Czar Theodore II assassinated, having ruled Russia for only 3 months
1709	Last of the Swedish army surrendered to Russia at Poltava
1723	William Blackstone, English jurist, born
1761	Whirlwind struck Cambridge, Massachusetts
1780	French support for the American revolution arrived in U.S.
1797	U.S. frigate United States launched at Philadelphia

```
1832        Abraham Lincoln mustered out of the Illinois
               militia
1834        James McNeill Whistler, artist, born
1860        Solar eclipse
1863        Clement Clark Moore, author of "A Visit from
               St. Nicholas," died
1890        Wyoming became a state
1915        Saul Bellow, author, born
1916        League of Nations proposed to the U.S. Senate
            Battle of the Somme ended
1919        Versailles Peace Treaty ratified by Germany
               and sent to the U.S. Senate
1920        David Brinkley, newscaster, born
1925        Scopes "Monkey Trial" began
1929        Current size of U.S. paper money made official
1940        Nazi bombing of England began
1943        Allied troops invaded Sicily
            Arthur Ashe, tennis great, born
1947        Don Black pitched a no-hitter and Cleveland
               beat Philadelphia 3-0
1951        Negotiations began for a truce along the
               38th parallel in Korea
1953        Beria dismissed as USSR secret police chief
1962        Telstar I, communications satellite, launched
1972        Solar eclipse
```

July 11th

```
            Southdown Sheep Fair at Lewes, Sussex, England
  969 AD    St. Olga died (Feast Day)
1274        Robert I, "the Bruce," King of Scotland, born
1276        Ottobuono Feischi elected Pope Adrian V
1302        Battle of the Spurs (Flemish infantry defeated
               French cavalry at Courtrai
1346        Charles IV chosen as King of Germany
1598        First settlement in New Mexico begun, San
               Juan de los Caballeros
1613        Michael I crowned first Romanov Czar of
               Russia
1657        Frederick I, first King of Prussia, born
1718        English defeated the Spanish fleet at Messina
1764        Nathaniel Ames, physician-almanac writer, died
1767        John Quincy Adams, U.S. President, born
1790        Spanish discovered Discovery Bay, Wisconsin
1791        American flag first raised over Detroit,
               Michigan
1804        Aaron Burr, Vice-President, killed Alexander
               Hamilton, Secretary of the
               Treasury, in a duel
1806        James Smith, signer of the Declaration of
               Independence, died
1814        Eastport, Maine, captured by the British
```

```
1838      John Wanamaker, merchant, born
1859      Treaty of Villafranca, French-Austrian
                    settlement over Italy
1869      "Buffalo Bill" and the Cavalry surprised
                    the Indians at Summit Spring,
                    Nebraska
1873      Bismarck Tribune, North Dakota newspaper,
                    first published
1877      Battle of the Clearwater in the Nez Perce
                    War began
1895      Thomas Mitchell, actor, born
1897      3 Swedes left Spitzbergen, Norway, in an
                    unsuccessful attempt to fly a
                    balloon over the North Pole
1899      E. B. White, humorist, born
1915      German cruiser Konigsberg sunk by the British
                    in the Rufiji River
1916      Second Battle of the Somme began
          First federal-aid Road Act for highway con-
                    struction passed by Congress
1917      King George II of Greece removed from
                    succession
1920      Eugenie, wife of Napoleon III, died
1927      Palestine shaken by a severe earthquake
1933      King Edward V of England and his brother,
                    murdered in 1438, reburied
1936      Hitler signed a treaty guaranteeing Austria's
                    frontier
1938      David Lawrence Pierson, originater of Con-
                    stitution Day, died
1955      U.S. Air Force Academy opened
1962      U.S. frogmen swam the English Channel under-
                    water, in 18 hr
          First U.S. television programs broadcast by
                    the BBC via satellite
1963      Argentine ship Ciudad de Asuncion burned in
                    the River Platte
1964      Elektrons III and IV, Russian satellites,
                    launched
1968      OV 1-15 and OV 1-16, atmospheric testing
                    satellites, launched
1970      Salmon Festival held at Arcata, California
          Green Corn Festival held at Bixby, Oklahoma
```

July 12th

```
          Feast of St. John the Iberian
          Feast of Sts. Nabor and Felix
          Feast of St. Veronica
100 BC    Julius Caesar born
526 AD    Felix III became Pope
1073      St. John Gaulberto died (Feast Day)
1153      Anastasius IV crowned Pope
```

1191	Acre taken by Richard the Lionhearted and the 3rd Crusade after a 2-year siege
1328	David II, infant King of Scotland, married Joanna, sister of King Edward III of England
1536	Erasmus, Dutch intellectual and writer, died
1645	Michael, first Romanov Czar of Russia, died
1691	Antonio Pignatelli was elected Pope as Innocent XII, a compromise candidate, due to a severe heat wave
1730	Lorenzo Corsini elected Pope (Clement XII)
1779	British burned Norwalk, Connecticut
1808	Missouri Gazette, the first in the state, founded in St. Louis and published till 1822
1817	Henry David Thoreau, writer, born
1849	Dolley Madison, heroic First Lady, died
1851	Louis Daguerre, daguerreotype photography inventor, born
1854	George Eastman, inventor and founder of Eastman Kodak, born
1859	Pawnee Indian camp in Nebraska attacked by the Cavalry
1861	"Wild Bill" Hickok shot it out with the McCanles gang at Rock Creek Station, Nebraska
1862	Congressional Medal of Honor established
1870	Celluloid, an early plastic, patented
1874	Lydd Fair in Kent, England held for the last time
1877	Battle of the Clearwater in the Nez Perce War ended
1887	Mound Bayou, Mississippi, settled, all residents being former slaves on cotton plantations
1895	Oscar Hammerstein II, composer, born
1912	First foreign movie shown in the U.S.
1917	Andrew Wyeth, artist, born
1918	Grand Duke Michael, brother of Russia's Czar, shot by Bolsheviks
1922	Senator Mark Hatfield born
1934	Van Cliburn, pianist, born
1942	Lidice, Illinois, changed its name
1951	Allie Reynolds pitched a no-hitter and New York beat Cleveland 1-0
1954	Federal highway program proposed
1961	Tiros III, weather satellite, launched
1970	Oldtime Fiddlers' Jamboree held at Shoshone, Idaho
	Green River Rendezvous held at Pinedale, Wyoming

July 13th

                  Feast of St. Mildred
                  Feast of St. Silas
                  Nathan Bedford Forrest's Birthday (Tennessee)
505 AD   St. Eugenius of Carthage died (Feast Day)
939   Pope Leo VII died
1590   Pope Clement X born
1608   Ferdinand III, Holy Roman Emperor, born
1610   St. Francis Solano died (Feast Day)
1771   Capt. Cook returned to England, ending his
                  first voyage
1772   Capt. Cook sailed from Plymouth, England, on
                  his second voyage of discovery
1785   Stephen Hopkins, signer of the Declaration of
                  Independence, died
1787   Northwest Ordinance governing the Northwest
                  Territories passed by Congress
1793   Jean Paul Marat, French revolutionist, stabbed
                  to death, supposedly in his bath
1794   Dr. James Lind, "founder of naval hygiene,"
                  died (England)
1811   James Young, petroleum pioneer, born
1843   Fremont's Rocky Mountain expedition reached
                  Ft. Laramie, Wyoming
1863   New York City draft riots began, lasting 3
                  days
1865   "Go west, young man" (Horace Greeley quoting
                  the Terre Haute (Indiana) Express)
1881   Billy the Kid shot and killed in Ft. Sumner,
                  New Mexico
1883   Queen Ranavalona II of Madagascar died
1890   John C. Fremont, author-explorer, died
1900   Allied troops took Tientsin, China (Boxer
                  Rebellion)
1905   Bosley Crowther, critic-journalist, born
1911   Edward, Duke of Windsor, invested as Prince
                  of Wales
1913   Dave Garroway, broadcaster, born
1930   First television broadcast aired
1941   Georgic destroyed in the port of Suez
1954   Grantland Rice, author, died
1967   "Dime a Dip" supper held at Essex Junction,
                  Vermont
1969   Luna 15 launched by USSR to collect moon soil
1971   Start of the Feast of Lanterns in Japan

July 14th

                  Feast of St. Madelgaire (or Vincent of
                          Soignies)
                  Feast of St. Phocas

Festival of Fandroana (Bathing in Madagascar)
Shinto Festival of Fans (Japan)
Nengaku dance performed, annually in Japan

1093 AD	St. Ulric of Zell died (Feast Day)
1223	King Philip II Augustus of France died
1254	Theobald IV, King of Navarre, died on Crusade
1274	St. Bonaventure died (Feast Day)
1531	King Henry VIII and his queen, Catherine of Aragon, parted for the last time
1570	Reformed missal went into use in Roman Catholic churches
1602	Jules Mazarin, French cardinal-statesman, born
1614	St. Camillus, patron of nurses, died (Feast Day)
1629	Pacification of Nimes granted tolerance to French Protestants
1634	King Charles I of England and his wife entered Oxford
1642	Japanese Empress Myosho moved into her sumptuous new Kyoto palace
1658	Falmouth, Maine, incorporated
1771	San Antonio de Padua Mission founded in California
1775	Spanish claimed Point Grenville, Washington
1779	George Ross, signer of the Declaration of Independence, died
1789	Corporal punishment abolished in the French Army
	Paris mob stormed the Bastille, starting the French Revolution (Bastille Day, French National Holiday)
1806	Lewis and Clark passed through the Gallatin Valley, becoming the first whites to enter Washington from the east
1809	St. Nicodemus of the Holy Mountain died (Orthodox Feast Day)
1820	First lightship in the U.S. stationed off Craney Island, Virginia
1825	Alexander Laing, Sahara explorer, married in Tripoli
1831	"Rocked in the Cradle of the Deep" written at sea by Emma Willard
1836	Milwaukee Advertiser began publication in Wisconsin
1847	A house in Braunau, Hungary, hit by a meteorite
1853	World's Fair in New York City opened for its first season, the first international exposition in the U.S.
1858	Perry landed in Japan and was received by the Lord of Toda
1864	Gold discovered near Helena, Montana

1865	Matterhorn first climbed
1868	First U.S. patent for a tape measure granted
	Second patent for a typewriter issued, this one the first efficient working model
1874	Lydd, Kent, England, fair closed for the last time
1880	Bastille Day became a French National Holiday
1887	Alfred Krupp, Germany's "cannon king," died
1902	Bell tower of St. Mark's Church fell (Venice, Italy)
1903	Irving Stone, author, born
1909	Edward P. Weston arrived, still walking in San Francisco, having left New York 105 days and 3,893 miles before
1914	Liquid fuel rocket patented
	Huerta, insurrectionist President of Mexico, resigned
1917	Douglas Edwards, broadcaster, born
1918	Ingmar Bergman, filmmaker, born
	French ship Djamnah torpedoed in the Mediterranean
1920	Arthur Laurents, playwright, born
1921	Sacco and Vanzetti murder trial ended in convictions
1940	Estonia, Latvia, and Lithuania annexed to USSR
1945	Italy declared war on her former ally, Japan
1947	Airline service begun between New York City and Asia
1953	Birthplace of George Washington Carver declared a National Monument
1956	Mel Parnell pitched a no-hitter and Boston beat Chicago 4-0
1957	Russian ship Eshghabad ran aground in the Caspian Sea
1958	Feisal II, King of Iraq, was assassinated and his country became a republic
1964	Mariner IV made its Mars "fly-by"
1965	Adlai E. Stevenson, statesman, died
1969	Fire Festival held at Nachi-Katsuura, Japan

July 15th

	Festival of Koza (procession of boats near Kochi, a Shinto shrine in Japan)
	Feast of Sts. Edith Polesworth and Edith of Tamworth
432 BC	Beginning of the Era of Metonic Cycle
303 AD	St. Felix of Thibiuca died
338?	St. James of Nisibus died (Feast Day)

668	Constans II, Eastern Roman Emperor, died in his bath
862	St. Swithin's Day (Rain today? Expect 39 more days of it!), commemorating his death
971	St. Swithin's body moved to a basilica
1015	St. Vladimir died (Feast Day)
1024	St. Henry II, Holy Roman Emperor died (Feast Day)
1099	Soldiers of the First Crusade captured Jerusalem
1189	Queen Eleanor of Aquitaine released from her husband's prison (King Henry II of England)
1240	Russia defeated Sweden at the Neva River
1291	Rudolph I, King of Germany, died
1381	John Ball, "mad priest of Kent," executed
1410	Battle of Gruenwald (Polish, Russian and Lithuanians defeated Germans)
1575	St. Philip Neri organized the Congregation of the Oratory
1606	Rembrandt van Rijn, artist, born
1678	Sweden defeated Denmark at Landskrona
1778	Anthony Wayne defeated the British at the Battle of Stony Point
1779	Clement Clark Moore, author of "A Visit from St. Nicholas," born
1782	Farinelli, male soprano, died
1788	Marietta, Ohio, capital of the Northwest Territories, got its first governor
1796	Thomas Bullfinch, author of Mythology, born
1806	William Clark passed through Bozeman Pass
1834	Inquisition ended in Spain
1848	John Donkey, comic weekly of New York and Philadelphia, ceased publication
1863	New York draft riots ended after 3 days
1870	Manitoba joined the Dominion of Canada Napoleon III declared war on Prussia
1877	Eten wrecked off Valpariaso, Chile
1883	"Tom Thumb," midget, died
1885	Niagara Falls reservation formally opened
1888	Printers' Ink, trade publication, founded
1903	Walter D. Edmonds, author, born
1921	Erroll Garner, jazz musician, born
1933	"Going to the Sun" highway dedicated in Montana
1936	Economic sanctions against Italy over its invasion of Ethiopia ended
1948	Gen. John J. Pershing died
1953	U.S. Consulate at Gibraltar closed
1958	U.S. Marines landed in Lebanon to prevent Communist takeover

```
1965        Mariner IV sent back the first close-up pic-
                 tures of another planet, Mars
1968        Direct flights began between New York and
                 Moscow
```

July 16th
_____

```
            Virgin of Carmen, celebrated in Venezuela,
                 Bolivia, Canary Islands and
                 British Honduras
            La Paz Day celebrated in Bolivia
            Feast of St. Raineld
 622 AD     Beginning of the Mohammedan Era when the
                 founder of Islam fled Mecca
 632        Beginning of the Persian Era
1212        Alfonso VIII, King of Castile, defeated the
                 Moors at Las Navas de Tolosa
1216        Pope Innocent III died
1342        King Charles I of Hungary died
1482        First world atlas printed
1661        Pierre d'Iberville, colonizer of Louisiana,
                 born
1668        French attacked Courtrai in Flanders
1723        Sir Joshua Reynolds, artist, born
1741        Bering discovered Alaska
1769        First Europeans settled in California at the
                 Franciscian Mission of San
                 Diego de Alcala
1779        Colonial troops captured Stony Point, New York
1790        District of Columbia established as the seat
                 of the U.S. government
1791        Club of the Feuillants, French political
                 association, formed
1798        Marine Hospital Service created by Congress
1821        Mary Baker Eddy, founder of Christian
                 Science, born
1825        Alexander Laing, Sahara explorer and a bride-
                 groom of 2 days, left for the
                 desert seeking the rumored
                 Timbuktoo
1846        St. Mary-Magdalen Postel died (Feast Day)
1848        Eben Rexford, composer of "Silver Threads
                 among the Gold," etc., born
1873        University of California at Berkeley founded
1876        Patent issued for a shaving mug with a soap
                 compartment
1880        Kathleen Norris, novelist, born
1886        Edward Z. C. Judson, a dime-novelist as Ned
                 Buntline, died
1896        Trygve Lie, first Secretary General of the
                 United Nations, born
1898        Santiago, Cuba, surrendered to U.S. forces
```

1906	Prince Franz Joseph II, ruler of Lichenstein, born

1906   Prince Franz Joseph II, ruler of Lichenstein,
            born
1908   Frances Horwich, creator of "Ding-Dong School"
            television show, born
1911   Ginger Rogers, actress, born
1917   July Uprising of the Bolshevik revolt in
            Russia failed
1918   Bolsheviks murdered the Russian royal family
1945   First atomic bomb tested at Alamagordo,
            New Mexico
1951   Leopold III, King of Belgium, abdicated
1960   John P. Marquand, novelist, died
1965   Proton I, Russian satellite, launched
        Mt. Blanc Tunnel through the Alps opened
1969   Three U.S. astronauts blasted off to land
            on the moon
1970   Tarpon Hunt held at Fort Meyers, Florida
        Gion Festival of Yasaka Shrine celebrated
            in Kyoto, Japan
1972   Eastern Turkey rocked by an earthquake

July 17th

Korean Constitution Day
Munoz Rivera's Birthday (Puerto Rico)
Dodge City Day (Kansas)
Feast of St. Marina (Greek Orthodox)
Feast of St. Alexis
Feast of St. Kenlem
180 AD Scillitan Martyrs, 12 North African Christians,
            murdered (Feast Day)
855   Pope St. Leo IV died (Feast Day)
1054   Henry IV, age 4, crowned King of Germany
1198   St. Narsus of Lampron died (Feast Day)
1203   Crusaders took Constantinople from the
            Moslems
1245   Frederick II, Holy Roman Emperor, excommuni-
            cated and deposed
1270   Louis IX, King of France, and the 8th Crusade
            landed at Carthage, North Africa
1385   King Charles IV of France married Isabella
            of Bavaria
1429   Charles VII crowned King of France
1453   English defeat at Castillon ended the 100
                Years' War and the claims of the
                English king to the throne of
                France
1744   Elbridge Gerry, signer of the Declaration of
            Independence, born
1754   First King's College class met (now Columbia
            University)
1763   John Jacob Astor, millionaire, born

1786	City of Panang on the Malay peninsula founded
1821	Spain ceded Florida to the U.S.
1850	First photograph (daguerreotype) of a star taken
1861	First U.S. paper money issued
1878	New Eddystone lighthouse begun (England)
1887	Dorothea Dix, poet-educator, died
1889	Erle Stanley Gardner, author, born
1895	First trolley made the trip to Old Town, Maine
1898	First Puerto Rican Parliament met
	Santiago, Cuba, surrendered to the U.S.
1903	James McNeill Whistler, artist, died
1904	James Cagney, actor, born
1912	Art Linkletter, author-broadcaster, born
1917	British royal family changed its surname to Windsor
1919	Finland became a republic
1925	Cornerstone of Puerto Rico's capitol laid
1928	Alvaro Obregon, Mexican president, assassinated
1936	Spanish Revolution began in Morocco
1938	"Wrong Way" Corrigan, flying to California, wound up in Ireland
1940	First passenger train left Bagdad for Istambul
1942	Maury H. B. Paul, original "Cholly Knickerbocker" columnist, died
1944	Pier exploded at Port Chicago, California
	Icelandic Republic established
1945	Potsdam, Germany, conference opened
1946	Gen. Mikhailovitch, Chetnik leader, shot for treason (Yugoslavia)
1947	Ferry Randas sank in a storm at Bombay, India
1955	Disneyland opened (California)
1959	Dr. Leakey discovered Zinjanthropus man (Olduvai Gorge, Africa)
1964	Vela 3 and TRS 6, U.S. satellites, launched

July 18th

	Feast of St. Camillus de Lellis, patron of the sick and infirm
	Feast of St. Symphorosa and her 7 sons
390 BC	Romans defeated by the Gauls at Allia
64 AD	Nero's Roman fire began
634	Mohammed died
641	St. Arnulf of Metz died
1100	Godfrey of Bouillon, "Advocate of the Holy Sepulchre," died
1216	Cencius Savelli elected Pope (Honorius III)
1289	Alfonso, King of Aragon, died

1374	Petrarch, Italian poet, found dead
1552	Rudolph II, Holy Roman Emperor, born
1635	Robert Hooke, scientist, born
1721	Antoine Watteau, French artist, died
1768	"The Liberty Song," first sheet music published in America, first appeared in The Boston Gazette
1770	Battle of Ismail in the first Russo-Turkish War
1792	John Paul Jones, U.S. naval hero, died
1811	First overland expedition to the Pacific left the Arikara Indian village in North Dakota (not Lewis and Clark; they went mostly by water) William Makepeace Thackeray, novelist, born
1817	Jane Austen, English novelist, died
1841	Pedro II crowned Emperor of Brazil
1863	Union victory at Buffington's Island, Ohio
1868	Dr. Livingstone discovered Lake Bangweulu, Zambia
1870	Doctrine of Papal Infallibility announced
1873	Oscar II crowned King of Sweden and Norway
1899	Horatio Alger, author, born
1906	Clifford Odets, playwright, born
1909	Don Carlos VII, claimant to the Spanish throne, died
1911	Hume Cronyn, actor, born
1913	Red Skelton, comedian, born
1915	Italian cruiser Giuseppe Garibaldi torpedoed in Mediterranean
1921	Astronaut John Glenn born
1936	Loyalists defeated insurgents in Madrid in Spain's Civil War
1938	Marie, widow of King Ferdinand of Rumania, died
1939	Edmund Heller, naturalist-explorer, died
1943	Vehicular traffic tunnel under the Mersey River opened in England
1951	"Jersey Joe" Walcott knocked out Ezzard Charles in 7 rounds for the heavyweight boxing title
1955	Start of a 5-day Geneva summit meeting of the "Big Four"
1965	Zond III, Russian solar orbiter, launched McCreary County Old Folks Day held in Whitley City, Kentucky
1970	Fife and Drum Corps Mustered at Deep River, Connecticut First sermon of the Buddha Festival made in Thailand

	Martyrs Day in Burma
	Feast of St. Arsenius
1580 BC	Sirius ascended to the throne of Egypt
379 AD	St. Macrina the Younger died (Feast Day)
711	Invading Moors defeated King Roderic of Spain
1333	Battle of Halidon Hill (English defeated the Scots)
1588	England coast-watchers sighted the Spanish Armada
1660	St. Vincent de Paul died (Feast Day)
1810	Queen Louise of Prussia died
1814	Samuel Colt, pistol maker, born
1821	George IV crowned King of England
1824	Augustin de Iturbide, Emperor of Mexico, killed
1834	Edgar Degas, French artist, born
1840	First Cunard steamship, Britannia, reached Boston
1848	First women's rights convention held (Seneca Falls, New York)
1869	Auburn, Maine, founded
1900	Main line of the Paris subway system opened
1912	Meteorite rain fell near Holbrook, Illinois
1917	William Scranton, Pennsylvania governor, born
1918	German retreat began
1924	Liverpool, England, cathedral consecrated
1936	Insurgents took control of Cadiz, Huelva, Seville, Cordoba, and Granada, Spain
1965	Clyde Beatty, animal trainer, died
	Syngman Rhee, Korean statesman, died
1968	Canada unveiled its population clock
1969	Feast of the Redeemer held in Venice, Italy
	Sinking Ra, Thor Heyerdahl's Egyptian reed boat, abandoned at sea
1970	Soyez 9, Russian space vehicle, landed after a record Earth orbit
	Buddhist Lent began in Thailand

	Feast of St. Margaret (invoked for cure of kidney diseases and in childbirth)
	Feast of St. Wilgefortis, invoked against troublesome husbands
	Wool Fair at Lewes, Sussex, England
	Colombia Independence Day
	Annual Fair at Campulung, Rumania
1031 AD	Robert II, King of France, died

1247	Mongol Emperor demanded that the Pope pay him homage
1290	Fair held at Neath, Glamorganshire, Wales
1304	Petrarch, Italian poet, born
1454	John II, King of Castile, died
1537	St. Jerome Emiliani, patron of orphans, died (Feast Day)
1764	New York given control of Vermont by the King
1796	Mingo Park, explorer, first saw the River Niger, Africa
1799	Fur traders de la Maissonneuve and Preneloupe became the first whites at Denver, Colorado
1845	300 business buildings in New York City destroyed by fire
1847	Max Liebermann, German artist, born
1857	Cavalry defeated Comanche Indians at Devil's River, Texas
1864	Union Victory at Peach Tree Creek, Georgia
1871	British Columbia joined the Dominion of Canada
1878	Final battle of the Bannock Indian War in Oregon
1881	Sitting Bull, Sioux Indian chief, surrendered
1890	King George II of Greece born
1897	Marconi's Wireless Telegraph Company formed
1903	Pope Leo XIII died
1907	Columbia and San Petro collided off California Salem, Michigan, train wreck
1914	French President Poincare made a state visit to Russia Oklahoma's capitol building begun
1917	Draft lottery in U.S. for World War I began Kerensky named Premier of Russia by provisional government
1919	Sir Edmund Hillary, mountain climber, born
1927	King Ferdinand I of Rumania died
1929	Mt. Washington's cog railway derailed (New Hampshire)
1937	Guglielmo Marconi, wireless inventor, died
1944	Attempt to assassinate Hitler with a bomb failed
1951	Abdullah ibn Hussein, King of Jordan, assassinated
1958	Jim Bunning pitched a no-hitter and Detroit beat Boston 2-0
1960	First undersea launching of a Polaris missile made
1963	Total eclipse of the sun, visible in northern North America
1969	"One small step for a man, one giant leap for mankind" (Neil Armstrong, as the first man on the moon)

	Liberation Day on Guam
	Feast of St. Victor of Marseilles, patron of cabinetmakers, invoked against lightning
	St. Daniel the Prophet's Day
356 AD	Mediterranean area swept by earthquake and tidal waves
905	Louis III, "the Blind," Holy Roman Emperor, blinded by a rival
1209	Slaughter at Beziers, Catholic heretics in France
1362	Louis I, "the Great," crowned King of Hungary
1402	Tamerlane defeated the Turks at Ankara, halting their eastward expansion
1411	Sigismund again chosen King of Germany
1552	Antonio de Mendoza, first Vicery of Mexico, died
1571	Inquisition created for the Portuguese Navy
1588	Sir Francis Drake and the British first met the Spanish Armada
1619	St. Lawrence of Brindisi died (Feast Day)
1758	Thomas Fleet, printer, died
1773	Jesiut Order dissolved
1779	Washington established his headquarters at West Point
1796	Robert Burns, Scottish poet, died
1809	Daniel Lambert died, age 30, height 5 ft. 11 in., weight 739 lbs.
1814	Inquisition restored in Spain following Napoleon's fall
1816	Baron de Reuter, founder of the news agency, born
1820	Electromagnet discovered
1831	Belgium and Holland separated, becoming two kingdoms
1832	Sir Walter Scott, novelist, died
1836	First Canadian railroad opened
1853	New York City authorized to acquire Central Park
1858	Christina, Queen-regent of Spain, born
1860	Chauncey Olcott, composer of "My Wild Irish Rose," born
1861	First Battle of Bull Run or Manassas, Virginia, was a Confederate victory
1873	Jesse James and gang held the first train robbery
1885	Frances Parkinson Keyes, author, born
1897	The Tate Gallery of British Art opened in London
1899	Ernest Hemingway, author, born

```
1902    Primus sank after a collision in the Elbe River
1920    Isaac Stern, violinist, born
1925    John Scopes found guilty of teaching evolution
1926    Illinois Central Railway opened its electric
                    passenger service in the Chicago
                    area
1930    Veterans' Administration created
1935    Mormon Monument dedicated at Palmyra, New York
1946    Bread rationing began in England
1949    First woman treasurer of the U.S. took office
        U.S. Senate ratified the North Atlantic Treaty
1953    First jet-powered fighter seaplane demonstrated
1954    Geneva Conference on Far Eastern Affairs ended
1957    Kenneth Roberts, novelist, died
1959    Savannah, first nuclear-powered merchant ship,
                    launched
1963    Giovanni Battista Montini elected Pope (Paul
                    VI)
1969    U.S. astronauts blasted off from the surface of
                    the moon
1970    Last power generator of the Aswan High Dam
                    dedicated in Egypt
```

July 22nd
_____

```
        Polish National Day
        Feast of St. Mary Magdalene, patron of per-
                    fumers, glove-makers, tanners, and
                    repentant women
 259 AD St. Dionysius became Pope
1099    Godfrey of Bouillon elected first Christian
                    ruler of Jerusalem
1212    King Otto IV of Germany married Beatrix of
                    Swabia
1227    Danes defeated at Bornhoved
1246    Carpini, papal legate, reached the Mongol
                    capital
1298    First use of the English longbow in war (Battle
                    of Falkirk; Scotland defeated)
1461    King Charles VII of France died
1478    Philip I, "the Handsome," King of Spain, born
1515    St. Philip Neri born
1587    "The Lost Colony" arrived at Roanoke, North
                    Carolina, island
1613    Michael, first Romanov Czar of Russia, crowned
1647    St. Marguerite Marie Alacoque born
1649    Pope Clement XI born
1676    Pope Clement X died
1686    Albany, New York, incorporated
1692    Papal Bull promulgated, cutting down on benefits
                    to relatives of the Pope
1708    Nathaniel Ames, physician and almanac-writer,
                    born
```

1779	Battle of Minisink (Colonial militia against British and Indians in New York)
1790	Lafayette took command of the French National Guard
1832	King of Rome, Duke of Reichstadt, son of Napoleon, died without ever ruling anywhere
1833	Benjamin R. Hanby, composer of "Darling Nellie Gray," born
1848	Emma Lazarus, poet, born
1861	Congress authorized a standing army of 500,000 men
1864	Gen. Sherman took Atlanta, Georgia, for the Union
1869	John A. Roebling, bridge designer, died of tetanus caught while constructing the Brooklyn Bridge
1871	Tweed Ring exposed by The New York Times
1882	Edward Hopper, artist, born
1884	Spanish ship Gigon collided with the British Lexham
1889	Morris Fishbein, medical author, born
1893	Dr. Karl Menninger, of the Clinic, born
1898	Alexander Calder, artist, born
	Stephen Vincent Benet, writer, born
1902	Gold discovered near Fairbanks, Alaska
1903	Cassius Clay, politician, died
1908	A fine charged to Standard Oil of Indiana for accepting rebates was set aside by the courts
	Amy Vanderbilt, etiquette authority, born
1916	James Whitcomb Riley, "The Hoosier Poet," born
	An explosion rocked a Preparedness Day parade in San Francisco
1928	Orson Bean, performer, born
1929	Bremen, a North German Lloyd liner, began her maiden voyage to New York
1933	First round-the-world solo flight completed by Wiley Post
1934	John Dillinger, escaped bank robber, shot in Chicago by the FBI
1948	First man swam the Straits of Gibraltar (a woman had done it 20 years before)
1950	King Leopold III of Belgium returned from exile
1956	Principals of the Organization of American States signed
1969	Thor Heyerdahl and the Ra crew landed in Barbados
1972	A Russian space vehicle landed on Venus
	Chi-Chi, the London Zoo's giant panda, died

		Ancient Roman festival honoring Neptune
		Feast of St. John Cassian
776	BC	First Olympic Games held
685	AD	John V became Pope
1227		Kiu Chang Chun, Taoist wise man and Chinese traveler, died
1343		Peace of Kalisz
1373		St. Briget of Sweden died
1623		Virginia colonists attacked by Indians
1664		Four British ships arrived in Boston on their way to oust the Dutch from New York
1711		Turks defeated and captured Czar Peter the Great of Russia at Falica
1759		Battle of Zullichau in the Seven Years' War
1766		First medical society in America organized
1793		Roger Sherman, signer of the Declaration of Independence, died
1794		Alexandre de Beauharnais, first husband of Napoleon's Josephine, guillotined for treason
1803		Insurrection began in Dublin, Ireland
1819		The Savannah, first American steamship to cross the Atlantic, left Liverpool, England, for St. Petersburg, Russia
1848		Battle of Somma Campaign, the Italian overthrow of the Austrian occupation
1865		Salvation Army founded
1870		Swedish immigrants arrived at New Sweden, Maine
1885		Ulysses S. Grant, U.S. President and Civil War commander, died and his Personal Memoirs were released
1892		Henry C. Frisk shot and wounded by anarchist Alexander Berkman
		Haile Selassie, Emperor of Ethiopia, born (National Holiday)
1896		Dale Van Every, author, born
1904		Ice cream cone invented
1912		Law effected requiring radio equipment for every steamship carrying 50 or more passengers
1945		Marshal Henri Pétain put on trial for treason in France
1951		Marshal Henri Pétain, convicted, died in his island prison
1954		Restoration and perpetual care of Old Ironsides authorized
1955		End of the Geneva summit meeting of the "Big Four"

1956	Bedloe's Island in New York harbor renamed Liberty after its resident
1964	Munitions explosion rocked the harbor at Bane, Algeria
1970	Intelstat III F 8, communications satellite, launched
	Muscat and Oman became the Sultanate of Oman after a coup

July 24th

	Feast of St. Christine
	Fast of Ab or Black Fast, commemorating the destruction of the temple (Hebrew)
	Tenjin Festival at Osaka, Japan
459 AD	St. Simeon the Stylite died, having spent most of his life atop a pillar
1015	Sts. Boris and Gleb (Feast Day)
1230	Start of the first Cheltenham, England, 3-day fair granted by King Henry III
1534	Jacques Cartier claimed Canada for France
1568	Don Carlos, mad prince of Spain, died
1567	James VI proclaimed King of Scotland after his mother's abdication
1704	Sir George Rooke took Gibraltar from Spain for England
1715	The ill-fated Spanish plate fleet sailed from Havana, Cuba
1783	Simon Bolivar, Venezuelan patriot, born (National Holiday)
1802	Alexandre Dumas, born
1827	Francisco Solano Lopez, dictator of Paraguay, born
1830	The Daily Evening Transcript first appeared in Boston
1847	Mormon pioneers reached Salt Lake City site (Pioneer Day, Utah State Holiday)
1851	England's window tax repealed
1862	Martin Van Buren, U.S. President, died
1863	Santee Sioux and Cavalry fought at Big Mound, Minnesota
1912	Delaware state flag design selected
1915	Eastland capsized in the Chicago River; 812 died
1936	Spanish insurgents set up a revolutionary government
1945	Four Japanese ships sunk off Kure by U.S. planes
1952	American steel strike ended
1969	Collins, Aldrin, and Armstrong came back to Earth
1970	Start of the Nordic Fest at Decorah, Iowa

	Constitution Day in Puerto Rico
	Supplication Day, start of the hurricane season in the Virgin Islands
	Feast of ex-St. Christopher, patron of archers, fruit dealers, and travelers, prayed to for prevention of sudden death and against storms
44 AD	St. James the Greater, one of the twelve Apostles, died (Feast Day)
306	Constintius I, Roman Emperor, died
1139	King Alphonso I of Portugal defeated the Moors at Ourique
1215	Frederick II crowned German king, again
1467	Battle of Ricardina, Italy, in which Florence, Milan, and Naples defeated Venice
1492	Pope Innocent VIII died
1535	Santiago de Guayaquil, Ecuador, founded (Foundation Day, national holiday)
1564	Ferdinand I, Holy Roman Emperor, died
1567	Caracas, Venezuela, founded
1593	Henry IV, Protestant King of France, became a Catholic
1666	England defeated the Dutch fleet that tried to sail up the Thames
1748	Solar eclipse
1766	Chief Pontiac and the Ottowa Indians made peace with the British
1806	William Clark camped at Pompey's Pillar, Montana, and carved his name
1812	Battle of Ostrovno
1814	Battle of Lundy's Lane, Vermont
	First steam train made a successful 9-mile trial run in England
1839	Francois Garnier, Mekong River explorer, born
1844	Thomas Eakins, artist, born
1868	Wyoming became a U.S. territory
1894	Sino-Japanese War began
1909	Louis Bleriot flew across the English Channel
1934	Engelbert Dollfuss, Austrian Chancellor, executed by the Nazis
1943	Mussolini resigned as Italian dictator
1952	Puerto Rico became a U.S. Commonwealth
1956	Andrea Doria, liner, and freighter Stockholm collided
1963	Limited nuclear test ban agreement signed
1970	Start of the Dutch Folk Festival at Schaefferstown, Pennsylvania
	End of the Wild Horse Chasing at Haranomachi, Japan

```
                83rd birthday party held for Ardmore, Oklahoma
1971            Teei (Monsoon Festival) celebrated in India
```

```
                Curacao Day in the Netherland Antilles
                Fair at Sherborne, England
                Fair at Tamworth, Staffordshire, England
                Festival honoring poet K. M. Bellman in
                        Stockholm, Sweden
                Feast of St. Ann, mother of the Virgin Mary
                        (patron of women in labor, miners,
                        dealers in used clothing, seam-
                        stresses, carpenters, stablemen,
                        and broommakers; invoked against
                        poverty and to find lost objects)
1139 AD         Portuguese defeated the Moors at Outique
1237            King Edward I of England did homage to King
                        Philip III of France for his
                        French holdings
1471            Pope Paul II died
1527            Coro, Venezuela, founded
1643            Excise taxes effected in England
1678            Joseph I, Holy Roman Emperor, born
1698            British settlers set out for Darien on the
                        Spanish Main
1757            Battle of Hastenbeck (Seven Years' War)
1758            French river Fort Louisbourg fell to the
                        British in Quebec
1775            Post Office established with Ben Franklin as
                        Postmaster General
1788            New York ratified the Constitution
1797            John Quincy Adams married Louisa C. Johnson
1799            Isaac Babbitt, inventor of alloys, born
1833            St. Bartholomea Capitaino died (Feast Day)
1845            Last sight of Sir John Franklin's expedition
                        seeking the Northwest Passage
1847            Liberia, settled in Africa by freed U.S. slaves,
                        became a republic (Liberian
                        Independence Day)
1848            Italians defeated Austrians at Volta
1856            George Bernard Shaw, playwright, born
1863            Santee Sioux and the Cavalry fought at Dead
                        Buffalo Lake, Minnesota
                Sam Houston, soldier-statesman, died
1865            Cavalry, on the way to rescue a wagon train
                        attacked by Indians, also
                        attacked at Platte Bridge
                Indians attacked Ft. Casper, Wyoming
1867            Otto, German-born King of Greece, died
1875            Carl Jung, psychologist, born
1894            Aldous Huxley, author, born
```

```
1897        Paul Gallico, journalist-author, born
1903        First transcontinental auto trip completed, San
                    Francisco to New York, at an
                    average of 175 miles per day
1904        Garland Roark, novelist, died
1919        British ratified the Versailles Peace Treaty
1922        Jason Robards, Jr., actor, born
1925        William Jennings Bryan, statesman, died
1944        Riza Khan Pahlavi, Shah of Iran, died
1945        Clement Atlee and the Labour Party elected in
                    England
1947        Department of Defense formed in U.S.
1948        Prince Charles of England born
1952        King Farouk of Egypt sent into exile
1953        Korean War armistice signed (Eastern Standard
                    Time)
1956        Egypt nationalized the Suez Canal
            Andrea Doria sank
1957        Carlos Armas, President of Guatemala,
                    assassinated
1958        Explorer 4 launched
1963        Skoplje, Yugoslavia, devastated by an earth-
                    quake
            Syncom 2 launched
1965        Eugene Burdick, author, died
1970        Barbershop Chorus Concert held at Guerneville,
                    California
1971        Apollo 15, lunar landing flight, launched
            Procession of Penitents at Furnes, Belgium
```

July 27th

```
            Barbarosa's Birthday, celebrated in Puerto Rico
            World Championship Pack Burro Race, Leadville
                    to Fairplay, Colorado
            Feast of St. Pantaleon, patron of doctors and
                    midwives, invoked against
                    tuberculosis
            Feast of the Seven Sleepers
  432 AD    St. Celestine I, Pope, died (Feast Day)
  852       Sts. Aurelius and Natalia died (Feast Day)
  916       St. Clement Slovensky died (Feast Day)
 1061       Pope Nicholas II, last German Pope, died
 1214       Battle of Bourines
 1276       James I, "the Conqueror," King of Aragon, died
 1582       Spanish fleet routed allied Portuguese, English,
                    and French
 1777       British at Detroit sent 15 Indian parties to
                    attack the settlements in Kentucky
 1779       Velocipede, an early bicycle, described in the
                    Journal de Paris
 1789       U.S. Department of Foreign Affairs founded
```

```
1791      Lafayette ordered the French National Guard to
                 fire on the crowds at Champ-de-
                 Mars
1796      Eliza H. Boardman born (she made Washington's
                 birthday a legal holiday)
1824      Alexandre Dumas fils, author, born
1872      Law of military conscription, the draft,
                 effected in France
1906      Leo Durocher, baseball personality, born
1916      Keenan Wynn, actor, born
1927      Spanish national flag adopted
1937      Japan attacked Tungchow, China
1944      Japanese occupation of Guam ended
1946      Gertrude Stein, author, died
1953      Korean truce agreement signed at Panmunjom
1967      Hinsburg, Vermont, "Dime a Dip" supper held
1970      Polka Festival held at New Ulm, Minnesota
          Antonio Salazar, Portuguese dictator, died
```

July 28th
_____

```
          Feast of Pope St. Innocent I
          Feast of Sts. Nazarius, Celsus, and Victor,
                 martyrs
          Feast of St. Samson
 388 AD   Battle of Aquileia
1057      Pope Victor II died
1330      Serbians defeated the Bulgarians and killed
                 their Tsar, Michael Sisman
1364      Battle of Pisa, Italy
1480      Turks made a sneak attack on Rhodes
1491      King Henry VIII of England born
1565      Settlers for Florida sailed from Spain
1575      Earl of Leicester was $3,000,000 poorer, having
                 played host to Queen Elizabeth I
                 of England at Kenilworth Castle
1576      Frobisher's expedition reached Labrador
1588      English sent fireships against the Spanish
                 Armada
1609      Admiral Sir George Somers discovered Bermuda
1611      Besieged Kalmar Castle surrendered (Sweden)
1746      Thomas Heyward, Jr., signer of the Declaration
                 of Independence, born
1750      Johann Sebastian Bach, composer, died of
                 apoplexy
1794      Robespierre, French revolutionist, was executed
                 and the Reign of Terror ended
1796      Jean Baptiste Corot, French painter, born
1812      Russians abandoned Vitebsk to Napoleon
1821      Gen. Jose de San Martin proclaimed the indepen-
                 dence of Peru from Spain
```

1847	Site chosen for Mormon temple in Salt Lake City, Utah
1862	First railway mail car in the U.S. went into service
	Gold discovered in Montana at Bismarck
	Speke discovered Ripon Falls, conjunction of the Nile Rivers
1863	Santee Sioux and Cavalry fought at Stony Lake, Minnesota
1866	Use of the metric measure system legalized in the U.S.
1874	Great dock completed at Liverpool, England, later to be consumed by fire
1892	Joe E. Brown, comedian, born
1893	Dr. Charles Mayo of the Mayo Clinic born
1896	Miami, Florida, with 260 inhabitants, incorporated
1898	U.S. forces completed the takeover of Puerto Rico
1901	Rudy Vallee, singer, born
1907	Ying King foundered off Hong Kong
1914	Austria declared war on Serbia, beginning World War I
1928	An egg was fried on the steps of the U.S. Capitol
1929	Jacqueline Bouvier (Kennedy) born
1933	First singing telegram, "Happy Birthday," sung to Rudy Vallee
1938	Mauretania, Cunard liner, launched
1943	Coffee rationing ended in the U.S.
1945	A B-25 bomber crashed into the Empire State Building
	Five Japanese ships sunk off Kure Island by U.S. planes
1948	Explosion at Farber works, Ludwigshafen, Germany
1958	U.S. Marines landed in Cuba to protect the Guantanomo Naval Base
	Building demolition begun of the site of Lincoln Center for the Performing Arts in New York City
1962	Steelton, Pennsylvania, train wreck
1971	Molinya 1/18, Russian communications satellite, launched

July 29th

Feast of St. Martha, patron of hotelkeepers
and laundresses
Last night of no sunset in Hammerfest, Norway
479 AD   St. Lupus of Troyes died (Feast Day)

1030	St. Olaf, King of Norway, killed in the Battle of Sticklestad (Feast Day) patron of Norway
1095	St. Ladislaus I, King of Hungary, died
1099	Pope St. Urban II, Founder of the First Crusade, died
1492	First almanac printed
1565	Mary, Queen of Scots, married Henry Stuart, Lord Darnley
1567	James VI, infant, crowned King of Scotland
1588	Final defeat suffered by the Spanish Armada
1644	Pope Urban VIII died
1703	Daniel Defoe, novelist, entered the pillory
1778	French fleet arrived at Rhode Island to help the colonial cause
1786	Pittsburgh Gazette, first newspaper west of the Allegheny Mountains, began publication
1857	Cavalry routed 300 Cheyenne Indians at Solomon's Fork on the Kansas River in Wyoming
1863	Venezuelan national flag became official
1867	Site for Nebraska's capitol chosen
1869	Booth Tarkington, author, born
1878	Total eclipse of the sun
1883	Mussolini, Italian dictator, born
1892	William Powell, actor, born
1899	Use of dum-dum bullets in war forbidden by the second Hague conference
1902	Umberto I, King of Italy, assassinated
1905	Dag Hammarsjkold, United Nations Secretary-General, born
1914	Cape Cod Canal opened to traffic (Massachusetts) First transcontinental telephone call made
1918	Edwin O'Conner, author, born
1937	Japan bombed Tientsin, China
1967	U.S. carrier Forstall burned off North Viet Nam Northern Venezuela rocked by an earthquake
1968	Pope Paul VI issued his edict against artificial birth control George Culver pitched a no-hitter and Cincinnati beat Philadelphia 6-1
1969	Frank Lesser, composer, died

July 30th

1178	Frederick Barbarosa crowned King of Burgundy
1511	Giorgio Vasari, Florentine artist, born
1538	Sir Humphrey Gilbert reached the coast of Newfoundland
1609	Iroquois Indians defeated by their first sight of firearms, used by the French and Hurons at Ticonderoga, New York

```
1619    Virginia Assembly, first legislative body in
            America, met at Jamestown
1683    Queen Marie Therese of France died, widow of
            Louis XIV
1684    Iroquois Indians submitted to rule by the
            English King
1718    William Penn, founder of Pennsylvania colony,
            died
1729    City of Baltimore, Maryland, founded
1733    Society of Freemasons opened its first lodge
            in America in Boston
1775    Capt. Cook's second voyage of exploration ended
1777    DeWitt Clinton inaugurated as Governor of New
            York
1818    Emily Bronte, English novelist, born
1844    The New York Yacht Club, oldest surviving in
            the U.S., organized aboard a yacht
1863    Henry Ford, inventor, born
1864    Confederates burned much of Chambersburg,
            Pennsylvania
        Petersburg, Virginia, mined by Union forces
1871    Ferry Westfield exploded at New York City
1891    Mozambique Company chartered by Portugal
        Casey Stengel, baseball personality, born
1896    Atlantic City, New Jersey, train wreck
1898    Henry Moore, British sculptor, born
1909    Mexico City rocked by earthquakes
        U.S. government bought its first airplane from
            the Wright brothers
1912    Meiji Tenno, 122nd Emperor of Japan, died
1915    Police Lieutenant Charles Becker, implicated in
            the Rosenthal murder, executed
1916    Munitions ship Black Tom sabotaged and
                        exploded at Jersey City, New
                        Jersey
1918    Joyce Kilmer, poet, killed in action
1921    Insulin discovered
1932    Start of Summer Olympics at Los Angeles,
            California
1936    Joyce Kilmer Memorial Forest dedicated in
            North Carolina
1941    Peace Treaty signed by Russia and Poland
1947    Thor Heyerdahl and his raft, Kon-Tiki, reached
                        Puka-Puka Island in Polynesia
                        after sailing from South America
1952    Chesapeake Bay Bridge dedicated
1956    "In God We Trust" officially became the U.S.
            motto
1963    First open-air crowning of a Pope held
                        (Paul VI)
1965    Pegasus 3 launched
```

```
1965       Medicare bill signed by the President
1970       Start of the Sioux Sun Dance at Pine Ridge,
               South Dakota
```

July 31st

```
           Feast of St. Neot
 432 AD    Sixtus III elected Pope
 448       St. Germanus of Auxerre died (Feast Day)
1315       Gates of Paris treacherously opened for
               Charles, King of Navarre
1367       Giovanni Colombini, founder of the Jesuit
               religious order, died
1527       Maximilian II, Holy Roman Emperor, born
1556       St. Ignatius of Loyola, founder of the Jesuit
               order, died (Feast Day)
1653       England sank 30 Dutch men-of-war off the coast
               of Holland
1703       Daniel Defoe, novelist, released from the
               pillory
1715       Spanish plate fleet wrecked off the coast of
               Florida by a hurricane
1750       King John V of Portugal died
1763       Ottowa Indians defeated the British at Bloody
               Run, Michigan
1790       First U.S. patent issued, for potash manu-
               facture
1792       First building of the U.S. government begun
1875       Andrew Johnson, U.S. President, died
1886       Franz Liszt, composer, died
1898       Otto von Bismarck, German statesman, died
1899       Use of incense forbade in Church of England
               worship
1909       Mexico City earthquakes ended
1914       War crisis in Europe closed the New York Stock
               Exchange
1940       Cuyahoga Falls, Ohio, train wreck
1945       U.S. cruiser Indianapolis torpedoed in the
               Philippine Sea
1954       K-2, highest unclimbed mountain in the world,
               climbed
1957       Pavel Tchelitchew, Russian artist, died
1964       Ranger 7 landed on the moon
1966       British launch Darwin vanished with 31 aboard
```

AUGUST

Full Moon - Sturgeon Moon, Grain Moon
Second Sunday - Family Reunion Day in the U.S.
First weekend - Governor's Day Celebration at Clear Lake,
        Iowa

August 1st

	Start of the Annual Trade Fair at Novgorod, Russia
	Lammas Day in England, heralding the wheat harvest
	St. Peter's deliverance from prison
	Feast of Sts. Faith, Hope, and Charity
10 BC	Claudius, Roman Emperor, born
527 AD	Justin I, Emperor of Eastern Rome, died
984	St. Ethelwold died (Feast Day)
1137	Louis VI, "the Fat," "the Wideawake," "the Bruiser," King of France, died of dysentery
1252	Carpini, papal legate and explorer of Mongolia, died
1291	First Everlasting League, Switzerland, founded (Swiss Independence Day)
1498	Columbus discovered Venezuela on his 3rd voyage
1589	Henry III, last Valois king of France, assassinated
1664	Christians defeated the Turks at St. Gottard, Hungary
1701	Canadians and their Indian Allies battled over "Firewater"
1714	Queen Anne of England died
1744	Jean Baptiste Pierre Antoine de Monet, Chevalier de Lamarck, naturalist, died

1769	Spanish explorer de Portola reached the site of Los Angeles
1779	Francis Scott Key, author of "The Star Spangled Banner," born
1790	Taking of the first U.S. census began
1819	Herman Melville, author, born
1834	Slavery outlawed in the British Empire
	Robert Morris, first Protestant missionary to China, died there
1843	Robert Todd Lincoln, son of the President, born
1846	200 Mormon pioneers arrived by ship in San Francisco
1849	Europeans first saw Lake Ngami, Africa
1859	Cornerstone laid for the monument to the fore-fathers at Plymouth, Massachusetts
1866	John Ross (Kooeskoowe), Cherokee Indian Chief, died
1873	First cable-car trip made in San Francisco
1876	Colorado became a state (Colorado Day, state holiday)
1885	Neutrality of the Congo Free State proclaimed
1889	Monument to the forefathers dedicated at Plymouth, Massachusetts
1893	King Alexander of Greece born
1903	First transcontinental auto trip ended in New York City, from California
1909	British ship Waratah vanished after leaving London with 300 aboard
1911	Michigan state flag adopted
1914	Germany declared war on Russia
1936	Start of the Summer Olympic Games at Berlin, Germany
	Yves St. Laurent, fashion designer, born
1944	U.S. troops attacked Germans around St. Lo, France
1950	Guam became a U.S. territory
1951	U.S. suspended all tariff concessions to Communist countries
1953	French ship Monique vanished off New Caledonia
1956	China struck by a typhoon
1960	Dahomey became independent of France (Independence Day, national holiday)
1962	Bill Monbouquette pitched a no-hitter and Boston beat Chicago 1-0
1970	Start of the 10-day feast of St. Domingo in Nicaragua

August 2nd

	Feast of Our Lady of the Angels
216 BC	Hannibal and his elephants routed the Romans at Cannae

47	"I came, I saw, I conquered" (Caesar upon the defeat of Pharnaces, King of Pontus, at Zela)
257 AD	Pope St. Stephen I died (Feast Day)
640	Pope Severinus died
686	Pope John V died
1100	William II, King of England, killed in a hunting accident
1274	King Edward I returned to England to be crowned
1552	St. Basil the Blessed died (Feast Day)
1754	Pierre L'Enfant, designer of Washington, D.C., born
1768	Samuel Hall founded the Essex Gazette in Salem, Massachusetts
1769	Los Angeles named, for Our Lady of the Angels
1787	St. Alphonsus de Liguori died, patron of professors of moral theology (Feast Day)
1788	Sir Thomas Gainsborough, English artist, died
1796	Napoleon defeated the Austrians at Lontano
1806	"Bloody Monday"
1811	William Williams, signer of the Declaration of Independence, died
1817	First steamboat put in at St. Louis, Missouri
1823	New York Mirror and Ladies' Literary Gazette founded as a weekly, eventually evolving into the daily New York Mirror
1829	Moray, Scotland, swept by floods
1830	The French revolted again, and King Charles X abdicated
1858	Administration of India transferred to the British government
1859	Horace Mann, educator-author, died
1862	Golden Age, Idaho's first newspaper, began publication
1867	The "Wagon Box Fight," where 3,000 Sioux Indians attacked 32 troopers and did not win
1868	King Constantine I of Greece born
1870	Subway opened in London, England
1876	"Wild Bill" Hickok killed while playing poker in Deadwood, South Dakota
1881	Federation of Organized Trades and Labor Unions formed, to become the American Federation of Labor in 1886
1887	Hodge Rowell patented his barbed wire
1914	Russia issued a proclamation of hostilities
1921	Enrico Caruso, singer, died of pleurisy
1923	Warren G. Harding, U.S. President, died
1924	Margaret Sidney, author, The Five Little Peppers and How They Grew, died
	James Baldwin, author, born

1934	President von Hindenburg of Germany died, opening the way to Hitler's takeover
1945	Potsdam, Germany, conference ended
1969	Navajo Trails Festival held at Durango, Colorado
1970	Festival of the Hungry Ghosts held in Singapore

August 3rd

National Guard Day in Venezuela
Feast of San Salvador (start of 3 days of celebration in El Salvador)

431 BC	Solar eclipse
30	Octavian captured Alexandria and Defender Antony, husband of Cleopatra, killed himself
1347 AD	Calais, France, surrendered to the English in 100 Years' War
1422	King Henry V of England died
1460	King James II of Scotland killed in a cannon explosion
1480	Turks gave up their unsuccessful siege of Rhodes
1492	Columbus sailed away from Spain
1576	Uranibourg Observatory construction began on Hveen Island, Denmark
1610	Henry Hudson entered Hudson's Bay, Canada
1645	French defeated the Holy Roman Empire's army at Nordlengen
1692	League of Augsburg fought the French at Steinkirk
1704	French defeated by the British at the Battle of Blenheim
1769	Europeans first noted the LaBrea tar pits at Los Angeles, California
1770	King Frederick William III of Prussia born
1792	Richard Arkwright, spinning-machine inventor, died
1795	Peace treaties signed with Indian tribes bordering on the U.S. boundaries, giving the U.S. the Ohio Territory
1804	Council held between U.S. and Nebraska Indians
1858	Speke discovered Lake Victoria, head of the White Nile
1867	Stanley Baldwin, English statesman, born
1868	St. Peter Eymard died (Feast Day)
1872	Haakon VII, King of Norway, born
1881	William G. Fargo, Wells-Fargo partner, died
1900	Ernie Pyle, journalist, born
1909	Walter V. Clark, author, born
1914	Germany declared war on France
	First ocean-going ship passed through the uncompleted Panama Canal

```
1916      Sir Roger Casement hanged (Irish Revolution)
          Second Battle of the Somme ended
1918      British ship Warilda torpedoed off the English
                          coast
1924      Leon Uris, author, born
          Joseph Conrad, novelist, died
1925      American Marines left Nicaragua
1926      Tony Bennett, singer, born
1955      Hurricane Connie began 11 days of devastation
                          in the U.S.
1958      Atomic submarine Nautilus crossed the North
                          Pole under the Arctic ice
1960      Republic of Nigeria became independent of France
1969      Navajo Trails Festival held at Durango, Colorado
1971      Lu Pan's Birthday celebration held in Hong Kong
```

August 4th

```
          Our Lady of the Snow, observed at Ciudad Bolivar,
                          Venezuela
          Emancipation Day in the Bahamas
  ? BC    Sodom and Gomorrah destroyed
1060 AD   Philip I, 8 years old, became King of France
1221      St. Dominic died (Feast Day)
1265      Battle of Evesham, England
1578      King Sebastian of Portugal killed in battle in
                          Morocco
1770      Machias, Maine, founded
1781      Corwallis's army retired to Yorktown, Virginia
1790      U.S. Revenue Cutter Service established, later
                          to become the Coast Guard
1792      Percy Bysshe Shelley, poet, born
1821      Saturday Evening Post, weekly magazine, founded
          William Floyd, signer of the Declaration of
                          Independence, died
1826      Last stocks for criminals removed from London
1854      Mt. Hood, Oregon, first climbed
1861      Jesse W. Reno, inventor of the escalator, born
1863      Custer and the Seventh Cavalry, guarding rail-
                          road surveyors, attacked by the
                          Sioux Indians
1875      Hans Christian Andersen, author, died
1886      Samuel Tilden, New York Governor and presi-
                          dential candidate, died
1892      "Lizzie Borden took an axe..." and was arrested
1900      Queen Mother Elizabeth, wife of King George VI
                          of England, born
1903      Giuseppe  Melchior Sarto elected Pope as Pius X
1906      Italian ship Sirio wrecked off Cape Palos
1914      England declared war on Germany for not
                          guaranteeing the neutrality of
                          Belgium
```

	Germany invaded Belgium and Russia
	U.S. proclaimed its neutrality
1916	U.S. purchased the Virgin Islands from Denmark
1928	Glacial ice dam on the Shyok River in India cracked
1939	Francisco Franco's party was proclaimed the only government in Spain
1944	Stockton, Georgia, train wreck
1952	Uranium "rush" began in Saskatchewan, Canada
1958	Potato-flake plant established at Grand Fork, North Dakota
1970	Start of 4 days of the International Ox-pulling Championships at Bridgewater, Nova Scotia, Canada

August 5th

	Feast of St. Afra
	Constitution Day in Iran
642 AD	King Oswald of Northumbria died
882	Louis III, King of France, died
1305	William Wallace, Scottish hero, captured by the British
1583	First English settlement in America founded at St. John's, Newfoundland
1604	John Elliott, missionary to the Indians, baptized
1620	Mayflower and Speedwell sailed from England
1633	George Abbott, Archbishop of Canterbury and preparer of the King James version of the Bible, died
1749	Thomas Lynch, Jr., signer of the Declaration of Independence, born
1764	Leopold II, Holy Roman Emperor, married Maria Louisa of Spain
1775	First white man, Don Juan Manuel Ayala, sailed through the Golden Gate into San Francisco Bay
1784	A 26-hour fire destroyed 10,000 buildings in Constantinople
1791	Peace signed at Sistova by Austria, Prussia, and Turkey
1796	Napoleon defeated the Austrians at Castiglione
1811	Hunt's overland expedition to the Pacific met the Cheyenne Indians
1827	Manuel Fonseca, first President of Brazil, born
1844	Cornerstone laid for the Statue of Liberty on Bedloe's Island
1850	Guy de Maupassant, French novelist, born
1858	First transAtlantic cable completed
1863	Sioux massacred 59 Pawnee Indians at Massacre Canyon, Nebraska

```
1864      "Damn the torpedoes!  Full speed ahead!"
                  (Adm. Farragut, victor at Mobile
                  Bay, Alabama)
1870      Philadelphia's public building commission
                  established
1886      Republic of Colombia founded
1906      John Huston, movie-maker, born
1909      First U.S. corporate income tax levied as part
                  of the Payne-Aldrich tariff bill
1910      Pilgrim Memorial dedicated at Provincetown,
                  Massachusetts
1911      Robert Taylor, actor, born
1914      Tipton Ford, Missouri, train wreck
          Woodrow Wilson offered the U.S. as mediator
                  between the warring Europeans
1915      Edith Cavell, British nurse, arrested by the
                  Germans and later executed as a spy
          Start of 20 days of flooding by storm tides on
                  the U.S. Gulf coast
          Warsaw,  Poland, fell to the Germans
1917      National Guard became a U.S. federal service
1922      Silver Springs, Missouri, train wreck
1925      An armament restrictions treaty was ratified
                  by Congress
1929      Dame Millicent Fawcett, British suffragist, died
1940      Talbot Mundy, novelist, died
          Start of 10 days of hurricane flooding in south-
                  east U.S.
1949      Peru and Ecuador rocked by earthquakes
1953      First prisoner exchange took place after the
                  Korean armistice
1960      Upper Volta became independent of France
1963      Craig Breedlove, in the Spirit of America, set
                  a land-speed record of 407.45 mph,
                  the first over 400 mph
1969      Mariner 7 flew by Mars, sending back pictures
1970      Bolivian Independence Day celebrated
          Princess Irene's birthday observed, a National
                  Holiday in Surinam
1972      Annual Magic Convention held at Colon, Michigan
```

<u>August 6th</u>

```
          Transfiguration (Protestant Episcopal and
                  Eastern Orthodox)
258 AD    St. Sixtus II, Pope, died (Feast Day)
317       Flavius Julius Constantius, Eastern Roman
                  Emperor, born
1221      St. Dominic of Spain, founder of the Dominican
                  Order, died
1223      Louis VIII crowned King of France
1272      King Stephen V of Hungary died
1284      Genoa defeated Pisa in the sea battle of Meloria
```

1458	Pope Colixtus III died
1514	Margaret of England, widowed Queen of Scotland, married the Earl of Angus
1538	Santa Fe de Bogata, Colombia, founded
1571	Cyprus fell to the Turks
1623	Anne, Mrs. William Shakespeare, died
1637	Ben Jonson, English playwright, died
1644	Louise de la Valliere, mistress of King Louis XIV of France, born
1660	Velazquez, Spanish artist, died
1697	Charles VII, Holy Roman Emperor, born
1774	First Shakers arrived in the U.S.
1777	Battle of Iriskany, New York
1806	Francis I abdicated as last Holy Roman Emperor
1809	Alfred, Lord Tennyson, poet, born
1825	Bolivia became independent of Spain
1846	New York, first subtreasury of the U.S., established
1855	"Know-Nothing" political party riot in Louisville, Kentucky
1876	Miller Hutchinson, inventor of the Dictograph and the Klaxon horn, born
1885	Manchester Ship Canal bill passed by the English Parliament
1889	Much of Spokane, Washington, destroyed by fire
1890	First execution by electrocution performed in the U.S. (New York)
1893	Louella Parsons, Hollywood columnist, born
1895	George Frederick Root, composer of "Battle Cry of Freedom," died
1911	Lucille Ball, comedian, born
1917	Robert Mitchum, actor, born
1926	Gertrude Ederle swam the English Channel
1927	Oriskany, New York, battle site and monument became a state park
1928	Italian submarine F-14 involved in a collision in the Adriatic Sea
1930	Bodies of North Pole-crossing Swedish balloonists found
	Judge Joseph Crater of the New York State Supreme Court disappeared
1932	Welland Canal, connecting Lake Erie to Lake Ontario, formally opened
1939	Princess Irene of Holland born
1941	Allied invasion of North Africa began
1945	Atomic bomb dropped on Hiroshima, Japan (Hiroshima Peace Festival, Japanese National Memorial Day)
1953	Korean War prisoner repatriation began
1961	Russia's Vostok II launched
1962	Jamaica became independent of Britain, remaining in the Commonwealth

1966   Salazar Bridge over the Targus River in Portugal
            opened to traffic

            Anniversary of the Battle of Boyaca, a Colombian
                National Holiday
            Southdown sheep fair held at Lewes, Sussex,
                England
            Feast of St. Victricius
461 AD   Majorian, Roman Emperor, died
1106   Henry IV, King of Germany and Holy Roman
                Emperor, born
1385   Joan, "The Fair Maid of Kent," mother of
                England's King Richard II, died
1479   Maximilian, Holy Roman Emperor, defeated the
                French at Guinegatte
1547   St. Cajetan died (Feast Day)
1743   Sweden ceded to Russia a large part of Finland
1782   Military Order of the Purple Heart founded (U.S.)
1783   John Heathcoat, lace-maker inventor, born
1789   Act of Congress established the U.S. Lighthouse
                Service
1803   Two ships left Kronstadt to make the first
                Russian globe-circling voyage
1821   Caroline, estranged wife of King George IV of
                England, died
1834   Joseph Jacquard, loom inventor, died
1846   Maine legislature passed an act restricting
                intoxicating beverages
1888   Mony Woolley, actor, born
1894   Pullman railroad car-manufacturing workers'
                strike ended
1904   Ralph Bunche, statesman, born
            Eden, Colorado, train wreck
1914   Liege, Belgium, fell to the Germans
1942   U.S. Marines landed on Guadalcanal
1947   Thor Heyerdahl and the Kon-tiki proved the
                possibility of South Americans'
                having gone to Polynesia
1955   Hurricane Diane began flooding the eastern U.S.
                coast
1959   Explorer VI took the first photos, via tele-
                vision, of the Earth from space
            A dynamite truck exploded in Roseburg, Oregon
1960   Ivory Coast became independent of France
1970   Third Annual Pea Harvest Festival held at
                Palmer, Alaska
1971   Apollo 15 splashed into the Pacific

Feast of St. Cyriacus, invoked against eye
diseases
Feast of St. Hormidz
Star Festival, a Korean holiday
117 AD   Trajan, Roman Emperor, died
676   St. Colman of Lindisfarne died
869   King Lothair of Lorraine died
870   Treaty of Mersen, France, divided Lothair II's
kingdom
1503   Margaret of England married King James IV of
Scotland
1540   King Henry VIII of England married Catherine
Howard, his 5th wife
1588   Last of the Spanish Armada destroyed
1829   Aberdeen, Scotland, devastated by floods
A locomotive was first operated in the western
hemisphere
1832   George, King of Saxony, born
Leopold I, King of Belgium, married Princess
Louise of France
1844   Sara Teasdale, poet, born
1846   Smithsonian Institution founded in Washington,
D.C.
1859   St. John-Baptiste Vianney, patron of parish
clergy, died (Feast Day)
1866   Matthew Henson, black member of Peary's polar
expedition, born
1896   Marjorie Rawlings, author of The Yearling, born
1900   First Davis Cup Tennis Tournament began
(Massachusetts)
1908   Arthur Goldberg, statesman, born
1923   Esther Williams, swimming actress, born
1945   Russia declared war on Japan
1963 $7,000,000 stolen in Britain's "Great Train
Robbery"
1968   Air Density Explorer and Injun 5 satellites
launched
1970   Maidens' Festival celebrated in Hong Kong and in
Malaysia, the Day of the Seven
Sisters
Watermelon Festival held at Rush Springs,
Oklahoma

Feast of St. Herman (Russian Orthodox)
Festival of St. Spyridon, patron of Corfu, Greece
48 BC   Battle of Pharsalus; Caesar defeated but failed
to capture Pompey

117 AD	Hadrian was told that he was heir to the Roman Empire
378	Valens, Roman Emperor, defeated and killed by the Goths at the Battle of Adrianople
642	St. Oswald, King of Northumbria, died (Feast Day)
1048	Pope Damascus II died
1332	English defeated the Scots at Dupplin Moor
1538	Idea for the Armada first mentioned to the Spanish king
1593	Isaak Walton, fisherman, born
1629	Quebec temporarily surrendered to the English
1832	Nathaniel Pitt Langford, one of the discoverers of the geysers at Yellowstone, born
1841	S.S. Erie lost
1842	British-U.S. extradition treaty signed
1843	First land sale held at Brisbane, Australia
1851	Gold discovered at Ballarat, Australia
1862	Confederate victory at the Second Battle of Bull Run or Manassas, Virginia
1870	England's Education Bill passed Parliament
1900	Umberto I, assassinated King of Italy, buried
1902	King Edward VII of England crowned
1928	Bob Cousy, basketball figure, born
1929	Breakwater at Antofagesta, Chile, which was almost completed, destroyed
1937	Japanese took formal possession of the capitol of China
	Finsler Comet passed within 45 million miles of Earth
1942	3 U.S. cruisers sunk in the Solomon Islands
1945	Atomic bomb dropped on Nagasaki, Japan
	Russia's declaration of war on Japan went into effect
	Michigan, North Dakota, train wreck
1962	Philippines hit by a typhoon
1964	Abieco, ancient Peruvian city, discovered
1965	Singapore separated from the Malaysian Federation (National Holiday in Singapore)
	A missile silo exploded at Searcy, Arkansas
1970	Start of the week-long Hobo Convention at Britt, Iowa

August 10th

258 AD	St. Lawrence died, patron of cooks, vineyards and restaurateurs; invoked against lumbago and fire
955	Otto I, "the Great," Holy Roman Emperor, defeated the Magyars at Lechfeld
1296	John, King of Bohemia, born

1385	Start of market days at Newport, Monmouthshire, England
1397	King Albert II of Germany born
1471	Francesco della Rovere elected Pope as Sixtus IV
1498	King Henry VII of England gave John Cabot a 10-pound reward for the discovery of Canada
1500	Diego Diaz sighted Madagascar
1519	Magellan left Spain to circle the world
1536	Cartier entered the Gulf of St. Lawrence, Canada
1628	Vasa, a Swedish warship, sank while being towed to the starting place of her maiden voyage
1644	French completed their conquest of the Rhine Valley from Basel to Coblenz
1720	Spaniards massacred by Pawnee Indians near Columbus, Nebraska
1741	Stellar discovered the Northern fur seal
1753	Edmund Randolph, U.S. statesman, died
1759	Ferdinand VI, King of Spain, died
1792	Paris mob stormed the Tuileries Palace, home of the king
	French revolutionary government suspended the king from any government functions
1804	Francis II became Emperor of Austro-Hungary
1807	Robert Fulton's steamboat Claremont made its first trip
1821	Missouri became a state
1845	Karl Wilhelm Naundorff, self-proclaimed son of King Louis XVI of France and claimant to the throne, died
1850	The Brewsterite wagon train started west, following the Santa Fe Trail
1861	Confederates victorious at Wilson's Creek, Missouri
1874	Herbert Clark Hoover, U.S. President, born
1875	Town of Custer, South Dakota, laid out
1885	First electric street railway opened (Baltimore, Maryland)
1887	Chatsworth, Illinois, train wreck
1900	Finals held in the first Davis Cup Tennis Tournament
1954	St. Lawrence Seaway hydroelectric power project begun
1960	Discoverer 13 launched
1968	ATS-4 satellite launched
1969	Mass swim across the Danube River at Ruse, Bulgaria

Hay fever season begins
Feast of St. Attracta
Feast of St. Blaun
Feast of St. Susan
Feast of St. Tiburtius (1)

490 AD   Theodoric and the Osgoths defeated the Roman army at Addua

1241   Ogedei, Mongol leader, died and his army withdrew from Hungary

1492   Roderigo Borgia elected Pope as Alexander VI

1494   Hans Memling, Flemish artist, died

1587   Sir Walter Raleigh's second expedition of colonists arrived in Virginia

1667   Moliere's comedy Tartuffe banned by the Archbishop of Paris

1674   European Allies under William of Orange defeated the French at Senef, Holland

1688   New Rochelle, New York, agreed to give a "fat calf" annually, to pay the Pell family for the land on which the Huguenot city was to be built

1733   Trustees of Georgia prohibited rum in the province

1778   Frederich L. Jahn, "father of gymnastics," born

1786   British took possession of Penang, Malaysia

1789   French decree abolishing feudalism proclaimed

1804   Austria became an Empire

1831   Barbados devastated by a hurricane

1834   "Old Zip Coon," minstrel song, introduced at the Bowery Theater, New York City

1855   Santa Anna, Mexican president, exiled

1860   First successful silver mill in the U.S. began operation (Virginia City, Nevada)

1862   Sarah Bernhardt made her acting debut

1863   Seventh Cavalry, guarding railroad surveyors, drove off attacking Sioux Indians

1872   Lowell Mason, author of "Nearer My God to Thee," died

1877   First satellite of the planet Mars discovered

1880   Mays Landing, New Jersey, train wreck

1919   Andrew Carnegie, industrialist-philanthropist, died

Constitutional Germany organized

1937   Edith Wharton, novelist, died

Japanese Marines landed in Shanghai, China, and shelled other major Chinese cities

1942   New Waterloo Bridge opened in London

1946   Mussolin's body, stolen from a pauper's grave in April, found

```
1950      Vern Beckford pitched a no-hitter and Boston
               beat Brooklyn 7-0
          Baudouin became King of Belgium, ending the
               restored reign of Leopold III
1953      New Rochelle, New York, paid its first calf to
               the Pells
1954      Armistice ended 7 1/2 years of war in Indo-
               China
          Cambodia and Laos became independent of France
1956      Jackson Pollock, artist, died
1960      Republic of Chad became independent of France
               (National Holiday)
1962      Russia's Vostok III launched
1964      Chile suspended diplomatic relations with Cuba
          Pope Paul VI became the first Pope to ride in
               a helicopter
1965      Five days of civil rights riots began in Los
               Angeles
1969      Dog Days ended
1970      Fox Hill Day celebrations held marking the
               anniversary of the end of slavery
               in the Bahamas
1972      Start of the Annual Hobo Convention at Britt,
               Iowa
```

August 12th

```
3113 BC   Starting date of the Mayan calendar
   49     Afranius, Petreius, and Varron, allies of
               Pompey, surrendered to Caesar in
               Spain
1099 AD   Moslems prevented from recapturing Jerusalem by
               Crusaders' having defeated them at
               Ascalon
1253      St. Clare of Assisi, founder of the Franciscan
               Order of Nuns, died; patron of
               embroidery workers, guilders, and
               washerwomen; invoked for good
               weather and against eye diseases
1350      Philip VI, King of France, died
1464      John Capgrave, English historian, died
1484      Pope Sixtus IV died
1515      Christian II, King of Norway and Denmark,
               married Isabella
1658      First police force in America established in New
               Amsterdam (New York City)
1676      King Philip's War, Pilgrims and Indians, ended
               with his death
1759      Battle of Kunersdorf in the Seven Years' War
1762      King George IV of England born
1765      British Indian Empire established by treaty
1782      Start of three days of fire in Constantinople
```

1792	Royalist newspapers suppressed in France
1839	First whites arrived at Sacramento, California
1850	Merriweather Lewis stood on the Continental Divide
1856	First patent issued for an accordion in the U.S.
1865	Joseph Lister became first doctor to use disinfectant during surgery
1881	Cecil B. DeMille, playwright and film director, born
1882	George Bellows, artist, born
1891	James Russell Lowell, poet-diplomat, died
1898	Spanish-American War armistice signed
1904	Alexis, heir to the Russian throne, born
1916	U.S. National Guard ordered to the Mexican border
1939	Harney, Nevada, train wreck
1953	Atomic Energy Commission reported a Russian H-bomb blast
1958	U.S. troop withdrawal from Lebanon began
	Atomic submarine Skate crossed the North Pole under the Arctic ice
1960	Echo I, communications relay satellite, launched
1962	Vostok IV launched by Russia
1969	Northern Japan rocked by a strong earthquake
1970	Start of the 250th anniversary celebrations at Plymouth, Massachusetts
	Queen Sirikit's Birthday celebrated as a National Holiday in Thailand

---

August 13th

	Feast of St. Cassian of Imola
	Feast of St. Hippolytus of Rome
	Ancient Romans sacrificed to Vertumnus and held a festival for Diana, goddess of the hunt on this, the Ides of August
29 BC	First of three Roman triumphs held for Octavian
523 AD	Pope John I elected; first Pope to leave Italy, visiting Constantinople
587	St. Radegund, Queen of the Franks, died (Feast Day)
622	St. Maximus the Confessor died
900	Zwendibold, King of Lorraine, killed in battle
1099	Paschal II elected Pope
1173	St. Narses the Gracious died (Feast Day)
1521	Cortez took Mexico, sacking the Aztec capitol of Tenochtitlan
1587	First American Indian converted to Protestantism baptized
1654	Folli transfused blood between animals

1704	English-Dutch allies defeated French and Bavarians at Hochstadt
1708	French sappers at siege of Turin were warded off by a countermine that breached the city's walls
1713	Prussian king's private estates became domains of the crown
1783	St. Tikhon of Zadonsk died (Orthodox Feast Day)
1784	U.S. legislature last met at Annapolis, Maryland
1792	French royal family taken to the Temple of the Tower in Paris as prisoners
1812	Essex captured the Alert
1818	Lucy Stine, abolitionist and suffragist, born
1844	New Jersey state constitution ratified
1846	First American flag raised in Los Angeles, California
1863	Eugene Delacroix, French artist, died
1868	Start of 3 days of earthquakes in Peru and Ecuador
1878	Luray Cavern discovered in Virginia
1884	Rufus Porter, founder of the Scientific American, died
1888	James L. Baird, television inventor, born
1890	First annual convention of mailmen held (Boston)
1895	Bert Lahr, comedian, born
1898	Manila surrendered to the Americans
1899	Alfred Hitchcock, "master of suspense," born
1907	Alfred Krupp, German industrialist, born
	First taxicab appeared in New York City
1910	Florence Nightingale, nursing pioneer, died
1912	Horace H. Furness, Shakespearean scholar, died
	Ben Hogan, golfer, born
1915	Marowijne sank in the Gulf of Mexico
1917	North Bedford, Connecticut, train wreck
1919	George Shearing, jazz musician, born
1927	Fidel Castro, Cuban dictator, born
1930	Governor Sulzer of New York impeached
1932	First double-decker railroad car began operating (Long Island, New York)
1935	American Child Health Association disbanded
1959	Ground broken in Staten Island for the Verrazano Narrows Bridge (New York)
1960	Central African Republic became independent of France
	First 2-way telephone conversation held via satellite
1963	Explosives dump exploded in Gauhiti, India

1385 AD	John I, King of Castile, defeated in battle over his claim to the Portuguese throne
1464	Pope Pius II died
1498	Columbus landed at the mouth of the Orinoco River, Venezuela
1642	Abel Tasman set sail to discover New Zealand
1721	New England Courant, Boston newspaper, founded
1782	Constantinople fires finally extinguished
1784	Iceland rocked by earthquakes
1794	Whiskey Insurrection Convention met at Monongohela, Pennsylvania
1814	Norway and Sweden united
1816	Britain annexed Tristan da Cunha, an Atlantic island
1842	Final defeat of the Seminole Indians in Florida
1848	Oregon became a U.S. territory
1860	Ernest Thompson Seton, naturalist-author, born
1867	John Galsworthy, author, born
1887	Ferdinand assumed the government in Bulgaria
1888	Ships Gersir and Thingvalla collided
1900	Islander, carrying $3,000,000 in gold, hit an iceberg and sank in Steven's Passage, Alaska
	Allied troops captured Peking in China's Boxer Rebellion
	Six-masted schooner George G. Wells launched
1903	John Ringling North, circus showman, born
1917	Russian imperial family sent to Siberia by Communists
1929	Graf Zeppelin began an around-the-world trip
1932	End of the summer Olympics at Los Angeles, California
1935	Social Security Act enacted by Congress
1941	Atlantic Charter drawn up
1944	Allies invaded France east of the Rhône River
1945	Japan surrendered, ending World War II (World War II Victory Day celebrated in Arkansas and Rhode Island)
1951	William Randolph Hearst, publisher, died
1955	Hurricane Connie ended 11 days of devastation in the U.S.
1962	Mail truck robbery near Plymouth, Massachusetts, netted the takers $1 1/2 million
1964	South Korea hit by flooding

	Dormition of the Virgin Mary (Eastern Orthodox)
	Feast of the Blessed Virgin Mary (Assumption)
	Feast of St. Tarcisus
	Madhu Festival held in Colombo, Ceylon
	Mid-autumn festival held in China, featuring moon viewing and moon-cookie eating
	Anniversary mass is said at Cataldo Mission, oldest European building in Idaho
	Anniversary of the moving of Guatemala's capitol
310 BC	Solar eclipse
383 AD	Gratian, Emperor of the western Roman Empire, killed
717	Siege of Constantinople raised
778	Charlemagne's rear guard, returning from Spain, attacked by the Basques
1038	St. Stephen, King of Hungary, died
1096	First Crusade set out for Jerusalem
1169	Henry VI crowned King of Germany
1195	St. Anthony of Padua born
1281	Mongol attack on Japan thwarted by a typhoon
1369	Philippa of Hainaut, wife of King Edward III of England, died
1416	British defeated the French at the naval battle of Harfleur
1461	French defeated English at Formigny
1534	Jesuit Order founded
	City of Santiago de Quito, Ecuador, founded
1548	Mary, Queen of Scots, arrived in France to marry the heir to the French throne
1549	First Christian missionaries arrived in Japan
1573	Asuncion, Paraguay, founded (Founding Festival held annually)
1688	Frederick William I, King of Prussia, born
1702	Battle of Luzzara, Italy, fought over succession to the Spanish throne
1760	Battle of Liegnitz in the Seven Years' War
1769	Napoleon Bonaparte born
1771	Sir Walter Scott, writer, born
1846	Mexican citizens at Las Vegas, New Mexico, took an oath of allegiance to the U.S.
1855	Battle of Traktir in the Crimean War
1860	Florence K. Harding, wife of the President, born
1870	Kansas Pacific Railroad completed to Denver, Colorado
1879	Ethel Barrymore, actress, born
1887	Edna Ferber, novelist, born
1889	Thomas Hart Benton, artist, born
1893	Final settlement reached in the seal-hunting dispute over the Bering Sea area

1896	"What's the Matter with Kansas?" editorial appeared in the _Emporia Gazette_
1914	Panama Canal formally opened
1935	Will Rogers, humorist, died in a plane crash
1940	End of 10 days of hurricane flooding in south-eastern U.S.
1947	India and Pakistan became independent of Britain (National Holidays in both countries)
1950	Princess Anne, only daughter of Queen Elizabeth II of England, born
	Assam, India, hit by earthquakes and floods
1960	Republic of the Congo (Brazzaville) proclaimed
1961	_Explorer 12_ launched
1967	Rene Magritte, Belgian artist, died
1970	Start of Awa Odori Holiday in Tokushima, Japan
1971	Festival of mountain guides held at Chamonix, France

August 16th

	Feast of St. Joachim
	Fiesta de la Nieve at Mendoza and Bariloche, Argentina
1327 AD	St. Roch died, patron of surgeons and tile-makers; invoked against or to heal plague, knee afflictions, and cattle diseases
1419	Wenceslaus, King of Germany, died
1728	Bering sighted the Diomede Islands
1777	British defeated the colonials at Bennington, Vermont (Bennington Battle Day, state holiday)
1784	Nathan Hale, journalist-author, born
1798	Mirabeau Buonaparte Lamar, second president of the Texas Republic, born
1812	Americans surrendered to the British at Detroit
1819	Peterloo or Manchester Massacre (England)
1830	Charles X, King of France, fled to England
1861	Edith Roosevelt, wife of President Theodore, born
1868	End of 3 days of earthquakes in Ecuador and Peru
	Bernarr MacFadden, publisher, born
1869	Ibarra, Ecuador, flattened by an earthquake
1894	George Meany, labor leader, born
1896	Peru and Ecuador rocked by an earthquake
	Gold discovered in the Klondike (Klondike Discovery Day, legal holiday in Yukon, Canada)
1899	Robert W. Bunsen, burner inventor, died
1915	106 died when 2 dredges were wrecked off Galveston, Texas

1916	Rumania joined the Allies against Germany
1921	Peter I, first King of the Serbs, Croats, and Slovenes, died
1924	Dawls Reparation plan, presented in London, accepted by the Allies and Germany
1930	Tony Trabert, tennis player, born
1936	Spanish insurgents took Badakoj
	Summer Olympics ended in Berlin, Germany
1949	Margaret Mitchell, author of Gone With the Wind, died
1960	Cyprus became independent of Britain
1965	Five days of civil rights rioting ended in Los Angeles
1968	ESSA-7, weather satellite, launched
1970	Coffee Festival held at Pereira, Colombia
	Festival of the Hungry Ghosts held in Malaysia

August 17th

	Our Lady of the Angels in Millanes, Venezuela
	Indonesian Independence Day
	Ancient Roman festival honoring Portunus, god of the gates and doors
	Feast of St. Mamas
754 AD	Carloman, Frankish King, died
1153	William, first son of King Henry II of England born, to die in infancy
1257	St. Hyacinth of Cracow died (Feast Day)
1424	British defeated French and Scots at Verneuil
1427	Gypsies were denied entry into Paris
1498	Caesar, Cardinal Borgia at age 18 by the appointment of his father, Pope Alexander VI, renounced his office to marry a French princess
1544	Lutheran University of Konigsberg founded
1585	Colony of English settlers established on Roanoke Island, North Carolina
1676	Sweden defeated Denmark at Fyllebro
1786	Davy Crockett, frontier hero, born
	King Frederick II, "the Great," ruler of Prussia, died, the result of watching a military review in the rain
1798	Désirée Clary married Bernadotte, Napoleon's appointee as King of Sweden and Norway
1805	Sacajawea, Indian woman who guided Lewis and Clark, reunited with her family
1820	Divorce trial of Caroline, estranged wife of King George IV of England, began in the House of Lords

```
1850      Jose de San Martin, liberator of Chile, died
1859      Blondin crossed Niagara Falls on a tightrope
1871      National flag of Guatemala adopted
1877      Second Martian moon discovered
          F. P. Cahill became the first man to be killed
               by Billy the Kid
1887      King Charles I of Austro-Hungary, born
1892      Mae West, actress, born
1914      Belgian government moved from Brussels to
               Antwerp
1915      German zeppelins attacked London
          Franklin D. Roosevelt, Jr., son of the
               President, born
1944      Canadians took Falaise, France, from the Germans
1945      Indonesia proclaimed its independence from
               Holland
1955      Ferdinand Léger, French artist, died
1959      Yellowstone National Park rocked by an earth-
               quake
1960      Gabon became independent of France
1967      Sugar-on-Snow Supper served at Cavendish,
               Vermont
1970      Beginning of the America's Cup yacht races
          Venus 7 space explorer left Russia for Venus
          National Flag Day celebrated in Bolivia
```

August 18th

```
          Feast of St. Helena, wife of Constantine
1227 AD   Genghis Khan, Mongol leader, died
1274      Edward I crowned King of England
1276      Pope Adrian V died, 6 weeks after his election
1477      Maximilian I, Holy Roman Emperor, married
               Mary, heiress to Burgundy
1503      Pope Alexander VI died of poison, accidentally
               (it was intended for a guest)
1559      Pope Paul IV died
1571      Valletta, capitol of Malta, completed and
               occupied by the Knights of
               St. John
1572      Henry of Navarre, to become King Henry IV of
               France, married Margaret, sister
               of King Charles IX of France
1587      First white child, Virginia Dare, born in
               America
1591      Governor of the Roanoke Island colony returned
               from England, only to find an
               empty fort
1642      First white man, a Jesuit missionary, saw Lake
               George, New York
          Guido Reni, Italian artist, died
1658      Leopold I elected King of Germany
```

```
1735     Boston's Evening Post newspaper founded
1765     Francis I, Holy Roman Emperor, died
1769     Don Alexander O'Reilly and his Spanish troops
                    took possession of Louisiana
1774     Merriweather Lewis, explorer, born
1786     Reykjavik, Iceland, founded (National Holiday)
1807     Napoleon established the Kingdom of Westphalia
1830     Franz Joseph I, ruler of Austro-Hungary, born
1862     Sioux Indian War began with the Massacre at
                    Yellow Medicine, Minnesota
1872     Foundation stone laid for Philadelphia's city
                    hall
1873     Mt. Whitney, California, first climbed
         Otto A. Harbach, musical playwright, born
1900     Madame Pandit, Indian stateswoman, born
1902     First unassisted triple play in baseball made
                    by Harry O'Hagen
1911     Bill passed admitting women to the Norwegian
                    Cabinet
1914     The first warship, Peruvian destroyer Teniente
                    Rodriguez, passed through the
                    Panama Canal
1924     French troops began evacuation of the Ruhr
                    valley
1954     St. Lawrence Seaway plans announced by U.S.
                    and Canada
1960     First mid-air recovery of a space vehicle made
                    with Discoverer 14
         Lew Burdette pitched a no-hitter and Milwaukee
                    beat Philadelphia 1-0
1961     Learned Hand, jurist, died
1963     James H. Meredith became the first black to
                    graduate from the University
                    of Mississippi
1966     Great Proletarian Cultural Revolution celebrated
                    in Peking, China
```

```
--------------------------------------------------------
August 19th
--------------------------------------------------------
```

```
         National Aviation Day in the U.S.
         Festival of the Seven Sisters in Singapore
         National Uprising Day in Iran
         Feast of St. Arnulf of Metz
14 AD    Octavius Augustus, Roman Emperor, died
440      Pope St. Sixtus III died
1399     King Richard II of England surrendered to Henry,
                    his cousin and heir, and abdicated
1458     Aeneas Sylvius Piccolomine elected Pope as
                    Pius II
1493     Frederick, III as Holy Roman Emperor, IV as
                    King of Germany, V as King of
                    Austria, died
```

1587	Sigismund III elected King of Poland
1646	John Flamsteed, father of modern astronomy, born
1680	St. John of Eudes died (Feast Day)
1757	First British-produced Indian coin made in Calcutta
1772	Swedish royal council arrested by order of the king
1779	British garrison at Jersey City, New Jersey, captured
1812	U.S.S. Constitution sank the British Guerriese, earning the nickname "Old Ironsides"
1819	James Watt, steam engine inventor, died
1830	Kyoto, Japan, suffered a severe earthquake
1835	Marshall Field, merchant, born
1843	Charles M. Doughty, Arabian explorer, born
1848	Report of the California gold strike appeared in the New York Herald
1854	Thirty U.S. soldiers were all killed when they attacked a Sioux Indian camp
1870	Bernard Baruch, financier-author, born
1871	Orville Wright, airplane inventor, born
1890	Daughters of the American Revolution organized
1893	Alfred Lunt, actor, born
1895	Wes Hardin, outlaw turned lawyer, killed in the Acme Saloon
1896	Charles Latin Hildreth, poet-novelist, died
1902	Ogden Nash, humorous poet, born
1903	James G. Cozzens, author, born
1915	Ocean liner Arabic sunk by the Germans
1916	Germans torpedoed 2 British cruisers
1917	Russian imperial family arrived in Siberia
1931	Willie Shoemaker, jockey, born
1939	Germany and Russia signed a trade agreement
1960	Gary Powers, pilot of a U.S. U-2 reconnaissance plane, was convicted of espionage by the Russian courts
	Russia orbited 2 dogs in Sputnik V
1964	Syncom 3, communications satellite, launched
1965	Jim Maloney pitched a no-hitter of 10 innings and Cincinnati beat Chicago 1-0
1966	Eastern Turkey rocked by an earthquake
1970	Skynet B, communications satellite, launched
1972	Natural Chimneys Jousting Tournament held at Mount Solon, Virginia

---

August 20th

	Miners'Day observations in Elena, Bulgaria
	Feast of St. Amadour
636 AD	Battle of Heiromax
651	St. Oswin, King of Deria (England), killed (Feast Day)

```
 684     St. Philibert died (Feast Day)
1153     St. Bernard of Clairvaux died (Feast Day)
1205     Henry crowned Emperor of Rumania
1597     First Dutch East India Company ships returned
             from the Far East
1648     French defeated the Dutch and the Holy Roman
             Empire at Lens
1694     William Penn restored to the governorship of
             Pennsylvania
1741     Bering discovered Alaska
1794     Anthony Wayne defeated the Indians at the
             Battle of Fallen Timbers
1823     Pope Pius VII died
1833     Benjamin Harrison, former U.S. President, died
1847     Americans defeated Santa Anna at Churubusco
1867     Abergele, England, witnessed the crash of a
             train and a petroleum wagon
1905     Al Lopez, baseball player, born
1910     Eero Saarinen, architect, born
1914     Giuseppe Melchior Sarto, Pope Pius X, died
         Carranza occupied Mexico City in the Mexican
             Revolution
         Germans entered Brussels, Belgium
1915     Italy declared war on Turkey
1919     Daylight Savings Time repealed in the U.S.
1940     Trotsky, exiled Russian, shot in Mexico
1941     Lon Warneke pitched a no-hitter and St. Louis
             beat Cincinnati 2-0
1953     Russia announced the H-bomb blast publicized
             by the U.S. Atomic Energy
             Commission on the 12th
1957     Bob Keegan pitched a no-hitter and Chicago
             beat Washington 6-0
1959     China hit by a typhoon
1968     Last imperial pheasant in a U.S. zoo died
             (Bronx, New York)
         "Rape of Czechoslovakia" (invasion by the Warsaw
             Pact Communist countries)
1972     Beginning of the Indian Fire-walking Exhibit
             at Suva, Fiji
```

August 21st
```
         Sacrifices offered to the Roman god Consus
         Feast of St. Jane Frances Chantal, founder of
             the Order of the Visitation
         Feast of St. Sidonius Apollinaris
 776 BC  Lunar eclipse
1044 AD  Battle of Nouy, France
1165     Philip Augustus, King of France, born
1214     England defeated France in a sea battle off
             Dover
```

1221	St. Abraham of Smolensk died (Feast Day)
1241	Pope Gregory IX, founder of the Inquisition, died
1400	Rupert elected to the throne of Germany
1567	St. Francis de Sales, patron of writers, died
1745	Czar Peter III of Russia married Catherine the Great
1765	William IV, King of England, born
1810	Bernadotte, Napoleon's appointee, elected crown prince of Norway and Sweden
1831	Nat Turner's Rebellion began
1858	Rudolph of Hapsburg, heir to Austria-Hungary, born .
	Lincoln and Douglas began debating
1863	Quantrell's raiders struck Lawrence, Kansas
1883	Rochester, Minnesota, severely struck by a tornado
1906	"Count" Basie, jazz musician, born
1919	Great dry dock completed at Pearl Harbor, Hawaii
1930	Princess Margaret Rose of England born
1935	Historic Sites Act became U.S. law
1936	Wilt Chamberlain, basketball star, born
1955	Hurricane Diane ended 2 weeks of flooding in eastern U.S.
1959	Hawaii became a state
1965	Gemini 5, manned orbital flight, launched
1968	USSR invaded Czechoslovakia
1970	Start of the 630th Annual Schubermess (amusement fair) at Luxembourg City, Luxembourg
1971	Festival of the Hungry Ghosts in Hong Kong, Malaysia, and Singapore

----
August 22nd

	Feast of the Assumption in Ethiopia
	Feast of St. Symphorian
634 AD	Abu Bakr, Moslem caliph, died
1138	Scots defeated by the English at the Battle of the Standard
1280	Pope Nicholas III died of a heart attack
1389	Isabella, wife of King Charles IV of France, crowned
1485	King Richard III of England killed at the Battle of Bosworth, ending the War of the Roses
1547	Bohemia's "Bloody Diet"
1642	England's War of the Reformation began, Royalists and King Charles I against the Parliamentarians

1787	John Fitch demonstrated his steamboat
1848	Ulysses S. Grant married Julia Boggs Dent
1851	Yacht America won England's major sailboat race, starting the America's Cup sailing challenges
1853	Leopold II, King of Belgium, married Marie Henriette, "the Rose of Brabant"
1854	Milan Obrenovic IV, King of Serbia, born
1862	Achilles Claude Debussy, composer, born
1869	Bruce Lancaster, novelist, born
1891	Park Place building collapsed in New York City
	Jacques Lipchitz, sculptor, born
1905	Georgia state seal added to its flag
1920	Ray Bradbury, author, born
1925	Sir George D. T. Goldie, founder of Nigeria, born
1927	Sacco and Vanzetti executed at the Charlestown, Massachusetts, prison
1932	The BBC had its first experimental television broadcast (England)
1936	Carl Yastrzemski, baseball player, born
1942	U.S. destroyer Ingraham involved in a collision in the Atlantic
1959	Philippine ship Pilar II sank in a storm off Palawan
1961	Goya's Duke of Wellington stolen from London's National Art Gallery
1964	Hurricane Cleo swept the Caribbean
1968	RAM C-B satellite launched
1969	World's tallest totem pole dedicated at Kake, Alaska
1972	Festival of the Hungry Ghosts in Hong Kong, Malaysia, and Singapore

----
August 23rd

	Ancient Romans made sacrifices to Vulcan, god of fire, and to Volcanalia
79 AD	Lava closed the harbor at Herculaneum, making escape from Pompeii and Mt. Vesuvius impossible
476	Odoacer proclaimed first barbarian king of Italy
1268	Charles of Anjou and Sicily defeated Conradin at Tagliatozza
1285	St. Philip Benizi died (Feast Day)
1328	King Philip VI of France defeated the Flemish, in revolt against their Count, at Cassel
1358	Isabella, widow of King Edward II of England, died
1754	King Louis XVI of France born

1775	Harpswell, Maine, incorporated
	American colonists publicly termed "rebels" by
	England's King George III
1776	British occupied Flatbush, New York
1785	Oliver Hazard Perry, naval hero, born
1818	First steamboat trip taken on Lake Erie
1833	Slavery abolished in the British colonies
1869	Edgar Lee Masters, poet of Spoon River
	Anthology, born
1877	Wes Hardin, Texas outlaw, captured near
	Pensacola, Florida
1883	Chester A. Arthur, U.S. President, entered
	Yellowstone National Park
1892	Manuel Fonseca, first President of Brazil,
	died
1902	Fanny Farmer opened her cooking school in
	Boston, Massachusetts
1912	Gene Kelly, musical actor, born
1914	Japan declared war on Germany
1926	Rudolph Valentino, actor, died
1939	Cobb, in a Railton, set a land-speed record of
	368.9 mph
1956	First non-stop transcontinental helicopter
	flight began
1960	Oscar Hammerstein II, musical playwright, died
1968	U.S. Virgin Islands received Home Rule
1970	Wedding of the Giants Procession held at Ath,
	Belgium

August 24th

	Feast of St. Bartholomew, patron of butchers,
	tanners, and bookbinders
	Our Lady of Luxembourg Annual Fair
	Ancient Romans opened the entrance to the
	Underworld
	Miners' Day in Bulgaria
	Flag Day in Liberia
79 AD	Two days of eruptions by Mt. Vesuvius destroyed
	Pompeii and Herculaneum
376	Gratian, Roman Emperor, received the title of
	Augustus
410	Alaric and his Goths entered and sacked Rome
684	St. Ouen died (Feast Day)
1113	Geoffrey Plantagenet, Count of Anjou, born
1246	Kuyuk crowned Emperor of the Mongols
1273	Rudolph of Hapsburg crowned King of Germany
1298	Albert I crowned King of Germany
1313	Henry VII, Holy Roman Emperor, died
1456	Printing of the Gutenberg Bible completed
1560	Papal jurisdiction and the Catholic mass
	abolished in Scotland

1572	Huguenots, French Protestants, massacred
1690	Calcutta, India, founded by the British East India Company
1772	King William I of the Netherlands born
1814	British burned Washington, D.C., including the Capitol
1821	New Mexico became independent of Spain
1826	St. Joan Thouret died (Feast Day)
1856	St. Emily de Vialar died (Feast Day)
1865	Ferdinand I, King of Rumania, born
	Eagle Speed foundered at sea off Calcutta, India
1867	Trusteeship incorporated for Johns Hopkins University in Maryland
1872	Aubry Beardsley, illustrator, born
1895	Richard, Cardinal Cushing, of Boston born
1896	German civil code of laws established
1912	Congress approved the Panama Canal Zone Administration
	Alaska became a U.S. territory
1928	Subway wreck under Times Square, New York City
1936	Spanish insurgents began aerial bombing of royalist Madrid
1939	Germany and Russia signed a 10-year non-aggression pact
1956	First nonstop transcontinental helicopter flight completed

August 25th

	Feast of St. Genesius the Actor
	Feast of St. Gregory of Utrecht
29 BC	Roman triumph held for Octavian
c. 250 AD	St. Genesius of Arles died (Feast Day)
383	Gratian, Roman emperor, assassinated
608	Boniface IV became Pope
716	Siege of Constantinople began
1248	King St. Louis IX of France and the Seventh Crusade set sail against Islam
1270	St. Louis IX, King of France, patron of builders, haberdashers, distillers, embroidery workers, hairdressers and barbers, died on Crusade of plague (Feast Day)
1282	St. Thomas of Hereford died
	St. Thomas de Cantilupe died
1284	King Edward II of England born
1530	Ivan IV, "the Terrible," Czar of Russia, born
1537	The Honorable Artillery Company chartered in England
1539	Glastonbury, England, abbey ordered dissolved as a Catholic institution

1558	King Francis II of France married Mary, Queen of Scots
1560	Protestantism formally effected in Scotland
1580	Antonio, claimant to the Portuguese throne, routed by the Spanish
1699	King Christian V of Denmark and Norway died in a hunting accident
1786	Louis I, King of Bavaria, born
1814	Library of Congress with 3,000 books destroyed by the British
1819	Allan Pinkerton, founder of the first U.S. detective agency, born
1825	Uruguay declared its independence from Brazil
1839	Bret Harte, author, born
1845	Louis II, King of Bavaria, born
1867	Michael Faraday, scientist, died
1908	Antoine Henri Becquerel, discoverer of radio-activity, died
1911	Train wreck at Manchester, New York
1913	Walt Kelly, creator of the cartoon "Pogo," born
1915	End of 20 days of flooding and storm tides on the Gulf coast
1916	U.S. National Park Service created
	Van Johnson, actor, born
1918	Leonard Bernstein, conductor-composer, born
1919	Commercial air service began between England and Paris
1921	American peace treaty with Germany and Austria signed in Berlin
1927	Althea Gibson, tennis player and golfer, born
	Two Japanese destroyers sunk near Bungo Straits
1944	German occupation of Paris ended
1950	U.S. hospital ship Benevolence and freighter Mary Luckenbach collided
1952	Virgil Trucks pitched a no-hitter and Detroit beat New York 1-0
1954	Hurricane Carol began flooding eastern U.S. coast
1964	Explorer 20 launched
1967	Dean Chance pitched a no-hitter and Minnesota beat Cleveland 2-1

August 26th
----

79 AD	Pompeii and Herculaneum buried by Mt. Vesuvius
1278	Attakar II, King of Bohemia, killed
1346	Battle of Crecy, in which English archers defeated the knights of France, and John, King of Bohemia, was killed
1444	Swiss defeated by the French at the Battle of St. Jacob

1498	Michelangelo commissioned to make the <u>Pieta</u>
1514	Turks defeated the Persians at Chaldrian and captured their queen
1618	Frederick V chosen king by the Bohemians
1676	Sir Robert Walpole, English statesman, born
1723	Anton van Leeuwenhoek, microscope inventor, died
1768	Capt. Cook left England to explore the Pacific
1776	U.S. offered half-pay pensions to disabled war veterans
1789	Declaration of the Rights of Man and the Citizen publicized in France
1791	Steamboat patents issued to John Fitch and Nathan Read
1801	Robert Morris, financier, released from debtors' prison
1818	First Illinois state constitution adopted
1819	Prince Albert of Saxe-Coburg-Gotha, husband of Queen Victoria, born
1838	St. Elizabeth Bichier des Ages died (Feast Day)
1843	First working typewriter patented
1850	Louis Philippe, King of France, died
1873	Lee DeForest, inventor of radio and television tubes, born
1908	Tony Pastor, discoverer of Lillian Russell, died
1914	German <u>Kaiser Wilhelm der Grosse</u> sank off Africa
1920	U.S. women given the right to vote
1922	Japanese cruiser <u>Nitaka</u> sank in a storm off Kamchatka
1925	Italian submarine V sank off Sicily
1929	Bridge over Lake Champlain opened
1937	Andrew Mellon, millionaire, died
1945	Russia and China signed a 30-year friendship treaty
1957	Russia announced a successful international ballistic missile test
1962	Mariner II launched at Venus
	Vilhjalmur Stefansson Arctic explorer, died
	Jack Kralick pitched a no-hitter and Minnesota beat Kansas City 1-0
1972	Start of the Summer Olympics at Munich, Germany

August 27th

Feast of St. Theresa
Start of the 30-day fair at Kensington-on-Hull, England as granted by King Edward I

```
550 or 551 BC   Confucius, Chinese philosopher, born
413       Lunar eclipse
423 AD    Flavius Honorius, Roman Emperor of the West,
                    died
543       St. Caesarius of Arles died (Feast Day)
824       Pope Eugenius II died
1172      Marguerite, wife of Henry Plantagenet, "the
                    Young King," crowned Queen of
                    England (he predeceased his
                    father, Henry II)
1310      King Charles I of Hungary crowned
1389      Battle of Kossova, Turkey
1576      Titian, Italian artist, died of the plague
1590      Pope Sixtus V died
1648      St. Joseph Calasanz died (Feast Day)
1776      New Jersey state legislature first met, at
                    Princeton
          Americans lost to the British at the Battle
                    of Long Island
1809      Hannibal Hamlin, U.S. Vice-President, born
1816      British bombardment of Algiers freed the
                    Christian captives
1824      Natal, Africa, declared a British territory
1858      Lincoln and Douglas debated at Freeport,
                    Illinois
1871      Theodore Dreiser, journalist-author, born
1872      Flathead Indians treatied away their Bitter
                    Root Valley lands in Montana
1889      C. S. Forrester, author, born
1900      Hurricane tides flooded southern Texas
1908      Lyndon Baines Johnson, U.S. President, born
1915      Italy declared war on Germany
1919      Group Captain rank introduced in the English
                    Air Force
1928      Kellogg-Briand Peace Pact signed, condemning
                    war
1935      Interstate Oil Compact Commission created in
                    U.S.
1938      Monte Pierson pitched a no-hitter and New York
                    beat Cleveland 13-0
1948      Charles Evans Hughes, jurist-author, died
1950      U.S. Army seized all railroads to prevent a
                    strike
1965      Le Corbusier, architect, died
1968      Mariana, Duchess of Kent, died
1971      Bennet Cerf, humorist-publisher, died
          Maidens' Festival celebrated in Hong Kong and
                    as the Seven Sisters in Malaysia
          Hunting World Exhibition opened in Budapest,
                    Hungary
          First crossing of the Atlantic by a speedboat
                    completed
```

	Daventry, Northamptonshire, England fair
	Ljubljana, Yugoslavia Wine Fair
	Feast of St. Hermes
	Feast of St. Julian of Brioude
	Feast of St. Moses the Black
430 AD	St. Augustine of Hippo died (Feast Day)
489	Goths defeated the Romans at the Battle of Isonzo
876	King Louis the German died
1413	St. Andrew's University, Scotland, chartered by a Papal Bull
1448	Francs-Archers, French regular infantry, created
1534	San Francisco de Quito, Ecuador, established
1565	Settlers arrived at St. Augustine, Florida
1619	Ferdinand II crowned Holy Roman Emperor
1654	Count Axel Oxenstjerna, Swedish statesman, died
1774	Mother Elizabeth Seton, founder of the Sisters of Charity of St. Vincent de Paul, born
1789	Enceladus, Saturn's moon, discovered
	Astronomical telescope at Slough, England, completed
1798	James Wilson, signer of the Declaration of Independence, died
1811	Percy Bysshe Shelley, poet, eloped with Harriet Westbrook
1828	Leon Trotsky, Russian writer, born
1830	"Peter Cooper," first U.S.-built locomotive, ran
1839	Tournament held at Eglinton, Scotland
1849	Venice, after siege and bombardment, surrendered to Austria
1850	Wagner's Lohengrin opera first performed
1854	St. Joaquina died (Feast Day)
1858	Charles Latin Hildreth, poet-novelist, born
1864	First setlers at Emigrant Gulch, Montana, arrived there
1876	Paul L. Haworth, historian-educator, born
1883	Krakatoa volcano ended two days of explosive eruptions in Indonesia
1894	Edison Marshall, novelist, born
	O. Henry's magazine The Rolling Stone or Iconoclast ceased publication
1899	Charles Boyer, actor, born
1903	Frederick Law Olmstead, traveler and landscape architect, died
1904	First jail sentence in the U.S. for speeding in an auto handed down in Newport, Rhode Island

```
1908     Roger Tony Petersen, ornithologist, born
1910     Nicholas proclaimed himself King of Montenegro
1913     Richard Tucker, opera singer, born
1914     Heligoland Bight, first serious naval engagement
                 of World War I, where Britain sank
                 3 German cruisers
1916     St. Louis-San Francisco Railway Company
                 incorporated
1922     First radio commercial broadcast
1926     Buryvestnik hit a pier and sank at Kronstadt,
                 Russia
1943     Boris III, King of Bulgaria, died
1957     U.S. Senate filibuster record-setting attempt
                 begun by Strom Thurmond
1963     Civil rights demonstration held in Washington,
                 D.C.
1965     Gemini V splashed down after orbiting the
                 Earth for a week
```

August 29th

```
         Feast of St. Sebbi
         Toth I on the ancient Egyptian calendar
5502 BC  Beginning of the Alexandrian Era
c.29 AD  John the Baptist beheaded
1261     Pantaleon Ancher, son of a French shoemaker,
                 elected Pope as Urban IV
1315     Pisa defeated Florence at Montecatini
1350     British defeated the Spanish fleet at Winchelsea
1475     England again invaded France
1484     Giovanni Battista Cibo elected Pope as Innocent VIII
1526     Louis II, King of Hungary and Bohemia, died
1533     Atahualpa, last Inca ruler, put to death
1632     John Locke born
1769     Edmund Hoyle of According to Hoyle . . . died
1780     Jean Auguste Dominique Ingres, French artist,
                 born
1809     Oliver Wendell Holmes, Sr., poet-physician, born
1833     England's "Factory Act," child-labor laws,
                 passed
1842     Britian received Hong Kong through the treaty
                 of Nanking
1877     Brigham Young, Mormon leader, died
1910     Japan announced the annexation of Korea
1914     Germany was victorious at the Battle of
                 Tannenberg
1916     U.S. cruiser Memphis wrecked at Santo Domingo
         Chinese passenger ship Hsin Yu sank off the
                 coast
         Wakatsu Maru wrecked off Japan
         Philippine legislature created
1917     Ingrid Bergman, actress, born
```

1922	Chilean ship <u>Itata</u> sank in a storm off Capumbo
1935	Beginning of 3 days of hurricane in Florida and the Keys
1943	Wayland, New York train wreck
1957	Senator Strom Thurmond set a Senate filibuster record of 24 hrs., 18 min.
1960	Hurricane Donna began 3 days of rampage in the eastern U.S.
1963	Pact signed for scheduled air service from Pakistan to Red China

August 30th

		Feast of Sts. Felix and Adauctus
		Huey P. Long Day, Louisiana holiday
		Victory Day in Turkey
30	BC	Cleopatra was bitten by an asp
257	AD	Sixtus III became Pope
410		St. Pammachius died (Feast Day)
526		Theodoric, King of the Osgoths, died
670		St. Fiacre, patron of gardeners and hemorrhoid sufferers, died (Feast Day)
1125		Lothair II chosen King of Germany
1181		Pope Alexander III died
1420		King Henry V of England died
1462		Pietro Barbro elected Pope as Paul II
1483		King Louis XI of France died
1617		St. Rose, first American saint, died the patron of Lima, Peru, her home (Feast Day)
1682		William Penn, founder of Pennsylvania, sailed from England
1748		Jacques Louis David, French artist, born
1757		Battle of Jagersdorf in the Seven Years' War
1797		Mary W. Shelley, author of <u>Frankenstein</u>, born
1806		<u>Daily Advertiser</u>, New York City's second daily newspaper, published its last issue
1820		George Frederick Root, composer of "Battle Cry of Freedom," born
1830		Baltimore and Ohio Railroad first ran its locomotive "Tom Thumb" powerer by steam
1842		Stromboli volcano erupted
1856		John Brown, abolitionist-raider, defeated
1864		Gold discovered at Emigrant Gulch, Montana
1869		Powell completed his boat trip through the Grand Canyon
1881		<u>Teuton</u> wrecked off the Cape of Good Hope, Africa
1896		Raymond Massey, actor, born
1901		John Gunther, correspondent-author, born
1905		Solar eclipse
1908		Fred MacMurray, actor, born
1916		Last survivors of Shackleton's Antarctic expedition rescued

1929	San Juan involved in a collision off Santa Cruz, California
1941	Stephen H. Horgan, inventor of half-toning for printing pictures, died
1965	Saas-Fee, Switzerland, hit by an avalanche
1970	Pageant of the Golden Tree held at Bruges, Belgium

August 31st

	Malaysian Day (National Holiday)
12 AD	Caligula, Roman emperor, born
161	Marcus Antoninus, Roman emperor, born
358	St. Paulinus of Trier died (Feast Day)
651	St. Aidan of Lindisfarne died (Feast Day)
1057	Leofric, husband of Lady Godiva, died
1240	St. Raymond Nonnatus, patron of midwives, women in labor, and little children, died (Feast Day)
1669	Henrietta Marie, widow of King Charles I of England, died
1688	John Bunyan, author of Pilgrim's Progress, died
1816	Delphian Club, a Baltimore, Maryland, literary group, founded
1821	Herman von Helmholtz, scientist, born
1823	French captured Trocadero, Spain
1873	Franz Joseph Land, Arctic Islands, discovered
1879	Yoshihito, 123rd Japanese emperor, born
1880	Queen Wilhelmina of Holland born
1881	First U.S. tennis championships played, at Newport, Rhode Island
1885	DuBose Heyward, novelist-playwright-poet, born
1886	Charlestown, South Carolina, rocked by an earthquake
1895	First professional football game played
1896	Japan rocked by an earthquake
1897	Fredric March, actor, born
1903	Arthur Godfrey, radio and television personality, born
1905	Dore Schary, playwright-producer, born
1908	William Saroyan, author, born
1914	St. Petersburg in Russia became Petrograd (now Leningrad)
1918	Alan Jay Lerner, playwright, born
	Ted Williams, baseball player, born
1932	Total eclipse of the sun
1935	End of 3 days of hurricane in Florida and the Keys
1949	Last Grand Army of the Republic encampment held at Indianapolis with 6 of the surviving Civil War veterans attending

1954	Steeple of the Old North Church in Boston, site of Paul Revere's lantern signals, fell during Hurricane Carol
1960	End of Hurricane Donna in the eastern U.S.
1962	Trinidad and Tobago became independent of Britain
1969	Rocky Marciano, boxer, died in a plane crash
1970	Midwest Old Settlers and Threshers Reunion held at Mount Pleasant, Iowa

SEPTEMBER

Full Moon - Harvest or Fruit Moon
First Sunday - Grandfather Day
First Monday - Labor Day
Labor Day Weekend - Annual Fiesta de Santa Fe in New
                    Mexico
           Antique Airplane Fly-in at Ottumwa, Iowa
First Wednesday - Fair at Lincoln, England
First Thursday - Watermelon Day in Rocky Ford, Colorado
First Saturday after the Full Moon - Indian Day in
                    Oklahoma
Second Saturday - Miss American winner announced
Third Tuesday - Opening of the Dutch Parliament
Third Wesnesday - Agriculture Show and Cheese Fair at
                    Frome, Somersetshire, England
Fourth Friday - American Indian Day
Monday after "Wakes Sunday" - Horn Dance performed at
                    Abbots Bromley, England
First weekend - Northern Navajo Fair at Shiprock, New
                    Mexico
Third weekend - Annual Fall Bird Migration Watch at
                    Silver City, New Mexico
Last weekend - Annual Harvest Festival at the "corn
                    palace" in Mitchell, South Dakota

September 1st
───

        Beginning of the Eastern Orthodox Church year
        Feast of St. Giles, patron of the indigent and
                    crippled and spur-makers; invoked
                    against cancer, sterility in women,
                    insanity, and night dangers
        Feast of St. Fiacre, hemorrhoid healer and patron
                    of gardeners in Ireland
5598 BC Beginning of the Grecian Mundane Era

5508		Beginning of the Civil Era of Constantinople
5492		Beginning of the Ecclesiastical Era of Antioch
312		Beginning of the Grecian or Syro-Macedonian Era
48		Beginning of the Caesarean Era of Antioch
69	AD	Beginning of the Destruction of Jerusalem
1159		Adrian IV, the only English Pope, died
1181		Ubaldo Allucingoli became Pope as Lucius III
1271		Tebaldo Visconti elected Pope as Gregory X while he was away on a Crusade
1315		Edmund the Butler given properties as rewards for putting down English rebels
1422		Henry VI, an infant, became King of England on the death of this father, Henry V
1513		Balboa set out from Darien to discover the Pacific
1557		Jacques Cartier, explorer of Canada, died
1640		Quinnipiack became New Haven, Connecticut
1689		Graduated tax imposed on beards in Russia
1715		Louis XIV, "the Sun King," ruler of France, died
1795		Museum of French Monuments opened in Paris
1807		Aaron Burr acquitted on charges of treason
1838		William Clark, expedition leader with Merriweather Lewis, died
1841		Nicholas I, King of Montenegro, born
1849		First section of the Pennsylvania Railroad opened
1852		Robert E. Lee appointed superintendant of West Point Academy
1854		Engelbert Humperdink, German composer, born
1858		U.S. Army ambushed Washington State Indians who had set an ambush for them
		British East India Company ceased government control of India
1862		First federal tax on tobacco effected
1864		Gen. Sherman captured Atlanta, Georgia
1875		Edgar Rice Burroughs, creator of "Tarzan," born
1878		First woman telephone operator began working, in Boston
1891		Fingerprint registry established in Argentina
1892		Harold Lamb, author, born
1900		Southern Texas began 15 days of hurricane flooding
1907		Walter Reuther, labor leader, born
		First night court held, in New York City
1914		Last passenger pigeon died, in the Cincinnati Zoo
1920		Lebanon gained its independence but was to be ruled under French mandate till 1941
1923		Earthquake shook Yokahama and Tokyo, Japan
1924		Rocky Marciano, boxer, born
1932		Jimmy Walker resigned as Mayor of New York City
1935		Southern Florida began to suffer 10 days of hurricane
1939		Germany invaded Poland, starting World War II and ending the Munich Pact
		BBC ceased television broadcasts for security reasons

```
1945      (Eastern Standard Time) Japan signed the World
                 War II surrender agreement
1956      First U.S. stamp honoring workers issued
1960      Entire work force of the Pennsylvania Railroad
                 went on strike
          Hurricane Donna began a 13-day trek from Florida
                 to New England
1962      Earthquakes rocked northwestern Iran
          Hong Kong hit by a typhoon
1969      Drew Pearson, columnist, died
          Libya declared a republic
1970      Harvest festivals held in Poland
          Settlers' Day held in Durban, South Africa
```

September 2nd

```
          Harvest dances held at Acoma Pueblo, New Mexico
          Feast of St. Stephen, King of Hungary
   31 BC  Octavian defeated Antony at Actium
  310 AD  Habbib, "Confessor of Edessa," martyred
   1057   Isaac Comnenus crowned emperor of Byzantium
c.1231    St. Brocard died (Feast Day)
   1666   The great fire began in London, England
   1752   New calendar adopted
   1789   Treasury Department established by Congress
   1792   168 French royalists murdered in Paris
   1807   British began three-day bombardment of
                 Copenhagen, Denmark
   1837   Morse's telegraph model exibited
   1850   Eugene Field, author of "Little Boy Blue," born
   1864   Sherman completed his occupation of Atlanta,
                 Georgia
   1871   Birchard Flour Mill in Phoenix, Arizona, burned
                 down
   1898   Mahdi's army defeated by Kitchener's British in
                 the Sudan, earning the 21st Lancers
                 an obelisk for their charge
   1910   Cities Service gasoline company incorporated
   1913   North Haven, Connecticut, train wreck
   1917   Cleveland Amory, author-critic, born
   1919   Start of 13 days of hurricane on the U.S. Gulf
                 coast
   1930   First nonstop flight, Europe to the U.S., completed
                 by 2 Frenchmen
   1940   Great Smoky Mountain National Park formally
                 dedicated
   1945   (Tokyo Time) Japan signed the surrender on
                 board the Missouri in Tokyo Bay
   1954   Hurricane Edna began 12-day assault against
                 northeastern U.S.
   1970   Union with Free France Day celebrated in Tahiti
```

Langport, Somersetshire, England fair
Feast of St. Cuthburga
Feast of St. Pius X. Pope

1189 AD Richard I, "the Lion-hearted" crowned King of
England

1192 Christian-Moslem truce left Crusaders with a
strip of coastline in Palestine

1650 Parliamentarians defeated "Bonnie Prince Charlie"
at Dunbar, Scotland, and issued
the first campaign medals

1685 Oliver Cromwell, leader of the anti-Royalists
in England, died, succeeded by his
son

1752 This became September 14th with the new calendar
in effect

1783 Treaty of Paris ended the Revolutionary War in
American and gave West Florida to
Spain

1807 Code Napoleon, French Civil laws, titled as
such

1833 The New York Sun newspaper first appeared, to
merge with The World Telegraph in
1950

1855 U.S. Army attacked the Sioux Indian camp at Ash
Hollow on the Platte River

1856 Louis Sullivan, architect credited with
inventing the skyscraper, born

1868 Santee Sioux village at White Stone captured by
the Army

1878 Princess Alice involved in a fatal collision in
the Thames

1888 British East Africa Company chartered

1894 Labor Day first observed as a legal holiday

1902 Soufriere volcano on the island of St. Vincent
erupted

1914 James delle Chiesa elected Pope as Benedict XV

1922 Seven U.S. destroyers wrecked off Honda Point,
California

1930 Santo Domingo wracked by a hurricane

1935 Campbell, in the Bluebird Special, set a land-
speed record of 301.13 mph, the
first to top 300 mph

1939 Britain, Australia, New Zealand, and France declare
war on Germany
British Athenia torpedoed off the Hebrides
Islands

1947 Bill McCahon pitched a ho-hitter and Philadelphia
beat Washington, 2-0

1954 Two U.S. Army officers killed on Quemoy in an
artillery duel between Free and
Red China

1961 Hurricane Carla began a 12-day rampage in Texas

```
                Vencedor capsized off the Colombia coast
1969            Ho Chi Minh, president of North Viet Nam, died


-------------------------------------------------------
September 4th
-------------------------------------------------------

                Fair at Crowland, Lincolnshire, England
                Southdown sheep fair at Lewes, Sussex, England
                Feast of St. Marinus of San Marino
 422 AD         Pope St. Boniface died
 476            Romulus Augustulus's reign as last Roman Emperor
                    of the West ended
 569            Lombards occupied Milan, Italy
1763            Gladwin attacked by Indians in the Detroit
                    River
1768            Chateaubriand, French author, born
1781            Settlers arrived to found the Spanish settlement
                    of Los Angeles, California
1813            Andrew Jackson wounded in a brawl in Nashville,
                    Tennessee
1847            Italian National Guard established
1852            First controlled airship flight made, in France
1855            Sioux Indians defeated the attacking Army at Ash
                    Hollow
1867            Charles D. Gibson, creator of the "Gibson Girl,"
                    born
1870            Third French Republic declared and Code Napoleon
                    changed to French Civil Code
1905            Pierre de Brazza, founder of the French Congo,
                    died
1907            Edvard Greig, composer, died
1908            Nicaraguan national flag adopted
1929            Graf Zeppelin completed its round-the-world trip
1936            Spanish insurgents captured Irun
1947            Start of 17 days of hurricane on the U.S. Gulf
                    coast
1948            Queen Wilhelmina of Holland abdicated, making her
                    daughter, Juliana, Queen
1951            Transcontinental television inaugurated in the
                    U.S.
1953            Florence Chadwick swam the English Channel
1957            School integration crisis began in Little Rock,
                    Arkansas
1964            OGO I satellite launched
1965            Albert Schweitzer, missionary-doctor, died


-------------------------------------------------------
September 5th
-------------------------------------------------------

                San Marino National Festival
                St. James Fair at Kelso, Scotland
                Feast of St. Bertin
                Feast of St. Lawrence Giustiniani
1187 AD         Louis VII, King of France, born
```

1316	Jacques Duese crowned Pope as John XXII, the second at Avignon, France
1566	Suleiman I, "The Magnificent," Sultan of Turkey, died
1569	Pieter Bruegel, Flemish artist, died
1638	Louis XIV, "The Sun King," ruler of France, born
1718	Date picked for the peaceful abandonment of piracy in the West Indies
1725	Marie Leszczynska of Poland married King Louis XV of France
1755	6,000 Accadians were deported from Nova Scotia, setting the theme for Longfellow's "Evangeline"
1774	First Continental Congress opened in Philadelphia
1781	French fleet, aiding the colonists, defeated the British outside Chesapeake Bay
	Grand Lodge of Free and Accepted Masons of the State of New York founded
1795	French army captured Dusseldorf, Germany
1807	After 3 days of bombardment, Copenhagen, Denmark, surrendered to the British
1813	"U.S.S. Enterprise" captured "H.M.S. Boxer"
1822	Aleppo, Syria, rocked by an earthquake
1847	Jesse James, outlaw, born
1877	Crazy Horse, Sioux Indian chief, killed at Ft. Robinson when troopers tried to confine him to the guardhouse
1879	Jeanette, Arctic exploration ship, caught in the polar ice pack
1904	Hamilton Basso, novelist-biographer, born
1905	Russo-Japanese War ended by the Treaty of Poetsmouth Naval Yard, New Hampshire
1914	Russian defeat by the Germans at Masurian Lakes began
	Beginning of the first Battle of the Marne
1916	Frank Yerby, novelist, born
1918	U.S. troopship Mt. Vernon sank
1920	Max Klinger, German artist, died
1926	Waco, Colorado, train wreck
1928	Johannesburg, South Africa, became a city
1939	U.S. procliamed its neutrality in World War II
1956	Explosion rocked Springer, New Mexico
1964	Kwangtung Province, China, hit by a typhoon
1967	Beginning of 18 days of devastation by Hurricane Beulah in Texas and Mexico
1968	Helicopter used to place the steeple on the First Congregational Church on Nantucket Island, Massachusetts
1970	Chamorro Night on Guam
	Cherokee National Holiday celebrated at Tahlequah, Oklahoma
1971	Grand Wine and Grape Festival held at Schwebsange, Luxembourg

```
            Feast of St. Cagnoald
 776 BC     Solar eclipse
 972 AD     Pope John VIII died
1298        Genoese captured Marco Polo in a sea battle
1565        Spanish landed at St. Augustine, Florida
1634        Swedish defeated at Nordlingen in the Thirty
              Years' War
1666        Great fire in London extinguished
1757        Lafayette, French hero of the American Revolution,
              born
1781        Slave ship Zong sailed from Africa for Jamaica
1782        Martha (Mrs. Thomas) Jefferson died
1796        Napoleon and the French defeated the Austrians
              at Bassano
1814        Hiram Fuller, author, born
1860        Jane Addams, Hull House founder, born
1886        Distinguished Service Order founded in England
1888        Joseph P. Kennedy, financier, born
1898        Wilhelmina became Queen of Holland in her own
              right
1901        William McKinley, U.S. President, shot by an
              assassin
1911        Stolypin, Russian Prime Minister, died of an
              assassin's bullet
1923        King Peter II of Yugoslavia born
            Edward P. Dutton, publisher, died
1928        Start of 2 weeks of hurricane in southern
              Florida
1939        Union of South Africa declared war on Germany
1943        Frankfort Junction, Pennsylvania, train wreck
1948        Juliana crowned Queen of the Netherlands
1953        Korean War prisoner repatriation ended
1968        Swaziland became an independent member of the
              British Commonwealth
1970        Independence Day celebrated in Pakistan
            Saracen Tournament held at Arezzo, Italy
1971        Gondola Regatta held in Venice, Italy
1975        Jewish New Year 5736 (Rosh Hashana)
```

```
            Feast of the Virgin of the Valley in Venezuela
            Feast of St. Cloud
            Feast of St. Evurtius (Episcopal)
            Fair at Ulverton, Lancashire, England
1151 AD     Geoffrey Plantagenet, Father of King Henry II
              of England, died of a chill
1295        Angels moved the home of Mary and Joseph to
              Loretto, Italy
1312        Ferdinand IV, King of Castile, died
1496        Ferdinand II, king of Naples, died
```

1502	Amerigo Vespucci returned to Lisbon, Portugal
1533	Queen Elizabeth I of England born
1548	Catherine Parr, widow of King Henry VIII of England, died
1701	Grand alliance formed against the Bourbon family, rulers of France
1764	Stanislaus II elected King of Poland
1797	U.S.S. Constellation launched at Baltimore, Maryland
1812	Naploeon defeated the Russians at Borodino
1822	Brazil proclaimed her independence from Portugal
1838	Forfarshire ran aground of Farne Island
1846	Board of Regents of the Smithsonian Institution first met
1859	Great Eastern steamship began its maiden voyage
1860	Grandma Moses, American painter, born
	Garibaldi, Italian nationalist, entered Naples
1870	British warship Captain foundered off Spain
1886	First America's Cup yacht race held in U.S. waters
1892	James J. Corbett took the heavyweight crown from John L. Sullivan in 21 rounds
	John Greenleaf Whittier, poet, died
1893	Collieres at Featherstone, England, destroyed by strikers
1900	Taylor Caldwell, author, born
1903	Margaret Landon, author of Anna and the King of Siam, born
1904	British-Tibetan treaty signed
1914	James A. Van Allen, rocket expert and godfather of the Van Allen Belts, born
1923	Peter Lawford, actor, born
1930	Badouin I, King of Belgium, born
1936	Hoover-Boulder Dam began operation
1963	Mrs. Prieto gave birth to 5 boys
1965	Hurricane Betsy began a 4-day visit to the Gulf coast

September 8th

	Feast of Sts. Adrian and Natalia, husband and wife
	Annual benediction pronounced on Lyons, France
70 AD	Jerusalem surrendered to Rome after a siege
1127	First Glastonbury, England, fair held
1198	Philip crowned King of Germany
1227	Frederick II, Holy Roman Emperor, sailed on 5th Crusade
1425	King Charles III, "the Noble," of Navarre, died
1429	Joan of Arc wounded in battle
1522	Last survivor of Magellan's 5 ships returned to Seville, Spain, having been around the world

1565	Spanish began construction of a fort at St. Augustine, Fla.
1592	Peter Stuyvesant, Dutch New York colonist, born
1625	Treaty of Southampton, English-Dutch pact against Spain, signed
1636	Harvard College established
1664	Peter Stuyvesant surrendered New Amsterdam to the British and it became New York
1685	Thomas Fleet, printer, born
1755	Colonists defeated the French and Indians at Lake George, New York
1781	Battle of Eutaw Springs, South Carolina
1818	Kansas City Star newspaper founded
1841	Antonin Dvorak, Bohemian composer, born
1865	U.S. Cavalry battled the Sioux, Arapahoe, and Cheyenne Indians at the Dry Fork of the Powder River
1892	"Pledge of Allegience" first published, in The Youth's Companion
1894	Herman von Helmholtz, scientist, died
1900	Southern Texas devastated by hurricane floods
1910	New York City's East River railroad tunnels opened
1917	Whiskey manufacture in the U.S. prohibited by federal decree
1922	Sid Caesar, comedian, born
1924	Grace Metalious, author of Peyton Place, etc., born
1926	Germany admitted into the League of Nations
1934	Morro Castle burned at sea off New Jersey
1935	Huey P. Long, Louisiana politician, assassinated
1939	President declared a limited national emergency
1943	Italy surrendered unconditionally
1944	Italian ship Rex, sunk in Trieste harbor by British planes
1945	U.S. forces invaded Japanese-held Korea
1946	Bulgaria abolished its monarchy, becoming a republic
1951	49 nations signed the Japanese Peace Treaty in San Francisco
1954	South East Asia Treaty Organization formed
1960	Radio-wave signals received from Saturn by the U.S. Navy
1964	Hurricane Dora hit Florida
	King Constantine II of Greece married Princess Anne Marie of Denmark
1968	Saundra Williams chosen the first "Miss Black America"
1969	Senator Everett Driksen died
1970	Orthodox canonization of St. Father Herman at Kodiak, Alaska, was the first such ceremony in North America
	Clothesline Show held in Sharon, Connecticut
	Our Lady of Aparecida honored at Aparecida del Norte, Brazil

Corn dances held at the San Ildefonso Pueblo,
New Mexico

	Feast of St. Ciaran of Clonmacnois
	Feast of St. Omer
	Swallows fly south from Korea
337 AD	Constantine II, Roman Emperor, granted title of Augustus
438	St. Isaac the Great died (Feast Day)
1000	Vikings fought at Swold
1409	University of Leipzig, Germany, founded
1492	Columbus resumed his voyage from the Canary Islands
1513	James IV, Kingof Scotland, killed in battle with the English at Flodden Field
1515	St. Joseph of Volokolamsk died (Russian Orthodox Feast Day)
1570	Cyprus surrendered to the Turks
1585	Cardinal Richelieu, French stateman, born
1598	First church in New Mexico completed
1654	St. Peter Claver, patron of the African missions, died (Feast Day)
1661	Quakers in Massachusetts released from prison
1737	Luigi Galvani, inventor of galvanized steel, born
1753	First steam engine in the colonies arrived from England to serve as a water pump
1754	William Bligh, captain of the Bounty, born
1776	The United Colonies became the United States
1791	Federal City became the Territory of Columbia and the City of Washington
1810	English gold war medals instituted for service in the Peninsula campaign
1815	John Singleton Copley, English artist, died
1826	Christian Advocate, Methodist weekly, founded
1850	California became a state
	New Mexico and Utah became U.S. territories
1853	Niagara Falls Table Rock fell
1861	Sally Tompkins became the only woman commissioned officer, a captain, in the Confederate Army
1863	Union forces captured Chattanooga, Tennessee
1873	Max Reinhardt, theatrical producer, born
1887	Alfred Landon, presidential candidate, born
1895	American Bowling Congress organized
1899	Dreyfus went on trial for the second time, accused of disclosing French government secrets
1900	James Hilton, English novelist, born
1901	Henri Toulouse.-Lautrec, French artist, died
1908	Congo Free State became the Belgian Congo

1909	Edward Harriman, financier, died
1919	Valbanera, a Spanish ship, lost off Florida with 500 lives
1932	Observation exploded in the East River, New York
1942	Coast Guard ship Muskeget vanished in the Atlantic
1943	Italian battleship Roma wrecked by German planes
1944	A week of hurricane began from the Carolinas to New England
1945	Gen. MacArthur took over the supervision of Japan Dick Fowler pitched a no-hitter and Philadelphia beat St. Louis 1-0
1948	Rex Barney pitched a no-hitter and the Dodgers beat the Yankees 2-0
1954	Start of 3 days of earthquakes in Algeria
1963	First giant panda born in captivity (Peking, China)
1964	Hurricane Dora left Florida
1965	Sandy Koufax pitched a perfect game and Los Angeles beat Chicago 1-0
1972	Jewish New Year 5733 (Rosh Hashana)

September 10th

	Feast of St. Aubert of Avranches who began the construction of Mont-St.-Michel, France
	Feast of St. Finnian of Moville
312 BC	Grecian calendar begins
9 AD	Three Roman legions destroyed by the Germans
422	Celestine elected Pope
453	St. Pulcheria, Empress of Byzantium, died (Feast Day)
1305	St. Nicholas of Tolentino died (Feast Day); patron of souls in purgatory
1382	Louis I, "the Great," King of Poland and Hungary, died
1401	Reconstruction of the burned Japanese imperial palace began
1419	John the Fearless, Duke of Burgundy, murdered
1533	Queen Elizabeth I of England christened
1543	DeSoto's expedition returned to Mexico
1547	England defeated Scotland at the Battle of Pinkie
1638	Marie Therese, Queen-consort of France, born
1733	Stanislaus I again elected King of Poland
1736	Carter Braxton, signer of the Declaration of Independence, born
1742	Faneuil Hall completed
1794	Middlesex Canal begun in England
1813	Perry sailed out of Put-in Bay for the Battle of Lake Erie and defeated the British
1839	Isaac K. Funk, Wagnalls' publishing partner, born
1846	Hand-crank sewing machine patented by Elias Howe

```
1849      Edwin Booth made his acting debut
1898      Elizabeth, wife of Franz Joseph, Emperor of
                     Austro-Hungary assassinated
1914      Russian defeat by the Germans at Masurian Lakes
                     completed
          First Battle of the Marne ended
1923      Solar eclipse
1929      Arnold Palmer, golfer, born
1935      Ten days of hurricane ended in Florida
1938      Twelve days of hurricane began  in northeastern
                     U.S.
1939      Canada declared war on Germany
1952      West Germany agreed to pay Israel for Nazi acts
1955      Hurricane Ione began 13-day stay in North
                     Carolina
1967      Gibraltar residents voted to remain British and
                     not return "the Rock" to Spain
          Joe Harlan pitched a no-hitter and Chicago beat
                     Detroit 4-0
1970      Start of the Honey Festival at Lebanon, Ohio
1971      Nikita Khrushchev, former Premier of Russia, died
```

===
September 11th
===

```
          Feast of Our Lady of Coromoto, patron of Venezuela
          Feast of St. Deinoil
          Feast of St. Paphnutius
          Feast of Sts. Protus and Hyacinth, martyrs
          Feast of St. Erik, patron of Denmark
 812 AD   Louis, son of Charlemagne, elected Holy Roman
                     Emperor to reign with his father
 813      Louis I, "the Pious," crowned himself Holy
                     Roman Emperor
1227      Pestilence hit Frederick II's forces and his
                     Crusade ended 3 days after it
                     began
1609      Henry Hudson discovered that Manhattan was an
                     island
1677      Maine passed the first law against liquor in
                     America
1697      Austrians defeated the Turks at Zenta in their
                     battle over control of Hungary
1777      British defeated Americans at Brandywine,
                     Pennsylvania
1814      McDonough's victory on Lake Champlain
1833      Royal William became the first steamboat to
                     cross the Atlantic
1850      Jenny Lind gave her first concert in the United
                     States
1851      Sylvester Graham, after whom graham flour is
                     named, died
1854      John Lee raided a wagon train, killing everyone
                     over 7 years old
```

```
1862    William S. Porter, short-story writer as O. Henry,
            born
1891    John H. B. Latrobe, artist-philanthropist, died
1917    Georges Guynemer, French air ace, killed in
            battle over Poelcappele
1923    First commercial long-distance short-wave
            message broadcast, a ringside
            account of a prizefight from Maine
            to Buenos Aires
1926    Eleven days of hurricane began in Florida and
            Alabama
1940    Hercules Powder Company plant exploded at
            Kenvil, New Jersey
1943    Conti di Savoina sunk by German bombs in Venice
            harbor
1950    Coshocton, Ohio, train wreck
1958    First atomic submarine, U.S.S. Swordfish, completed
1965    Hurricane Betsy ended a four-day stay on the U.S.
            Gulf coast
1970    Ethiopian New Year
        Witches Sabbath celebrated in Oudewater, Holland
1971    Cache Valley Threshing Bee held in Utah
```

September 12th

```
c.1021 AD  St. Guy of Anderlecht died (Feast Day)
1213    Peter II, King of Aragon, killed in the battle
            of Muret, part of the crusade to
            unite France
1494    Francis I, King of France, born
1683    German-Polish army broke the Turkish siege of
            Vienna
1687    John Alden, last of the Mayflower Puritans, died
1703    Pactum Mutuae Successionis set down inheritances
            within the Hapsburg family
1722    First commencement held at Yale University, for
            a class of eight
1805    Duke of Wellington, Waterloo victor over
            Napoleon, met Adm. Nelson, victor
            over Napoleon at Trafalgar, for
            the only time
1813    Edmund Randolph, U.S. statesman, died
1814    Americans defeated the British at the Battle
            of Baltimore (Defenders' Day,
            Maryland state holiday)
1818    Richard Gatling, machine-gun inventor, born
1847    Battle of Chapultepec
1877    The Chase National Bank founded (New York City)
1888    Maurice Chevalier, performer, born
        Italian steamer and La France
1892    Alfred A. Knopf, publisher, born
1898    Ben Shahn, artist, born
1904    Neuguen, Argentian, founded
```

1908	Winston Churchill married his Clementine
	Wright brothers flew their plane for 1½ hours
1913	Jesse Owens, athlete, born
1914	German cruiser Hela sunk by a British submarine off Heligoland
1918	British Galway Castle torpedoed in the Atlantic
	Americans began the assault at the St. Mihiel salient
1936	Spanish insurgents captured San Sebastian and Toledo
1943	Mussolini, Italian dictator, escaped to German lines
1950	Solar eclipse
1953	John F. Kennedy married Jacqueline Bouvier
1954	End of three days of earthquakes in Algeria
1955	Endurance record set for riding a unicycle
1959	Russia's Lunik II landed on the moon
1968	Second Delaware Memorial Bridge dedicated
1970	Stahlstown, Pennsylvania, held its Flax Scutching Festival
	Start of Plymouth, Massachusetts, 350th anniversary celebration
	Luna 16, Russian unmanned moon inspector, launched

September 13th

	Ides of September
	Feast of St. Notburga, patron of hired hands in Austria and Germany
	Dedication of Jupiter's Temple on Capitol Hill, Rome
81 AD	Domitian became Roman Emperor on the death of Titus
533	Romans defeated the Vandals near Carthage, Africa
604	Sabinian elected Pope
608	St. Eulogius of Alexandria died (Feast Day)
1125	Lothair II crowned King of Germany
1254	Hayton, King of Little Armenia, entered Mongolia
1409	Isabella of France, Queen to Richard II, King of England, died
1509	Andrea Mantegna, Italian artist, died
1598	King Philip II of Spain died
1619	Dulwich College opened at Dulwich, England
1745	Francis I elected Holy Roman Emperor
1759	Battle of Quebec
1782	English defeated Spanish-French fleet at Gibraltar
1791	Louis XVI took an oath as constitutional monarch of France
1814	Francis Scott Key wrote "The Star-Spangled Banner" as the British shelled Ft. McHenry, Baltimore

1851	Dr. Walter Reed, discoverer of cause of yellow fever, born
1847	Battle of Chapultepec continued
1854	Escorial Palace completed in Spain
	British and French forces landed in the Crimea
1857	Milton S. Hershey, candy-maker, born
1860	Gen. John J. Pershing born
	Shoshone Indians attacked a wagon train on the Oregon Trail
1899	Mt. Kenya, Africa, first climbed by a white man
1948	Margaret Chase Smith elected as a senator by Maine voters
1960	Hurricane Donna's 13-day march through the eastern U.S. ended
	Funds approved for the Theodore Roosevelt Memorial
1964	Women citizens of San Marino allowed to vote for the first time
1969	Jewish New Year 5730 Rosh Hashana
	Swap, Talk, and Brag Day held at Intervale, New Hampshire
1970	Expo '70, Osaka, Japan World Fair, closed
	Folklore Festival held at Salzburg, Austria

September 14th

	Elevation of the Holy Cross (Eastern Orthodox)
	Exaltation of the Cross
	Feast of Our Lady of Sorrows in Gibraltar
	Start of a week-long fair in Chesterfield, England
413 BC	Part of the Athens army surrendered to Sparta
258 AD	St. Cyprian beheaded
407	St. John Chrysostom died
786	Hadi, Moslem caliph, killed by his mother
891	Pope Stephen VI died
1131	Fulk became King of Jerusalem
1307	Leading Knights Templar arrested in France
1321	Dante, writer, died
1437	Transylvania united
1523	Pope Adrian VI died
1607	"Flight of the Earls" in Ireland
1742	James Wilson, signer of the Declaration of Independence, born
1759	Gen. Montcalm died defending Quebec from the British
1769	Alexander von Humboldt, explorer, born
1788	John Penn, signer of the Declaration of Independence, died
1812	Napoleon entered Moscow
1814	Britist took Fr. McHenry, Baltimore, Maryland
	General Society of the War of 1812 formed
1836	Aaron Burr, Vice-President, died
1845	National Police Gazette founded, lasting till 1932

```
1849        Ivan Pavlov, psychologist, born
1851        James Fenimore Cooper, author, died
1852        Sir Arthur Wellesley, Duke of Wellington, victor
                      at Waterloo, British soldier-
                      statesman, died
1857        Financial panic in the U.S.
1859        Jan Tschakste, first president of Latvia, born
1862        Battle of South Mountain, Maryland
1882        Asia foundered near the Sault Ste. Marie locks
1883        Margaret Sanger, birth control advocate, born
1886        American Philatelic Society formed
1899        Hal Wallis, film producer, born
1901        William McKinley, President of the United States,
                      died 8 days after being shot by
                      an assassin
1909        A week of hurricane flooding began in Mississippi
                      and Louisiana
1910        Jack Hawkins, actor, born
1921        Election of Judges began for the Permanent Court
                      of International Justice
1927        Isadora Duncan, dancer, died in an auto accident
1943        Italian ship Conte Verdi scuttled at Shanghai,
                      China
1944        Dewey, Indiana, train wreck
1954        Hurricane Edna's 12 days in northeastern U.S.
                      ended
1963        Fischer quintuplets, four girls and a boy, born
1964        Third session of the Second Ecumenical Council
                      began
1965        Fourth and final session of the Second Ecumenical
                      Council opened
1966        First pharaoh's head reunited with its body at
                      the new Abu Simbel site overlooking
                      the Nile
1969        Tanker Manhattan  opened up the Northwest
                      Passage
1970        Jicarilla Apache Annual Festival held at Horse
                      Lake in New Mexico


========================================================
September 15th
========================================================

            Respect for the Elderly, a Japanese Holiday
            Independence Day in Mexico, Costa Rica, El
                      Salvador, Nicaragua, and Guatemala
            Final day of the Annual Trade Fair at Novgorod,
                      Russia
            Feast of St. Nicetas the Goth
            Feast of St. Nicomedes
 863 AD     Iwashimizu Shrine held its first festival (Japan)
1159        Alexander III crowned Pope
1492        Columbus saw a meteor fall into the sea
1510        St. Katherine of Genoa died (Feast Day)
1655        Indians attacked settlements on and near Staten
                      Island
```

1789	James Fenimore Cooper, author, born
	U.S. Department of Foreign Affairs became the Department of State
1793	All colleges and universities abolished in France
1794	James Madison married Dorthea (Dolley) D. P. Todd
	Abram Clark, signer of the Declaration of Independence, died
1795	Zachariah Allen, inventor of the first home hot-air furnace, born
1807	Aaron Burr was acquited on charges of treason
1811	Hunt's overland expedition to the Pacific sighted the Teton Mountains of Wyoming
1830	Liverpool and Manchester Railway, the first wholly locomotive-powered line, opened in England
1844	Iron ore discovered in the Mesabi Mountains, Minnesota
1851	Honduras became independent of Spain (National Holiday)
1854	Kansas Weekly Herald founded at Leavenworth, the first English-language newspaper in the state
1857	William Howard Taft, 27th President of the U.S., born
1859	Isambard Kingdom Brunel, English civil engineer, died
1862	Union victory at Battle of Antietam, fought at Sharpsburg, Maryland
1864	John Speke, discoverer of the source of the Nile River, died in a hunting accident
1872	Patent granted for the first sprinkler system
1874	First session of the Universal Postal Union opened, at Bern, Switzerland
1890	Louise Blanchard Methune became the first woman to join the American Institute of Architects
1898	Teddy Roosevelt's "Rough Riders" were mustered out of the army
	Robert Benchley, humorist, born
1899	Dr. Milton Eisenhower, "Ike's" brother, born
1900	15 days of hurricane floods ended in southern Texas
1907	Canaan, New Hampshire, train wreck
1914	Lebanon, Missouri, train wreck
1916	First tanks in the world, British, went into battle in the Somme
1919	End of 13 days of hurricane on the U.S. Gulf coast
1922	Jackie Cooper, actor, born
1928	Beginning of the Jewish Year 5689
1935	Swastika became the German national emblem
1938	Thomas Wolfe, novelist-playwright, died
1942	U.S. aircraft carrier Wasp torpedoed in the Solomon Islands

```
1947       Start of 4 days of typhoon flooding in Japan
1950       U.S. Marines landed at Inchon, Korea
1951       New law center at New York University dedicated
1958       Port Elizabeth, New Jersey, train wreck
1959       Start of a state visit to the U.S. by Premier
                     Nikita Khrushchev of Russia
1961       Hurricane Carla ended a 12-day rampage in Texas
1968       Zond 5, unmanned lunar orbiter, launched by
                     Russia
1969       St. Louis Cardinals' pitcher Steve Carlton struck
                     out 19 of the opposing New York Mets,
                     setting a record
1970       Moon Cake Festival held in Singapore, the Mid-
                     Autumn Festival in Hong Kong
1975       Yom Kippur, Hewbrew holiday
```

```
============================================================
September 16th----------------------------------------------
============================================================
```

```
           Feast of St. Cornelius
           Feast of St. Euphemia
           Feast of St. Ninian
  ? BC     God created the sun, moon, and stars
  335      Alexander the Great destroyed Thebes, Egypt
  258 AD   St. Cyprian died (Feast Day)
  655      Pope St. Martin I died
  681      Sixth Ecumenical Council, held in Constantinople,
                     ended
  921      St. Ludmilla murdered (Feast Day)
  984      St. Edith of Wilton died (Feast Day)
 1087      Pope St. Victor III died
 1226      Pandulph, papal legate to England, died
 1379      University of Erfurt, Germany, chartered
 1380      Charles V, "the Wise," King of France, died
 1485      "Beefeaters," or Yoemen of the Guard, English
                     ruler's bodyguard, established
 1619      Another group of colonists left England, bound
                     for Virginia
 1620      The Mayflower Puritans sailed from England
 1736      Gabiel Farenheit, degree system namer, born
 1751      Charity Grammar School opened in Philadelphia
 1776      Washington defeated Howe at the Battle of Harlem
                     Heights, New York
 1777      British siege of Philadelphia began
 1782      Great seal of the United States first used
 1810      Mexican Revolution against Spain began (Mexican
                     Independence Day)
 1824      Louis XVIII, King of France, died
 1847      Shakespeare's house at Stratford-on-Avon purchased
                     to be preserved as a memorial
 1848      Saturn's moon Hyperion discovered
 1858      Butterfield's Overland Mail Coach began service
 1859      Europenas discovered Lake Nyassa, Africa
```

1875	James C. Penney, founder of the department store chain, born
1880	Alfred Noyes, English poet, born
1893	Cherokee Strip in Oklahoma opened for home-steading (Cherokee Strip Day, state holiday)
1903	Gwen Bristow, novelist-poet, born
1907	United Methodist Church in the U.S. united
1908	General Motors Corporation incorporated
1915	Haiti signed a treaty gaining U.S. protection
1917	Russia proclaimed itself a republic
1919	Congressional act incorporated the American Legion
1920	Wall Street New York City bomb explosion killed 38 people
1923	First Catholic Seminary for the education of black priests founded in Mississippi
1938	Eyston, in a Thunderbolt, set a land-speed record of 357.5 mph
1944	A week of hurricane on the U.S. east coast ended
1947	Cobb, in a Railton-Mobil, set a land-speed record of 394.2 mph
1955	Civil war agianst dictator Juan Peron began in Argentina
1956	Periagia, a U.S. freighter, sank in a storm off Norway
1960	Warren Spahn pitched a no hitter and Milwaukee beat Philadelphia 5-0
1961	Start of two days of typhoon damaging in Japan
1963	Federation of Malaysia formed
1965	Dave Morehead pitched a no-hitter and Boston beat Cleveland 2-0
1970	Yabwsame (horseback archery) Day held in Kamakura, Japan

September 17th

Immigrants' Day, celebrated in Caracas, Venezuela

Feast of St. Lambert of Maastricht
Feast of Sts. Socrates and Stephen

284 AD	Beginning of the ra of Diocletian
853	St. Columba of Cordoba died (Feast Day)
1156	Investiture of Regensburg (Austria)
1179	St. Hildegard died (Feast Day)
1374	Compact of Kassa signed between Polish nobles and their king
1621	St. Robert Bellarmine died
1630	Boston, Massachusetts, founded and named
1631	Swedish victory near Leipzig in the Thirty Years' War
1665	King Philip IV of Spain died
1701	James II, exiled King of England, died

```
1717      The Presbyterian Synod first met in America, in
                    Philadelphia
1730      Baron Frederick von Steuben, Prussian General
                    who served in the American Revolution,
                    born (Memorial Day observed in the
                    U.S.)
1776      Presidio of San Francisco founded (California)
1789      Mimas, Saturn's seventh moon, discovered
1847      U.S. forces captured Mexico City and Santa Anna
1850      San Francisco, California, partially burned
1890      Gabriel Heatter, broadcaster, born
1894      Battle of the Yalu in the Sino-Japanese War
1907      Oklahoma citizens approved their state's constitutio
1908      Wright brothers' plane crashed
1911      First transcontinental airplane flight, New York
                    to Pasadena, California, began
1928      Roddy McDowell, actor, born
1929      Sterling Moss, racing-car driver, born
1930      Ceremony held beginning the construction of
                    Hoover-Boulder Dam
1935      Commonwealth of the Philippines elected its
                    first president
1939      Russia invaded Poland
          British aircraft carrier Courageous torpedoed
1949      Canadian Noronic burned at Toronto
1951      French landing craft hit a mine at Cochin,
                    China
1952      World nonstop helicopter flight record set by
                    Elton J. Smith
1953      Beginning of three days of typhoon in South
                    Korea
1957      Malaysia joined the United Nations
1961      End of two days of typhoon in Japan
1967      Mt. Washington's cog railway derailed (New
                    Hampshire)
1968      Gaylord Perry pitched a no-hitter and San Francisco
                    beat St. Louis 1-0
1970      Start of Johnny Appleseed Days in Lisbon, Ohio
1974      Jewish New Year 5735 (Rosh Hashana)
```

September 18th
```
          Fair at Bury, Lancastershire, England
          Feast of St. Methodius of Olympus
 53 AD    Trajan, Roman emperor, born
 96       Marcus Nerva became Emperor of Rome when Domitian
                    was stabbed to death
1180      King Louis VII of France died
1663      St. Joseph of Copertino died (Feast Day)
1679      New Hampshire colony separated from Massachusetts
1705      Privateers took over New York City for a day
                    before the British artillery drove
                    them out
```

```
1709       Samuel Johnson, English writer, born
1733       George Read, signer of the Declaration of
                 Independence, born
1769       First piano, a spinet, manufactured in America
1784       Last volume, number 181, of the second edition
                 of Encyclopaedia Britannica
                 published
1786       King Christian VIII of Denmark and Norway born
1793       Philadelphia Journal or Weekly Advertiser ceased
                 publication
           President George Washington laid the cornerstone
                 for the U.S. Capitol
1845       Nord de France, transportation company, founded
1851       The New York Times began publication as The New
                 York Daily Times
1870       Germans began besieging Paris in the Franco-
                 Prussian War
1872       King Charles XV of Sweden died
1877       Sam Bass and his gang held up a Union Pacific
                 express train at Big Springs,
                 Nebraska
1905       Greta Garbo, actress, born
1906       Hong Kong hit by a typhoon
1914       Francis H. Leggett wrecked in the Columbia River
1931       Mukden Incident (Japanese troops overran the
                 garrison in Manchuria)
1951       Gelett Burgess, author of "I never saw a purple
                 cow . . . ,"died
1959       Vanguard III launched
1961       Dag Hammarsjkold, United Nations Secretary-
                 General, killed in a plane crash
1962       Tiros VI, weather satellite, launched
           Burundi, Jamaica, and Rwanda joined the United
                 Nations, along with Trinidad and
                 Tobago
1968       Ray Washburn pitched a no-hitter and St. Louis
                 beat San Francisco 2-0
1972       Yom Kippur
```

September 19th

```
           Battle of Britain commemoration
           Fair at Cardiff, Wales
           Harvest festival at Laguna Pueblo, New Mexico
           Fair at Sutton Coldfield, Warwickshire, England
           Feast of St. Januarius or Gennaro
 690 AD    St. Theodore of Canterbury died (Feast Day)
1180       Philip II became King of France
1356       England defeated the French at Poitiers and
                 captured John, their King
1551       King Henry III of France born
1703       Charles VI, Holy Roman Emperor, proclaimed King
                 of Spain
```

1734	French defeated the army of the Holy Roman Empire at Guastally, Italy, in the war over the Polish succession
1737	Charles Carroll, signer of the Declaration of Independence, born
1757	Elizabeth, Empress of Russia, suffered a fainting fit
1760	Last French military man in Michigan surrendered to the British
1775	Benedict Arnold and the American forces began their trek to attack Quebec
1777	First Battle of the Stillwater fought
1783	Hot-air balloon flight took place, with animal passengers, at Versailles, France
1790	Holy Roman Emperor Francis II married Marie Theresa
1796	Washington made his farewell address as President
1799	Rene Auguste Caillie, French explorer, born
1803	Robert Emmet executed in Ireland for treason by the British
1852	St. Emily de Rodat died (Feast Day)
1864	Union Cavalry victory at Winchester, Virginia
1881	James A. Garfield, U.S. President, died of an assassin's bullet received in July
1890	Ertogul, a Turkish frigate, foundered off Japan
1894	Rachel Field, novelist-poet-playwright, born
1899	Dreyfus pardoned by public demand in France
1904	Bergen Evans, educator-author, born
1926	"Duke" Snyder, baseball player, born
1928	Mickey Mouse made his acting debut in the cartoon feature "Steamboat Willie" by Walt Disney
1942	Conde Nast, publisher, died
1944	Russia signed an armistice with Finland
1947	End of four days of typhoon flooding in Japan
1955	Juan Peron deposed as President of Argentina
	Tampico, Mexico, hit by a hurricane
1957	First U.S. underground nuclear explosive tested
1959	Three-day typhoon in South Korea ended
1965	Winston Chruchill Memorial unveiled in Westminster Abbey, London, England
1970	Cherokee Strip celebration held at Perry Oklahoma
	Flax-sketching festival held at Stahlstown, Pennsylvania

===
September 20th
===

	Feast of St. Eustace, invoked in fighting fires and for protection from hell
2348 BC	Noah's ark uncovered
256	Alexander the Great born
331	Alexander the Great crossed the Tigris River to attack Persia

Lunar eclipse
451 AD Roman victory over the forces of Atilla the Hun
        at Chalons-sur-Marne, France
622   Mohammed changed the name of his city from
        Yathrib to Medina
833   Caliph Mu'tasim entered Baghdad
1276   John Peter Juliani crowned Pope John XXI, though
        there had been no John XX
1319   "The Chapter of Myton," Scots victory over the
        English
1410   Treaty of Arras, reuniting France and Burgundy
1519   Magellan's expedition sailed from Spain
1546   Royal College of Physicians in London received
        its Grant of Arms
1553   Fair held at Lyme Regis, Dorsetshire, England
1565   French Ft. Caroline in Florida taken by the
        Spanish
1643   First Battle of Newberry, England
1771   Mungo Park, African explorer, born
1792   French defeated the Prussians at Valmy, France
1797   U.S.S. Constitution ("Old Ironsides") launched
        at Boston
1808   Covent Garden Theater in London burned down
1832   Charles Carrol, signer of the Declaration of
        Independence, died
1840   Jose Francia, "El Supremo," Paraguaian dictator,
        died
1841   Horace Greeley's New Yorker weekly ceased
        publication
1857   Delhi, India retaken by the British
1865   Vassar College for Women opened (Poughkeepsie,
        New York)
1870   Patent issued for a shaving mug with drain holes
        in the soap compartment
        Italian nationists occupied Rome in the name of
        the Kingdom of Italy
        Natoleon III surrendered the Papal States to
        Italy
1873   Bank failures in New York City caused a financial
        panic
1878   Upton Sinclair, author, born
1915   Igor Cassini, columnist "Cholly Knickerbocker,"
        born
1917   Quebec Bridge in Canada completed
        Transcaucasia, Russia, declared itself a
        republic
1918   Americans captured St. Mihiel salient
1928   End of two weeks of hurricane in southern
        Florida
1932   English Methodist sects united
1934   Sophia Loren, actress, born
1947   Fiorello LaGuardia, New York City Mayor, died
1957   Jean Sibelius, composer, died

1958	Hoyt Wilhelm pitched a no-hitter and Baltimore beat New York 1-0
1960	Central African Republic, Chad, both Congos, Cyprus, Dahomey, Gabon, Ivory Coast, Madagascar, Niger, Somalia, Togo, and Upper Volta all joined the United Nations
1966	Guyana, formerly British Guiana, joined the United Nations
1969	Bob Moose pitched a no-hitter and Pittsburgh beat the New York Mets 4-0
1970	Our Lady of Penafrancia honored at Naga, Philippines Harvest dances held at the San Juan Pueblo, New Mexico
1971	Jewish New Year 5732 (Rosh Hashana)

September 21st

	Independence Day celebrations in Merida, Venezuela
	Feast of St. Matthew
	Spring Celebration in Argentina
	New Year's Day to the Ancient Egyptians, Persians, and Phoenicians
	Fair previously held at Guildford, Surry, England
	Tivoli Gardens, Copenhagen, Denmark, closes for the season
490 BC	Battle of Marathon, Greece
19	Vergil, Roman poet and author of the _Aeneid_, died
1237 AD	King Edward II of England murdered
1397	Richard, Earl of Arundel and Surry, beheaded (England)
1415	Frederick, III as Holy Roman Emperor, IV as King of Germany, V as Archduke of Austria, born
1549	Marguerite d'Anguoleme, Queen of Navarre, died
1645	Louis Joliet, explorer, born
1676	Benedetto Odescalchi elected Pope as Innocent XV
1737	Francis Hopkinson, signer of the Declaration of Independence, born
1756	John McAdam, paving-material inventor, born
1784	First daily newspaper in the U.S., _Pennsylvania Packet and General Advertiser_, founded
1798	George Read, signer of the Declaration of Independence, died
1814	"Star-Spangled Banner" published as a poem in the _Baltimore American_
1826	Alexander Laing became the first European to reach Timbuktu
1832	Sir Walter Scott, poet-novelist, died Treaty signed at Rock Island, Illinois, ended the Black Hawk War

1853	Phara Paramindr Maha Chulalongkorn, King of Siam, born
1861	Belian government secretly decreed its monopoly on rubber from the Congo and ivory from everywhere
1866	H. G. Wells, novelist, born
1867	New York Evening Mail newspaper founded
1897	"Yes, Virginia, there is a Santa Claus" editorial appeared in the New York Sun
1898	Pavel Tchelitchew, Russian artist, born
	Champlain monument unveiled in Quebec, Canada
1909	End of a week of hurricane flooding in Louisiana and Mississippi
1922	Solar eclipse
1931	England abandoned the gold standard
1934	Honshu Island, Japan, hit by a typhoon
1941	Solar eclipse
1947	End of 17 days of hurricane of the Gulf coast
1949	People's Rupublic of China proclaimed by its Communist leaders
1954	India withdrew all its forces from Tibet
1956	Beginning of 9 days of hurricane Flossy in the Gulf states
1957	King Haakon VII of Norway died
	West German bark Pamir sank in a storm off the Azores
1964	Malta became an independent part of the British Commonwealth (Independence Day)
1965	Twentieth session of the United Nations General Assembly convened
	Gambia, Maldive Islands, and Singapore joined the United Nations
1968	Chester F. Carlson, inventor of Xerography, died
1969	Festival of Hops held in Belgium

September 22nd

	Feast of St. Maurice, patron of infantrymen, weavers, and sword-makers; invoked against gout
	Feast of the Martyrs of Agaunum
	Feast of St. Phocas, patron of sailors
530 AD	Pope St. Felix III died
880	King Carloman of Bavaria and Italy died
1241	Snorri Sturleson, Icelandic poet, killed
1503	Francesco Todeschini de Piccolomini elected Pope as Pius III
1521	Selim, Sultan of Turkey, died
1555	St. Thomas of Villanueva died (Feast Day)
1609	Moors expelled from Spain
1692	Seven witches hanged at Salem, Massachusetts
1762	British bombarded Manila in the Philippines
1774	Pope Clement XIV died

```
1776    Nathan Hale hanged by the British as a spy
1791    Michael Faraday, scientist, born
1792    First French Republic proclaimed
1825    La Chasse et l'amour produced, first viewing of
                      an Alexandre Dumas play
        The New York Star, daily newspaper, established
1862    Santee Sioux defeated by the Minnesota Militia
                      at Wood Lake
1864    Union Cavalry victory at Fisher's Hill, Virginia
1912    Alfred G. Vanderbilt, financier, born
1914    Three British cruisers sunk by a German submarine
1915    Beginning of 8 days of hurricane devastation on
                      the Gulf coast
1926    Eleven days of hurricane ended in Florida and
                      Alabama
1927    Slavery abolished in Sierra Leone
1932    Ingemar Johansson, boxer, born
1938    Twelve days of hurricane ended in the north-
                      eastern U.S.
        Partially completed Fort Penn Dam on the Missouri
                      River badly damaged
1940    Japanese troops invaded French Indo-China
1955    Hurricane hit Mexico and the West Indies, lasting
                      6 days
1958    Mary Roberts Rinehart, mystery writer, died
1959    Baby gorilla born at the zoo in Basel, Switzerland
1960    Sudan became the Republic of Mali
1968    New site for Abu Simbel temple dedicated (Egypt)
1969    Yom Kippur
1970    Emancipation Day in the U.S. celebrated
```

September 23rd

```
        Feast of St. Thecla of Iconium
        Feast of St. Linus, first Pope after St. Peter
  ? BC   Euripides born
   63    Octavian Augustus, first Roman Emperor, born
  704 AD  St. Adamnan died (Feast Day)
  918    Conrad I, King of Germany, died
 1459    Battle of Blore Heath in the War of the Roses,
                      England
 1578    Sir Humphry Gilbert sailed in search of the
                      Northwest Passage
 1642    First Bachelors of Arts degrees conferred in
                      America, at Harvard
 1648    Cossacks defeated the Poles at Pildawa
 1713    Ferdinand VI, King of Spain, born
 1776    British occupied Jersey City, New Jersey, then
                      known as Powel's Hook
 1779    Bonhomme Richard captained by John Paul Jones,
                      defeated H.M.S. Serapis
 1780    Major John Andre, British spy, captured
```

1800	William McGuffy, creator of the McGuffy Readers, born
1806	Lewis and Clark expedition returned to St. Louis, Missouri
1828	Chaka, Zulu chief, murdered
1845	The Knickerbocker Baseball Club of New York City, first in the U.S., founded
1846	J. G. Gaulle discovered the planet Neptune
1847	Komei crowned Emperor of Japan
1862	James W. Blake, composer of "Sidewalks of New York," born
1870	Prosper Merimee, French writer, died
1873	Detroit News newspaper founded
1889	Walter Lippmann, columnist, born
1898	Walter Pidgeon, actor, born
1902	John Wessley Powell, Grand Canyon explorer, died
1905	Japanese warship Mikasa sank with 599 aboard
1910	Elliott Roosevelt, son of the President, born
1911	First air mail pilot sworn in, to deliver mail from Garden City to Mineola, Long Island, New York
1912	Russian Obnevka sank in the Dvina River
1913	First plane flight across the Mediterranean completed
1920	Mickey Rooney, actor, born
1926	Gene Tunney beat Jack Dempsey in 10 rounds for the heavy weight boxing title
1937	National Foundation for Infantile Paralysis created
1939	Sigmund Freud, psychologist, died
	Time capsule buried at Flushing Meadow Park, New York, to be opened in 6939 A.D.
1945	Sgt. Joe Louis, heavyweight boxing champion, awarded the Legion of Merit medal
1949	U.S. President announced an atomic explosion in Russia
1952	Rocky Marciano knocked out "Jersey Joe" Walcott for the heavyweight boxing title in 13 rounds
1955	Hurricane Ione ended a 13-day stay in the northeastern U.S.
1962	Lincoln Center for the Performing Arts opened in New York City with Philharmonic Hall completed
1967	Hurricane Beulah blew itself out
1970	University Day and Farmers' Day celebrations in Iran

September 24th

Our Lady of Mercy, Patron of Caracas, Venezuela
Feast of St. Thecla (Orthodox)

15 AD	Aulus Vitellius, Roman emperor, born

366	Pope Liberius died
768	Pepin III, "the Short," ruler of France and father of Charlemagne, died
784	Second Council of Nice began, dealing with the use of images in Roman Catholic churches
1046	St. Gerard of Csanad died (Feast Day)
1066	Vikings entered York, England
1143	Pope Innocent II died
1332	Baliol crowned King of Scotland
1541	Paracelsus, Swiss physician, born
1621	First newspaper in England debuted
1657	First autopsy and coroner's jury verdict recorded in America (Maryland)
1664	First convention between the English and the Iroquois Indians held at Albany, New York
1705	Stanislaus I crowned King of Poland
1755	John Marshall, U.S. Supreme Court Justice, born
1780	Benedict Arnold escaped to the British after his attempt to betray West Point
1784	Zachary Taylor, 12th President of the U.S., born
1789	U.S. Attorney-General's office established
1817	Colgate University at Hamilton, New York, organized
1820	Central Asia opened to British trade by a treaty with Ladakh
1821	Jose Carrera, first president of Chile, shot
1826	Alexander Laing left Timbuktu
1847	U.S. Army entered Mexico City
1854	British-French victory at the Battle of Alma in the Crimean War
1869	"Black Friday" financial disaster in New York City
1896	F. Scott Fitzgerald, novelist, born
1904	New Market, Tennessee, train wreck
1906	Devil's Tower National Monument created
1924	Boyce Thompson Institute for Plant Research, Inc. founded at Yonkers, New York
1952	Romania adopted a Communist constitution
	French submarine La Sibylle lost off Toulon
1966	Start of hurricane Alma in southeastern U.S. and the islands
1968	Swaziland joined the United Nations
1970	Luna 16 returned to Russia from the Moon
1971	American Indian Day celebrated

September 25th

Southdown sheep fair at Lewes, Sussex, England
Start of a two-day fair at Dover, England
Feast of St. Euphrosyne (Greek Orthodox)
Feast of St. Cadoc

	Feast of St. Finbarr or Barr
	Feast of St. Vincent Strambi
1066 AD	King Harold of England routed the Vikings at York and King Harald III of Norway was killed
1392	St. Sergius of Radonezh died (Russian Orthodox Feast Day)
1396	Crusaders defeated by the Turks at Nicopolis, Bulgaria
1492	False cry of "Land" rang out over Columbus' ship
1493	Columbus began his second voyage to America
1506	Philip I, "the Handsome," King of Spain, died
1555	Peace of Augsburg recognized the Lutheran religion in Germany
1690	Publick Occurences, Both Foreign and Domestic, first newspaper in America, published its only issue
1711	Ch'ien Lung, Emperor of China, born
1849	Johann Strauss, composer, died
1857	King Charles XV became Regent of Sweden
1866	St. Francis of Camporosso died (Feast Day)
1890	Sequoia National Park created
	Polygamy banned by the Mormon Church
1894	Robert Briscoe, first Jewish mayor of Dublin, Ireland, born
1897	William Faulkner, author, born
1905	Red Smith, sportswriter, born
1909	Hudson-Fulton Celebration held in New York
1911	French battleship Liberty exploded at Toulon
1918	Phil Rizzuto, baseball player, born
1922	Johnson Oatman, hymn composer ("Count Your Blessings"), died
1926	International slavery convention signed by 20 African nations
1928	R. F. Outcault, creator of "Buster Brown," died
1933	Ring Lardner, humorist, died
1956	First transAtlantic telephone cable system went into use
	Sal Maglie pitched a no-hitter and Brooklyn beat Philadelphia 5-0
1962	Sonny Liston took the heavyweight title from Floyd Patterson by a knockout in one round
1970	Indian dances held at Santo Domingo Pueblo, New Mexico
1971	Hugo Black, retired Supreme Court Justice, died

Feast of St. Flavian I (Orthodox)
Feast of St. Cornelius, Pope
Feast of Sts. Cyprian and Justina
Feast of the Martyrs of North America, Jesuit
missionaries

611 AD   St. Colman of Lann Elo died (Feast Day)
1004   St. Nilus of Rossano died (Feast Day)
1087   William II, "Rufus," sone of the Conqueror,
         crowned King of England
1143   Pope Celestine II took office
1480   First Inquisitors appointed to serve in Spain
1580   Sir Francis Drake returned to England with a
         shipload of plunder from the
         Spanish
1651   Francis D. Pastorius, founder of Germantown,
         Pennsylvania, born
1777   British captured Philadelphia after a ten-
         day siege
1815   Holy Alliance of Russia, Austria, and Prussia
         signed in Paris
1826   Alexander Laing, Sahara explorer, murdered in
         the desert
1841   Henri Le Caron, British spy, born
1870   King Christian X of Denmark born
1888   T. S. Eliot, poet, born
1898   George Gershwin, composer, born
1914   Federal Trade Commission established
1917   Edgar Degas, French artist, died
1918   Tampa torpedoed off the English coast
1925   U.S. submarine S-51 collided with City of Rome
         off Block Island
1934   Cunard liner Queen Mary launched
1947   Hugh Lofting, creator of "Dr. Dolittle," died
1952   George Santayana, poet-philosopher, died
1953   Viet Nam hit by a typhoon and flooding
1954   Northern Japan struck by a typhoon that sank
         the ferry Toya Maru with 1200
         aboard
1959   Japan hit by a typhoon
1960   Emily Post, etiquette authority, died
1965   Jewish year 5726 (Rosh Hashana)
1968   OV-2-5, 5-2, 5-4, LES-6 all launched by one
         rocket
1970   Start of the Grape Jamboree held at Geneva, Ohio
1971   Hirohito became the first Japanese Emperor to
         step on U.S. soil
1974   Yom Kippur

Feast of Sts. Cosmas and Damian, patrons of
          physicians, druggists, mid-wives:
          invoked for good health
1066 AD William the Conqueror set sail from France
1130   Roger II appointed King of Sicily
1290   Chihli, China, rocked by an earthquake
1323   St. Elezear died (Feast Day)
1540   Society of Jesus (Jesuit order) recognized by
          the Pope
1660   St. Vincent de Paul died
1696   St. Alfonso Maria Dei Liquori born
1700   Pope Innocent XII died
1722   Samuel Adams, signer of the Declaration of
          Independence, born
1777   U.S. Congress met at Lancaster, Pennsylvania
1781   William I, King of Wurttemberg, born
1783   Augustin de Iturbide, Emperor of Mexico, born
1821   Mexico declared its independence from Spain
1825   First passenger-carrying railway opened,
          traveling from Stockton to
          Darlington, England
1860   Milos Obrenovic I, ruler of Serbia, died
1915   Gasoline tank railway car exploded at Ardmore,
          Oklahoma
1917   Louis S. Auchincloss, novelist, born
1919   Adelina Patti, singer, died
         Charles S. Percy, Illinois senator, born
1922   George II became King of Greece
1923   Lockett, Wyoming, train wreck
1938   Cunard liner Queen Elizabeth launched
1958   Start of two days of typhoon Ida's crossing
          Japan
1959   Japan hit by a typhoon
         Russian Premier Khrushchev ended his visit to
          the U.S.
1961   Sierra Leone joined the United Nations
1964   Warren Commission report on the assassination
          of President John F. Kennedy
          released
1965   Mt. Taal, Philippine volcano, erupted
1969   Hebrew celebration of Succoth
1973   Jewish New Year 5734 (Rosh Hashana)

Feast of St. Thiemo, patron of engravers
Feast of St. Eustochium
480 BC Battle of Salmis
235 AD Pontian resigned as Pope

```
351 AD   Roman empire reunited after the battle at Mursa
            on the Drave
780      St. Lioba died (Feast Day)
876      Louis, founder of the German kingdom, died
929      St. Wenceslas, patron of Czechoslovakia, died
            (Feast Day)
1066     William the Conqueror and his Normans landed in
            England
1106     Battle of Tinchebrai
1197     Henry VI, Holy Roman Emperor, died of a cold
            caught while hunting
1238     King James I, "the Conqueror," defeated the
            Moors at Valencia, Spain
1322     Battle of Muhldorf over the throne of Germany
1542     Juan Cabrillo discovered San Diego Bay,
            California
1781     Americans attacked the British at Yorktown,
            Virginia
1791     Jews in France given full citizenship
1795     Britain, Russia, and Austria formed the Triple
            Alliance
1803     Prosper Merimee, French writer, died
1839     Frances Willard, temperance leader, born
                  (Frances Willard Day, Minnesota
                  state holiday)
1840     George W. Peck, author of Peck's Bad Boy,
            born
1841     George  Clemenceau, French statesman, born
1850     U.S. Navy abolished flogging as punishment
1863     Carlos I, King of Portugal, born
1887     Avery Brundage, head of the U.S. Olympic
            Committee, born
1891     Herman Melville, author, died
1892     Elmer L. Rice, playwright-novelist, born
1901     William S. Paley, broadcast executive, born
         Ed Sullivan, columnist-television emcee, born
1909     Al Capp, creator of "Li'l Abner," born
1912     Japanese Kickermaru sank off Japan
1917     Kellyville, Oklahoma, train wreck
1920     Eight players on the Chicago White Sox team
                  indicated for "throwing" the 1919
                  World Series to Cincinnati
1934     Bridgette Bardot, actress, born
1951     Allie Reynolds pitched a no-hitter and New York
            beat Boston 8-0
1954     James Street, author, died
1955     End of 6 days of hurricane in Mexico and the
            British West Indies
1958     France adopted a new constitution
         Typhoon Ida left Japan after a two-day stay
1960     Mali and Senegal joined the United Nations
1962     Alovelle I, first Canadian satellite, launched
```

```
1969      Gold Star Mothers' Day celebrated in the U.S.
1970      Confucius' Birthday celebrated on Taiwan
1971      Luna 19, Russian moon probe, launched
```

==

```
          Michaelmas, an English Quarter Day - rents due,
                 people move in or out
          Feast of St. Michael, patron of policemen,
                 swordsmen, hat-makers, mariners,
                 grocers, and the sick; invoked for
                 a peaceful death
          Feast of Sts. Rhipsime and Gaiana (Armenian)
          Constitution Day in Brunei
  48 BC   Pompey the Great murdered in Egypt
 219 AD   Egalabalus, boy-emperor, entered Rome
 440      Pope Leo I, "the Great," elected to office
 557      St. Cyriacus the Recluse died (Feast Day)
 855      Lothair I, Holy Roman Emperor, died
 996      Gregory V, first German Pope, driven from the
                 throne by a revolt
1227      Frederick II, Holy Roman Emperor, excommunicated
1273      Rudolph I elected King of Germany
1560      Gustavus I Eriksson, King of Sweden, died
1582      St. Theresa died
1620      Acarigua, Venezuela founded
1703      Francois Boucher, French artist, born
1720      South Sea Bubble burst the English speculators'
                 market
1725      Robert, Baron Clive, founder of England's
                 Indian Empire, born
1758      Lord Horatio Nelson, English naval hero, born
1820      King Henry Bourbon of France born, never to
                 reign
1829      Police took over the duties of London's Night
                 Watch
1833      Ferdinand VII, King of Spain, died
1842      The Order of the Sons of Temperance organized
          in New York City
1877      Nez Perce Indian camp in the Bear Paw Mountains
                 attacked by the U.S. Army
1879      Meeker Massacre   Ute Indian attack on the Army
                 on the White River Reservation in
                 Colorado
1901      Enrico Fermi, physicist, born
1902      Emile Zola, French novelist, died of
                 asphyxiation
1908      Gene Autry, singing movie cowboy, born
          Greer Garson, actress, born
1911      Italian-Turkish war began
1913      Rudolf Diesel, engine inventor, lost overboard
                 from the mail steamer and presumed
                 drowned
```

```
1916      Trevor Howard, actor, born
1927      Telephone service began between U.S. and Mexico
1956      Anastasio Somoza, President of Nicaragua,
              assassinated
1963      Second session of the Ecumenical Council began
1967      Start of the Water Dowsers' Convention at
              Danville, Vermont
1968      Cape of Good Hope, Africa, rocked by an earth-
              quake
1969      Earthquake shook western South Africa
1970      Dancing held at Taos Pueblo, New Mexico
1971      Yom Kippur
          OSO-7, U.S. sun-study satellite, launched
```

```
          Feast of St. Otto of Bamberg
          Feast of St. Sophia
          World Championship Goose-calling Contest,
              Missouri Valley, Iowa
106 BC    Pompey the Great, enemy of Caesar, born
420 AD    St. Jerome died, patron of students (Feast Day)
653       St. Honorius of Canterbury died (Feast Day)
1139      Empress Matilda landed in England to claim her
              throne
1207      Rumi, Persian poet, born
1399      King Richard II of England, imprisoned by his
              cousin in the Tower of London,
              abdicated
1560      King Gustavus Vasa of Sweden died
1568      Insane Eric XIV deposed as Swedish king
1572      St. Francis Borgia died
1619      The baronetage established in Ireland
1673      Mary of Modena became by proxy the second wife
              of King James II of England
1745      Prussians under Frederick the Great beat the
              Austro-Saxons at Soor
1787      The Columbia left Boston to be the first to
              carry the U.S. flag around the
              world
1812      A Russian fort established near Bodega Bay,
              California
1846      Ether first used, for a tooth extraction
1855      Bechuanaland became a British protectorate
1880      First photograph taken of a nebula, in Orion
1890      Revolutionary War widows' pension raised from
              $12 to $30 per month
1897      St. Therese of Lisieux died
1906      New York Central Railroad began using electric
              locomotives
1915      End of eight days of hurricane on the U.S.
              Gulf coast
```

1918	Bulgaria surrendered
	Ticonderoga torpedoed in the Atlantic
1921	Germany ratified a peace treaty with the U.S.
	Deborah Kerr, actress, born
1924	Truman Capote, author, born
1938	Munich agreement signed; peace declaration between Hitler and England in which Germany gained Sudetenland from Czechoslovakia
1945	U.S. returned to Standard Time from War Time
1946	Nuremberg Tribunal convicted 22 Nazi leaders of war crimes
1947	Pakistan and Yemen joined the United Nations
1948	Edith K. C. (Mrs. Theodore) Roosevelt died
1949	Blockade of Berlin removed after the Berlin Airlift
1954	First atomic-powered U.S. vessel, submarine Nautilus, commissioned
1956	End of nine days of Hurricane Flossy in the Gulf states
1961	Syria withdrew from the United Arab Republic, leaving Egypt as the only member
1962	Third revision of the English Bible since 1611 published
	James Meredith became the first black student at the University of Mississippi
1966	Botswana (Bechuanaland) became independent of Britain
	Hurricane Alma ended its devastating stay in the southeast U.S.
1969	England's general post office became a public corporation
1970	Festival of Lights held in Singapore
1971	Hunting World Exhibition, at Budapest, Hungary, closed

OCTOBER

Full Moon - Travel Moon
          Palolo worms surface and mate in the South Pacific
1st Monday - Court Day in Maysville, Kentucky
          Child Health Day (U.S.)
2nd Monday - Columbus Day Observance (U.S.)
3rd Monday - Court Day in Mt. Sterling, Kentucky
4th Monday - Veterans' Day Observance (U.S.)
1st Sunday - Feast of the Rosary of the Blessed Virgin Mary
2nd weekend - Peanut Festival at Holdenville, Oklahoma
3rd week - National Macaroni Week (U.S.)
4th week - National Pretzel Week

October 1st
_____

          Korean Armed Forces Day
          Feast of St. Bavo
          Feast of St. Gregory the Enlightener
          Feast of St. Nicetius of Trier
          Feast of St. Remi (or Remigus)
          Feast of St. Romanus the Melodist
4008 BC   Beginning of the Mundane Era
3761   Beginning of the Jewish Mundane Era
2051   Beginning of the Era of Abraham
 331   Alexander the Great defeated Darius and the
                    Persians at Gaugamela
 110   Beginning of the Sidonian Era
1136 AD   Siege of LaSap, France
1207   King Henry III of England born
1273   Rudolph of Hapsburg elected King of Germany

1404	Pope Boniface IX died
1410	Jobst chosen King of Germany
1528	Papal legates arrived in England to discuss King Henry VIII's divorce from Catherine of Aragon
1685	Charles VI, Holy Roman Emperor, born
1730	Richard Stockton, signer of the Declaration of Independence, born
1754	Paul I, Emperor of Russia, born
1800	A secret treaty with Spain gave Louisiana to France
1851	Construction of Chicago, Rock Island and Pacific Railway began
1868	Phra Paramindr Maha Chulalongkorn born, and became King of Siam immediately, under a Regency
	7 Cavalry companies began a campaign against hostile Plains Indians, leaving Ft. Hacker, Kansas, guided by "Buffalo Bill" Cody
1869	Austria issued the first postcard
1872	First daily weather charts made
1873	Sir Edwin Landseer, English artist, died
1884	First U.S. theatrical school, ancestor of the American Academy of Dramatic Arts, formed
1885	Special delivery mail service began
1890	Yosemite National Park established
1893	Faith Baldwin, author, born
1896	Rural Free Delivery mail service begun, in West Virginia
1904	Vladimir Horowitz, pianist, born
1907	Plaza Hotel, New York City, opened
1908	"Model T" Ford introduced
1910	Dynamite explosion at the Los Angeles Times building, blamed on a labor dispute
1915	Gulf coast of the U.S. hit by a hurricane
1925	Texas Technology College opened
1928	Newark, New Jersey, airport established
	Air service began between U.S. and Mexico
1938	Germans began occupation of Sudetenland, Czechoslovakia
1940	Pennsylvania Turnpike opened to traffic
	Solar eclipse
1946	Nuremberg War Trials sentenced 11 Nazi criminals to hanging
1949	Mao Tse-Tung declared his Communist Government in China (National Foundation Day)
1961	Former British and French Cameroon colonies formed the Federal Republic of Cameroons, Africa (Reunification Day)

1963	Nigeria became a republic within the British Commonwealth
1968	New railway station in Nanking, China, opened to the public
	Marcel Duchamp, French artist, died
1969	Santa Rosa, California, rocked by an earthquake
1970	Jewish New Year (Rosh Hashana)
1972	New Van Gogh Museum opened in Amsterdam, Holland

October 2nd

	Start of a 2-day fair at Lymington, Hampshire, England
	Gandhi's birthday celebrations held in India
48 BC	Caesar sailed to Egypt to support Cleopatra
534 AD	Athalaric, King of the Ostrogothics, died
679	St. Leger died (Feast Day)
815	The Bishop of Munich received food and a cartload of beer as interest on a loan
1187	Jerusalem fell to the Moslems led by Saladin
1263	Scots attacked Norwegians living in Largs, Scotland
1326	King Edward II of England fled London, his barons, and his wife
1452	King Richard III of England born
1501	Catherine of Aragon arrived in England to marry Arthur, Prince of Wales, heir to Henry VII
1780	Major John Andre, British spy, hung
1803	Samuel Adams, signer of the Declaration of Independence, died
1869	Mahatma Gandhi, Hindu spiritual leader, born
1870	Plebiscite annexed Rome and the Papal States to the Kingdom of Italy
1895	Groucho Marx, comedian, born
1898	Bud Abbott, of Abbott and Costello comedy team, born
1902	Elizabeth Cody Stanton, suffragist, died
1909	Hudson Fulton Celebration in New York closed
1934	Navy of India inaugurated
1935	Italy invaded Ethiopia over a border dispute with Somaliland
1942	British cruiser Curacao involved in a fatal collision off England
1954	First large oil refinery in North Dakota dedicated
1958	Guiana became independent of France
1962	U.S. launched Explorer 14
1964	Hurricane Hilda paved a path through the southeast U.S.

```
1967      Thurgood Marshall sworn in as first black U.S.
               Supreme Court Justice
1968      President signed the Redwood National Park bill
1970      Hallingdal Peasant Wedding Festival held at
               Hol, Norway
```

October 3rd

```
          Korean National Foundation Day Celebration
          Feast of St. Josepha Rossello
          Feast of St. Thomas of Hereford
 695 AD   Sts. Hewalds (or Ewalds) the 2, patrons of
               Westphalia, died (Feast Day)
 959      St. Gerard of Brogne died (Feast Day)
1568      Isabel de Valois, 3rd wife of King Philip II of
               Spain, died
1574      Spanish occupiers evacuated Leyden, Holland
               (Liberation Day)
1656      Miles Standish, Massachusetts colonist, died
1700      Charles II of Spain rewrote his will, leaving
               all to Philip of Anjou, 2nd son
               of King Louis XIV of France
1776      New Jersey's great seal authorized
1860      Rembrandt Peale, artist, died
1863      First modern Thanksgiving holiday proclaimed by
               President Lincoln
1866      Evening Star foundered with 250 aboard sailing
               out of New York
1876      Johns Hopkins University's first classes met
1897      St. Therese of Lisieux ("Little Flower"),
               patron of the missions, died
               (Feast Day)
1900      Thomas Wolfe, novelist-playwright, born
1908      Australian national flag adopted
1928      French submarine Ondine sank off Portugal
1931      Start of the first transPacific flight, Tokyo
               to Wenatchee, Washington
1962      Wally Schirra made his flight in Sigma 7 as
               part of the U.S. Mercury space
               program
          Telephone company office exploded in New York
               City
1968      European Satellite Research Organization
               launched a study of the northern
               lights
1969      Last wooden passenger train car taken out of
               service (Myrtle Avenue Elevated,
               Brooklyn, N.Y.)
1970      Annual Fredericksburg, Virginia, Dog Mart held,
               continuously since 1698
1971      Mid-Autumn Festival held in Hong Kong
```

	Fast of Ceres celebrated in Ancient Rome
	Closing of the Gate of Mercy in the Church of the Holy Sepulchre, Duggendorf, Germany
1209 AD	Otto IV crowned Holy Roman Emperor
1226	St. Francis of Assisi, founder of the Franciscan Friars, died (Feast Day)
1289	King Louis X, "the Quarreller," of France born
1550	King Charles IX of Sweden born
1669	Rembrandt van Rijn, Dutch artist, died
1693	League of Augsburg defeated by the French at Marsaglia, Italy
1769	Bangor, Maine, settled
1777	British took Philadelphia, occupying it for a year
1822	Rutherford B. Hayes, 19th U.S. President, born
1853	Turkey's declaration began the Crimean War
1861	Frederic Remington, artist, born
1866	Fire swept the city of Quebec, Canada
1884	Damow Runyon, writer, born
1896	Buster Keaton, dead-pan comedian, born
1905	Calvin Coolidge, U.S. President, married Grace A. Goodhue
1915	Dinosaur National Monument created
1918	King Ferdinand of Bulgaria abdicated
	A munitions plant exploded at Morgan Station, New Jersey
1924	Charlton Heston, actor, born
1944	Alfred E. Smith, governor of New York and presidential candidate, died
1957	Sputnik I, Russian satellite, launched
1958	BOAC began first jet transAtlantic air service
1959	Lunik III, Russian lunar probe, took pictures of the unseen side of the moon
1960	Courier 1B, communications satellite, launched
	A chemical plant exploded at Kingsport, Tennessee
1963	Gambia, smallest country in Africa, became independent of Great Britain
1965	Pope Paul VI visited the New York World's Fair
1966	Basutoland, on gaining its independence from England, became Lesoatho
1972	Confucius' Birthday celebrated in Hong Kong

October 5th

```
          Ancient Romans opened the door of the Underworld
          Feast of St. Maurus
          Feast of St. Placid
1056 AD   Henry III, "the Black," Holy Roman Emperor, died
1285      Philip, "the Bold," King of France, died
1685      Mary of Modena, wife of King James II of England,
              born
1740      Ivan VI declared heir to the Russian throne
1762      The British took Manila, Philippines
1763      Augustus III, King of Poland, died
1787      Thomas Stone, signer of the Declaration of
              Independence, died
1789      William Scorsby, Arctic explorer, born
1813      Tecumseh, Shawnee Indian chief, killed battling
              the British in the War of 1812
1823      Leo XII crowned Pope
1830      Chester A. Arthur, 21st U.S. President, born
1837      Hortense, Queen of Holland and stepdaughter of
              Napoleon, died
1864      Calcutta, India, hit by a cyclone
1877      Chief Joseph of the Nez Perce Indians surrendered
              to the U.S. Army
1879      First Salvation Army meeting in the U.S. held
              in Philadelphia
1897      Sir John Gilbert, English artist, died
1908      Joshua Logan, filmmaker, born
1915      Allies landed at Salonika
1929      Beginning of the Jewish Year 5690
1931      First nonstop transPacific flight completed,
              Tokyo to Wenatchee, Washington
1938      Czechoslovakian President Benes resigned
1941      Louis Brandeis, Supreme Court Justice, died
1954      Hurricane Hazel began a 13-day rampage from the
              Carolinas to New York
1962      French Assembly dissolved
1964      First attempt made to dig into the tomb of Imhotep,
              an Egyptian Pharoh
          Janice Pepper married Francis Salt in England
1968      Atlanta, Georgia, Memorial Arts Center opened
```

October 6th

```
          Feast of St. Faith (or Foi, or Foy)
  69 BC   Romans defeated Armenians at Tigranocerta
 891 AD   Formosus elected Pope
1101      St. Bruno died (Feast Day)
1238      Cathedral of St. Peter, Petersborough, Northamptonshire,
              England, dedicated
1536      William Tyndale, New Testament publisher,
              executed for heresy
```

```
1764        Johann Ebel, author of the first Swiss guidebook,
                born
1773        Louis Philippe I, King of France, born
1789        March of the Women on Versailles moved the French
                government to Paris
1809        John W. Griffiths, clipper ship developer, born
1820        Jenny Lind, singer, born
1837        Samuel F. B. Morse filed for a patent on his
                improved telegraph
1846        George Westinghouse, inventor, born
1863        Quantrill's Raiders defeated the Cavalry at
                Baxter Springs, Kansas
            First Turkish bath in the U.S. opened but it
                had only one customer the first day
1866        First chapter of the Order of the Eastern Star
                organized
1867        Henry Timrod, "Poet Laureate of the Confederacy,"
                died
1868        First Maine State Fair held
1874        27th Exhibition of American Manufacturers
                opened in Philadelphia
1876        American Library Association organized
1884        Naval War College established in Newport,
                Rhode Island
1889        Thomas Edison exhibited his kinetoscope
1890        Mormon Church abolished polygamy
1892        Alfred Lord Tennyson, poet, died
1908        Austria annexed Bosnia and Hercegovina
1914        Thor Heyerdahl, explorer, born
1917        War Risk Insurance Act became law
            Peru severed diplomatic relations with Germany
1918        French and U.S. forces crossed the Aisne
            431 died when the British ship Otrano was in-
                volved in a collision off Scotland
1958        Nuclear submarine Seawolf surfaced after a 60-
                day underwater cruise
1968        Hemisfair '68 San Antonio, Texas, opened
1969        Labor Day celebrated in New South Wales, Australia
1973        Yon Kippur
```

October 7th

```
            Feast of St. Justina
            Feast of St. Osyth, Queen of the East Saxons
            Feast of St. Sergius
            Commemoration of the enthronement of Our Lady
                of Europe in Gibraltar
            Ancient Athenian festival honoring Apollo
3761 BC     The world was created (according to some
                authorities)
 336 AD     Pope St. Mark died
 929        Charles III, "the Simple," King of France died
1425        Treaty of Saumur signed by France and Brittany
```

```
1492      A false cry of "Land ho" and sighting of land
                      birds made Columbus change course
                      and miss Florida
1542      Cabrillo discovered Catalina Island, off
                      California
1571      Battle of Lepanto Gulf, Greece, where the Turks
                      were defeated by the Spanish
1573      Archbishop William Laud, persecutor of English
                      Puritans, born
1728      Caesar Rodney, signer of the Declaration of
                      Independence, born
1745      Henry Rutgers, patriot and philanthropist, born
1748      King Charles XIII of Sweden and Norway born
1763      Royal proclamation made against American
                      colonists settling west of the
                      Allegheny Mountains
          Cape Breton Island made part of Nova Scotia
1769      Captain Cook sighted New Zealand
1777      Second Battle of Saratoga, New York
1840      William I, ruler of Holland, abdicated
1849      Edgar Allan Poe, author, died
1849?     James Whitcomb Riley, "the Hoosier Poet," born
                      (he would never reveal his age)
1858      William I became regent of Germany and Prussia
1868      Cornell University opened
1870      Leon Gambetta escaped from Paris by balloon
1889      Barnard College for Women opened
1891      14 Barnard graduates became the first women to
                      earn college degrees in New York
                      City
1894      Oliver Wendell Holmes, Sr., physician-author,
                      died
1911      Vaughn Monroe, singer, born
1913      First air passenger flight made, Albany to New
                      York City
1918      Lost Batallion, 194 men still alive, rescued
1919      KLM Royal Dutch Airline, first commerical
                      airline, founded
          Versailles Peace Treaty ratified by Italy
1949      "Tokyo Rose" sentenced for propaganda broadcasts
1954      U.S. ship Mornackite sank in a storm off Virginia
          Marian Anderson became the first black hired by
                      the Metropolitan Opera Company
1955      U.S. Navy received its smallest submarine, 50 ft.
                      long, crewed by 5 men
1972      Start of a week of the Festival of the 9 Emperor
                      Gods in Singapore
```

October 8th

          Feast of St. Pelegia the Penitent
          Feast of St. Bridget
          Feast of St. Demetrius

```
                Feast of St. Keyne
                Feast of St. Margaret
                Feast of Sts. Sergius and Bacchus, patrons of
                        desert wanderers
                Feast of St. Thais
    451 AD      4th Ecumenical Council opened
    876         King Charles II, "the Bald," of France was
                        defeated by the Germans at Andernach
    1191        Prince John picked to replace Longchamp as head
                        of the English government while the
                        King crusaded
    1559        Remainder of Valladolid (Spanish Protestants
                        burned by the Inquisition)
    1754        Henry Fielding, English novelist, died
    1769        Captain Cook anchored at New Zealand
    1790        Start of 45 days of earthquakes in Algeria
    1793        John Hancock, signer of the Declaration of
                        Independence, died
    1810        Serfdom abolished in Prussia
    1829        First U.S. locomotive trip began
    1830        Johann Ebel, author of the first Swiss guidebook,
                        born
    1838        John M. Hay, statesman-writer, born
    1840        First Hawaiian constitution publicized
    1869        Franklin Pierce, U.S. President, died
    1871        If the legend is true, Mrs. O'Leary's cow kicked
                        the lantern, starting the Great
                        Chicago Fire
    1890        Eddie Rickenbacker, aviator, born
    1910        Religious orders expelled from Portugal
    1912        Balkan War began (Montenegro, Bulgaria, Serbia,
                        and Greece against Turkey)
    1918        Allies occupied Beirut
    1932        Cornerstone laid for new North Dakota capitol
    1940        Eagle Squadron formed for American volunteers
                        in the British Air Force
    1944        Wendell Willkie, U.S. presidential candidate,
                        died
    1956        Don Larsen pitched a perfect game in the World
                        Series and the Yankees beat the
                        Dodgers 2-0
    1962        Algeria joined the United Nations
    1965        Thomas B. Costain, author, died
    1969        Our Lady of the Immaculate Conception Procession
                        held on Guam
```

October 9th

```
                Feast of St. Denis, patron of France (or
                        Dionysius)
                Feast of St. John Leonardi
                Hangul - Korean National Alphabet Holiday
    709 AD      Abdalmalik, Islamic caliph, died
```

1000	Lief Ericson landed in North American (Lief Ericson Day)
1047	Pope Clement II died
1192	King Richard I of England began his ill-fated return from his Crusade
1390	King John I of Castile died
1469	Fra Filippo Lippi, Florentine artist, died
1547	Miguel Cervantes, Spanish novelist, baptized
1557	Trujillo, Venezuela, founded
1562	Fallopius, anatomist, died
1576	Frobisher, not finding the Northwest Passage, returned to London
1581	St. Louis Bertrand died (Feast Day)
1635	Roger Williams banished from Massachusetts, to found Rhode Island
1642	First commencement exercises held at Harvard University
1662	Connecticut Colony got its Royal Charter
1767	Mason and Dixon, surveyors, forced to end their "line" when their Indian guides would go no farther west
1812	U.S. captured 2 British merchant ships at Ft. Erie, Ontario
1854	Yakima Indians defeated the U.S. Infantry in Washington
1871	Great Chicago Fire ran out of fuel and went out
1888	Washington Monument opened
1899	Bruce Catton, author, born
1903	Walter O'Malley, baseball personality, born
	"Great Deluge" rainstorm hit New York City
1913	Volturno exploded in mid-ocean
1914	Antwerp, Belgium, fell to the Germans
1924	Association of Professional Ballplayers of America formed
1933	Great meteor shower
1934	Alexander I, King of Yugoslavia, assassinated
1949	Sadler Wells Ballet Company made its U.S. debut
1958	Pope Pius XII died
1962	Uganda became independent within the British Commonwealth
1963	Uganda became a republic (Independence Day)
1964	Explorer 22 launched by the U.S.
1967	U.S. freighter Panoceanic Fait sank in a Pacific storm
1969	Mi'Raj, Muslim Festival
1970	Confucius' Birthday celebrated in Hong Kong
	Cambodia became the Khmer Republic
	Our Lady of the Nazarene (Brazil)

October 10th

Oklahoma Historical Day
National Chinese Day in Surinam

	Fair at Tewkesbury, Gloucestershire, England
	Fair at Sherborne, England
	Feast of St. Gereon
644 AD	St. Paulinus of York died (Feast Day)
680	Hosain, heir to the Caliphite of Mohammed, killed in battle
1227	St. Daniel and companions martyred (Feast Day)
1486	Bartholomew Diaz, discoverer of the Cape of Good Hope, received a Portugese Royal annuity
1510	St. Francis Borgia, invoked against earthquakes, born
1572	St. Francis Borgia died (Feast Day)
1573	Spanish captured Tunis
1614	New Netherlands Company given a 3-year monopoly on the Dutch fur trade in America
1738	Benjamin West, artist, born
1765	Last French flag on the North American continent lowered for good
1794	Russians defeated Poles at Maeiejowice in the 2nd War of Polish Succession
1813	Guiseppi Verdi, Italian composer, born
1830	Queen Isabella II of Spain born
1845	U.S. Naval Academy at Annapolis opened
1858	First Butterfield Overland Mail Coach reached San Francisco from St. Louis
1861	Fridtjof Nansen, Norwegian Arctic explorer, born
1862	Stuart's Confederate Cavalry raided Chambersburg, Pennsylvania
1868	Cuba proclaimed its independence, resulting in a 10-year war with Spain
1874	Britain annexed the Fiji Islands
1885	John McClosky, first U.S. cardinal, died
1888	Mud Run, Pennslyvania, train wreck
1900	Helen Hayes, actress, born
1909	Battle monument unveiled at Point Pleasant, West Virginia
1911	Wuchang uprising began in China to overthrow the Royal family
1914	King Carol I of Rumania died
1918	Irish ship Leinster torpedoed in the St. George Channel
1938	German occupation of the Sudetenland completed as authorized by the Munich conference
	Withdrawal of 10,000 Italian troops from Spain began
1963	Limited nuclear test ban treaty went into effect
1964	Olympic Games opened in Tokyo, Japan
1969	Festival of lights celebrated in Singapore
1970	Yom Kippur
	Fiji Islands got their independence from Britain
	Double 10th National Day in Taiwan, commemorating the 1911 revolution

```
            Princess Anne Day in Maryland
            Lowestoft, Suffolk, England, fair
            Feast of St. Canice (or Cainnech or Kenneth)
  961 AD   St. Bruno died (Feast Day)
  1347     Louis IV, Holy Roman Emperor, died at a bear
               hunt
  1405     King T'aejong arrived in Seoul, Korea
  1492     Columbus's fleet sailed into debris from land
               and saw a light
  1521     Pope Leo X named King Henry VIII of England
               "Defender of the Catholic Faith"
  1586     Mary, Queen of Scots, tried for plotting
               against Queen Elizabeth I of
               England
  1592     St. Alexander Sauli died (Feast Day)
  1698     Frist Partition Treaty made, dividing Spanish
               possessions among the European
               powers, on the death of King
               Charles II
  1726     Benjamin Franklin arrived in Philadelphia
  1737     Calcutta, India, earthquake
  1746     Allies defeated by the French at Rocoux over
               the Austrian succession
  1776     British fleet on Lake Champlain defeated at
               Valcour Island
  1780     Bermuda settlements destroyed by a hurricane
  1797     Naval battle of Camperdown fought
  1799     Gen. Pulaski, Revolutionary War hero, died
               (Memorial Day)
  1809     Meriwether Lewis, of Lewis and Clark expedition,
               died
  1811     Franz Liszt, composer, born
            First steam-propelled ferry service began (New
               York City)
  1815     Pennsylvania Gazette, Philadelphia newspaper,
               ceased publication
  1853     Morrissey knocked out Sullivan in 37 rounds
  1860     Start of a U.S. Army campaign against the Navajo
               Indians of Arizona
  1865     Morant, Jamaica, swept by a slave uprising
  1870     Germans captured Orleans, France (Franco-
               Prussian War)
  1878     Santana, Kiowa Indian Chief, committed suicide
               in prison
  1880     Buffalo Evening News, New York newspaper, founded
  1884     Eleanor Roosevelt, First Lady and ambassador,
               born
  1899     Boer War began
  1910     Joseph Alsop, Jr., writer, born
  1914     Ferdinand I ascended the Rumanian throne
  1928     Graf Zeppelin left Friedrichshafen, Germany for
               Lakehurst, New Jersey
```

```
1946      Archbishop Aloysius Stepinac, Catholic Primate
                   of Yugoslavia, imprisoned for Nazi
                   collaboration
1958      Pioneer I, lunar probe, launched
1962      Second Vatican Ecumenical Council began (first
                   was in 1869)
1968      First pygmy hippo born at the Brookfield Zoo
                   (Chicago)
1968      Apollo 7, first manned flight in this series,
                   launched for 163 orbits
1970      White Sunday celebrated on Samoa
```

```
October 12th
```

```
          Feast of St. Ethelburga of Barking
          Feast of St. Wilfrid
 638 AD   Pope Honorius I died
 678      St. Leger put to death after torture
1263      Battle of Largs (Scotland and Norway)
1303      Pope Boniface VIII died
1307      15,000 Knights Templar arrested in France
1492      Columbus sighted the Bahamas (Columbus Day)
1537      King Edward VI of England born
1576      Maximilian II, Holy Roman Emperor, died, refusing
                   the last rites
1604      St. Serafino died (Feast Day)
1822      Don Pedro became constitutional emperor of Brazil
1825      Louis I became King of Bavaria
1844      George Washington Cable, author, born
1860      Elmer A. Sperry, inventor of the gyro-compass,
                   born
1861      Keel laid for the Union ironclad Monitor
1875      Granville Fortescue, soldier-playwright, born
1914      First troops from Newfoundland reached England
1915      Edith Cavell, British nurse, executed as a spy
                   by Germany
1944      Start of 11 days of hurricane in Florida
1954      Hurricane hit southwest Haiti
1955      Bernarr MacFadden, publisher, died
1964      Russia launched Voskhod I
1968      Equatorial Guinea, Spanish African colony,
                   became independent
          Mexico City Summer Olympics began
1969      Sho-de-o at Wagoner, Oklahoma
          Sonja Henie, ice skater, died of leukemia
1971      Start of the week-long celebration of Persia's
                   2,500th birthday at Persepolis,
                   Iran
          Dean Acheson, Secretary of State, died
```

	Thanksgiving Day (Canadian Holiday)
	Fair at Winchester, England
	Feast of Sts. Januarius, Faustus, Martialis, and Cordovan, martyrs
54 AD	Nero became Emperor of Rome when his mother, Agrippa, poisoned his father, Claudius
902	Great meteor shower
909	St. Gerard of Aurillac died (Feast Day)
1066	St. Edward the Confessor, King of England, died (Feast Day)
1307	59 Knights Templar burned in Paris
1399	Henry IV crowned King of England
	Geoffrey Chaucer, writer, granted a larger English royal pension
1769	Horace H. Hayden, founder of the first dental college, born
1778	First Masonic Grand Lodge organized (Williamsburg, Va.)
1792	George Washington laid the cornerstone for the White House
1812	Battle of Queenston Heights, Niagara
1825	Maximilian I, King of Bavaria, died
1838	Meteorites showered on Cold Bokkeveld, South Africa
1857	Minnesota state constitution adopted
1860	First aerial photograph in the U.S. taken, from a balloon over Boston
1894	First U.S. amateur golf championship played (Yonkers, N.Y.)
1910	Ernest Gann, author, born
1913	National Safety Council organized
1916	General Motors incorporated
1919	France ratified the Versailles Peace Treaty
1921	Yves Montand, actor, born
1924	Anatole France, French writer, died
1928	Telephone service begun between U.S. and Spain
	Marie Feodorovna, Empress Dowager of Russia, died
1932	Cornerstone laid for the new Supreme Court building
1937	Germany signed a treaty of sovereign respect with Belgium
1940	Italy declared war on Germany
1945	Milton S. Hershey, candy maker, died
1947	Largest American flag ever flown hung on the George Washington Bridge
1959	Explorer 7 launched
	Ground broken for Eisenhower Presidential Library at Abeline, Kansas
1966	A chemical plant exploded at LaSalle, Quebec
1967	St. Genevive's Apple Frolic held at Shoreham, Vermont

	Feast of St. Justus of Lyons
222 AD	Pope Callixtus I, Saint, died (Feast Day)
931	Great meteor shower
934	Great meteor shower
1002	Great meteor showers
1066	Battle of Hastings (William the Conquerer took England)
1466	Second Peace of Thorn gave Prussia to Poland
1633	King James II of England born
1644	William Penn, founder of Pennsylvania, born
1734	Francis Lightfoot Lee, signer of the Declaration of Independence, born
1773	Tea-carrying ship burned at Annapolis, Maryland
1781	American and French troops attacked the British at Yorktown, Virginia
1783	Political Intelligencer founded
1784	Ferdinand VII, King of Spain, born
1790	William Hooper, signer of the Declaration of Independence, died
1793	Marie Antoinette's trial by the French Revolutionists began
1806	Napoleon's armies were victorious at Jena and Averstadt, Prussia
1809	Peace of Schonbrunn signed by Napoleon and Austria
1834	First patent granted to a black, to Henry Blair for his seeding corn planter
1842	Croton Aqueduct system opened, bringing water to New York City
1854	First baby show in the U.S. held in Ohio
1855	Henry Wheeler Shaw, alias "Josh Billings," humorist, died
1890	Dwight D. Eisenhower, U.S. President, born
1894	E. E. Cummings, author-artist, born
1895	Paul Muni, actor, born
1899	Dismal Swamp Canal, "Washington's Ditch," reopened in Maryland
1915	Bulgaria declared war on Serbia
1923	Ankara became the capitol of Turkey
1933	Germany quit the League of Nations
1939	British battleship Royal Oak torpedoed
1949	Eleven leaders of the U.S. Communist Party convicted of a plot to overthrow the U.S. government
1954	William Willis completed his solo raft sail from Peru to Samoa
1957	Mitchel College, first on a military base, dedicated (New York)
	Queen Elizabeth II became the first reigning sovereign to open Canada's Parliament
1958	Madagascar proclaimed itself the Malagasy Republic (National Day)

1970   King's Birthday celebrated in Afghanistan

October 15th

            Romans sacrificed a war horse to Mars, god of
                war
            Feast of St. Thecla of Kitzingen
            National Poetry Day
   70 BC   Vergil, Roman poet and author of the Aeneid,
                born
  898 AD   St. Euthymius the Younger died (Feast Day)
 1106   King Philip I of France and Bertrada, his kid-
                naped bigamous wife, visited Fulk
                of Anjou, her husband
 1389   Pope Urban VI died
 1538   Royal decree exempted all but Spanish colonists
                from the Inquisition in America
 1582   St. Theresa of Avila died (Feast Day)
 1590   Giambattista Castagna elected Pope as Urban VII
 1783   First ascent by a man in a balloon made, in
                France
 1785   Jose Miguel Carrera, first President of Chile,
                born
 1795   King Frederick William IV of Prussia born
 1852   Friedrich Jahn, "father of gymnastics," died
 1856   Oscar Wilde, English author, born
 1858   Lincoln-Douglas debates ended
 1899   Dr. William C. Menninger, psychiatrist, born
 1902   Soufriere volcano on St. Vincent Island, erupted
 1903   James Street, author, born
 1904   George, King of Saxony, died
 1905   C. P. Snow, scientist-writer, born
 1908   John Kenneth Galbraith, author-statesman, born
 1910   Edwin O. Reischauer, diplomat, born
 1914   British cruiser Hawke sunk by a submarine off
                Scotland
            Mohammed Zahir Shah, King of Afghanistan, born
 1917   Arthur Schlesinger, Jr., author, born
 1922   Ferdinand I and his wife Marie crowned rulers
                of Rumania
 1923   Continental Illinois National Bank & Trust
                Company of Chicago chartered
 1924   Statue of Liberty declared a National Monument
 1928   Graf Zeppelin arrived at Lakehurst, New Jersey,
                from her home port in Germany
 1946   Hermann Goering, Nazi war criminal, committed
                suicide
 1964   Nikita Khrushchev ousted from his Soviet
                government posts
            Cole Porter, composer, died
 1969   Pumpkin Festival held at Circilville, Ohio
 1970   Sukkoth, Jewish harvest feast
            Deliverance Day in Afghanistan

1971   Confucius' birthday celebrated in Hong Kong
Bad earthquake rocked southeastern Peru

October 16th

	Gallus Day - if it is dry, so will be Spring (Feast of St. Gall)
709 AD	Mont Ste. Michael Church dedicated (France)
786	St. Lull died (Feast Day)
1080	Rudolph, King of Germany, died of his battle wounds
1243	St. Hedwig died (Feast Day)
1291	Zurich joined the Swiss Confederation
1430	James II, King of Scotland, born
1443	Unsuccessful attempt made to usurp the Japanese throne
1536	The "Pilgrimage of Grace" occupied York, England
1555	Bishops Risley and Latimer burned for their efforts to return England to Catholicism
1591	Pope Gregory XIV died
1671	Start of a weekend of earthquakes in Peru
1690	New England colonists attacked Quebec
1725	First newspaper issued in New York City
1755	St. Gerard of Majella died (Feast Day)
1758	Noah Webster, dictionary writer, born
1793	Marie Antoinette, Queen of France, guillotined
1813	Start of "The Battle of Nations" at Leipzig, Germany, where Napoleon defeated the Allies
1815	Napoleon landed in exile on St. Helena Island
1846	Ether first demonstrated as an anesthetic in surgery
1859	John Brown and his abolitionists raided Harpers Ferry, Virginia
1869	"Cardiff Giant" unearthed
1872	William H. Seward, Secretary of State and buyer of Alaska, died
1888	Eugene O'Neill, playwright, born
1891	Clark Sellers, handwriting expert, born
1898	William O. Douglas, Supreme Court Justice, born
1906	Varina Davis, "First Lady of the Confederacy," died
1909	Alaska-Yukon-Pacific Exposition in Seattle closed
1914	British repulse of the Germans at Ypres began
1925	Treaty of Locarno signed over German demilitarizati of the Rhineland
1926	1200 killed in a troopship explosion in the Yengtze River in China
1942	Bengal, India, Struck by a cyclone
1953	U.S. aircraft carrier <u>Leyte</u> damaged in Boston Harbor

1964	Communist China exploded its first atomic device
1968	Alvin, oceanograpic research submarine, sank
1971	National Newsboy Day (U.S.)

October 17th

	Feast of Sts. Ethelbert and Ethelred of Kent
	Feast of St. Etheldreda (or Audrey)
	Feast of St. Shushanik
532 AD	Pope St. Boniface II died
732	Arabs defeated at Poitiers, France, and drive back to Spain
1101	Great meteor shower
1171	Henry II, King of England, arrived in Ireland
1346	English defeated Scots at Neville's Cross
1683	Charter of Liberties and Privileges, basis of New York City government, framed
1690	St. Margaret Mary died (Feast Day)
1696	Augustus III, King of Poland, born
1740	Anne, Empress of Russia, died
1777	Burgoyne's British army surrendered at Saratoga, New York
1781	American and French forces defeated the British at Yorktown, Virginia
	Richard M. Johnson, U.S. Vice-President, born
1797	Treaty of Campo Eormio ended Napoleon's Italian campaign
1805	Napoleon defeated Austria at Ulm
1829	Chesapeake-Delaware Canal opened
1849	Frederick Chopin, composer, died
1854	British-French bombardment of Sevastopol began (Crimean War)
1879	Georgia state flag adopted
1892	First trainload of iron ore shipped out of the Mesabi Mountains of Minnesota
1893	Charles Gounod, composer of Faust, died
1900	Rosamond Marshall, novelist, born
1908	Jean Arthur, actress, born
1910	Julia Ward Howe, composer of "The Battle Hymn of the Republic," died
1915	Arthur Miller, playwright, born
1917	U.S. transport ship Antilles torpedoed
	Western Australia became connected to the other states by railroad
1918	Unsinkable Lucia became the last vessel sunk by a German submarine in World War I
1919	Radio Corporation of America incorporated
1921	Louis III, former King of Bavaria, died
1923	Bournemouth, England, radio station first broadcast
1936	Siege of Oviedo lifted in the Spanish Civil War

1965	New York World's Fair closed after its second season
1966	Lesotho, formerly Botswana, joined the United Nations
1969	National Harvest Festival held in Japan
	Indian Summer Festival held at Stillwell, Oklahoma

October 18th

	Feast of St. Luke, patron of doctors, painters, glassmakers, lacemakers, and artists
	Feast of St. Justus of Beauvais
614 AD	France got a constitution
629	Clotaire II, King of France, died
707	Pope John VII died
768	Charlemagne and his brother, Carloman, crowned co-rulers of the Frankish Empire
1417	Pope Gregory XII died, 2 days after resigning from office
1503	Pope Pius III died after less than a month on the throne
1636	New Book of Canons ordered to be used in Anglican churches
1697	Canaletto, architectural scene painter, born
1715	Peter II, Czar of Russia, born
1775	British burned Portland, Maine
	St. Paul of the Cross died
1810	Code Napoleon becmae law in Holland
1812	Wasp captured Frolic in the War of 1812
1817	National flag of Chile adopted
1818	Charles Mudie, founder of a chain of English lending libraries, born
1831	Frederick III, Emperor of Prussia and Germany, born
1833	James Clark Ross returned to England after 4 years in the Arctic
1854	Ostend Manifesto issued
1865	Peace drawn up between U.S. and the Kiowa and Comanche Indians, sending the latter to reservations
1869	La Prensa, Argentine newspaper, first published
1893	Lucy Stone, abolitionist and suffragist, died
1898	Puerto Rico surrendered to the U.S.
1908	Belgian Congo chartered as a colony
1916	Eben Rexford, composer ("Silver Threads Among the Gold") died
1919	William Waldor, Viscount Astor, author, died
1921	Pilot Club International organized
	Congress ratified the peace treaty with Germany and Austria

```
1945    Public opening ceremony for Connecticut
                governor's mansion held
1954    Hurricane Hazel's 13 days of devastation ended
1962    Ranger 5, lunar probe, launched
1964    First season of the New York World's Fair ended
1970    Monkey God Festival held in Singapore
1971    Festival of Lights held in India
```

October 19th
```
        Ancient Romans held a ceremony honoring Mars,
                the god of war, storing their
                weapons for the winter
        Feast of St. Frideswide, patron of Oxford, England
202 BC  Solar eclipse
        Romans defeated Hannibal at Zama (Second Punic
                War)
125     Beginning of the Tyrian Era
439 AD  Vandals took Carthage, Africa
615     Deusdedit elected Pope
946     St. John of Rila died (Feast Day)
1202    Great meteor shower
1216    King John "Lackland" of England died of eating
                too many peaches washed down
                with beer
1314    Frederick III chosen King of Germany
1469    Isabella of Castile married Ferdinand of Aragon,
                uniting Spain
1552    Siege of Metz begun by Charles V, Holy Roman
                Emperor
1562    George Abbott, Archbishop of Canterbury and
                preparer of the King James version
                of the Bible, born
        St. Peter of Alcantara died (Feast Day)
1630    First general court held at Boston, Massachusetts
1745    Jonathan Swift, writer, died
1749    William Ged, stereotype inventor, died
1781    British surrender at Yorktown, Virginia, ended
                the Revolutionary War
1790    Lyman Hall, signer of the Declaration of
                Independence, died
1810    Cassius Clay, American politician, born
1812    Napoleon began the retreat from Moscow
1813    Allies, after a 3-day battle, defeated Napoleon
                at Leipzig, Germany
1818    Chickasaw Indians treatied away their lands
                east of the Mississippi River
1850    Richmond Dispatch newspaper founded in Virginia
1864    Union Cavalry victorious at Cedar Hill, Virginia
        St. Albans, Vermont, raided by Confederate
                soldiers
1870    Cambria lost off Inishtrahull
1889    Fannie Hurst, novelist, born
```

```
                King Louis I of Portugal died
1911            Manchu dynasty power in China ended in revolution
1915            Carranza's government in Mexico recognized by
                        the U.S.
1920            First scheduled airline service in the West begun,
                        Barranquilla to Giradot, Colombia
1945            N. C. Wyeth, illustrator, died
1950            Edna St. Vincent Millay, poetess, died
1951            War with Germany formally ended by the U.S.
1954            Mt. Cho Oyu (26,750 ft.) on the Nepal-Tibet
                        border climbed by an Austrian team
1956            Beginning of a 3-day Polish uprising to be more
                        independent of Moscow
1958            Brussels, Belgium World Fair closed
```

```
October 20th ───────────────────────────────────────────────
```

```
                On the Tuesday following, a 2-day fair opens at
                        Gainsborough, Lincolnshire, England
                Kenyatta Day celebrations in Kenya, Africa
                Feast of St. John of Kanti
 766 AD         St. Andrew of Crete died (Feast Day)
1187            Pope Urban III died of dysentery
1314            Louis IV crowned King of Germany
1382            St. Mary's College founded at Westminster, England
1518            Florence, Italy, requested the remains of the
                        writer Dante be moved there
1536            "Pilgrimage of Grace" captured Pontefract Castle,
                        England
1616            Thomas Bartholin, Danish physician and tracer
                        of the lymphatic system, born
1632            Sir Christopher Wren, English architect, born
1740            Charles VI, Emperor of Austria and last male
                        Hapsburg, died
                Prussians under Frederick the Great captured
                        Breslau, Austria
1791            Williams College, Williamstown, Massachusetts,
                        opened
1827            Naval battle of Navarino fought
1853            Benjamin Harrison, U.S. President, married
                        Caroline L. Scott
1859            Minerva Society, first U.S. women's club,
                        organized at New Harmony, Indiana
1869            Cochise's Apache Indians attempted to ambush
                        the U.S. First Cavalry at
                        Chiricahua Pass
1880            Lydia Child, novelist-abolitionist, died
1883            First vocational school in the U.S. established
                        (Baltimore)
1884            France declared a blockade of Formosa
1890            Sir Richard Burton, explorer, died
                Pike's Peak railroad completed
1894            Second French Panama Canal company formed
```

1900	Senator Wayne Morse born
1911	Amundsen and his dog sleds set out for the South Pole
1918	Germany accepted Wilson's "14 Points" and withdrew its submarines
1922	St. Bertilla Boscardin died (Feast Day)
1925	Art Buchwald, columnist-author, born
1926	Havana, Cuba, hit by a hurricane
1931	Mickey Mantle, baseball star, born
1936	Women given full rights in the United Lutheran Church
1943	Two U.S. Navy tankers collided off Palm Beach, Florida
1944	Gen, MacArthur kept his "I will return" promise to the Philippines
1950	North Korean captial, Pyongyang, captured by U.N. forces
1960	New York Times published simultaneously in New York and Paris
	Mechanized post office experiment effected in Providence Rhode Island
1964	Herbert Clark Hoover, U.S. President, died
1968	Jacqueline Kennedy, widowed First Lady, married Aristotle Onassis

October 21st

	Formerly Feast of St. Ursula, patron of educators of young girls; invoked for a good death
	Feast of St. Hilarion
	Feast of St. Viator
	Ancient Greek festival held honoring Thesis
635 AD	St. Fintan of Taghmon died (Feast Day)
1096	French and German members of the First Crusade defeated by the Turks at Nicaea
1187	Alberto diMora became Pope Gregory VIII
1379	St. John of Bridlington died (Feast Day)
1422	King Charles VI of France died
1520	Magellan entered the Straits of Magellan
1600	Battle of Sekigahara, Japan
1639	Dutch defeated Spaniards at the Battle of the Downs
1669	Arlington National Cemetery grounds presented to Robert Howsen for services
1692	William Penn was deposed as Governor of Pennsylvania
1772	Samuel Taylor Coleridge, poet, born
1803	U.S. Senate ratified the Louisiana Purchase
1805	Nelson and the British fleet defeated the combined French and Spanish off Trafalgar (Trafalgar Day in England)
1808	Samuel F. Smith, composer of "America," etc., born

```
1822       Russians were 6 months to get out of California
1833       Alfred B. Nobel, inventor of dynamite and donor
               of the Nobel Prizes, born
1854       Florence Nightingale set out for the Crimea
1868       Sir Ernest Dunlop Swinton, "father of the
               military tank," born
1872       Germany gave the San Juan Islands to the U.S.
1879       Thomas A. Edison invented the electric light
1892       Grounds dedicated for the World Columbian
               Exposition in Chicago
1917       Oil discovered at Ranger, Texas
           "Dizzy" Gillespie, jazz musician, born
1921       Austrian national flag adopted
1928       "Whitey" Ford, baseball player, born
1929       First air ambulance service organized
1930       Solar eclipse
1935       Haiti hit by a terrific storm
1936       Siege of Madrid begun by Spanish insurgents
1940       New York World's Fair closed after its second
               season
1944       A liquid gas tank exploded at Cleveland, Ohio
1954       Cornerstone laid for New York City's coliseum
1958       Two peeresses inducted as the first women in
               England's House of Lords
1959       Solomon R. Guggenheim Museum in New York City,
               designed by Frank Lloyd Wright,
               dedicated
1960       Queen Elizabeth II launched England's first
               nuclear-powered submarine
1962       Century 21 Exposition, Seattle, Washington,
               closed
1965       An explosion on a bridge at Tila Bund, Pakistan
1969       Jack Kerouac, novelist, died
1970       John T. Scopes, defendant in the "Monkey Trial,"
               died
           Zond 8, Russian lunar orbiter, launched
           Black Christ Festival held at Portabello, Panama
1971       ITOS-2, U.S. weather satellite, launched
```

October 22nd

```
           Feast of St. Donatus of Fiesole
2137 BC    Solar eclipse
 304 AD    St. Philip of Heraclea died (Feast Day)
 685       Two giant pandas were presented to the Japanese
               emperor by the Chinese emperor
 741       Charles Martel, "the Hammer," Frankish ruler,
               died
 995       First saints canonized
1303       Nicholas Boccasini elected Pope as Benedict XI
1383       Ferdinand I, King of Portugal, died
1707       English ship Association sank with 800 aboard
1715       Peter II, Czar of Russia, born
```

```
1721      First birthday of the Russian Empire celebrated
1746      Princeton University chartered
1766      Settlement at Pensacola, Florida, hit by a
               hurricane
1797      First public parachute descent made at Paris,
               France
1799      Raleigh Register, North Carolina newspaper,
               founded
1806      Thomas Sheraton, English furniture maker, died
1811      Franz Liszt, composer, born
1844      Date predicted for the second coming of Christ
1845      Sarah Bernhardt, actress, born
1882      N. C. Wyeth, illustrator, born
          New York, Chicago & St. Louis Railroad ran its
               first train
1883      Metropolitan Opera's grand opening presented
               Faust
1894      Shonai, Japan, rocked by an earthquake
1905      Constance Bennett, actress, died
1917      Joan Fontaine, actress, born
1918      Height of the great flu epidemic that killed about
               20 million people all over the
               world
1944      Battle of Leyte Gulf, Philippines, began, the
               largest naval battle ever
1952      Philippine Islands hit by a typhoon
1954      West Germany was accepted as a member of NATO
1962      President Kennedy announced a missile buildup
               in Cuba
1965      Roger Williams National Memorial established
1966      U.S. freighter Golden State and Philippine
                    Pioneer Leyte collided in Manila
                    Bay
1969      Cajun Yam Festival held in Louisiana
```

October 23rd

```
          Feast of St. James (Iakovos - Eastern Orthodox)
          Swallows leave Capistrano, California
4004 BC   Earth created at 9 a.m. according to James
               Ussher, 17th Century Irish
               churchman
 304 AD   St. Severus died
 877      St. Ignatius of Constantinople died (Feast Day)
1157      Valdemar I, King of Denmark, defeated a rival,
               Sweyn III, at the battle of Grathe
               Heath
1260      Kotuz, Egyptian caliph, murdered by an aide who
               assumed his office
1366      Great meteor shower
1385      University of Heidelberg, Germany, founded
1456      St. John of Capistrano died
1520      Charles V crowned Holy Roman Emperor
```

1526	Ferdinand I elected King of Bohemia
1717	Compulsory education effected in Prussia
1764	British defeated Indian forces at Buxar, India
1799	William Paca, signer of the Declaration of Independence, died
1835	Adlai Stevenson, U.S. Vice-President, born
1844	Robert Bridges, English Poet Laureate, born
1850	National Women's Rights Convention held (Worcester, Mass.)
1870	St. Anthony Claret died (Feast Day)
1871	Dr. Livingston reached Ujiji, Africa, to pick up supplies, again
1899	Emily Kimbrough, author, born
1910	Phra Paramindr Maha Chulalongkorn, King of Siam, died
1917	First U.S. shot fired in World War I
1921	John Boyd Dunlop, pioneer in pneumatic rubber tires, died
1925	Gore Vidal, novelist-dramatist, born
	Johnny Carson, television personality, born
1937	Suiyvan Province declared independent of China
1939	Zane Grey, western author, died
1942	British defeated Germans at El Alamein, North Africa
1944	End of 11 days of hurricane in Florida
1945	Vidkun Quisling, pro-Nazi Norwegian Premier, executed
1946	Ernest Thompson Seton, naturalist-author, died
1956	Hungarian Revolt against Communism began
1961	Giant nuclear blast set off by Russia in spite of world protests

---

October 24th

	Feast of St. Raphael the Archangel
	Feast of St. Felix of Thibiuca
	U.N. Day - Korean National Holiday
51 AD	Domitian, Roman Emperor, born
996	Hugh Capet, King of France, died
1147	King Alfonso I of Portugal captured Lisbon from the Moors
1273	Rudolph I crowned King of Germany
1375	Valdemar III, King of Denmark, died
1533	Great meteor shower
1537	Jane Seymour, 3rd wife of King Henry VIII of England, died
1605	Jahangir crowned Emperor of India
1632	Anton Van Leeuwenhoek, microscope pioneer, born
1648	Peace of Westphalia ended the 30 Years' War between the Holy Roman Empire and France
1774	Edenton, North Carolina, tea party held

```
1788        Sarah J. B. Hale, author of "Mary Had a Little
                    Lamb," born
1808        Gaceta de Caracas, Venezuelan newspaper, first
                    published
1852        Daniel Webster, statesman-orator, died
1897        Chittagong, India, hit by a cyclone and flood
1904        First real subway in New York City opened
            Moss Hart, playwright, born
1926        Charles M. Russell, artist, died
1944        Japanese battleship Musashi sunk by U.S. planes
            U.S. aircraft carrier Princeton exploded off
                    Leyte
1945        Argentina, Brazil, Chile, China, Cuba, Czechoslavakia
                    Denmark, Dominican Republic,
                    Egypt, El Salvador, France, Great
                    Britain, Haiti, Iran, Lebanon,
                    Luxembourg, New Zealand, Nicaragua,
                    Paraguay, Philippines, Poland, Russia,
                    Saudi Arabia, Syria, Turkey, United
                    States, and Yugoslavia all joined
                    the United Nations (U.N. Day in
                    U.S.)
            Viet Nam established in French Indo-China
1949        U.S. Consul General at Mukden, Manchuria,
                    arrested by the Communists
1966        President Johnson's meetings on Viet Nam opened
                    in Manila
1969        Southern California rocked by earthquakes
            King Tutankamen of Egypt was discovered to have
                    died of a blow to the head about
                    3,000 years ago
1970        Pumpkin Festival held at Circleville, Ohio
1972        Jackie Robinson, first black major league baseball
                    player, died


October 25th
----------------------------------------------------------

            Thanksgiving Day in the Virgin Islands, marking
                    the end of the hurricane season
            Feast of Sts. Chrysanthus and Daria
            Feast of Sts. Crispin and Crispinian, patrons of
                    leatherworkers and shoemakers
            Feast of St. Gaudentius of Brescia
            Feast of St. Isadore the Farm-servant
  39 BC     Roman triumph held for Pollio
 625 AD     Pope Boniface V died
 721        St. John of Beverly died (Feast Day)
1147        German segment of the Second Crusade defeated by
                    the Saracens at Dorylaeum
1154        Stephen, King of England, died
1241        Godfrey di Castigione became Pope as Celestine IV
1314        Frederick III crowned King of Germany
1340        Geoffrey Chaucer, English writer, born
```

1400	Geoffrey Chaucer, English writer
1415	Battle of Agincourt (Henry V of England defeated France)
1555	Charles V, Holy Roman Emperor and King of Spain, resigned all titles to live in a monastery
1692	Elizabeth Farnese, Queen of Spain, born
1764	John Adams, U.S. President, married Abigail Smith
	William Hogarth, English artist, died
1779	British evacuated Newport, Rhode Island
1781	Johnstown, New York, became the site of the last Revolutionary War battle
1812	U.S.S. United States defeated British Macedonian
1825	Johann Strauss, composer, born
1838	Georges Bizet, French opera composer (Carmen, etc.) born
1854	The Light Brigade charged at Balaklava in the Crimean War
1859	Chester A. Arthur, U.S. President, married Ellen L. Heredon
	Royal Charter was shipwrecked
1870	Postcard first used in the U.S.
1881	Pablo Picasso, artist, born
1888	Richard E. Byrd, polar explorer, born
1901	Northwest Province, frontier of British India, created
1918	Canadian ship Princess Sophia sank off Alaska
1920	King Alexander of Greece died
1921	King Michael I of Yugoslavia born
1924	Shenandoah completed the first transcontinental airship voyage
1927	Italian ship Principessa Mafalda exploded off Brazil
1931	George Washington Bridge, connecting New York and New Jersey, opened
1944	10 Japanese ships sunk in the Second Battle of the Philippine Sea
1945	Greece joined the United Nations
1947	Bar Harbor, Maine, ravaged by a forest fire
1960	A gas explosion blew up a Windsor, Ontario, store
1962	Uganda joined the United Nations
1966	End of President Johnson's meetings on Viet Nam in Manila, Philippines
1970	40 martyrs of the English Reformation canonized
	Restoration (to China) Day celebrated on Taiwan
	Czechoslovakian folk activities performed at Masaryktown, Florida
1971	United Nations voted Communist China in and Nationalist China out of its membership

October 26th

	Stock fair held at Grantham, Lincolnshire, England
1289 AD	Montpellier, France, medical and law schools united into a university
1529	The Papal legate left England without agreeing to give King Henry VIII his divorce
1644	Second Battle of Newbury, England
1664	Marines organized in England
1673	Demetrius, Prince of Moldavia, born
1676	"Bacon's Rebellion" in Virginia ended with his death
1764	William Hogarth, British artist, died
1784	Pennsylvania Evening Post & Daily Advertiser, first U.S. daily newspaper, ceased publication
1793	National Gazette newspaper ceased publication
1803	Joseph A. Hansom, cab inventor, born
1860	Victor Emmanuel, King of Italy, and Garibaldi, liberation fighter, shook hands
1868	Illinois state seal first used
1896	Italian-Abysinnian War ended
1902	Elizabeth Cady Stanton, suffragist, died
1914	Jackie Coogan, child actor, born
	British battleship Audacious mined off Lough Swilly
1919	Shah Mohammed Reza Pahlavi of Iran born (national holiday)
	Senator Edward Brooke born
1923	Charles Steinmetz, electrical engineer, born
1940	Empress of Britain torpedoed off Ireland
1942	President Coolidge hit a mine in the South Pacific
	U.S. aircraft carrier Hornet damaged in the Battle of the Santa Cruz Islands
1966	Fire broke out aboard the aircraft carrier Oriskany off North Viet Nam
1967	Shah of Iran crowned
1968	Flusing Meadow Park Zoo opened (New York City)
	Soyus III, Russian manned orbiting space vehicle, launched
1972	Igor Sikorsky, helicopter inventor, died

October 27th

	Feast of St. Frumentius
	Feast of St. Procula, wife of Pontius Pilate (Orthodox)
	Navy Day held at McAlester, Oklahoma
97 AD	Nerva, Roman Emperor, adopted Trajan as his successor

312	Maxentius, Roman Emperor, drowned
1401	Catherine, wife of King Henry V of England, born
1439	King Albert II of Germany died
1553	Michael Servetus, Spanish physician, burned for heresy
1590	Pope Urban VII died
1602	Great meteor shower
1650	William II, stadtholder of Orange (ruler of Holland), died
1659	Two Quakers hanged for returning to Massachusetts Bay Colony after expulsion
1682	William Penn, Pennsylvania founder, first landed in America
1776	A Danish fort in the Virgin Islands became the first foreign nation to salute the U.S. flag when it exchanged salutes with a U.S. schooner
1780	Solar exlipse
1793	Eliphalet Remington, firearms manufacturer, born
1829	First baby carriage patent in the U.S. issued
1834	Don Carlos, Carlist claimant to the Spanish throne, was deprived of his inheritance
1858	Theodore Roosevelt, 26th U.S. President, born
1868	First meeting of the Ancient Order of United Workmen held, at Meadville, Pennsylvani
1869	The "Stonewall" burned near Cairo, Illinois
1880	Theodore Roosevelt, U.S. President, married Alice H. Lee
1904	First electric New York subway opened, running from the Brooklyn Bridge to midtown Manhattan
1914	Dylan Thomas, poet, born
1915	Shakleton's party abandoned their ice-crushed ship in the Antarctic
1918	Theresa Wright, actress, born
1919	Versailles Peace Treaty ratified by Japan
1920	40,000 Philadelphia textile workers were discharged to get the radicals out of the factories
1925	Train wreck near Victoria, Mississippi
1931	Cornerstone laid for Theodore Roosevelt Memorial Hall at the Museum of Natural History, New York
1936	(Wallis) Warfield Simpson, Duchess of Windsor, got a divorce
1938	DuPont announced the invention of nylon
1944	Battle of Leyte Gulf ended in the destruction of Japan's naval power
1947	"Last" Japanese soldier on Guadal Canal captured, for the third time
1949	Southeastern India hit by a cyclone
1952	Jigme Dorji Wangchuk became the Dragon King of Bhutan

```
1959      Mexico hit by a hurricane
1961      Mauritania and Mongolia joined the United
               Nations
          Super aircraft carrier Constellation commissioned
1962      Thailand hit by a terrific storm
1964      Art Afrons in his "Green Minster" set a land-
               speed record of 536.71 mph, the
               first over 500 mph
1967      Expo '67, in Montreal, Canada World's Fair,
               closed
          Theodore Roosevelt Monument on his Potomac
               Island dedicated
1968      Mexico City Summer Olympics ended
1969      Northern Yugoslavia rocked by a strong earth-
               quake
1970      Zond 8, Russian lunar orbiter, returned to
               earth
```

October 28th

```
          Greek National Day
          Fair at Walsall, Staffordshire, England
          Annual fair at Rochdale, Lancashire, England
          Feast of St. Faro
          Feast of St. Jude Thaddeus, patron of the
               impossible
          Feast of St. Simon, patron of curriers
 312 AD   A bridge of boats over the Tiber River in
               Italy collapsed
1017      Henry III, "the Black," Holy Roman Emperor,
               born
1348      Third wave of the Great Plague hit the Old
               World
1351      Fair held at Droitwich, England
1359      King Edward III of England landed at Calais,
               France
1412      Margaret, Queen of Scandinavia, died
1435      Ladislaus V crowned King of Bohemia
1492      Columbus discovered Cuba
1636      Harvard College founded by the Massachusetts
               Bay Colony
1646      John Eliot, apostle to the New England Indians,
               preached his first sermon
1701      Pennsylvania's colonial charter revised
1707      Oweri and Mino, Japan, rocked by an earthquake
1709      St. Demetrius of Rostov died (Russian Orthodox
               Feast Day)
1726      Gulliver's Travels first published
1776      British defeated Americans at the Battle of
               White Plains, New York
1865      Florida repealed its secession
1875      Gilbert H. Grosvernor, author and National
               Geographic editor, born
```

1880	Fingerprints first advocated in print for criminal identification
1886	Statue of Liberty dedicated by President Cleveland
1891	Japan rocked by an earthquake
1892	Roumania wrecked off Portugal
1902	Elsa Lancaster, actress, born
1906	Train wrecked near Atlantic City, New Jersey
1914	Dr. Jonas Salk, polio vaccine discoverer, born
1918	Czechoslovakia proclaimed a free, independent republic (Nationalization Day)
1919	Congress passed the Volstead Prohibition Act over the presidential veto
1922	Fascists took over the Italian government
1937	Spanish Loyalist government moved to Barcelona
1945	The Stage Door Canteen closed, having entertained 3.2 million servicemen
	Shoe rationing in the U.S. ended
1949	First U.S. woman ambassador, Eugenie Anderson, sworn in
1958	Angelo Guiseppe Roncalli was elected Pope as John XXIII
1960	Chartres Cathedral celebrated its 700th anniversary
1962	Kennedy and Khrushchev came to an agreement on the Cuban missile crisis

---
October 29th

Turkey Republic Day
Fair day at Midhurst, Sussex, England
Annual livestock fair at Marlow, Buckinghamshire, England
Feast of St. Colman of Kilmacduagh

1185 AD	Henry, heir to Gemany and the Holy Roman Empire, betrothed to Constance, daughter of the King of Sicily
1268	Conradin, contender for the throne of Sicily, executed
1591	Gianntonio Faschinetii elected Pope as Innocent IX
1618	Sir Walter Raleigh, courtier, explorer, and colonizer, executed for conspiring against James I
1709	First Barrier Treaty between England and Holland signed
1795	John Keats, poet, born
1808	Last punishment for witchcraft administered in England
1814	Demologos or Fulton the First, first steamship of war, launched
1815	Daniel D. Emmett, composer of "Dixie," born
1838	Mormons massacred at Hanu's Mill, Missouri
1858	First store opened in Denver, Colorado

1863	International Red Cross flag adopted
1867	50 vessels wrecked in a hurricane in the Virgin Islands
1881	The Judge, a New York comic weekly, founded
1889	British South African Company chartered
1900	Westminster became a city within London, England
1908	Comet Morehouse photographed
1911	Joseph Pulitizer, publisher and prize founder, died
1912	Size of the U.S. flag set by presidential order
1918	King George V of England named an honorary Japanese field marshall
1924	Frances E. H. Burnett, author of Little Lord Fauntleroy, died
	Ends of the Holland Tunnel met under the Hudson River, New York City
1928	Graf Zeppelin left Lakehurst, New Jersey, to return to Germany
1929	Wall Street crash began the U.S. Great Depression
1939	Golden Gate International Exposition, San Francisco, closed
1950	Gustav V, King of Sweden, died
1956	Israel invaded Egypt's Sinai Peninsula
1958	Jet flights between New York and Paris began
1970	Deepavali or Festival of Lights celebrated in India and Ceylon

---

October 30th

? BC	Noah began to fill the ark, according to some authorities
298 AD	St. Marcellus the Centurion died (Feast Day)
1536	Lutheranism became the official religion in Denmark
	Frederick II named heir to Norway and Denmark
1611	King Charles IX of Sweden died
1617	St. Alphonsus Rodriguez died (Feast Day)
1735	John Adams, 2nd U.S. President, born
1764	Gorham, Maine, incorporated.
1812	Juvenile Port Fol o, a children's weekly, founded in Philadelphia by a fourteen-year-old
1823	Edmund Cartwright, power-loom inventor, died
1864	Town of Helena, Montana, organized
1885	Ezra Pound, author, born
	Force Publique, Congo's policing army, established
1893	World's Columbian Exposition, Chicago, closed
	Charles Atlas, ex-97-lb.-weakling, born
1905	Imperial Manifesto made Russia a semi-constitutional monarchy

1918	Turkey, defeated, signed the World War I armistice
	Ted Williams, baseball player, born
1922	Italian Fascists marched on Rome
1938	Orson Wells did his "War of the Worlds" radio broadcast
1945	India joined the United Nations
1957	Jamestown, Virginia's 350th anniversary celebration ended
1961	Russia fired another giant nuclear blast over world opposition
1965	An explosion leveled the marketplace at Cartagena, Colombia

---

October 31st

	Halloween or All Hallow's Eve
	Protestant Reformation Day
	Youth Honor Day (Iowa)
	Feast of St. Bee
	Feast of St. Quentin, invoked against coughs
655 AD	St. Foillan died (Feast Day)
994	St. Wolfgang died (Feast Day)
1345	Ferdinand I, King of Portugal, born
1442	Wladislaus III, King of Poland, born
1512	Michelangelo's Sistine Chapel ceiling unveiled
1517	Luther nailed his 95 Theses on the Church door
1623	Jan Vermeer, Dutch artist, born
1705	Pope Clement XIV born
1740	William Paca, signer of the Declaration of Independence, born
1776	British fell back from the Battle of White Plains because of a storm (New York)
1791	National Gazette newspaper founded
1800	National Intelligencer, a tri-weekly political newspaper, founded
1861	Missouri seceded from the Union
1864	Nevada became a state
1867	Bakargani, India, flooded
1868	Meiji Tenno crowned Emperor of Japan
1876	Noak Hali, India, devastated by a storm wave
1886	First service held in the first Christian Science Church to be built
1887	Generalissimo Chiang Kai-Shek, Chinese Statesman, born
1898	Trans-Mississippi International Exposition at Omaha, Nebraska, closed
1900	Ethel Waters, actress, born
	National flag of Ecuador adopted
1902	Cable completed from Brisbane, Australia, to Vancouver, British Columbia, Canada
1907	Royal University of Ireland became the National University of Ireland

1928	Graf Zeppelin arrived in Friedrichshafen, Germany, from U.S.
1934	Century of Progress Exposition, Chicago, closed after its second season
1939	New York World's Fair ended its second season
1941	U.S. destroyer Reuben James torpedoed in the North Atlantic
1945	Peru joined the United Nations
1949	Philippine Islands hit by a typhoon
1956	British and French bombarded Cairo when Egypt refused a ceasefire with Israel
	Cardinal Mindszenty of Hungary released from prison
1960	East Pakistan hit by a cyclone and tidal waves
	Crown Prince Reza Pahlavi of Iran born
1961	British Honduras hit by a hurricane
1963	Explosion damaged the State Fair Coliseum at Indianapolis, Indiana
1968	Ramon Novarro, silent screen star, murdered

NOVEMBER

Full Moon - Beavers' Moon, Hunters' Moon
First week - International Cat Week
First Tuesday after the first Monday - U.S. Election
                Day
First Saturday after the 11th - Sadie Hawkins Day
                (U.S.)
Second Sunday - World Fellowship Sunday, beginning
                World Fellowship Week
Second weekend - Black Leggings Warrior Society
                Meeting, Anadarko, Oklahoma
Fourth Thursday - Thanksgiving (U.S.)
Sunday nearest the 30th - Beginning of the Christian
                Advent

November 1st

```
          Ancient Roman Festival of Pomona honoring
                Nike-Victoria
          Druid harvest celebration
          Liberty Day (Virgin Islands)
          Feast of St. Benignus
          All Saints' Day
 79 AD    Pompeii buried by a Mt. Vesuvius eruption
                (Italy)
 670      St. Omer died
 846      King Louis II, "The Stammerer," of France born
1216      Fourth Lateran Council began
1500      Benevenuto Cellini, Italian artist, born
1503      Guiliano della Rovere bargained for and was
                elected Pope as Julius II
```

1636	Nicholas Boileau-Despreaux, French poet, born
1700	King Charles II of Spain died, their last Hapsburg king
1755	Lisbon, Portugal, destroyed by an earthquake
1756	Casanova, jailed as a spy, escaped
1765	Stamp Act went into effect in the American colonies
1778	King Gustavus IV of Sweden born
1835	Texas independence from Mexico proclaimed
1839	Seminole Indians attacked, protesting their removal from Florida
1861	George B. McClellan became Union Commander in Chief
1800	Stephen Crane, author of Red Badge of Courage, born
1880	Grantland Rice, author, born
1881	State of North Borneo chartered by Britain
1894	Alexander III, Czar of Russia, died
	Waipara wrecked off New Zealand
1905	Rasputin first met the Russian Imperial family
1908	"Brighton Belle," celebrated British train, made its first run
1914	Two British cruisers sunk in the Battle of Coronel
1917	Union Carbide and Carbon Corporation organized
1918	Austria and Hungary formed separate republics
1919	John H. Secondari, broadcaster-author, born
1922	Turkish Assembly abolished the Sultanate
1929	Albert Fall, U.S. Secretary of the Interior, sentenced for his part in the Teapot Dome scandal
1939	First commercial oil well in Nebraska came in
1945	Australia joined the United Nations
1948	Solar eclipse
1950	Two Puerto Rican separatists attempted to assassinate President Truman
1952	First hydrogen bomb exploded (Eniwetok Atoll, Pacific)
1958	Beginning of 5 days of severe storms in East Pakistan
1962	Mars I launched by Russia to study Mars
1963	First U.S. Christmas stamp went on sale
	Russia launched the Polyot I satellite
	President Diem of Viet Nam assassinated
1969	Chesapeake Appreciation Day
	Queen Elizabeth II of England began a South American tour
1972	Ezra Pound, writer, died

All Souls' Day
1328 AD James the Butler named Irish Earl of Ormonde
1470   King Edward IV of England born
1697   Transit of Mercury
1734   Daniel Boone, frontiersman, born
1795   James K. Polk, 11th U.S. President, born
1800   Pope Pius VII left Rome to crown Napoleon
                    Emperor
1833   Horace H. Furness, Shakesperean scholar, born
1865   Warren G. Harding, U.S. President, born
1866   First encampment of the Grand Army of the
                    Republic held at Indianapolis
1867   Harper's Bazaar magazine founded
1878   Cleveland Penny Press newspaper began
                    publication
1887   Jenny Lind, singer, died
1889   North and South Dakota became states
1901   Pan American Exposition, Buffalo, New York
                    closed
1909   William Powell Firth, English artist, died
1913   Burt Lancaster, actor, born
1917   Balfour Declaration favored the establishment
                    of a Jewish state in Palestine
                    (England)
         Modern Norwegian army founded
1918   Malbone Street subway tunnel wrecked (Brooklyn,
                    New York)
1920   First commercial radio station established
1930   Haile Selassie crowned Emperor of Ethiopia
1936   BBC began regular television broadcasts in
                    England
1938   Partition of Czechoslovakia completed by the
                    Vienna Council
1945   Costa Rica and Liberia joined the United
                    Nations
1949   Indonesia granted its independence by the
                    Netherlands
1961   James Thurber, author-artist, died
1962   Dismantling of the Cuban missile sites began
1965   Proton II satellite launched by Russia
1969   Veteran Autos Run held, London to Brighton,
                    England
1970   Richard, Cardinal Cushing, of Boston died

November 3rd

         Feast of St. Hubert, patron of hunters, forest-
                    ers, furriers, smelterers, makers
                    of precision instruments; invoked
                    against rabies and for the protec-
                    tion of dogs

```
              Feast of St. Silvia
              Feast of St. Winifred
              Panama Independence Day (Canal Zone)
    361 AD    Flavius Julius Constantius, Roman Emperor,
                  died
   1002       English, led by Ethelred the Unready,
                  massacred the Danes
   1148       St. Malachy died (Feast Day)
   1493       Columbus discovered Dominica
   1591       City of Guanare, Venezuela, founded
   1616       Charles I, future ill-fated King of England,
                  made Prince of Wales
   1639       St. Martin de Porres, patron of integration
                  workers, died (Feast Day)
   1640       England's Long Parliament met (dissolved
                  by Cromwell in 1653)
   1749       Daniel Rutherford, discoverer of nitrogen,
                  born
   1760       Battle of Torgou (Seven Years' War)
   1782       Britain recognized the United States
   1783       Continental Army disbanded by Congress
   1794       William Cullen Bryant, editor-poet, born
   1801       Vincenzo Bellini, opera composer, born
   1811       First steamboat trip on the Ohio River began
   1814       Napoleon's trial, the Congress of Vienna,
                  opened
   1839       Beginning of the Opium War between England
                  and China
   1844       Mohammed V, Sultan of Turkey, born
   1852       Meiji Tenno, Emperor of Japan, born
   1859       San Francisco vigilante committee disbanded
              First business college in U.S. opened
                  (Poughkeepsie, N.Y.)
   1865       Harvard Club of New York City founded
              Mescalero Apaches disappeared, not to be
                  seen again for 7 years
   1879       Vilhjalmur Stefansson, Arctic explorer, born
   1883       Women's Christian Temperance Union founded
              American Indians declared aliens and depen-
                  dents by the U.S. Supreme Court
   1900       First U.S. auto show opened, in New York City
   1901       King Leopold III of Belgium born
   1903       Republic of Panama, independent of Colombia,
                  proclaimed, starting a war
   1914       British bombarded the forts at the Dardanelles
   1916       Connemara and Retriever collided in the Irish
                  Sea
   1917       First U.S. soldiers were killed in World War I
   1918       Bob Feller, baseball pitcher, born
   1928       Latin alphabet introduced in Turkey
   1935       Greece voted to restore the monarchy
   1940       Laurentic torpedoed
   1942       U.S.-Alaskan highway completed
```

1953	First U.S. coast-to-coast color television broadcast
1960	U.S. launched the Explorer VIII satellite
1962	Britain's first woman ambassador, Barbara Salt appointed to Israel
1964	Citizens of Washington, D.C., first got to vote in a presidential election
1969	Japanese Culture Day

November 4th

	Thanksgiving Day in Liberia
1031 AD	St. Emeric killed in a hunting accident (Feast Day)
1212	St. Felix of Valois died
1520	Christian II of Denmark and Norway crowned King of Sweden
1575	Guido Reni, Italian artist, born
1576	"Fury of Antwerp" (Spanish settlers in the Low Countries raided their leaders' treasuries and paid themselves)
1584	St. Charles Borromeo died (Feast Day)
1650	William III, King of England and ruler of Holland, born
1677	William III and Mary, co-rulers of England, married
1698	British settlers arrived at Darien on the Spanish Main
1743, 1822, 1868	Transits of Mercury
1766	King Gustavus III of Sweden married Sophia Magdalena of Denmark
1769	Don Gaspar discovered San Francisco Bay
1790	Carlos Antonio Lopez, ruler of Paraguay, born
1791	St. Clair fought and defeated the Miami Indians (Ohio)
1794	Russians defeated Poles at Praga in the Second War of Polish Succession
1814	Norway declared an independent kingdom that shared Sweden's king
1825	First boat to use the Erie Canal arrived at New York City from Buffalo
1841	First California emigrants reached the Stanislaus river from St. Louis, Missouri
1842	Abraham Lincoln married Mary Todd
1847	Felix Mendelssohn, composer, born
1854	Florence Nightingale arrived in the Crimea
1862	Gatling patented his machine gun
1875	Ship collision involving the Pacific off Cape Flattery

```
1876      James Earl Fraser, U.S. sculptor, born
1879      Will Rogers, humorist, born (Will Rogers
               Day in Oklahoma)
1889      World's Fair opened at Paris, France
          Menelek II elected Emperor of Ethiopia
1890      Zanzibar became a British Protectorate
1893      United Boy's Brigades of American organized
1895      Eugene Field, author of "Little Boy Blue,"
               died
1906      Sterling North, author, born
          Robert Considine, journalist-author, born
1908      Tomas Palma, first President of Cuba, died
1912      Pauline Trigere, fashion designer, born
1914      German cruiser Karlsruhe exploded
1915      Austria surrendered
1916      Walter Cronkite, newscaster, born
1918      Art Carney, actor, born
1922      Entrance to Tutankhamen's tomb discovered
               (Egypt)
1942      Battle of El Alamein in North Africa ended
               in German defeat
1954      Henri Matisse, French artist, died
1956      Russian army crushed the Hungarian anti-
               communist revolt
1965      England's Princess Margaret began a tour of
               the United States
1966      Flooding began in Florence, Italy
1971      Four men completed a raft ride across the
               Pacific from Ecuador to Australia
```

November 5th

```
          Feast of Sts. Zachary and Elizabeth, parents
               of John the Baptist
1193 AD   Council of Compigne nullified King Philip II
               of France's marriage to Ingeborg
               of Denmark
1370      Casimir III, "the Great," King of Poland, died
               following a hunting accident
1380      Wat Tyler's Rebellion began when English
               peasant protested a poll tax
1492      Spanish discovered corn on Cuba
1513      Pope Leo X reformed the Roman University
1514      Mary, wife of King Louis XII of France,
               crowned Queen
1605      Appointed day for the "Gunpowder Plot" to
               blow up the English Parliament
               (Guy Fawkes' Day)
1688      King William III of England arrived there from
               Holland to take his father-in-
               law's throne away
```

```
1757       Prussians defeated the French at Rossbach (Seven
                Years' War)
1786       Necker Island in the Pacific discovered
1789, 1993   Transits of Mercury
1852       American Society of Civil Engineers organized
1854       Battle of Inkerman, a Russian defeat in the
                Crimean War
1872       Thomas Sully, English artist, died
1885       Will Durant, historian-author, born
1889       Idaho's constitution adopted
1895       George B. Selden got a patent on a "road
                engine," the first gasoline
                automobile
           Charles MacArthur, playwright, born
1903       Duray, in a Gabon-Brillie, set a land-speed
                record of 84.73 mph
1905       Independent Norway's king entered Oslo
1911       First transcontinental airplane flight arrived
                at Pasadena, California from New
                York (air time 82 hrs., 4 min.)
1912       Roy Rogers, movie cowboy, born
1913       Louis III became King of Bavaria
1914       Britain annexed Cyprus and declared war on
                Turkey
1942       George M. Cohan, theatrical great, died
1945       Colombia joined the United Nations
1956       Britain and France invaded Egypt when they
                wouldn't agree to a ceasefire with
                Israel
           A United Nations police force was organized to
                supervise the Middle-East truce
1970       Ex-king Peter of Yugoslavia died
```

November 6th

```
           Feast of St. Leonard, patron of prisoners,
                coppersmiths, blacksmiths, lock-
                smiths, porters, coalminers,
                greengrocers, and barrel makers
           Feast of St. Illtyd
2948 BC    Noah born
1406 AD    Pope Innocent VII died
1429       Henry VI crowned King of England
1479       Joanna the Mad, Queen of Castile, born
1632       King Gustavus II Adolphus of Sweden died
1650       William II, governing Prince of Holland, died
                of smallpox
1656       King John IV, "the Fortunate," of Portugal died
1710, 1756   Transits of Mercury
1817       Charlotte, daughter of King George IV of England
                and heir to the throne, died in
                childbirth
```

```
1836       Charles X, exiled King of France, died
1854       John Philip Sousa, march composer, born
1860       Ignace Paderewski, composer, born
1861       Dr. James A. Naismith, founder of basketball,
               born
1869       First college football game played
           Cairo, Egypt, opera house opened
           New Blackfriars Bridge opened in London
1889       Universal Exposition, Paris, closed
1893       Tchaikovsky, composer, died of cholera
1908       Taish sank in a storm, taking 150 lives
1914       Japan captured Tsingtau
1921       James Jones, author, born
1928       Arnold Rothstein, New York gambler, shot, his
               killer yet to be found
1936       Spanish Loyalist government left Madrid for
               Valencia
1937       Italy joined Germany and Japan in an anti-
               Comintern pact
1966       The floods ended; assessment of the damage to
               Florence, Italy began
1968       Viet Nam War peace talks began in Paris
```

November 7th

```
 630 AD    Constans II, Eastern Roman Emperor, born
 680       Sixth Ecumenical Council opened, at Constan-
               tinople
 739       St. Willibrord died (Feast Day)
1225       St. Engelbert died (Feast Day)
1598       Francisco de Zurbaran, Spanish artist, born
1619       Frederick and Elizabeth crowned rulers of
               Bohemia
1629       New Hampshire named
1631       First passage of a planet across the sun
               observed (Mercury)
1677, 1776, 1835, 1881, 1914, 1960   Transits of Mercury
1776       Warren, Maine, incorporated
           "Crossing of the Fathers," Utah, a fording place
               on the Colorado River, discovered
1800       Platt Rogers Spencer, handwriting expert, born
1811       U.S. Army defeated the Shawnee Indians at the
               Battle of Tippecanoe
1867       Marie Curie, scientist, born
1872       Mary Celeste left New York for Italy, later
               found abandoned in the Atlantic
1874       Elephant first used as the Republican Party
               symbol
1885       Last spike driven for the Canadian-Pacific
               Railroad
```

1901	Li Hung Chang, Chinese statesman, died
1906	Colorado River flow into the Salton Sink closed
1913	Beginning of the "Great Storm" on the Great Lakes
	Albert Camus, author, born
1915	Italian ship Ancona torpedoed in the Mediterranean
1917	Bolsheviks overthrew Kerensky's provisional government in Russia
1918	Billy Graham, evangelist, born
	U.S. troops reached Sedan
1935	"Chic" Sale, humorist-author, died
1942	(Eastern Standard Time) Allies invaded North Africa
1945	Mexico and the Union of South Africa joined the U.N.
1956	All fighting in Egypt stopped
1962	Eleanor (Mrs. Franklin D.) Roosevelt died

===

November 8th

===

	Fair at Sutton Coldfield, Warwickshire, England
	Ancient Romans opened the entrance to the Underworld
	Feast of St. Cuby
35 AD	Marcus Nerva, Roman Emperor, born
306 (?)	The Four Crowned Ones martyred (Feast Day)
618	Pope St. Deusdedit died
641	Alexandria, Egypt, fell to the Muslims
789	St. Willehad died (Feast Day)
911	Conrad I chosen King of Germany
1115	St. Godfrey (or Geoffrey) of Amiens died (Feast Day)
1286	King Pedro III of Aragon died
1307	Rebellion erupted in Switzerland to oust Austrians
1333	Start of the first two-day autumn fair at Kendal, England
1519	Cortez entered Tenochtitlan, capitol of the Aztecs
1620	Bohemia defeated at White Mountain in the Thirty Years' War
1622	King Charles X of Sweden born
1674	John Milton, English poet, died
1725	New York Gazette, weekly newspaper, founded
1726	King Louis XIII of France died
1793	Louvre Museum, Paris, opened
1802	Transit of Mercury
1837	Mr. Holyoke Female Seminary opened (Massachusetts)
1838	First Wabash Railroad train ran
1889	Montana became a state

```
1900        Margaret Mitchell, author of Gone With The Wind,
                born
1909        Katherine Hepburn, Oscar-winning actress, born
1910        Tolstoy, Russian novelist, died
1917        Bolshevik "November Revolution" declared
                successful in Russia
1918        Republic of Brunswick proclaimed in Germany
1919        Zonta International formed
1923        Beer Hall Putsch, Munich, Germany, the start of
                Hitler's rise
1934        Bremen, North German Lloyd liner, began her
                100th transAtlantic voyage
1937        Chinese abondoned Shanghai to the Japanese
1942        (Local Time) Allies invaded German-held North
                Africa
            British aircraft carrier Avenger sunk off North
                Africa
1966        Edward Brooke of Massachusetts elected, the
                first black senator since
                Reconstruction
1968        U.S. launched Pioneer D, a solar-orbiting
                satellite
1969        Lord Mayor's Procession held in London, England
```

```
November 9th
```

```
            Feast of St. Theodore the Recruit
1225 AD     Frederick II, Holy Roman Emperor, married
                Yolande, Princess of Jerusalem
1313        Battle of Gammelsdorf
1389        Pietro Tomacelli crowned Pope as Boniface IX
            Isabella of France, wife of King Richard II of
                England, born
1620        Pilgrims sighted Cape Cod, Massachusetts
1690, 1723, 1848, 1927, 1973    Transits of Mercury
1698        Great meteor shower sighted
1775        Benedict Arnold and his American forces arrived
                to attack Quebec
1817        Harriet Shelley, estranged wife of the poet,
                drowned herself
1831        The Post, a daily newspaper, begun in Boston
1841        King Edward VII of England born
1853        Stanford White, architect, born
1866        Czar Alexander III of Russia married Dagmar of
                Denmark
1872        Start of a two-day fire in Boston, Massachusetts
1884        Ivan Krylov, Russian fable writer, died
1886        Ed Wynn, actor-comedian, born
1901        George V invested as Prince of Wales
1911        Howard Pyle, American artist-writer, died
1913        "The Great Storm" destroyed 10 Great Lakes
                steamships
```

	Spiro T. Agnew, U.S. Vice-President, born
1914	German cruiser Emden sank off Cocos Island
1918	The Kaiser abdicated and fled Germany
1920	St. Nectarius Kephalas died (Orthodox Greek Feast Day)
1924	"Ma" Ferguson elected Governor of Texas
	Nellie Taylor Ross elected Governor of Wyoming
1927	Propeller Club of the U.S. organized
1935	Congress of Industrial Organizations formed
1936	Giant panda captured in China for the Chicago Zoo
1940	Neville Chamberlain, British statesman, died
1945	Canada joined the United Nations
1953	Cambodia became independent of France (Independence Day)
	Dylan Thomas, poet, died
	Saud ibn Abdul Aziz became King of Saudi Arabia
1965	All the lights went out in the northeastern United States
1969	Eastman House, Rochester, New York, became a national landmark
1970	Charles de Gaulle, former President of France, died

November 10th

	Hero Day in Indonesia
461 AD	Pope Leo the Great died
627	St. Justus of Canterbury died (Feast Day)
1241	Pope Celestine IV died after 2 weeks in office
1444	Wladislaus III, King of Poland, died fighting the Turks
1483	Martin Luther, German religious reformer, born
1526	John Zapolya elected King of Hungary
1549	Pope Paul III died
1608	St. Andrew Avellino died, invoked for a holy death and against apoplexy or sudden death (Feast Day)
1635	Massachusetts colonists settled Saybrook, first English settlement in Connecticut
1674	New Amsterdam and other Dutch colonial holdings in North America formally given to England
1697	William Hogarth, English artist, born
1736, 1894	Transits of Mercury
1766	Queens College (Rutgers), New Jersey, chartered
1775	U.S. Marine Corps created
1776	Joseph Hewes, signer of the Declaration of Independence, died
1790	Daniel Houghton set out from Gambia to find Timbuktu
1806	Shah Alam, Mogul Emperor of India, died

```
1820      King George IV of England gave up trying to
                divorce his wife, Caroline of
                Brunswick
1834      Franklin Pierce, U.S. President, married Jane
                M. Appleton
1843      John Trumbull, English artist, died
1869      Horace Mann School for the Deaf opened in Boston
1879      Vachel Lindsay, poet, born
1880      Jacob Epstein, sculptor, born
1889      Claude Raines, actor, born
1890      British cruiser Serpent sank in a storm off Spain
1891      First Women's Christian Temperence Union
                convention opened (Boston)
1893      John P. Marquand, novelist, born
1908      London Times reported on the cutting of the
                Cullinan diamond, 3,025.75 carats
1914      Start of the Seventh Annual Cactus Derby auto
                race from Los Angeles to Phoenix
1917      Lenin made Premier of Russia
1918      British battleship Britannia torpedoed off Cape
                Trafalgar
1920      Armistice Day in England
1925      Richard Burton, actor, born
1926      King Leopold III of Belgium married Astrid of
                Sweden
1935      King George II returned to the Greek throne
1951      Transcontinental telephone dialing established
                in U.S.
1954      Marine Memorial showing the flag-raising on
                Iwo Jima dedicated in Washington,
                D.C.
1961      Stalingrad, Russia, renamed Volvograd
1968      Zond 6, Russian lunar probe, launched
```

November 11th

```
          Maracaibo, Venezuela, fetes honoring the Virgin
                of Chiquinquira
          Fairs held at Halifax, Yorkshire and Dover,
                England, as well as Langport in
                Somersetshire
          Fair date of old at Guilford, Surrey, England
          Feast of St. Menas
          Start of Advent in the Ethiopian Christian Church
307 AD    Lucinius, Roman Emperor, became Augustus
397       St. Martin of Tours died; patron of reformed
                drunkards (Catholic Feast Day;
                Martinmas in England)
619       St. John the Almsgiver died
826       St. Theodore the Studite died (Feast Day)
1012      Date of a supposed Viking carving near
                Heavener, Oklahoma
1050      Henry IV, Holy Roman Emperor, born
```

```
1055      St. Bartholomew of Grottaferrata died (Feast Day)
1208      Otto IV again elected King of Germany
1404      Cosmo Megliorati crowned Pope as Innocent VII
1417      Odo Colonna elected Pope as Martin V
1522      John Zapolye crowed King of Hungary
1647      King Charles I of England escaped from Hampton
               Court
1661      King Charles II of Spain born
1748      Charles IV, King of Spain, born
1788      First settlement made at Cincinnati, Ohio,
               called Columbia
1815, 1861, 1940   Transits of Mercury
1831      Nat Turner, leader of a slave revolt, hanged
1851      First U.S. patent for a telescope issued
1855      Tokyo, Japan, rocked by an earthquake
1858      James A. Garfield, U.S. President, married
               Lucretia Rudolph
1861      Pedro V, King of Portugal, died of cholera
1868      New York Athletic Club held the first indoor
               track meet
1869      Victor Emmanuel III, King of Italy, born
1871      "Tammany Tiger" cartoon character first appeared
1882      Gustav VI, King of Sweden, born
1887      Roland Young, actor, born
          Manchester Ship Canal construction began in
               England
1889      Washington became a state
1897      F. Van Wyck Mason, author, born
1899      Pat O'Brien, actor, born
1913      Robert Ryan, actor, born
1914      Howard Fast, author, born
          Barney Oldfield won the 7th Annual Cactus Derby
               in a Stutz
1918      World War I armistice signed (Rememberance Day
                    in Canada; Veterans' Day in U.S.)
          Poland declared itself independent
          Charles I retired as ruler of Austria
1921      Unknown Soldier of World War I buried at
               Arlington Cemetery
1924      British submarine M-1 involved in an English
               Channel collision
1925      Discovery of cosmic rays announced
1932      Completed Tomb of the Unknown Soldier dedicated
               at Arlington
1935      Explorer II, a manned U.S. balloon, studied the
               stratosphere
1942      Germany invaded Italy and unoccupied France
1954      Armistice Day, U.S. holiday, became Veterans'
               Day
          Eisenhower Memorial Museum dedicated at Abilene,
               Kansas
1957      Jamaica became the first British West Indies
               colony to receive home rule
1961      Venezuela severed diplomatic relations with Cuba
```

```
1965        Rhodesia declared its independence from Britain
1969        Fly-in breakfast held at Fairview, Oklahoma
```

November 12th

```
            Feast of St. Lebuin
            Feast of St. Martin I, Pope
            Feast of St. Nilus of Ancyra
 295 AD     Beginning of the Era of Ascension
 607        Pope Boniface III died
 956        Lothair crowned King of France
1035        King Canute I of Denmark, Norway, and England
                died
1202        King Canute VI of Denmark died
1439        Plymouth, England, became the first town
                incorporated by Parliament
1459        University of Basel, Switzerland, chartered
1662        Robert Hooke appointed curator of experiments
                by London's Royal Society
1715        Battle of Sheriffmuir, English against Bonnie
                Prince Charlie
1770        Joseph Hopkinson, author of "Hail Columbia,"
                born
1776        North Carolina's Constitutional Convention first
                met
1782, 1986   Transits of Mercury
1799        Great meteor shower witnessed
1815        Elizabeth Cady Stanton, suffragist, born
                (holiday in U.S.)
1840        Auguste Rodin, French sculptor, born
1867        Fort Laramie Conference began to settle western
                Indian problems
1893        St. Juan de Avila, Apostle of Andalusia,
                beatified
1906        Madame Butterfly, Puccini's opera, first produced
                in New York
1912        Bodies of Scott's Antarctic expedition found
1913        "The Great Storm" ended, having destroyed 19
                Great Lakes ships
1915        Haiti approved the treaty making it a U.S.
                protectorate
1918        Republic of Austria founded
1921        Limitation of Armament Conference met in
                Washington, D.C.
1923        Hitler arrested and imprisoned, and while there
                wrote Mein Kampf
1928        British ship Vestris sank in a storm off Virginia
1929        Grace Kelly, actress-princess, born
1933        Century of Progress Exposition in Chicago ended
                its first season
1936        San Francisco-Oakland Bay Bridge opened to
                traffic
1944        German battleship Tirpitz lost off Norway
```

1951	Wyuta, Wyoming, train wreck
1956	Morocco, Sudan, and Tunisia joined the United Nations
1966	Total eclipse of the sun
1969	Annual fiesta and harvest dances held at Jemes and Tesuque pueblos in New Mexico
	Tanker Manhattan completed her voyage through the Northwest Passage

November 13th

	Ancient Roman Ides of November
	Indian summer begins
	Feast of St. John Chrysostom (Orthodox)
444 AD	St. Brice died; invoked against stomach diseases (Feast Day)
867	Pope St. Nicholas I died (Feast Day)
1179	St. Homobonus, patron of tailors, clothmakers and Cremona, Italy died (Feast Day)
1312	King Edward III of England born
1460	Prince Henry the Navigator of Portugal died
1463	St. Diego (or Didacus) died (Feast Day)
1568	St. Stanislaus Kostka died (Feast Day)
1775	American forces captured Montreal, Canada
1779	Thomas Chippendale, cabinetmaker, buried
1799	Republic of Rome ended when Napoleon evacuated Italy
1832, 1833	Great meteor showers witnessed
1833	Edwin Booth, actor, born
1850	Robert Louis Stevenson, author, born
1853	Maria II, Queen of Portugal, died
1856	Louis Brandeis, jurist, born
1868	Gioacchino Rossini, opera composer, died
1889	Graduate School of the Sacred Sciences opened at the Catholic University of America
1900	Alexander King, artist-author, born
1907	First Central American Conference held (Washington, D.C.)
1908	Hsuan T'ung, infant, chosen to succeed his uncle as Emperor of China
1917	St. Francis Cabrini, patron of emigrants, died
1918	Charles I retired as ruler of Hungary
	King Louis III of Bavaria abdicated
1941	British aircraft carrier Ark Royal sunk in the Mediterranean
	Japanese battleship Hiyei sunk in the Solomon Islands
1945	Ethiopia and Panama joined the United Nations
1955	A military junta took over the government of Argentina

```
1965       Yarmouth Castle, a cruise ship, burned off
                Nassau
1968       HL-10, an experimental controlled-flight
                satellite, launched
```

November 14th

```
           Feast of St. Dubricius
 565 AD    Justinian I, the Great, Eastern Roman Emperor,
                died
1180       St. Lawrence O'Toole died (Feast Day)
1305       Bertrand de Got crowned the first Avignon Pope
                as Clement V
1359       St. Gregory Palamas died (Orthodox Feast Day)
1501       Arthur, heir to England, married Katherine of
                Aragon
1525       Pizarro left Panama to conquer Peru
1587       Cavendish, a British sea rover, captured Great
                St. Anne, a Spanish treasure
                galleon
1623       St. Josaphat of Polotsk died (Feast Day)
1698       King Charles II of Spain wrote his will, leaving
                all to Joseph Ferdinand of Bavaria
1734       Louise de Keroualle, mistress of King Charles
                II of England, died
1765       Robert Fulton, inventor, born
1803       Jacob Abbott, author of the Rollo books, born
1814       Norway annexed to Sweden by the Treaty of Kiel
1832       Charles Carroll, signer of the Declaration of
                Independence, died
           Trolley service began in New York City
1840       Claude Monet, French artist, born
1851       Herman Melville's Moby Dick published
1866, 1867, 1868   Great meteor showers witnessed
1888       Meeting held that evolved into St. Andrew's,
                the first U.S. golf club
1889       Jawaharlal Nehru, Indian statesman, born
           Nellie Bly began her attempt to go around the
                world in less than 80 days, and
                succeeded
1896       Mamie Dowd, Mrs. Dwight D. Eisenhower, born
1900       Aaron Copeland, composer, born
1907, 1953   Transits of Mercury
1908       King Hsu, Emperor of China, died
1912       Barbara Hutton, heiress, born
1915       Booker T. Washington, educator-author, died
1918       Tomas Masaryk elected first President of
                Czechoslovakia
1922       First BBC radio broadcast aired in England
           Latvia elected its first president
1935       King Hussein I of Jordan born
1939       William I. Hull, educator-author, died
```

1940	Coventry, England, cathedral damaged by Nazi bombs
1945	Bolivia joined the United Nations
1948	Prince Charles Philip Arthur George, heir to the throne of England, born
1955	Robert Sherwood, playwright, died
1963	Volcanic island of Surtsey born off Iceland
1968	Equatorial Africa joined the United Nations
1969	Apollo 12 blasted off to land on the Moon
1970	Annual elephant roundup held at Surin, Thailand
	Twenty-fifth birthday concert performed by the Rhode Island Philharmonic Orchestra at Providence
	End of the Water Festival at Bangkok, Thailand

November 15th

	Feast of St. Malo
2349 BC	Methuselah born
309 AD	Sts. Shmona and Garia, the "Confessors of Edessa," martyred (Feast Day)
878	St. Fintan of Rhienau died (Feast Day)
1136	St. Leopold, Prince of Austria, died (Feast Day, celebrated in Klosternburg by sliding down a huge wine barrel)
1280	St. Albert the Great, patron of students of natural history, died (Feast Day)
1316	John I, King of France, posthumous son of Louis X
1533	Spaniards entered the Incas' holy city, Cuzco
1630	Johann Kepler, German astronomer, born
1712	Duke of Hamilton and Lord Mohun killed each other in a duel (England)
1741	British captured Patia, on San Fernandez Island
1763	Mason and Dixon began surveying their line
1777	Articles of Confederation adopted by the Continental Congress
1790	Leopold II, Holy Roman Emperor, crowned King of Hungary
1794	John Witherspoon, signer of the Declaration of Independence, died
1802	George Romney, English portrait painter, died
1806	Zebulon Pike discovered his Peak (Colorado)
1819	Daniel Rutherford, discoverer of nitrogen, died
1838	Grand Caledonian Curling Club founded in Scotland
1860	New Minot Ledge Lighthouse lit (Massachusetts)
1864	General Sherman burned Atlanta, Georgia
1881	American Federation of Labor organized
1882	Felix Frankfurter, Supreme Court Justice, born
1887	Marianne Moore, poet and baseball fan, born
1889	Manoel II, King of Portugal, born
1891	W. Averell Harriman, U.S. diplomat, born
1896	Power from Niagara Falls turned on in Buffalo, New York

1899	Pedro II, second Emperor of Brazil, dethroned
1901	Great meteor shower
1907	"Mutt and Jeff" comic strip first appeared
1908	Empress Dowager Tzu-Hsi of China died
	Belgium annexed the Independent State of the Congo
1920	Danzig, Germany, proclaimed a free city
1929	Ambassador Bridge, connecting Detroit, Michigan, and Windsor, Ontario, Canada, opened to traffic
1939	Cornerstone of the Jefferson Memorial laid in, Washington, D.C.
1940	Queens-Midtown Tunnel opened to Manhattan
1942	Japanese battleship Kirishima lost off the Solomon Islands
1945	Venezuela joined the United Nations
1960	George Washington, first U.S. nuclear-powered submarine, began its maiden voyage
1961	Transet 4-Band TRAAC satellites launched by the U.S.
1965	Craig Breedlove in the "Spirit of America" set a land-speed record of 600.601 mph, first to break the 600 mark
1966	Gemini 12, U.S. orbital manned flight, splashed back to Earth
1969	Beginning of the Eastern Orthodox Advent
	Annual Elephant Roundup held in Thailand
1999	Transit of Mercury

November 16th

	Feast of St. Eucherius of Lyons
2348 BC	Noah's flood ended
42 AD	Tiberius, Roman Emperor, born
1093	St. Margaret, Queen of Scotland, died (Feast Day)
1240	St. Edmund of Abingdon died (Feast Day)
1272	King Henry III of England died
1302	St. Gertrude of Helfta died (Feast Day)
1326	King Edward II of England captured by his wife and his barons
1532	Inca Empire fell to Pizarro and the Spanish
1632	Swedish King Gustavus Adolphus killed at the Battle of Lutzen
1665	Oxford Gazette first published in England
1715	Prussia defeated Sweden at Rugen
1724	John Sheppard, famed English thief, hanged
1797	Frederick William II, King of Prussia, died
1801	New York Post newspaper founded
1855	Turks surrendered to Russia at Kars, Armenia
1873	W. C. Handy, blues composer, born
1882	Milwaukee Journal, Wisconsin newspaper, founded

```
1889        George S. Kaufman, playwright, born
1895        Paul Hindemith, German composer, born
            Samuel F. Smith, composer of "America," died
1899        Mary Margaret McBride, author, born
1907        Gila Cliff Dwellings became a national monument
            Oklahoma became a state
1908        Burgess Meredith, actor, born
1914        Federal Reserve Banking Act effected (U.S.)
1926        First New York City production of Puccini's
                         Turandot opened
1932        Great meteor shower seen
1933        U.S.-Russian diplomatic relations established
1963        Moving of the Abu Simbel temple began at Aswan,
                         Egypt
1969        Turkey Day celebrated in Millstadt, Illinois
            A "moon rock" first went on public display
            (Museum of Natural History, New York City)
```

November 17th

```
            Feast of St. Dionysius of Alexandria
            Feast of St. Gregory the Wonderworker or of
                         Neocaesarea
   3 BC     Christ born, according to Clement of Alexandria
 375 AD     Valentinian I, Roman Emperor, died
    594     St. Gregory of Tours died (Feast Day)
    680     St. Hilda died (Feast Day)
   1200     St. Hugh of Lincoln died (Feast Day)
   1303     Sea coal first used
   1326     Edmund, Earl of Arundel, executed
   1370     Louis I, "the Great," crowned King of Poland
   1553     Two written works on Spain's New World conquests
                         banned in Spain
   1558     Queen "Bloody Mary" Tudor of England died
   1603     Sir Walter Raleigh imprisoned for treason
   1629     Laconia Company given a charter to establish
                         the colony of New Hampshire
   1745     French and Indians attacked Saratoga, New York
   1755     King Louis XVIII of France born
   1785     Seth Boyden, inventor of patent leather, born
   1794     Eli Terry's clock patented, the first
   1796     Napoleon and the French defeated the Austrians
                         at Arcole
   1800     Congress first met in the U.S. Capitol
   1830     Hungarian Academy of Sciences established
   1896     Suez Canal opened to traffic
   1878     King Humbert I of Italy warded off an assassin's
                         blow with his sabre
   1880     U.S. and China signed an immigration treaty
   1889     Pedro II, Emperor of Brazil, went into exile
   1891     Paderewski, Polish pianist, made his American
                         debut
   1902     Augieres, in a Mars, set a land-speed record of
                         77.13 mph
```

```
1904        Isamu Noguchi, sculptor, born
1914        German cruiser Yorck hit a mine at the mouth
                of the Jade River
1917        Auguste Rodin, sculptor, died
1922        Deposed Sultan Mehmed VI fled Constantinople
1925        Rock Hudson, actor, born
1926        Carl Akeley, museum-supplying naturalist, died
1934        Lyndon Baines Johnson married Claudia A.
                (Ladybird) Taylor
1941        Speical Japanese envoys received in Washington, D.C.
1970        Student's Day celebrated in Czechoslovakia
            Luna 17 landed a wheeled, self-propelled Russian
                vehicle on the Moon
```

November 18th

```
            Our Lady of Chiquinquira (Venezuela)
            Feast of St. Mawes
            Feast of St. Romanus of Antioch
            Start of the sunless period in Hammerfest, Norway
   94 AD    Vespasian, Roman emperor, born
   942      St. Odo of Cluny died; invoked for rain (Feast
                Day)
  1188      Richard, heir to England, did homage to Philip
                Augustus of France for his French
                possessions
  1210      Otto IV, Holy Roman Emperor, excommunicated
  1307      William Tell shot the apple off his son's head
  1414      Sigismund crowned King of Germany
  1518      Cortez set out from Cuba to conquer Mexico
  1626      St. Peter's Basilica at the Vatican consecrated
  1755      American northeast rocked by earthquakes
  1776      Colonial army evacuated Fort Lee and retreated
                across New Jersey
  1789      Louis J. M. Daguerre, photographic-process
                inventor, born
  1837      Missouri capitol destroyed by fire
  1840      Last transported British convicts landed in
                Australia
  1841      Rhode Island's People's Constitution completed
  1860      Ignace Jan Paderewski, Polish pianist-statesman,
                born
  1865      Mark Twain's first fiction, "The Celebrated
                Jumping Frog of Calaveras County"
                appeared in the Saturday Press
  1870      Elizabeth Meriwether Gilmer, Dorothy Dix of
                newspapers, born
            Postal delivery by pigeon began of English mail
                to besieged France
  1872      New Hampshire rocked by an earthquake
            Susan B. Anthony and 12 suffragists arrested
                for trying to vote
  1874      Clarence Day, author of Life with Father, born
```

```
1883    U.S. adopted Standard Time
1886    Chester A. Arthur, U.S. President, died
1890    Battleship U.S.S. Maine launched
1899    Eugene Ormandy, conductor, born
1901    George H. Gallup, pollster, born
        Hay-Paunceforte Treaty signed over the Panama
                Canal
1903    Treaty about the Panama Canal ratified by the U.S.
1910    First guns of the Mexican Revolution fired
1911    Ruth McKenny, author of My Sister Eileen, born
1913    First airplane "loop the loop" flown (San Diego,
                California)
1923    Alan B. Shepard, first U.S. astronaut, born
1935    Economic sanctions against Italy went in effect,
                supported by the League of Nations
1946    Jimmy Walker, flamboyant mayor of New York City,
                died
1958    U.S. freighter Carl D. Bradley sank in a Lake
                Michigan storm
1962    Norwegian Tharald Brovig and Japanese Munakata
                Maru collided
1965    Henry A. Wallace, U.S. Vice-President, died
1969    Joseph P. Kennedy, diplomat and financier, died
```

November 19th

```
        Feast of St. Barlaam of Antioch
461 AD  St. Hilarius became Pope
766     Ecgbert, founder of the Cathedral School of
                York, died
1231    St. Elizabeth, Princess of Hungary, died (Feast
                Day)
1298    St. Mechtilde of Hackeborn died (Feast Day)
1317    Philip V, "the Tall," proclaimed himself King
                of France
1493    Columbus discovered Puerto Rico
1497    Vasco da Gama discovered the water route to
                India
1600    King Charles I of England born
1616    Eustache LeSueur, French artist, born
1692    Thomas Shadwell, English poet laureate, died
1703    "The Man in the Iron Mast" died in the Bastille
                prison (Paris)
1744    New York Gazette, a weekly newspaper published
                since 1725, expired
1805    Ferdinand de Lesseps, Suez Canal builder, born
1810    Jean Georges Noverre, French dancer, died
1813    William I, King of Holland, arrived in his country
1828    Franz Schubert, composer, died
1831    James A. Garfield, 20th U.S. President, born
1847    Mary H. Foote, author-illustrator, born
1850    Alfred, Lord Tennyson, made poet laureate of
                England
```

	Richard M. Johnson, U.S. Vice-president, died
1858	Francis Hobart Herrick, naturalist-author, born
1863	Lincoln gave his Gettysburg Address at the founding of that national cemetery
	Billy Sunday, evangelist, born
1867	Fitz-Greene Halleck, poet, died
1868	William Sidney Mount, American artist, died
	William I. Hull, educator-historian, born
1869	Griffith O. Ellis, publisher, born
	Canada purchased the Northwest Territories from the Hudson's Bay Company
1874	"Boss" Tweed convicted of fraud in New York City
1880	Hiram Fuller, author, died
1887	W. A. Sholten involved in an English Channel collision
	Emma Lazarus, ooet, died
1889	First North Dakota legislature met in Bismarck
	Brazilian national flag adopted
1890	Helen J. Ferris, editor-author, born
1905	Tommy Dorsey, bandleader, born
1909	Peter F. Drucker, author-educator, born
1919	Versailles Peace Treaty rejected by the U.S. Senate
1921	Roy Campanella, baseball player, born
1923	Beer Hall Putsch, the beginning of Hitler's rise, ended in Munich, Germany
1937	Eyston, in the Thunderbolt 1, set a land-speed record of 311.42 mph
1939	Cornerstone laid for the Roosevelt Museum at Hyde Park, N.Y.
1940	Beginning of the Nazi bombing of Birmingham, England
1946	Afghanistan, Iceland, and Sweden joined the United Nations
1950	John H. Fahey, publisher, died
1961	Dorothy Heyward, playwright-novelist, died
1969	Apollo 12 astronauts landed on the moon
1970	National Festival held in Monaco

November 20th

	Indian summer ends
	Feast of St. Felix of Valois
	Feast of St. Fabian
	New Year's Day in Hawaii, prior to its discovery by Captain Cook
869 AD	St. Edmund, King of the East Angles, killed by the Danes (Feast Day)
1022	St. Bernward died (Feast Day)
1376	Richard II invested as Prince of Wales
1564	Spanish expedition set out to colonize the Philippines
1620	Peregrine White, first baby among the New England colonists, born

1703	Eddystone Lighthouse swept away by a storm (England)
1737	Queen Caroline of England, wife of George II, died
1819	Arkansas Gazette, first newspaper west of the Mississippi, founded
1820	Whaling ship Essex sunk by a sperm whale
1850	Conference of Olmutz met for agreements between Austria and Prussia
1851	Panic in a New York public school killed 45 students
1866	First Great Army of the Republic convention held
1884	Norman Thomas, perenniel Socialist presidential candidate, born
1888	Nathaniel Currier, Ives' lithography partner, died
1925	Senator Robert Kennedy born
1927	Handball rules set by the AAU
1937	Chunking became the wartime capitol of China
1946	U.S. soft-coal miners went on strike
1947	Queen Elizabeth II of England married Prince Philip
1950	U.S. forces fighting in Korea reached the Manchurian border
1967	U.S. population reached 200 million
1970	Indians occupied the former Alcatraz prison

November 21st

	Presentation of the Blessed Virgin Mary (Orthodox)
235 AD	St. Anthesus became Pope
496	St. Gelasius I, Pope, died (Feast Day)
615	St. Columban died
1555	Georg Agricola, "father of mineralology," died
1643	Rene Robert Cavalier de la Salle, Mississippi River explorer, born
1694	Voltaire, French writer, born
1729	Josiah Barttell, signer of the Declaration of Independence, born
1783	First flight in a hydrogen-gas balloon made (Paris)
1787	Sir Samuel Cunard, steamship line founder, born
1789	North Carolina ratified the U.S. Constitution
1806	Napoleon's Berlin Decree announced, blockading and prohibiting trade with England
1846	The first steamboat sailed on the St. Lawrence River
1877	Thomas A. Edison invented the phonograph
1898	René Magritte, Belgian artist, born
1899	Garret A. Hobart, U.S. Vice-President, died
1907	Jim Bishop, columnist, born
1916	British ship Britannic torpedoed in the Aegean Sea

	Emperor Franz Joseph I of Austro-Hungary died
1918	German fleet surrendered to the British
1920	Stan Musial, baseball player, born
1921	Canadian coat-of-arms adopted
1924	Mrs. Warren G. Harding, wife of the President, died
1944	Japanese battleship Kongo sunk off China by a U.S. submarine
1945	Guatemala joined the United Nations
	Robert Benchley, humorist, died
1964	Second Ecumenical Council ended
	U.S. launched Explorer satellites 24 and 25
	Verrazano Bridge opened linking Staten Island and Brooklyn

November 22nd

	Feast of St. Cecilia (or Cecily), patron of musicians and makers of musical instruments
	Independence Day in Lebanon
1220 AD	Frederick II crowned Holy Roman Emperor
1316	John I, King of France, died, after living and reigning only a week
1515	Mary of Guise, wife of King James V of Scotland, born
1633	First settlers for Maryland sailed from England
1652	York, Maine, incorporated
1774	Robert, Baron Clive, founder of Britain's Indian Empire, committed suicide
1790	End of 45 days of earthquakes in Algeria
1791	Society for Establishing Useful Manufactures incorporated
1819	Mary Ann Evans, a writer as George Eliot, born
1868	John Nance "Cactus Jack" Garner, U.S. Vice-President, born
1871	James W. Garner, author-educator, born
	Sidewheeler City of New London burned in the Thames River, Connecticut
1890	Charles de Gaulle, French statesman, born
1899	Hoagy Carmichael, composer, born
1900	Sir Arthur Sullivan, Gilbert's composing partner, died
1913	Charles F. Berlitz, language instructor and author, born
1916	Jack London, novelist, died
1924	Geraldine Page, actress, born
1926	Baseball's Lew Burdette born
1935	Railroad service began between Ankara and Dierbekr, Turkey
1938	National Cotton Council of America formed
1939	New York City took over its subway system
1940	End of the German bombing of Birmingham, England

```
1950       Train wreck at Richmond Hill, New York
1963       John F. Kennedy, President of the U.S.,
               assassinated
1971       Elgin Long became the first man to fly over both
               Poles
```

November 23rd

```
           Tasting of the First Fruits Ceremony (Rice, in
               Kyoto, Japan)
           Feast of St. Clement IV of Rome, Pope, patron of
               boatmen, invoked for sick children
           Feast of St. Felicity
 912 AD    Otto the Great, Holy Roman Emperor, born
 955       King Edred of England died
1263       St. Alexander, Prince Nevsky died (Orthodox
               Feast Day)
1407       Duc d'Orleans, brother of King Charles VI of
               France, murdered
1457       Ladislaus V, King of Hungary and Bohemia, died
1470       Guru Nanak, founder of the Indian religion of
               Sikhism, born
1476       University of Mainz, Germany, granted a Papal
               charter
1744       Abigail, wife of President John Adams, born
1749       Edward Rutledge, signer of the Declaration of
               Independence, born
1765       Twelve county judges in Maryland took the first
               official action against the Stamp
               Act
1774       Massachusetts began organizing the Minute Men
1804       Franklin Pierce, U.S. President, born
1814       Elbridge Gerry, signer of the Declaration of
               Independence, died
1837       House of Commons committee appointed to study the
               penny postage (England)
1848       Bark Eliza left Salem, Massachusetts, for the
               California gold fields
1863       Battle of Orchard Knob, Tennessee
1873       Ville de Havre involved in a collision in the
               Atlantic
1887       Boris Karloff, movie monster actor, born
1890       William III, King of Holland, born
1893       Harpo Marx, comedian, born
1902       Walter Reed, yellow fever researcher, died
1903       Enrico Caruso made his American debut at the
               Metropolitan Opera
1960       Tiros II weather satellite launched by the U.S.
1965       Elizabeth, Belgiun Queen Mother, died
1969       Fossil bones discovered in the Antarctic
```

```
          Feast of St. Colman of Cloyne
          Feast of St. John of the Cross
 166 AD   Beginning of the Era of Maccabees
 304(?)   St. Chrysogonus martyred (Feast Day)
 851      Sts. Flora and Mary martyred (Feast Day)
 1504     Queen Isabella of Spain, sponsor of Columbus,
              died
 1642     Abel Tasman sighted Tasmania
 1643     Holy Roman Empire defeated the French at
              Tuttlingen
 1655     King Charles XI of Sweden born
 1775     Father Ricci, head of the suppressed Jesuit order,
              died in prison
 1784     Zachary Taylor, U.S. President, born
 1807     Joseph Brant, Mohawk Indian Chief, died
 1819     Lake Champlain Canal opened to boat traffic
 1830     Kentucky's Louisville Daily Journal, forerunner
              of Louisville Times, founded
 1849     Frances E. H. Burnett, author of Little Lord
              Fauntleroy, born
 1864     Henri Toulouse-Lautrec, French artist, born
 1868     New Metropolitan Meat Market opened in London
 1875     Britain purchased enough shares to control the
              Suez Canal
 1877     Huron wrecked off North Carolina
 1880     Uncle Joseph involved in a fatal collision off
              Spezzia
 1885     King Alphonse XII of Spain died
 1914     British repulsed the Germans at Ypres
 1921     John V. Lindsay, mayor of New York City, born
 1925     William F. Buckley, conservative, born
 1929     Georges Clemenceau, French statesman, died
 1944     Swedish ship Hansa exploded off Gotland
 1965     Explosion destroyed the armory at Keokuk, Iowa
          Sir Abdullah as-Salam as-Sabah, Emir of Kuwait,
              died
 1969     Apollo XII splashed down in the Pacific on
              returning from the moon
```

November 25th

```
          Feast of St. Catherine of Alexandria, patron
              of philosophers, scholars, spinsters,
              millers, tanners, and spinners
          Feast of St. Catherine of Audley
          Feast of St. Mercury
 1177 AD  Christian Kingdon of Jerusalem fell to the
              Sultan of Egypt
 1185     Pope Lucius III died and Urban III elected to
              replace him
 1277     John Gaetano Orsini elected Pope as Nicholas III
```

1314	Louis IV crowned King of Germany
1413	Sigismund crowned King of the Lombards
1491	Treaty signed between Spain and the Moors in Granada
1542	English defeated the Scots at Solway Moss
1609	Henrietta Marie of France, Queen to King Charles I of England, born
1638	Catherine of Braganza, wife of King Charles II of England, born
1758	Americans routed the French from Fort Duquesne (Pittsburgh)
1759	Construction of Fort Pitt on the ruins of Fort Duquesne begun
1764	Stanislaus II crowned King of Poland
1771	Albany Gazette, New York newspaper, founded
1783	British evacuation of New York completed
1795	William Henry Harrison, U.S. President, married Anna T. Symmes
1799	U.S. brig Nancy confiscated by the British for carrying goods to France
1834	A three-course meal could be obtained at Delmonico's, a New York hotel, for 12¢
1835	Andrew Carnegie, industrialist-philanthropist, born
1846	Carrie Nation, temperance agitator, born
1851	First Young Men's Christian Association in North America organized
1863	Union victory at Missionary Ridge, Tennessee
1870	Paraguay's Assembly adopted a constitution
1881	Angelo Guiseppe Roncalli, Pope John XXIII, born
1914	Joe DiMaggio, baseball great, born
1921	Hirohito became Regent of Japan
1931	Kill van Kull Bridge opened, connecting Staten Island to New Jersey
1936	Japan and Germany signed an anti-Comintern pact
1941	British battleship Bacham torpedoed in the Mediterranean
1947	U.S. freighter Clarksdale Victory sank off western Canada
1951	Train wreck near Woodstock, Alabama
1960	John F. Kennedy, Jr., son of the President, born
1969	Niagara Falls, stopped for a disintegration study, started again

---

November 26th

---

311 AD	St. Peter of Alexandria martyred (Feast Day)
399	Pope St. Siricius died, not to be canonized for 1,400 years
885	Vikings attacked Paris
1237	Second Lombard League smashed by Frederick II, Holy Roman Emperor

```
1267      St. Silvester Gozzolini died (Feast Day)
1346      Charles IV crowned King of Germany
1377      Charter issued for the founding of St. Mary's
                College at Oxford, England
1621      St. John Berchmans died (Feast Day)
1706      King Frederick William II of Prussia married
                Sophia Dorthea of Hanover
1751      St. Leonard of Porto Maurizio died (Feast Day)
1780      900,000 gold guineas sank in New York harbor
1783      Annapolis, Maryland, became the capitol of the
                United States
1789      Thanksgiving, as appointed by George Washington
1807      William Sidney Mount, artist, born
1818      Encke's comet discovered
1825      Kappa Alpha, first social fraternity, organized
1836      John MacAdam, road-paving inventor, born
1847      Marie Feodorovna, Empress of Russia, born
1869      Maud Charlotte Mary Victoria of England,
                Queen of Norway, born
1875      Grand Sable on Reunion Island buried by a rock-
                slide
1879      Charles W. Goddard, serial author ("Perils of
                Pauline"), born
1894      Nicholas II, last Czar of Russia, married Alix
                of Hesse
1898      Portland sank off Cape Cod
1907      Turkish ship Kaptan sank in the North Sea
1912      Eric Sevareid, author-newscaster, born
1914      British battleship Bulwark exploded at Sheerness
1922      Charles M. Schulz, creator of "Peanuts," born
          King Tutankhamen's tomb opened (Egypt)
1926      John M. Browning, inventor of a machine gun, died
1934      Duke of Kent married Princess Mariana of Greece
1941      Lebanon was declared an independent nation
1943      British ship Rohna bombed off Algeria
1950      Communist Chinese allies of North Korea crossed
                the Yalu River
1964      Norwegian tanker Stoldt Dagali and Israeli liner
                Shalom collided off New Jersey
1966      First tidal-powered hydroelectric dam went
                into use (France)
1969      BTHS-West Hobo Day held at Belleville, Illinois
```

```
=================================================
November 27th
=================================================
```

```
          Labor-Thanksgiving Day in Japan
          Feast of  Sts. Barlaam and Josaphat
   43 BC  Octavius, Antonius and Lepidus formed a Roman
                triumverate
  784 AD  St. Virgil of Salzburg died (Feast Day)
1198      Constance, widow of Holy Roman Emperor Henry IV,
                died
1308      Henry VII elected King of Germany
```

```
1346    St. Gregory of Sinai died (Feast Day)
1382    French defeated the Flemish at Roosebeke
1635    Marquise de Mainteon, mistress and 2nd wife of
              King Louis XIV of France, born
1868    Custer attacked a Cheyenne-Arapaho Indian
              village in Kansas
1872    Meteor shower seen
1885    Meteorite feel near Mazapil, Mexico
1895    Alexandre Dumas, fils, author, died
1908    San Pablo sank off the Philippines
1912    Albanian national flag adopted
        David Merrick, theatrical producer, born
1941    Syria became an independent nation
1945    Norway joined the United Nations
1953    Eugene O'Neill, playwright, died
1957    Caroline Kennedy, daughter of the President,
              born
```

November 28th

```
        Feast of St. Katherine Laboure
 749 AD Abu-l-Abbas declared Caliph
 765    St. Stephen the Younger died (Feast Day)
1360    Outlaws almost stole the ransom for King Rene
              of Provence
1476    St. James of the March died (Feast Day)
1582    William Shakespeare married Anne Hathaway
1660    First meeting held of England's Royal Society,
              a scientific group
1678    Catherine of Braganza, wife of King Charles II
              of England, accused of treason for
              having no children
1680    Giovanni Bernini, builder of St. Peter's,
              Vatican, died
1720    Mary Read, woman pirate, sentenced to hang
1785    William Whipple, signer of the Declaration of
              Independence, died
        Samuel Hall founded the Massachusetts Gazette
              in Boston
1794    Baron Von Steuben, hero of the U.S. Revolution,
              died
1795    U.S. government bought off the Barbary pirates
1811    Maximilian II, King of Bavaria, born
1857    Alphonso XII, King of Spain, born
1859    Washington Irving, author, died
1863    Thanksgiving first observed in U.S., modern-
              style
1894    Brooks Atkinson, critic and author, born
1899    Peter J. Steincrown, physician-author, born
1904    Jeremiah E. Rankin, hymn composer, died
        Nancy Mitford, author, born
1919    Lady Nancy Astor became the first woman elected
              to the English House of Commons
```

```
1922      "Hello, U.S.A." was the first skywriting message
1929      Richard E. Byrd began his flight across the
              South Pole
1933      Morrocan-Tunisian Railroad opened
1937      Spanish insurgents proclaimed a blockade of
              all the Loyalist ports
1940      Inter-American Coffee Agreement signed by 14
              producing nations
1942      Coconut Grove nightclub fire in Boston killed
              491
1962      Queen Wilhelmina of Holland died
1964      U.S. launched Mariner IV
1969      Pecos Valley Pecan Festival began (New Mexico)
```

November 29th

```
          Yugoslav Republic Day
 496 AD   Pope St. Gelasius died
 741      Pope St. Gregory III died
 799      Charlemagne returned Pope Leo III to Rome
1198      al-Aziz, Caliph of Egypt, died in a hunting
              accident
1226      Louis IX crowned King of France
1268      Pope Clement IV died
1314      King Philip the Fair of France died
1348      New vicar appointed at Shaftesbury, England, to
              replace one who had died of plague
1378      King Charles IV of Germany died
1484      Convention of Spanish Inquisitors held
1489      Margaret, wife of the King of Scotland, born
1503      Cesare Borgia, son of Pope Alexander IV,
              imprisoned
1519      Magellan sighted South America
1612      British defeated the Portuguese over control of
              Swally, India
1652      Dutch destroyed the British fleet in the Dover
              Strait
1777      First Spanish pueblo, San Jose, founded in
              California
1807      Portuguese royal family set sail for Brazil to
              escape Napoleon
1832      Louisa May Alcott, author, born
1847      Cayuse Indians attacked the Whitman Mission
              School in Washington, killing 11
              and abducting 50
1864      Cheyenne and Arapaho Indians massacred at Sand
              Creek, Colorado
1872      Horace Greeley, editor-author, died
1878      Louis A. Godey, publisher of The Ladies' Book,
              died
1910      Penn Station opened to railroad traffic in New
              York City
```

```
1916     U.S. government protested the deportation of
              Bulgarian workers to Germany
1929     Richard E. Byrd flew across the South Pole
1944     Japanese aircraft carrier Shanano sunk off
              Japan by a U.S. submarine
1959     Explosion at Jamuri Bazar, India
1961     U.S. Mercury-Atlas spaceship with chimpanzee
              passenger recovered
```

November 30th

```
         Start of 8-day fair at Warrington, Lancashire,
              England
         Annual Eaton Wall game played, goalless since
              1909 (England)
         Feast of St. Andrew, founder of Ecumenical
              Patriarchate of Constantinople
              (Orthodox); patron of fishermen
              and fish dealers and Scotland,
              invoked for motherhood
 538 AD  St. Gregory of Tours born
1016     Edmund Ironside, King of England, died
1292     John Baliol crowned King of Scotland
1521     Pope Leo X died without receiving the last
              sacraments
1608     Cardiff, Wales, granted a third annual fair
1616     The Margaret, loaded with colonists, landed at
              Hampton, Virginia
1667     Jonathan Swift, English writer, born
1700     King Charles XII of Sweden defeated Russia at
              Narva in a half hour and captured
              6,000
1785     Standish, Maine, incorporated
1830     Pope Pius VIII died
1835     Samuel Clements, author as Mark Twain, born
1874     Winston Churchill, British statesman, born
1900     Oscar Wilde, English author, died
1904     Port Arthur, Russia, fell to the Japanese
1926     Sesquincentennial Exposition, Philadelphia,
              closed
1936     Crystal Palace, London, destroyed by fire
1939     Russia invaded Finland
1944     Albert Fall, U.S. Secretary of the Interior
              convicted in the Teapot Dome
              scandal, died
1953     Francis Picaba, French artist, died
1956     Floyd Patterson knocked out Archie Moore in the
              fifth round for the heavyweight
              boxing title
1964     Zond 2, Russian Mars probe, launched
1966     Barbodos got full independence from Britain
              (Independence Day)
1967     Southern Yemen became independent of Britain
```

DECEMBER ♑

Full Moon - Hunters' Moon, Ice Moon
First Friday - Arbor Day in Georgia

December 1st

0	Feast of St. Natalia
66 AD	St. Eligius, patron of metalworkers, black-smiths, wheelwrights, veterinar-ians, saddlers, miners, lock-smiths, clock, carriage, and tool makers, cabdrivers, farmers, jockeys and laborers, died (Feast Day)
659	St. Eloi, patron of goldsmiths, died
1135	King Henry I of England died
1170	Thomas a Becket, Archbishop of Canterbury, returned to England from exile
1372	Geoffrey Chaucer left England for Rome on a royal mission
1715	Christians in Venice, Italy, declared war on the Turks
1726	Oliver Wolcott, signer of the Declaration of Independence, born
1764	French government ordered suppression of the powerful Jesuit Order
1797	Oliver Wolcott, signer of the Declaration of Independence, died
1822	Dom Pedro crowned Emperor of Brazil
1825	Czar Alexander I of Russia died
1844	Alexandra of Denmark, wife of King Edward VII of England, born
1878	First telephone installed in the White House
1886	Rex Stout, mystery author, born
1887	China ceded Macao to Portugal

1898	Cyril Ritchard, actor, born
1901	Tina Lesser, designer, born
1904	Louisiana Purchase Exposition, St. Louis, Missouri, closed
1909	First Christmas Club account opened, in a New York bank
1911	Walter Alston, baseball figure, born
1917	Father Flanagan founded Boys' Town in Nebraska
1919	Lady Astor became the first woman to take a seat in the British Parliament
	Iceland became an independent kingdom but sharing the King with Denmark (Independence Day)
1920	Obregon became President of Mexico after Carranza's assassination
1939	LaGuardia Airport, New York City opened to the public
1941	U.S. Civil Air Patrol established
1945	Gen. Anton Dostler, Nazi war criminal, hanged in Rome
1956	Virgin Islands National Park dedicated
1959	Twelve-nation pact signed, making Antarctica a scientific preserve
	Construction of Sea Dragon completed, the atomic submarine that sailed under the Arctic ice
1964	Malawi, Malta, and Zambia joined the United Nations
1965	Second attempt begun to find the tomb of Egyptian Pharoh Imhotep
1970	Italy again got divorce laws, lacking since 1851
1972	Beginning of Hanukkah (Jewish holiday)

December 2nd

	Feast of St. Viviana
537 AD	Pope St. Silverius died
1001	Danish invading settlers massacred in England
1547	Cortez, conqueror of the Aztecs, died in obscurity in Spain
1697	New St. Paul's Cathedral, London, dedicated
1742	Publication of the Weekly Advertiser or Philadelphia Journal began
1784	George Washington nicknamed New York the Empire State
1795	Mungo Park began his exploration of central Africa
1804	Napoleon crowned himself Emperor of France
1805	Napoleon defeated Austria and Russia at Austerlitz
1814	Marquis de Sade, writer, died

1823	Monroe's Doctrine proclaimed in an annual message to Congress
1825	Pedro II, second and last Emperor of Brazil, born
1848	Emperor Ferdinand I of Austro-Hungary abdicated in favor of Franz Josef
1852	Louis-Napoleon proclaimed France a hereditary empire and himself Emperor Napoleon III
1859	John Brown, raider of Harper's Ferry, hanged
	George Seurat, French artist, born
1863	Statue of Freedom placed atop the U.S.Capitol
	Ground broken for the Union-Pacific Railroad at Omaha
1873	The Reformed Episcopal Church organized in the U.S.
1879	Borusia sank off Spain
1885	Dr. George R. Minot, discoverer of liver as an anemia cure, born
1886	Theodore Roosevelt married Edith K. Carow
1892	Jay Gould, financier, died
1901	British ship Condor vanished off Esquemalt, British Columbia
1914	Austrians captured Belgrade, Yugoslavia
1915	Adolph Green, playwright, born
1916	Permanent all-over lighting of the Statue of Liberty begun
1919	Henry Clay Frick, millionaire, died
1925	Amalgamation of Dyeworks and Chemical Industries of Germany founded
1927	Ford "Model A" introduced
1934	Palomar telescope's giant mirror cast by the Corning Glass works
1941	Australian cruiser Sydney lost in home waters
1942	First sustained atomic chain reaction performed on the squash court of the University of Chicago
1945	Government ordered nationalization of France's major banks
1952	First birth of a baby publicly televised
1954	Senator Joseph McCarthy and his subcommittee condemned by the Senate
1967	Francis Cardinal Spellman of New York died
1969	Start of the Poultry Show at Kingfisher, Oklahoma
	Christmas Parade held at Bakersfield, California
	Root's Country Market and Auction held at Petersburg, Pennsylvania
1970	Last anti-evolution teaching law, that of Mississippi, voided by the courts
1972	Start of the Festival of Whirling Dervishes at Konya, Turkey

Feast of St. Cassian of Tangier
Feast of St. Lucius, King

1154 AD Pope Anastasius IV died
1368   King Charles VI of France born
1552   St. Francis Xavier died, patron of foreign
         missions, invoked against
         plague (Feast Day)
1564   Ivan the Terrible and the Russian royal
         family left Moscow
1639   Bronx, New York, purchased from the Indians
         by Jonas Bronck
1714   Planet Uranus discovered by John Flamsteed
1738   Verendrye and his French explorers reached
         the site of Bismarck, North
         Dakota, seeking a water route
         to the Pacific
1750   Beggar's Opera became the first produced in
         America
1753   Samuel Crompton, spinning-mule inventor, born
1755   Gilbert Stuart, artist, died
1775   First U.S. flag, "The Grand Union," raised
         over a U.S. ship
1783   New York Gazette founded
1787   Rumsey demonstrated his first steamboat on
         the Potomac
1795   Sir Rowland Hill, organizer of England's
         penny postal system, born
1805   Clark, Lewis' partner, carved his name and
         this date on a Pacific pine tree
1813   William I proclaimed Prince Sovereign of the
         Netherlands
1818   Illinois became a state
1833   Oberlin, first fully coeducational college,
         opened (Ohio)
         Carlos Juan Finlay, originator of the mos-
         quito-yellow-fever theory, born
1836   Madison selected as the capitol of Wisconsin
1838   Cleveland Abbe, father of the U.S. Weather
         Bureau, born
1868   Jefferson Davis' treason trial began
1892   Dahomey, Africa, became a French protectorate
1894   Robert Louis Stevenson, writer, died of
         tuberculosis
1905   John Bartlett, compiler of Familiar Quotations,
         died
1912   Balkan War ended (Turkey against Greece,
         Montenegro, Bulgaria, and
         Serbia)
1917   A roof in Strathmore, Scotland, was de-
         stroyed by a meteorite

1935	Italian school day shortened to 3 hours to save coal
1948	Kiangya exploded in the China Sea
1952	Eleven Communists hanged in Czechoslovakia for treason and espionage
1956	Explosion of a Brooklyn, New York, pier
1967	First heart transplant operation performed, by Dr. Christiaan Barnard in South Africa; patient lived 18 days
	Twentieth Century Limited train made its last run
1969	Nature walk opened at Calaway Gardens, Georgia

December 4th

	Feast of St. Peter Chrysologus
	Feast of St. Barbara, invoked against lightning and sudden death; patron of gunners, miners, mathematicians, architects, smelters, brewers, oilers, and masons
	Feast of St. John of Damascus (Orthodox)
	National Day in Burma
265 AD	Last of the wall around Verona, Italy, built
771	Carloman, coruler of France with Charlemagne, died
1075	St. Anno martyred
1099	St. Osmund died (Feast Day)
1154	Nicholas Breakspear became the only Englishman elected Pope (Adrian IV)
1214	William the Lion, King of Scotland, died
1334	Pope John XXII, second Avignon Pope, died
1383	Amadeus, Pope as Felix V, born
1604	Champlain reached the St. Croix River, Maine
1619	Colonists for Berkley Grant, Virginia, celebrated Thanksgiving
1680	Thomas Bartholin, Danish physician and tracer of the lymphatic system, died
1775	Esek Hopkins, Brigadier General of the Rhode Island Army, took command of the U.S. Navy
1781	Prosperity fought off a privateer
1789	Mission of Santa Barbara dedicated in California
1793	King Frederick William III of Prussia married Louise
1841	King Edward VII of England invested as Prince of Wales
1866	Wassily Kandinsky, abstract artist, born
1867	National Granges, farmers' organization, founded

	America and the United States burned on the Ohio River
1875	"Boss" Tweed, New York politician, escaped from jail
1915	San Francisco's World's Fair closed
1917	Battle of Cambiae ended
1918	Woodrow Wilson sailed to attend the Paris Peace Conference
1923	Maria Callas, opera singer, born
1936	Construction of Oregon's new capitol began
1947	Bulgaria adopted a Communist constitution
1963	Ecumenical Council changed the Roman Mass from Latin to the local language
1969	Start of Weslaco, Texas, 50th anniversary celebration

December 5th

	Feast of St. Birinus
63 BC	Lentulus, Roman conspirator, executed
304 AD	St. Crispina died (Feast Day)
532	St. Sabas died (Feast Day)
1212	Frederick II chosen King of Germany, again
1484	Pope set severe penalties against German witches and magicians
1560	King Francis II of France died
1757	Prussians defeated the Austrians at Leuthen (Seven Years' War)
1776	Phi Beta Kappa fraternity formed
1777	Constitution Gazette, first newspaper in New Jersey, began publication
1782	Martin Van Buren, U.S. President, born
1791	Wolfgang Mozart, composer, died
1833	Philadelphia and Reading Railroad Company incorporated
1842	Site chosen for the first Catholic mission in Idaho
1848	California gold discovery announced by President Polk in a message to Congress
1866	American Watercolor Society formed
1901	Walt Disney, filmmaking cartoonist, born
1902	Senator Strom Thurmond born
1906	Otto Preminger, filmmaker, born
1912	Presidential order created the Panama Canal Zone under U.S. control
1921	Train wrecked at Woodmont, Pennsylvania
1926	Claude Monet, French artist, died
1931	Vachel Lindsay, poet, died
1932	Japanese destroyer Sawarab sank in a storm off Formosa

```
1933        Twenty-first Amendment repealed the Eighteenth,
                and liquor was legal in the U.S.
                again
1936        Marii, one of the Union of Soviet Socialist
                Republics, created and Kurghiz
                joined the Union
1955        American Federation of Labor and Congress of
                Industrial Organizations merged
1957        Gas line exploded near Villa Rica
```

```
            Feast of St. Abraham of Kratia
            Feast of former St. Nicholas, patron of sail-
                ors, children, merchants, pawn-
                brokers, coopers, brewers, unjust
                losers in lawsuits, scholars,
                dock workers, Greece, Sicily,
                Lorraine (part of France); invoked
                against thieves
1185 AD     King Alphonso I of Portugal died
1352        Pope Clement VI died
1362        Guillaume de Grimoard crowned Pope as Urban V
1421        Henry VI, King of England, born
1492        Columbus landed on Haiti
1648        "Pride's Purge," English government reform
                movement, took place
1741        Elizabeth declared Empress of Russia after
                a coup
1792        William II, King of Holland, born
1799        Feudal system abolished in Denmark
1811        North American earthquake
1835        New York City business district swept
                by a fire
1857        Joseph Conrad, novelist, born
1865        Thirteenth Amendment, abolishing slavery,
                ratified
1872        William S. Hart, actor-author, born
1874        Cospatrick burned and 470 died
1875        Deutschland wrecked at the mouth of the Thames
1877        Washington Post newspaper founded
            Imprisonment for debt ended in Italy
1884        Capstone of the Washington Monument put in
                place
1886        Joyce Kilmer, poet, born
1889        Jefferson Davis, President of the Confeder-
                acy, died
1896        Ira Gershwin, composer, born
1906        Agnes Moorehead, actress, born
1917        Explosion of the Mont Blanc loaded with TNT
                practically destroyed Halifax,
                Nova Scotia
```

	Finland became independent of Russia (Independence Day)
	U.S. destroyer Jacob Jones torpedoed off Scilly Islands
1918	Americans entered Mainz, Germany
1920	Dave Brubeck, jazz musician, born
1921	"British Commonwealth of Nations" title first used in an official document
	Irish peace agreement signed
1922	English flag lowered for the last time at Dublin Castle, Ireland
1942	British ship Ceramic torpedoed off the Azores
1958	U.S. launched Pioneer III
1967	Metropolitan Museum of Art announced that its Greek bronze horse was a forgery (New York City)

December 7th

	Feast of St. Ambrose, patron of bees and domestic animals
	Start of a 2-day fair at Clitheroe, Lancashire, England
43 BC	Cicero, Roman politician, slain
521 AD	St. Columba born
983	Otto II, Holy Roman Emperor, died
1254	Pope Innocent IV died
1545	Tocuyo, Venezuela, founded
1550	Barbara crowned Queen of Poland
1598	Giovanni Bernini, builder of St. Peter's Basilica, Rome, born
1682	"Great Law of Pennsylvania" passed
1738	Verendrye, exploring French fur trader, reached the site of his National Monument in North Dakota
1787	Delaware ratified the U.S. Constitution
1793	Mme. Du Barry, mistress of King Louis XV of France, guillotined
1816	Juvenile Port Folio of Philadelphia ended after four years of weekly publication
1835	First railroad in Germany opened, Nurnberg to Furth
1840	Illinois legislature first met in the new capitol
1848	The Independent, New York City weekly magazine, founded
1869	The News began publication in Indianapolis
1873	Willa Cather, author, born
1880	St. Josepha Rosello died
1887	Irving Crump, author of stories for boys, born

```
1888      Pneumatic rubber tire for tricycles patented
1894      Ferdinand de Lesseps, Suez Canal builder,
                died
1896      Antonio Maceo, leader of the Cuban insurrec-
                tion, killed
1911      Louis Prima, musician, born
1915      Eli Wallach, actor, born
1917      U.S. declared war on Austro-Hungarian Empire
1941      Britain declared war on Finland, Hungary, and
                Rumania
          Japanese planes attacked Pearl Harbor, Hawaii
          Japanese troops occupied Shanghai, China
1949      Nationalist Chinese government fled to
                Formosa, escaping the Communists
1965      Roman and Orthodox churches reconciled,
                cancelling their excommunications
                of each other in 1054
1969      Bodhi Day, Buddhist day of Enlightenment
          Annual Holly Tour held in Baltimore, Maryland
1970      Start of Whirling Dervishes Festival at
                Konya, Turkey
1971      Rube Goldberg, cartoonist-inventor, died
```

December 8th

```
          Feast of the Immaculate Conception
          Feast of St. Budoc
  65 BC   Horace, Roman poet, born
 877 AD   Louis II, "the Stammerer," crowned King of
                France
1626      Queen Christina of Sweden born
1644      Christina became the first reigning Queen
                of Sweden
1708      Francis I, Holy Roman Emperor, born
1741      Vitus Bering, discoverer of Alaska, died
                in the Aleutian Islands
1765      Eli Whitney, cotton-gin inventor, born
1767      Guiria, Venezuela, founded
1776      Washington and the American troops crossed
                the Delaware
1787      La Purisima Concepcion Mission founded in
                California
1828      Henry Timrod, "poet laureate of the Confed-
                ercy," born
1840      Dr. David Livingstone sailed for Africa
1854      Doctrine of the Immaculate Conception
                announced by Pope Pius IX
1859      American College in Rome, Italy, founded
1861      Bay of Naples shaken by an earthquake (Italy)
1865      Jean Sibelius, composer, born
1868      Jesuit church packed with worshipers burned
                in Santiago, Chile
```

1885	Kenneth Roberts, novelist, born
1886	American Federation of Labor founded with Samuel Gompers as president
1889	Hervey Allen, novelist, born
1905	American Bison Society organized to protect the remaining buffalo
1907	King Oscar II of Sweden and Norway died
1911	Lee J. Cobb, actor, born
1914	Four German cruisers lost in the Battle of the Falkland Islands
1919	Sons of Norway store at St. Petersburg, Alaska burned down
1929	Royal Gorge Bridge, the highest above water as it crosses the Arkansas River, opened to traffic
1934	Weekly air mail service began between England and Australia
1941	Siam (Thailand) fell to the Japanese
	Japan bombed Manila, Philippines
	U.S., Britain, and Free France declared war on Japan
1950	U.S. banned all shipments to Communist China
1962	Beginning of a 114-day newspaper strike in New York City
	First session of the Ecumenical Council ended
1965	Ecumenical Council, begun in 1962, closed
1966	Greek ferry Herakhon sank in an Aegean storm

December 9th

297 AD	Sts. Hipparchus and Philotheus martyred (Feast Day)
861	Mutawakkil, Caliph of Baghdad, murdered
1165	Malcolm IV, King of Scotland, died
1212	Frederick II crowned King of Germany
1315	Second Everlasting League founded in Switzerland
1437	Sigismund, King of Hungary, Bohemia, Germany, and Lombardy, as well as the Emperor of Rome, died
1482	Frederick the Wise, elector palatine of the Rhine, born
1561	Sir Edmund Sandys, founder of a Virginia colony, born
1565	Pope Pius IV died
1594	Gustavus II Adolphus, King of Sweden, born
1608	John Milton, poet, born
1640	St. Peter Fourier died (Feast Day)
	Hugh Bewitt banished from the Massachusetts Colony for declaring himself free of original sin
1641	Sir Anthony Van Dyck, artist, died

1669	Pope Clement IX died
1706	Pedro II, King of Portugal, died
1721	Irish House of Commons rejected the establishment of a national bank
1777	Charter drafted for the first French government pawnshop
1778	British captured Savannah, Georgia
	Illinois Territory became a county of Virginia
1792	First formal cremation of a human in America performed
1793	The Globe, New York City newspaper, established
	America Minerva newspaper began publication
1824	Defeat at Ayacucho, Peru, ended Spain's domination in South America
1842	Peter A. Kropotkin, Russian geographer, born
	First Christmas card created, in England
1845	Fremont expedition reached Sutter's Fort, California
1854	Alfred, Lord Tennyson's "Charge of the Light Brigade" published
1856	Dr. David Livingstone, African explorer, returned to London
1862	Karel Kovarovic, Czech composer, born
1864	Battle of Deveraux's Neck ended
1877	Women given the right to witness documents in Italy
1880	James B. Hendryx, author, born
1898	Emmett Kelly, clown, born
1902	Lucius Beebe, journalist, born
1905	Law signed in France separating Church and state
1909	Douglas Fairbanks, Jr., actor, born
1919	Petersberg, Alaska, got a volunteer fire department
1920	Karel Kovarovic, Czech composer, died
1932	Willie Hartack, jockey, born
1935	Peking, China, students demonstrated against Japanese rule in Manchuria
1938	James W. Garner, author-educator, died
1941	Two British ships sunk by the Japanese off Malaya
1947	Rocking F Ranch in Nevada laid claim to all the water in clouds passing over it
1958	John Birch Society organized
1965	Baseball's Branch Rickey died
1966	Barbados joined the United Nations
1969	Festival of Trees held in Honolulu, Hawaii
1970	Peru and Ecuador shaken by an earthquake
1971	Ralph Bunche, United Nations official, died

Aviation Day in Venezuela
Human Rights Day (United Nations)
Albatrosses nest
Feast of St. Miltiades

304 AD	?St. Eulalia died (Feast Day)
1348	Third vicar appointed to Shaftsbury, England, to replace those who had died of plague
1607	Capt. John Smith left Jamestown on the trip that involved him with Pocahontas
1672	Monthly postal service established between Boston and New York
1792	Insurance Company of North America organized
1805	William Lloyd Garrison, abolitionist, born
1817	Mississippi became a state
1830	Emily Dickinson, poet, born
1831	Spirit of the Times, sporting journal, founded
1848	Louis Napoleon, nephew of the Emperor, elected President of France
1862	West Virginia became a state
1865	Leopold I, a German elected King of Belgium, died
1869	Women in Wyoming granted the right to vote
1896	Alfred Nobel, chemist and prize donor, died
	Ira Gershwin, composer, born
1898	Spain ceded Puerto Rico and the Philippines to the U.S. in the treaty ending the Spanish-American War
1901	First Nobel Prizes awarded
1902	First Aswan Dam stopped the flow of the Nile River
1904	Bethlehem Steel Company organized
1911	Chet Huntley, broadcaster, born
1914	Dorothy Lamour, actress, born
1915	Millionth Ford automobile built, a "Model T"
1923	Egyptian flag adopted
1934	New York City got a 2 percent sales tax
1936	King Edward VIII of England announced his intention to abdicate
1945	Netherlands joined the United Nations
1946	Damon Runyan, writer, died
1958	Jet passenger airline service began between New York and Miami
1969	Tortugas Indian Pilgrimage held at Las Cruces, New Mexico
	Pancake Days Festivals held at Hazelton and Wilkesbarre, Pennsylvania

Beast market held at Boston, England
Ancient Roman festival honoring all the gods

361 AD Julian, Roman Emperor, entered Constantinople
384   St. Damascus I, Pope, died (Feast Day)
493   St. Daniel the Stylite died (Feast Day)
1241   Ogedei, Mongol leader, died and his army
            withdrew from Hungary
1282   Llywelyn ap Gruffydd, Welsh leader, killed
1521   Wladislaus II, King of Hungary and Bohemia,
            died
1695   Captain Kidd received his English commission
            as a privateer
1718   King Charles XII of Sweden killed at the
            siege of Fredriksten, Norway
1787   Rumsey again demonstrated his steamboat
            on the Potomac
1816   Indiana became a state
1843   Robert Koch, bacteriologist, born
1844   Laughing gas first used for a tooth extraction
1845   First Sikh War between England and India began
1882   Fiorello LaGuardia, New York City mayor, born
1905   Gilbert Roland, actor, born
1922   Irish Free State, a British Dominion, adopted
1924   Duke University founded (North Carolina)
1936   King Edward VIII of England abdicated to
            marry the woman he loved
1937   Italy withdrew from the League of Nations
1941   Germany, Italy, and the U.S. exchanged
            declarations of war
        Japanese troops occupied Guam
1950   U.S. Supreme Court made its Fifth Amendment
            ruling (no one could be forced
            to testify against himself)
1969   Start of the Centennial celebrations at Fort
            Sill, Oklahoma

Antarctic whaling season begins
Feast of St. Finnian of Clonard
Day of Our Lady of Guadalupe, Mexico

751 AD St. Edburga of Minster died (Feast Day)
1154   St. Vicelin died (Feast Day)
1189   King Richard the Lionhearted left England for
            the Third Crusade
1254   Rinaldo Conti elected Pope as Alexander IV
1293   Khalil, sultan of Egypt, murdered by Baidara,
            his replacement, who was also
            murdered
1574   Selim II, Sultan of Turkey, died

1586	Stephen Bathory, King of Poland, died of apoplexy
1710	Shipwreck on Boon Island, Maine
1745	John Jay, first U.S. Chief Justice, born
1787	Pennsylvania became a state
1791	Marie Louise of Austria, second wife of Napoleon, born
1818	Mary Todd Lincoln, wife of the President, born
1863	Edvard Munch, Norwegian artist, born
1870	Solar eclipse
1871	"Wild Bill" Hickok fired as marshall of Abeline, Kansas
1893	Edward G. Robinson, actor, born
1899	The wooden golf tee was invented
	Winston Churchill escaped from a prison camp (Boer War)
1901	Marconi signaled "S" from England to Newfoundland via his wireless
1911	Coronation durbar for King George V of England held at Delhi, India
1912	Louis III became Regent of Bavaria
1913	Stolen "Mona Lisa" recovered
1915	Frank Sinatra, singer-actor, born
1916	Germany and its allies called for peace negotiations
1917	Train wrecked at Modane, France
	Suffrage granted to all Dutch citizens over 25 years of age
1922	John Wanamaker, merchant, died
1936	Spanish submarine torpedoed off Malaya
1937	U.S.S. Panay sunk in China's Yangtze River by Japan
	Chinese Premier Chiang Kai-shek moved to Hankow
1946	"Big Four" meeting in New York ended, setting peace terms for Germany's allies
1958	Guinea joined the United Nations
1963	Kenya got its independence from England (Independence Day)
1964	Jomo Kenyetta, Maumau leader, became President of Kenya
1968	Tallulah Bankhead, actress, died
1969	Matachines Dance held at Jemez Pueblo, New Mexico
	Pecan Perfection Day held at Monahans, Texas
	All-Poinsettia Show held at Mission, Texas
1970	Last steam train in France left Paris for the last time

Ides of December
Feast of ex-Saint Lucy (or Lucia), patron of
        Syracuse, Sicily; invoked against
        eye diseases, dysentery, and
        hemorrhages
Feast of St. Odilia

1124 AD	Pope Colextus II died
1204	Maimonides, Jewish philosopher, died
1250	Frederick II, deposed Holy Roman Emperor, died of dysentery
1294	Pope Celestine V abdicated
1402	Emperor Go-Komatsu moved into the rebuilt Japanese Imperial Palace
1476	First item, a Papal indulgence, printed in England
1503	Nostradamus, French astrologer, born
1545	Council of Trent opened to discuss Catholic Church reform
1557	Sir Francis Drake left England to sail around the world
1640	John IV crowned King of Portugal
1641	St. Jane Frances de Chantel died
1642	Abel Tasman discovered New Zealand
1769	Dartmouth College chartered (New Hampshire)
1784	Samuel Johnson, English writer, died
1806	Aaron Burr's attempt to set up a kingdom on the Mississippi classed as war against the U.S.
1819	Tuscaloosa, Alabama, incorporated
1835	Philip Brooks, composer ("O Little Town of Bethlehem"), born
1839	Christian VIII became King of Denmark
1862	Confederates were victorious at Fredericksburg, Virginia
1884	First wagon train of emigrants to California reached Sutter's Mill
1890	Marc Connelly, playwright, born
1897	Drew Pearson, columnist, born
1918	American forces crossed the Rhine
1922	Train wrecked near Humble, Texas
1924	Samuel Gompers, author and labor leader, died
1925	Pahlavi dynasty invested with sovereignty in Persia (Iran)
1927	Yehudi Menuhin, violinist, made his New York debut at the age of 10
	Poland officially adopted its flag
1937	Karim Aga Khan, Moslem religious leader, born
1941	Britain declared war on Bulgaria
1944	Wassily Kandinsky, abstract artist, died
1947	Maine Turnpike opened to traffic

1952	Two apartment buildings exploded at Dortmund, Germany
1957	Western Iran rocked by earthquakes
1961	U.S. launched Relay I, communications satellite
	Grandma Moses, American primitive artist, died
1968	Part of El Paso, Texas, became Mexican by returning the Rio Grande River to its original bed
1969	Santa Claus Bowl game played at Lakeland, Florida
1971	Hanukkah (Jewish festival)

December 14th

	Feast of St. Spiridiron
867 AD	Adrian II elected Pope
872	Pope Adrian II died and John III elected to replace him
1542	James V, King of Scotland, died
1553	Henri IV, Protestant King of France, born
1591	St. John of the Cross died
1719	Boston Gazette founded as a weekly publication
1788	King Charles III of Spain died
1799	George Washington, first U.S. President, died
1819	Alabama became a state
1871	George Hudson, English "railway king," died
1895	King George VI, brother of abdicated Edward VIII of England, born
1896	James Doolittle, leader of the U.S. bombing raids on Japan in World War II, born
1897	Senator Margaret Chase Smith born
1901	Paul I, King of Greece, born
1911	Roald Amundsen, with 4 men and dog teams, reached the South Pole
1934	Women given the right to vote in Turkey
1945	Eleven Nazi war criminals hanged for their concentration-camp atrocities
1955	Albania, Austria, Bulgaria, Cambodia, Ceylon, Finland, Hungary, Ireland, Italy, Jordan, Laos, Libya, Nepal, Portugal, Rumania, and Spain all joined the United Nations
1960	Tankers Peter Zoranic from Yugoslavia and World Harmony of Germany collided in the Bosporus
1967	Southern Yemen, formerly Aden, joined the United Nations
	King Constantine of Greece went into exile
1969	HO Model Train Open House held at Aurora, Illinois

Around the World Christmas Party held at
West Lafayette, Indiana
Nickomo Indian Giveway Ceremony held at
Hopkinton, Rhode Island

December 15th

	Netherlanda Antilles Kingdom Day
	Festival of Consus, an ancient Roman deity
	Feast of St. Nino
37 AD	Nero, Roman Emperor, born
687	Sergius I elected Pope
1268	Haakon IV, "the Old," King of Norway, died
1476	Matthias I, King of Hungary, married Beatrice of Naples
1675	Jan Vermeer, Dutch artist, died
1683	Izaak Walton, fisherman, died
1745	Prussians routed Saxons at Kesselsdorf
1785	King George IV of England married his mistress, Catholic Maria Fitzherbert
1791	U.S. Bill of Rights went into effect (Bill of Rights Day)
1792	First life insurance policy in the U.S. issued
1811	Mississippi River Valley hit by a strong earthquake
1836	U.S. Patent Office destroyed by fire
1852	Antoine Henri Becquerel, discoverer of radio-activity, born
1855	Frank Leslie's Illustrated Newspaper, a weekly, began publication in New York
1888	Maxwell Anderson, playwright, born
1890	Sitting Bull, leader of the Sioux Indians, killed by the U.S. Army
1892	J. Paul Getty, millionaire, born
1902	Henry Field, anthropologist, born
1904	Betty Smith, author, born
1914	Russians drove Austrians out of Belgrade, Yugoslavia
1917	Armistice signed for World War I's Russian front
1938	Ground broken for the Jefferson Memorial, Washington, D.C.
1944	U.S. troops landed on Mindoro Island
	U.S. rank of Admiral of the Fleet created by Congress
1957	Start of two days of earthquakes in western Iran
1960	King Badouin of Belgium married Dona Fabiola de Mora y Aragon of Spain
1964	San Marcos I, first Italian satellite, launched
1965	U.S. spaceships Gemini VI and VII rendezvoused in orbit

Queen Salote of Tonga died
Oosterscheldeberg, a 3-mile causeway crossing
        an arm of the Zeeland, opened
        in the Netherlands

1969   Sixty-eighth anniversary of the Sindia Wreck
        celebrated at Ocean City,
        New Jersey
"Nut Day" fair held at Bastogne, Belgium

December 16th

370 AD	St. Eusebius of Vercelli died (Feast Day)
714	Pepin II, ruler of France, died
882	Pope John VIII murdered and Marinus I elected to replace him
1431	Henry VI, King of England, crowned King of France
1631	Mt. Vesuvius volcano erupted (Italy)
1653	Oliver Cromwell became Lord Protector of Britain
1770	Ludwig von Beethoven, composer, born
1773	Boston Tea Party held
1775	Jane Austen, English novelist, born
1811	Missouri rocked by an earthquake
1835	Wall Street area of New York City destroyed by fire
1838	The Boers defeated the Zulus in South Africa ("Dingaan's Day")
1851	Patent for brass spinning granted
1852	The Evening Star began publication in Washington, D.C.
1860	Burke and Wells expedition completed their crossing of the Australian continent
1868	Daniel Douglas Home levitated out one window and into another 70 feet above the ground
1870	Cape Hatteras Lighthouse first lit
1880	Transvall, South Africa, again proclaimed a republic
1893	Railroad reached Cripple Creek, Colorado
1897	First practical sunken-treasure submarine demonstrated
1899	Noel Coward, theatrical personality, born
1901	Margaret Mead, anthropologist-author, born
1919	Shakespeare's Merchant of Venice barred from the Youngstown, Ohio, schools
1920	Kansu, China, rocked by an earthquake
	Permanent Court of International Justice created
1922	Florence E. Allen became the first woman justice of a state supreme court, in Ohio

1928	Uruguay adopted its flag
1941	British cruiser <u>Galatea</u> torpedoed in the Mediterranean
1943	Train wreck near Buie, North Carolina
1944	Germans counterattacked at the Ardennes Bridge
1946	Thailand joined the United Nations
1951	Elizabeth Meriwether Gilmer, journalist as Dorothy Dix, died
1953	Delaware Water Gap Bridge between New Jersey and Pennsylvania opened to traffic
1963	Kenya joined the United Nations
1968	Edict that had banned Jews from Spain since 1942 rescinded

---

December 17th

	International Students' Day in Czechoslovakia
	Stock fair at Grantham, Lincolnshire, England
	Feast of St. Olympias
63 AD	Lazarus died for the second time
693	St. Begga died (Feast Day)
779	St. Sturm died (Feast Day)
942	William Longsword, Duke of Normandy, assassinated
1187	Pope Gregory VIII died
	Paolo Scalari elected Pope as Clement III
1213	St. John of Matha died
1232	Crusaders gathered to free Burriana, Spain, from the Moors
1273	Rumi, Persian poet, died
1734	William Floyd, signer of the Declaration of Independence, born
1770	Ludwig von Beethoven, composer, baptized
1778	Sir Humphry Davy, inventor of the safety lamp, born
1807	Napoleon announced his Milan Decree, legalizing the seizure of ships trading with Britain
	John Greenleaf Whittier, poet, born
1819	Colombia and Venezuela became one country
1830	Simon Bolivar, South American revolutionary hero, died
1843	Charles Dickens' <u>A Christmas Carol</u> first published
1894	Arthur Fiedler, orchestra conductor, born
1903	The Wright brothers had their first successful flight, 120 ft. in 12 sec.
	Erskine Caldwell, author, born
1907	William Thomas, inventor of the submarine cable, died

```
1908        Los Angeles bombed with confetti from balloons
1909        King Leopold II of Belgium died
1919        Picatinny Arsenal in New Jersey exploded
            August Renoir, French artist, died
1927        U.S. submarine S-4 involved in a collision
                        off Cape Cod
1938        Construction of the Chicago subway began
1939        German battleship Graf Spee blown up by its
                        crew off Uruguay
1944        German offensive began the Battle of the Bulge
1945        Honduras joined the United Nations
1969        Senior Citizens' Holiday Festival held at
                        Newark, New Jersey
            Old San Diego Posada celebrated in California
            Twenty-one year study of unidentified flying
                        objects ended with no conclusions
1970        End of the Whirling Dervishes Festival at
                        Konya, Turkey
```

December 18th

```
 761 AD     St. Winebald died (Feast Day)
1127        Conrad III elected King of Germany
1644        Antonio Stradivari, violin-maker, born
1709        Elizabeth, Empress of Russia and daughter of
                        Czar Peter the Great, born before
                        her parents married
1790        Leopold I, German-born King of Belgium, born
1819        Father Isaac Hecker, founder of the Paulist
                        Fathers, born
1829        Jean Baptiste Lamarck, naturalist, died
1845        First battle of the First Sikh War fought by
                        India and Britain at Moodkee, India
1847        Marie Louise of Austria, second wife of
                        Napoleon, died
1861        Edward MacDowell, composer, born
1863        Francis II, Archduke of Austria, born
1879        Paul Klee, Swiss-born artist, born
1886        Ty Cobb, baseball star, born
1898        Chasseloup-Laubat in a Jeantaud set a land-
                        speed record of 39.24 mph
1910        Abe Burrows, playwright-author, born
1913        Willie Brandt, German statesman, born
1915        Woodrow Wilson, U.S. President, married
                        Edith B. Galt
1916        Betty Grable, actress-pinup girl, born
1936        First live giant panda arrived in the U.S.
1944        Three U.S. destroyers sunk by a Pacific storm
1945        Uruguay joined the United Nations
1956        Japan joined the United Nations
1958        Atlas-Score, first communications sattelite,
                        launched by the U.S.
```

1969   Capital punishment ended in England

December 19th

        Adam's Day (Roman Catholic)
        Feast of St. Anastasius
        Ancient Roman festival of Saturn, god of the
                seed-corn
  960 AD Reconstruction of Kyoto, Japan's Imperial
                Palace, begun after a fire
 1075   Edith, wife of King Edward the Confessor of
        England, died
 1154   Stephen, King of England, died
 1155   Henry II and Eleanor of Aquitaine crowned
                rulers of England
 1170   St. Thomas a Becket martyred on the orders of
                King Henry II of England
 1370   Pope Urban V died
 1406   Angelo Coraorrio crowned Pope as Gregory XII
 1606   Jamestown, Virginia, colonists sailed from
                England
 1675   Narragansett Indians made their last stand
                against the English in King
                Philip's War
 1683   King Philip V of Spain born
 1722   Ostend Company, Dutch East Indies traders,
                chartered
 1732   Benjamin Franklin's Poor Richard's Almanac
                printed
 1777   American troops camped at Valley Forge,
                Pennsylvania
 1787   New Jersey ratified the U.S. Constitution
 1790   Sir William Parry, Arctic explorer, born
 1813   British captured Fort Niagara (War of 1812)
 1851   J. M. W. Turner, English artist, died
 1859   Mirabeau Buonaparte Lamar, second President
                of the Texas Republic, died
 1871   Birmingham, Alabama, incorporated as a city
 1901   Oliver L. Farge, novelist, born
 1903   Williamsburg Bridge, New York City, opened
                to traffic
 1915   Allies began the evacuation of Gallipoli on
                the Dardanelles
 1923   King George II of Greece and his family left
                their country
 1934   Al Kaline, baseball player, born
        Border dispute began between Ethiopia and the
                Italian colony of Somaliland
 1944   U.S. Army advances into Germany pushed back
 1946   French and Communists began fighting in Viet
                Nam

1960	U.S. aircraft carrier Constellation burned in the Brooklyn Navy Yard
	Maryland's State House designated a registered national landmark
1963	U.S. launched the 19th Explorer satellite

December 20th

(?) BC	Romulus, founder of Rome, conceived
1192 AD	King Richard the Lionhearted, returning from the Third Crusade, captured and held for ransom by Austria
1334	Jacques Fournier elected the third Avignon Pope as Benedict XII
1620	Samuel Fuller became the first doctor to arrive in New England
1686	British founded Calcutta, India
1699	Russia adjusted its calendar so that New Year's Day would be January 1st instead of September 1st
1792	Kentucky's state seal accepted by the state legislature
1803	U.S. took title to the Louisiana Purchase Lands
1832	Crete ceded to Egypt by Turkey
1835	Cherokee Indians driven from Georgia because gold was discovered on their lands
	Texas declared itself independent of Mexico
1860	South Carolina seceded from the Union
1864	Gen. Sherman completed his "March to the Sea"
1880	First electric lights lit on Broadway, New York
1917	Train wrecked at Shepherdsville, Kentucky
1919	Train wrecked near Onawa, Maine
1922	Assorted Russian republics united as the Union of Soviet Socialist Republics
1928	Ethel Barrymore Theater opened (New York City)
1961	Moss Hart, playwright, died
1963	Berlin Wall opened for the first time
1968	John Steinbeck, author, died
1969	Christmas Afloat held at San Pedro, California
	Sheepherders' Ball held at Boise, Idaho

December 21st

	Feast of St. Thomas Didymus, apostle
	Fair at Penryn, Cornwall, England
	New Year's Day to the ancient Greeks and Romans
1124 AD	Honorius II confirmed as Pope

1375	Giovanni Boccaccio, Italian poet, died
1491	Five-year truce began between England and Scotland
1557	St. Peter Canisius died
1605	Spanish expedition left Callao, Peru, in search of Australia
1620	Pilgrims landed at Plymouth, Massachusetts (Forefathers Day in New England)
1671	Isaac Newton was proposed for membership in London's Royal Society
1725	Russian Imperial Academy of Science founded
1767	Boston Chronicle newspaper founded
1790	Samuel Slater's thread-spinning factory went into production
1804	Benjamin Disraeli, British statesman, born
1864	Gen. Sherman reached Savannah, Georgia, and it surrendered
1866	Sioux Indians attacked the Cavalry at Ft. Philip Kearny, Wyoming
1872	Albert Payson Terhune, author, born
1873	Garnier, explorer of the Mekong River in Indochina, died
1876	Irenee du Pont, head of the chemical firm, born
1879	Joseph Stalin, Russian dictator, born
1928	Boulder (Hoover) Dam construction act approved by Congress
1929	Chinese ship Lee Cheong sank off Hong Kong
1940	F. Scott Fitzgerald, author, died
1944	American troops pinned down at Bastogne rescued
1945	Ecuador and Iraq joined the United Nations
1946	Coastal Japan hit by tidal waves
1947	Mark Hellinger, journalist-author, died
1958	Charles deGaulle elected President of France's 5th Republic
	Lion Feuchtwanger, author, died
1963	U.S. launched the Tiros VIII weather satellite
1964	Explorer 26 launched by the U.S.
1967	First heart-transplant patient died, 18 days after surgery
1968	U.S. launched Apollo 8 to fly around the moon
1969	Christmas Boat Parade at Pompano Beach, Florida
	Santa arrived in Dieterich, Illinois, and all the town's porch lights were turned on

---

December 22nd

69 AD	Audus Vitellius, Roman Emperor, murdered
1216	Papal Confirmation given to the Dominican Order of Friars

1668	Stephen Daye, first printer in the Colonies, died
1719	American Weekly Mercury newspaper founded in Philadelphia
1727	William Ellery, signer of the Declaration of Independence, born
1770	Father Gallitzin, "Apostle of the Alleghenies," born
1775	Continental Navy organized under Ezek Hopkins
1820	Daniel Webster made a speech at the Plymouth, Massachusetts, Bicentennial Celebration
1859	"Brown of Osawatomie" by John Greenleaf Whittier, was published in the New York City Independent
1872	George Catlin, Western artist, died
1880	Mary Ann Evans, writer as George Eliot, died
1888	J. Arthur Rank, filmmaker, born
	Father Isaac Hecker, founder of the Paulist Fathers, died
1894	U.S. Golf Association formed
	Dreyfus found guilty of betraying French secrets
1901	Andre Kostelanetz, conductor, born
1911	Harriet J. H. Robinson, suffragist, died
1912	"Lady Bird" Johnson, First Lady, born
1913	Menelik II, Emperor of Ethiopia, died
1938	Coelacanth, a fish thought to have been extinct for 65 million years, caught off South Africa

December 23rd

619 AD	Boniface V became Pope
1096	Parts of the First Crusade arrived in Constantinople
1193	St. Thorlac died (Feast Day)
1466	King George Podiebrad of Bohemia excommunicated
1569	St. Philip of Moscow, Primate of the Russian Church, martyred by Ivan the Terrible
1588	Duc de Guise and Cardinal de Tournon murdered in France
1688	King James II of England escaped to France from his Protestant subjects
1732	Richard Arkwright, "father of the factory system," born
1783	George Washington retired to Mount Vernon
1805	Joseph Smith, founder of Mormonism, born
1817	William Goddard, founder of the U.S. postal system, died

1823	"The Night Before Christmas" first published
1854	Shikoku, Japan, rocked by an earthquake
1858	Puccini, opera composer, born
1870	Battle of Pont-Noyelles (Franco-Prussian War)
1903	Train wrecked at Laurel Run, Pennsylvania
1913	Federal Reserve Banking System put into effect
1918	Jose Greco, Spanish dancer, born
1933	Crown Prince Akihito Tusugu No Miya of Japan born
1938	Final victorious push begun by the Spanish insurgents
1944	Charles D. Gibson, creator of the "Gibson Girl," died
1948	Tojo and six other Japanese military leaders hanged as war criminals
1953	Beria, former head of the Soviet Secret Police, executed
1963	Greek liner Lakonia burned in the Atlantic
1968	North Korean forces seized the U.S.S. Pueblo
1969	Night of the Radishes in Oaxaca, Mexico

December 24th

	Christmas Lantern Festival at San Fernando, Philippines
	Feast of St. Ignatius of Loyola
5 BC	Servius Galba, Roman Emperor, born
640 AD	Pope John IV elected to office
820	Leo V the Armenian, Eastern Roman Emperor, assassinated
877	St. Odo born
1167	John I "Lackland," King of England, born
1473	St. John of Kanti died
1524	Vasco da Gama, explorer, died
1728	Universal Instructor in All Arts and Sciences and Pennsylvania Gazette founded in Philadelphia
1745	Benjamin Rush, signer of the Declaration of Independence, born
1784	Methodist Episcopal Church formed in Maryland
1799	Napoleon was declared First Consul of France
1809	"Kit" Carson, frontiersman, born
1814	Treaty of Ghent ended the War of 1812
1818	"Silent Night" composed and first sung
1837	Elizabeth, wife of Emperor Franz Joseph of Austro-Hungary, born
1849	San Francisco caught fire
1863	William Makepeace Thackeray, novelist, died
1870	Punchinello, New York comic magazine, folded after 8 months of publication
1871	Aida opera had its world premier in Cairo, Egypt

```
1873    John Hopkins, merchant-philanthropist, died
1880    Johnny Gruelle, creator of "Raggedy Ann," born
1905    Howard Hughes, millionaire, born
1914    First German air raid on England
        John Muir, naturalist-explorer, died
1920    John Meridith Langstaff, author of "Frog Went
            a'Courting," born
1940    "Billy" (William Joseph) Hill, songwriter,
            died
1944    Belgian ship Leopoldville torpedoed
1950    Hungnan, Korea, evacuated of civilians and
            U.N. forces
1968    Apollo 8 flew around the Moon, broadcasting a
            Christmas message back to Earth
1969    Luminaria Caravan Tour held at Albuquerque,
            New Mexico
```

```
=================================================================
December 25th
=================================================================
```

```
        Feast of St. Eugenia
        New Year's Day in England before 1066
        Quarter Day in England - rents due, move in
            or out
   0 BC/AD  Jesus Christ born (according to the Bible)
 304 (?) St. Anastasia died (Feast Day)
 496    Clovis, King of France, baptized a Christian
 800    Charlemagne, King of France, crowned Holy
            Roman Emperor
 967    Otto II crowned Holy Roman Emperor
 983    Otto III crowned King of Germany
1046    Henry III, "the Black," crowned Holy Roman
            Emperor
1066    William, "Bastard of Normandy," Conqueror of
            England, crowned King in
            Westminster Abbey
1075    Pope Gregory VII kidnapped while saying Mass
1100    Baldwin I crowned King of Jerusalem
1130    Roger II crowned King of Sicily
1145    King Louis VII of France vowed to go on a
            Crusade
1194    Henry VI, Holy Roman Emperor, crowned King
            of Sicily
1241    Mongols captured Budapest, Hungary
1406    King Henry III of Castile died
1497    Vasco da Gama sighted Natal, South Africa
1541    From this day forward, only archery can be
            played on Christmas (England's
            Unlawful Games Act)
1620    Pilgrims began construction of a meeting house
            at Plymouth, Massachusetts
1635    Champlain, Canadian explorer and settler, died
1641    Preliminary peace signed ending the Thirty
            Years' War
```

1642	Sir Isaac Newton, discoverer of gravity, born
1644	Observance of Christmas forbidden in England
1667	Ehrengarde, Duchess of Kendal and mistress of King George I of England, born
1800	King Francis II of Austria signed an armistice with France
1821	Clara Barton, Red Cross founder, born
1830	First scheduled steam-powered passenger railroad service in the U.S. began
1847	James D. Kelly, author of the Naval Academy song, born
1883	Maurice Utrillo, French artist, born
1887	Conrad Hilton, hotelman, born
1891	Diphtheria antitoxin first used on humans
1893	Robert Ripley, creator of "Believe It or Not," born
	Natural gas discovered at Iola, Kansas
1907	Cab Calloway, jazz musician, born
1924	Rod Serling, television writer, born
1926	Hirohito became Emperor of Japan on the death of Yoshihito, his 123rd predecessor
1929	Marine Historical Association, developers of Mystic Seaport, Connecticut, organized
1936	Princess Alexandra of England born
1944	Nazi counterattack repulsed
1951	"Stone of Destiny" stolen from Westminster Abbey, London
1954	Liberty Hyde Bailey, horticulturalist-author, died
1967	Apartment building explosion in Moscow killed 20

December 26th

		Boxing Day – European gift-giving day
		Feast of St. Stephen the Apostle, patron of smelters and stonecutters
?	AD	Judas, betrayer of Jesus, born
268		Pope Dionysuis died
795		Leo III elected Pope
1076		Boleslav II crowned King of Poland
1194		Frederick II, Holy Roman Emperor, born
1519		Tapestries, designed by Raphael, first hung in the Sistine Chapel
1530		Baber, founder of the Mogul Dynasty in India, died
1559		Giovanni Angelo de Medici elected Pope as Pius IV
1734		George Romney, English artist, born

1783	Thomas Nelson, Jr., signer of the Declaration of Independence, died
1805	Treaty of Pressburg recognized the Kingdom of Italy
1845	Marthasville changed its name to Atlanta (Georgia)
1862	38 Santee Sioux Indians hanged in Minnesota
1891	Henry Miller, author, born
1901	First train of the Uganda Railway reached Lake Victoria
1912	Electric-lighted Christmas tree lit on the Boston Common
1921	Steve Allen, humorist, born
1930	The Diamond Match Company incorporated
1932	Kansu, China, rocked by an earthquake
1941	U.S. Congress set the date for future Thanksgivings
1943	German ship Scharnhorst torpedoed off Norway by the British
1969	Turtle Dance held at San Juan Pueblo, New Mexico
	Tangerine Bowl football game played at Orlando, Florida

December 27th

	Feast of St. John the Evangelist (or Divine), patron of theologicians; invoked against poisons and burns and for forming friendships
388 AD	St. Fabiola died (Feast Day)
1571	Johann Kepler, German astronomer, born
1587	Sigismund III crowned King of Poland
1722	Bradley measured Venus via telescope
1726	St. John of the Cross canonized
1793	Alexander Laing, Sahara explorer, born
1822	Louis Pasteur, scientist, born
1831	The Beagle, with Charles Darwin, set out to survey the coast of South America
1872	U.S. Cavalry victorious in the last important engagement of the Apache Indian War
1890	Shanghai burned in the China Sea
1894	Francis II, last Bourbon King of Naples, died
1896	Louis Bromfield, author, born
1903	"Sweet Adeline" first sung publicly
1904	Marlene Dietrich, performer, born
1917	Russian banks nationalized
1918	U.S. President Wilson was honored at a banquet at Buckingham Palace, London
1932	Radio City Music Hall opened (New York City)

1939	Anatolia, Turkey, hit by an earthquake and floods
1941	Intramuros Museum, Manila, destroyed by Japanese bombs
1942	Train wrecked at Almonte, Ontario, Canada
1945	Belgium joined the United Nations
1947	First "Howdy Doody" television show aired
1948	Joseph Cardinal Mindszenty, Primate of Hungary, arrested for espionage
1960	The Robin (Turdus migratorius) became the U.S. national bird
1968	Apollo 8 returned to Earth after spending Christmas at the Moon
1969	Basque Festival held at Boise, Idaho
	Surfing Tournament held at Ocean City, New Jersey

December 28th

	Feast of the Holy Innocents (celebrated in Venezuela like our April Fool's Day)
418 AD	Boniface I became Pope
1531	Ruiz sailed from Panama to conquer Ecuador
1622	St. Francis de Sales died
1694	Mary II, Queen of England, died of smallpox
1734	Rob Roy, Scots outlaw, died
1777	Czar Alexander I of Russia born
1788	Second settlement made at what is now Cincinnati, Ohio
1800	George XIII, ruler of Georgia, Russia, died
1828	Honshu Island, Japan, rocked by an earthquake
1836	Colony of South Australia proclaimed under a eucalyptus tree
1846	Iowa became a state
1856	Woodrow Wilson, 28th U.S. President, born
1872	Fifth Cavalry defeated the Tonto Apaches in the Salt River Canyon
1879	73 drowned when a North Britain Railway train was blown off a bridge
1895	Public motion picture theater opened in Paris
1897	Cyrano de Bergerac first produced (Paris)
1908	Southern Italy and Sicily shaken by an earthquake
1911	Sam Levene, teacher turned TV personality, born
1930	Fire destroyed North Dakota's capitol
1935	Clarence Day, author of Life With Father, died
1945	Theodore Dreiser, journalist-author, died
1949	Hervey Allen, author, died
1963	Paul Hindemith, German composer, died
1966	Train wrecked at Everett, Massachusetts

1969   Last day of the National Senoir Women's Indoor
                          Polo Meet at Quincy, Illinois
              Miss Cheerleader U.S.A. competition held at
                          Cypress Gardens, Florida

December 29th
───

              Feast of St. David
              Feast of St. Marcellus the Righteous
              Feast of St. Thomas of Canterbury (or a Becket)
1331 AD   Frist Droitwich, England, fair chartered
1616   Stephen Bocskay, Prince of Transylvania, died
1721   Marquise de Pompadour, mistress of King Louis XV
                          of France, born
1766   Charles Macintosh, inventor of waterproof
                          fabrics, born
1774   Captain Cook passed Cape Horn, discovering the
                          Isle of Georgia
1778   British captured Savannah, Georgia
1788   New York Daily Gazette newspaper founded
1792   French convention voted to guillotine King Louis XVI
1800   Charles Goodyear, inventor, born
1808   Andrew Johnson, 17th U.S. President, born
1809   William Gladstone, British statesman, born
1812   U.S.S. Constitution captured the British Java
1835   Cherokee Indians sold all their lands east of
                          the Mississippi for $5 million
1843   Elizabeth, Queen of Rumania, born
1845   Texas became a state
1848   Gaslights installed in the White House
1851   First YMCA in the U.S. opened in Boston, Massachusett
1876   Train wreck at Ashtabula, Ohio
1879   Billy Mitchell, aviator, born
1890   U.S. Army massacred Sioux Indians at Wounded
                          Knee Reservation
1895   Jameson Raid took place in South Africa
1897   Seal-killing in the northern Pacific prohibited
1913   First movie serial, 13 installments, released
1915   Robert Ruark, novelist, born
1934   U.S. given control of Wake Island in the
                          Pacific
1937   Ireland's Constitution went into effect
1940   Many London churches damaged by Nazi bombs,
                          including historic St. Mary's
1952   Alan N. May, a British scientist convicted of
                          espionage, released from prison
1967   Paul Whitman, bandleader, died

December 30th
───

              Feast of St. Egwin
40 AD   Titus, Roman Emperor, born

274	Pope St. Felix died
961	The Japanese Emperor moved into his rebuilt house in Kyoto
1591	Pope Innocent IX died
1604	St. John Regis died
1703	Yedo and Tokyo, Japan, shaken by an earthquake
1775	Americans attacked the British at Quebec, Canada
1803	Francis Lewis, signer of the Declaration of Independence, died
1809	Masked balls were forbidden from now on in Boston
1852	Rutherford B. Hayes, U.S. President, married Lucy W. Webb
1853	Gasden Purchase of Arizona and New Mexico from Mexico completed
1865	Rudyard Kipling, poet-writer, born
1873	Alfred E. Smith, New York governor-presidential candidate, born
1894	Amelia Bloomer, suffragist, died
1896	Jose Rizal, Philippine hero, executed by a Spanish firing squad (Rizal Day holiday)
1903	Iroquois Theater in Chicago burned
1904	Barras, in a Darracq, became the first to go over 100 mph, setting a record of 109.65 mph
1906	Train wreck at Washington, D.C.
1912	Minerological Society of America founded
1914	Bert Parks, master of ceremonies, born
1917	British Aragon torpedoed in the Mediterranean
1926	Census results showed that there were 2,517 silver fox farms in Canada
1935	Sandy Koufax, baseball pitcher, born
1947	The Communist Peoples' Republic of Rumania proclaimed
1963	John F. Kennedy 50¢ piece authorized by Congress

==

December 31st
==

"Touch a Pig for Luck" Day in Austria
Feast of St. Columba of Sens
Hogmanay in Scotland
"Serving of the Seasons" drives out devils in Japan
All Koreans must hear a cock crow before going to sleep

192 AD	Marcus Antonius, Roman emperor, died
335	Pope St. Silvester I died (Feast Day)
406	German Vandals invaded Roman Gaul (France)
439	St. Melanai the Younger died (Feast Day)
1097	Dekak failed to break the Crusaders siege of Antioch

1499	Jacques Cartier, French discoverer of Canada, born
1514	Andreas Vesalius, anatomist, born
1539	Henry VIII, King of England, met Anne of Cleves, his 4th wife
1600	British East India Company chartered
1705	Catherine of Braganza, wife of King Charles II of England, died
1719	John Flamsteed, father of modern astronomy, died
1812	Astor's overland expedition to the Pacific went into winter camp on the North Platte River
1834	John Wycliffe, English religious reformer, died
1859	Vanity Fair, comic weekly, began in New York City
1862	Start of the Battle of Murfreesboro or Stone's River, Tennessee
	Monitor, an ironclad ship, sunk off Cape Hatteras
1869	Henri Matisse, French artist, born
1876	Circassian, a whaling ship, wrecked at Southampton, New York
	St. Katherine Laboure died
1890	Ellis Island opened as an immigration depot
1909	Manhattan Bridge, Manhattan to Queens, opened to traffic
1926	Houdini, escape-artist and magician, died of a ruptured appendix
1934	Augsburger Abendseitung, German newspaper, ceased publication after 300 years
1936	International treaty limiting the size of the navies of the U.S., England, France, Italy, and Japan expired
1939	Chicago and Northwestern Railway opened
1944	Train wreck at Bagley, Utah
1945	Fort Niagara abandoned as a U.S. Army post
1946	President Truman declared a cessation of the hostilities of World War II
1969	Deer Dance held at Sandia Pueblo, New Mexico
	Pikes Peak Fireworks displayed at Colorado Springs, Colorado
1970	International scuba-diving meet held at Mali-Losinj, Yugoslavia
	Ice Yachting Competition held at Hamburg, Germany